THE
TRIUMPH
ZI*of*ON

OUR PERSONAL QUEST FOR THE
NEW JERUSALEM

THE TRIUMPH
of ZION

OUR PERSONAL QUEST FOR THE
NEW JERUSALEM

JOHN M.
PONTIUS

CFI
Springville, Utah

ISBN 13: 978-1-59955-230-9

Published by CFI, an imprint of Cedar Fort, Inc., 2373 W. 700 S., Springville, UT 84663
Distributed by Cedar Fort, Inc., www.cedarfort.com

LIBRARY OF CONGRESS CATALOGING-IN-PUBLICATION DATA

Pontius, John M.
 The triumph of Zion : our personal quest for the New Jerusalem / John M. Pontius.
 p. cm.
 Includes bibliographical references.
 ISBN 978-1-59955-230-9 (alk. paper)
 1. Zion (Mormon Church) 2. Second Advent. I. Title.
 BX8643.Z55P66 2009
 230'.9332--dc22

                                                  2008044138

Cover design by Angela D. Olsen
Cover design © 2010 by Lyle Mortimer

Printed in the United States of America

10 9 8 7 6 5

Printed on acid-free paper

In Gratitude:

To Jesus Christ,
for all things bright and beautiful.

To my loving wife, Terri, my soulmate and friend, my cheerleader and
fellow dreamer, for teaching me the most important thing I know.

To my friend, Joshua Mariano,
for inspired research that
greatly enhanced this book.

To my earthly father.
I hear you even still:
"It's all true, it's all true."

To many friends and editors
whose comments and inspired input
were indispensable.

BOOKS BY JOHN M. PONTIUS

Following the Light of Christ
into His Presence

Millennial Quest Series:
Spirit of Fire
Angels Among Us
Angels Forged in Fire
Angels and a Flaming Sword, Part 1
Angels and a Flaming Sword, Part 2

We Three Kings

The Triumph of Zion

CONTENTS

INTRODUCTION

My interest in Zion, and what it truly implies for Latter-day Saints, has evolved through my spiritual life from indifference to rich excitement. It has taken the Spirit of the Lord many years to penetrate the traditional thinking I inherited as a child, and in its place to cast a celestial light upon a far more glorious view of Zion.

It was never my intention to write a book about Zion. I saw the subject as universally cut and dried. I was of the opinion that Zion is what I assumed most people thought it was, to be completed when the prophet tells us to return to Missouri and build the New Jerusalem. That seemed simple enough.

I hope you will forgive a personal reference, but it is the best way I can explain the existence of this book.

When I was a child I believed that God existed, that Jesus was the Christ, and that the restored gospel was true. This seems to be almost genetically encoded into my soul. But I only had a vague idea what this implied. I didn't know what difference it made, except that my parents took me to church twice a week, we had family prayer and family home evening, and I couldn't watch TV on Sunday. Beyond that, the gospel was mostly inconsequential in my life.

As I grew older I realized there were blessings to be obtained: serving a mission, temple marriage, opportunities to serve, and other things. I looked forward to and accomplished each phase of my gospel life with determination and satisfaction.

But the gospel was still largely inconsequential. I say that because I read the scriptures and somehow saw myself in a different gospel program than the one I read about in the lives of the ancient faithful. I assumed that Adam lived in a different gospel pattern; that Enoch did things nobody else would do; that Lehi, Nephi, the brother of Jared, and all the other ancient faithful enjoyed something far more intimate and spiritually profound than I could. That conclusion was patently simple to draw primarily because I could read about it in their lives, but I didn't see it in my life or in the lives of those I idealized in the gospel.

It has only recently burst into my soul with a thunderclap of power that not only is the gospel true, but it also works. The gospel works today the same as in any dispensation of the past. It withholds nothing from our grasp. Any blessing, vision, miracle, or manifestation, whether it be angelic visitations or the appearance of God himself, is in fact ours to enjoy—today—now. We will examine how this is possible later on in this book. It wasn't until this truth distilled upon my soul that the gospel came alive to me. It was at that moment of realization that the gospel became powerfully, eternally, and immediately consequential in my life.

From that moment to this, my quest has not been to find the faith to believe, but rather to find the belief that will place my faith into operation. In other words, I had faith that these things were true about the faithful in antiquity, but I didn't necessarily believe that they applied to me. I needed to learn how to believe with all my heart that the things my faith said were true were actually mine to claim and not just inspiring accounts of God's one-of-a-kind dealings with righteous souls who lived in the past.

With the belief in my soul that the gospel was offering me the same blessings it offered Nephi, Moroni, and John the Beloved, the scriptures became a type of spiritual mail order catalog, and I began pondering which of the great blessings the Lord ordained for me to personally seek and obtain.

As a result of this belief, I prayed for many years for a certain gift. At one lofty moment I heard a reply that without words conveyed the thought, "This is a righteous request, and I will surely grant it, but it is not the greatest gift that you should seek."

A couple of years passed with me pondering this response until I thought I had identified a greater gift, and so I prepared, fasted, and asked. I received basically the same response—something greater should be my request. In all, it took fifteen years of climbing the ladder of belief to arrive at what is, at least for me personally, the greatest gift I can receive while still a mortal, which is to finally stand in the presence of Christ and to personally request a place in the latter-day Zion. It is a joyful destination yet before me. We will explore further on in this book why this is the greatest request and how to qualify for it.

The immediate effect of this understanding upon my soul was an intense curiosity about what Zion is to be. Since I intended to be a part of it, I wanted to know how to get there, what it would be like once I arrived, and what I would be doing there.

In searching for further and brighter light and knowledge on these things, it seemed to me that the scriptures hinted that our latter-day Zion was to be like Enoch's Zion, which meant that our Zion would eventually need to be a translated city, like Enoch's. I later learned, and have included in this book, that there are many scriptures and authoritative statements to establish this principle. But at that time in my search I was unaware of them, and hence, unsure.

The idea that our latter-day Zion was to be translated troubled me, because I had never heard the latter-day Zion described in that way.

I asked a friend of mine, Joshua Mariano, a remarkable researcher, to see if he could find a connection between translation and the latter-day Zion. I was thinking he might find little, if anything. Joshua also doubted that there was a connection, but he agreed to look. Several months passed before he emailed me the result of his labors. The document I received was 143 pages long. Joshua's information opened important doors for my own research into the doctrine of the latter-day Zion. Our combined efforts ultimately produced 540 scriptural citations and 248 doctrinal quotes for a total of 888 undergirding references included in this book. To be honest, after completing this research I was overwhelmed and just a little frightened.

The fear I felt at first flowed from the fact that Joshua's and my own research contained so much authoritative evidence about Zion that was completely unknown to me. Even though the research corroborated my earlier view that our latter-day Zion was to become a translated city, the reality that this vision of Zion had at one time been commonly understood and then had become lost to view was troubling to me. It seemed at that time to be obvious evidence that we as a people had collectively forgotten what Zion is to be, and having forgotten such a precious truth, we could never succeed in eventually building it. This truth struck me as a white-hot tragedy. This should in no way be interpreted as a criticism of our latter-day Church, because the information was readily available and easily found once I knew what to look for. We found hundreds of authoritative statements, which indicates that the information is not lost at all, even though I was not aware of most of it.

I have since changed my estimation, and my fear has melted in the warm embrace of faith—and hence the reason for this book. What I found in Joshua's research was so compelling to my soul, so empowering to my faith, and so beautifying to my view of the future, that I felt moved to re-illuminate these compelling truths about Zion. These principles changed everything I thought I knew about Zion, and from that moment to this, it continues to change my entire worldview. These truths have the potential to open one's eyes to the same faith-rendered view of our latter-day Zion that Enoch saw before he built his great Zion, and that God-inspired view of Zion empowers any person to seek and obtain those blessings whether it is time to build and populate an actual city of Zion or not.

Zion will eventually triumph. Most of us believe this. What I did not realize until I encountered the principles within this book is that the triumph of Zion will largely be a personal victory. It will be a glorious day when the prophet commands us to recommence the actual building of the latter-day cities of Zion. That will be a day of days. But the larger triumph will be that you and I are worthy, prepared and empowered to be called to join that last great effort; that we will be there, worthy to walk and talk with Christ, to be called to join the 144,000 in reaping the earth, to defend Zion and those who seek her protection with the power of God. This will be the true triumph of Zion and one that will ring across the eternities with everlasting consequence. This is the triumph that will cause the angels to spontaneously burst into songs of exquisite joy.

Zion is a principle that prophets throughout all recorded history have correctly understood. In the latter days, Joseph Smith, Brigham Young, John Taylor, and many others extensively spoke and wrote about Zion, though most of what they taught is presently little understood. This expanded vision of Zion speaks to me personally, as if in a voice of thunder, bearing witness that there is so much we must still do to establish the Latter-day Zion. But in a much louder voice of joy, it speaks of promise and privilege and power that is well within our reach. We have such a sweeping challenge and obligation before us that we should feel deeply honored, and not just a little overwhelmed. Yet we are scarcely cognizant of our privileges regarding Zion. The promises are so incredible that mortal minds can scarcely take them in, and hence we seem to be more or less oblivious to our potential. We are somewhat like children merrily playing in a sandbox filled with diamonds; we have played in them for so long that we esteem them merely as sparkling sand.

The premise of this book is that these promises regarding Zion are ours to claim. Only the prophet can begin building the city and society of Zion. But as individual seekers and spiritual pilgrims, we have fantastic promises and opportunities in the palms of our hands that we have only to close our fingers around to claim. We have the potential, the right, and the obligation to reach far beyond our present belief, and even further beyond our present view of our capacity, and claim gifts that are so exceedingly rare and so celestially precious as to make them the most desirable of all possible blessings in mortality. Everything we require has already been revealed and given to us. Every necessary priesthood, power, and key is operative in our lives. We have only to realize their purpose and make inspired use of them to become a Zion individual.

This book is not an encyclopedia about Zion. It is not intended to be a definitive work detailing every aspect of what Zion is to be. It is not about Zion's government, laws, or economy. It does not presume to know when or how the city of Zion will be built. Rather, this book is looking at a specific principle, which is the connection between Zion and the doctrine of translation, how they are connected, how translation affects the latter-day Zion, and how to qualify for it.

In this book we will certainly not be "revealing" anything doctrinally new. Everything we will discuss comes from the scriptures and from the prophets of this dispensation. All of it was known in Joseph's day, though these principles surrounding Zion may be somewhat obscure today.

What we will be doing is shining light upon specific threads of our understanding to make what was once subtle become vividly beautiful and realistically obtainable.

I humbly acknowledged that this book is not intended to be a voice of warning, neither is it a "steadying of the ark." It is not a call to action of any kind for the latter-day Church. Instead, it is a voice of joy: Joy in the promises to us as individuals and as a people, joy in our individual possibilities, joy in the approaching day when Christ will suddenly come in glory to His latter-day Zion that we will yet build; joy in the long-awaited day when He will end the heartaches of this world and sit down as King of Kings and Lord of Lords to rule the earth for a thousand years of peace.

Chapter One

UNDERSTANDING ZION

What Zion Is and Is not

Zion is much more than what we as Latter-day Saints seem to think it is. Definitions range in our minds anywhere from the geography in and around Jackson County, Missouri, to the area of Salt Lake City, Utah, to the "true Church" in general, to the New Jerusalem as it will exist in the Millennium. Each of these things can be correctly called Zion in some sense of the word. We understand that Zion is a little bit of each of these, and far more than any of them. We know that Zion will receive Christ when He returns, and we know that Zion will be the City of the Living God during the Millennium and the capital city of His kingdom during that era.

It may take most of a lifetime to understand Zion—what it is, where it is, what it has to do with the dispensation in which we live, and how we personally fit into this amazing vision. When the truths of Zion are instilled into a soul by the Holy Spirit of God, what is gained is a truth so astonishing that it changes souls. The truth whereof we speak is twofold: First, it is the astonishing facts of what Zion actually is, and second, it is the sure knowledge that we—you and I—can obtain a place within it without waiting for an actual city to be built in Missouri. We will discuss these things in depth as we continue.

When one at last understands what Zion truly is, the obligation of obtaining citizenship in that great society may seem overwhelming to the humble soul—and well it should. It is a journey intended to take a lifetime, to tug at one's heartstrings; to test to the utmost, and to purify and refine the already clean. Yet, this journey is one that millions will walk, and it is not beyond us. Even more important, doing so is vital to our salvation.

Why is it vital to our salvation? Because we have been tasked with building Zion prior to the Lord's Second Advent, and as we will discuss in detail, the Lord will not return until Zion is here to receive Him. Can we ignore such a divine responsibility and still hope to be counted valiant?

Though the journey to Zion may seem astronomical without the lens of great faith, there truly is a well-marked path to becoming part of Zion today. This realization is startling and life-changing to everyone who understands it.

The way into Zion has always existed. We have been on that path our entire gospel lives. We are just now rediscovering our personal place there and our obligations relative to establishing Zion. As has been mentioned, the doctrine of Zion is not new. It is, in fact, as old as Adam. We are just now coming to believe what our faith has already taught us.

It may well seem paradoxical to think of having to learn to believe what our faith has already taught us. One would think if we had faith in something, we would also believe it. But a mental inventory will reveal that much of what we know by faith, we actually don't believe applies to us. Speaking personally, I have found that I have faith that these great miracles are true and possible, but at times have also believed that they don't apply to me, or that they were meant for other people, or another day and age. I have had to teach myself to believe that those things which I know are true are all available to me when I follow an inspired path to obtain them.

Examples may include revelation, visions, miracles, and healings. As the miracles become greater, our faith remains strong, but our belief that they apply to us grows weaker. Examples of these greater miracles may include speaking in tongues, raising the dead, walking on water, building Zion, becoming translated, speaking with angels and God, and all other profound blessings of the gospel. Yet the scriptures repeatedly promise them to us. Further on we will discuss in depth the convergence of faith and belief. For now, the point being made is that we know many details about the latter-day Zion and have faith that it truly will be built prior to the Lord's return, but our belief structure may not include us personally building it.

This much is astonishingly true—one cannot discover what Zion actually is without yearning to be a part of it. To catch a glimpse of Zion in its true light and glory is to suddenly see the mind of God, to understand the meaning of mortality and the mystery of godliness, to view the purposes of the latter-day gospel in a far brighter light, and to finally comprehend those things which . . .

> 9 Eye hath not seen, nor ear heard, neither have entered into the heart of man, the things which God hath prepared for them that love him. (1 Corinthians 2:9)

Much more than a place, a city, or a society, Zion is a state of being. To be a part of a perfected Zion society in any dispensation, we have to become a Zion individual. It is roughly like saying, to live in the air, one must become a bird. To enter the unique environment of the latter-day Zion, when it has reached its full potential, requires a specific and powerful change to transform a body and soul into the Zion format.

As we continue to explore Zion throughout this book, it will become apparent that to be a participant in Zion is to be become pure, to be endowed with the fullest priesthood power, to rise above the mortal sphere, to be endowed with power that transcends life and death, to have authority in heaven and on earth, and to quite literally dwell with God.

Having said all that, I am convinced that the previous paragraph is a textbook example of knowing things by faith without believing them. As we read such statements, each assertion "feels" true, so little thought is given to translating them from truisms into belief. Consider for a moment one of the statements just above. "To be a participant in Zion is to rise above the mortal sphere." What an amazing statement! What does it mean to you? Consider the raw power in those words. To rise above the mortal sphere is not to leave mortality, but as a mortal to no longer be subject to the trials of mortality, to live beyond pain, hunger, even death. Such privileges have belonged to past generations of Zion individuals, and will belong to this dispensation of those who seek and obtain Zion.

We are speaking of the powers of godliness, power that transcends life and death, power over personal injury, immunity to disease and sickness, and to literally have power over our own death.

Such a Zion lifestyle so powerfully exceeds our present paradigm that it becomes inconceivable—not in the perception of Zion someday being like this for someone, but in the perception of Zion being like this in our day, for you and me. We can't conceptually place ourselves in that Zion.

In other words, we don't believe what our faith actually tells us. Thus we have ceased to strive for the very thing which would bring us our greatest triumph in mortality, and our greatest joy.

What we may not also grasp is that Zion is not unlike the celestial kingdom in that one must meet rigorous qualifications to enter. Zion is in fact the "City of the Living God," and Christ will live there and rule the earth from Zion during the Millennium. This makes Zion a function of the divine presence, and those who dwell there will of necessity be changed to endure—or better stated, to enjoy the presence of Christ.

Unlike the celestial kingdom though, Zion is not on a celestialized globe. Zion will begin on this earth in this day of wickedness, before the world is cleansed prior to the Second Coming. The Latter-day Zion is a phenomenon of mortality and will be established among living mortals— you and I, we hope—on this earth prior to the Lord's return in glory. We will discuss and document these assertions in detail later.

The blinding truth before us is that Zion is not beyond our reach. God does not task us with impossible assignments. Zion is a state that has been obtained in the past, and will be obtained again in this dispensation, possibly by hundreds of thousands prior to the Lord's return. The question before us is only whether we—you and I—are willing to pay the price to be a part of it.

What can be more fantastic that this? One truth in fact transcends even the glorious possibilities of Zion. We will discuss this fully later, but in brief, it is that it is within our capability to establish Zion in our lifetime. Everything we need, every doctrine, every priesthood ordinance, every truth and power and principle that is required of a mortal to person- ally qualify for and enter Zion exists today within the latter-day Church. Nothing is missing. Nothing remains to be revealed. No statement or proclamation of the living prophets needs to be made. It is all present, now, in its complexity and completeness. All we must do is see what we already possess with an eye of faith. We must obtain an inspired belief that it is ours to claim and then be willing to pay the price to do so. Of course, only the living prophet can tell us when it is time to gather and build the city of Zion. But we can, and must, obtain a Zion stature and privilege before we will be invited to become a part of that great city of holiness.

When we as individuals enjoy the full effect of every ordinance and covenant available to us, we will become a Zion individual—not just in the Millennium—but now, in this life, in this pre-millennial world. We are the seeds that the Sower has scattered upon the landscape of mortality. Those seeds that take root in this dispensation and weather the storms that refine and define us will attain their divine birthright and bring forth the full fruit, and we will become Zion.

We trouble ourselves a great deal about the timing of the Second Coming and preparing to endure the rigors we assume must precede it. We want to be among the "wise virgins" whose lamps are full, so we store food like squirrels and pay our tithing, which we humorously refer to as fire insurance. We often rehearse to ourselves that no man knows the day or hour when the Lord will return. Yet, we do know that He won't return until Zion has been established. So we may say with certainty that we do know that as long as Zion does not exist, the time is not accomplished for His return. In this sense we do know when He will come. He will come when we have built and populated Zion.

Zion Must Be Built before Christ Returns

As Enoch stood prior to the cleansing of the wicked earth by the flood, we stand in approximately the same position relative to the Second Coming and the cleansings that must precede it. At the beginning of Enoch's ministry, no city of righteousness glowed in the evening darkness. He boldly preached to the spiritually unwashed and impure. Certainly other believers were upon the earth, and many who understood at least a part of God's dealings with man. Enoch undoubtedly went to these people first, and many believed and joined him. Those who believed were taught and received the ordinances of salvation and exaltation. As individuals they grew until they were worthy of the divine presence, and thereafter, because of their collective purity, they were instructed to build a city upon whose gilded streets Deity walked and talked on a familiar basis.

Just as Enoch had to build his Zion to save the righteous from the universal destruction of the flood, we must build Zion in our day to save the righteous from the universal cleansing by fire that will accompany Christ's glorious return. Since He will not return until after we build Zion, can it be that the Lord isn't delaying His return—but we are?

Moses spoke of the New Jerusalem this way:

62 And righteousness will I send down out of heaven; and truth will I send

forth out of the earth, to bear testimony of mine Only Begotten; his resurrection from the dead; yea, and also the resurrection of all men; and righteousness and truth will I cause to sweep the earth as with a flood, to gather out mine elect from the four quarters of the earth, unto a place which I shall prepare, an Holy City, that my people may gird up their loins, and be looking forth for the time of my coming; for there shall be my tabernacle, and it shall be called Zion, a New Jerusalem. (Moses 7:62)

Observe the sequence of events:

- Righteousness and truth will sweep the earth as with a flood.
- The elect will be gathered from the four quarters of the earth.
- A Holy City, the New Jerusalem will be built.
- The elect may gird up their loins (take courage) in Zion.
- The Second Coming will occur.

The implication of this is that we, the stewards of the latter-days, cannot be intelligently looking for the Second Coming until we have built Zion. Zion is the highest blessing of this dispensation, and because it is the greatest, building it is the greatest challenge we will ever face.

It is also worth noting that righteousness and truth sweeping the earth will expose the world to the principles of righteousness, causing many to become the elect of God, which will cause the gathering net of Zion to enclose them in its safety. This is in fact the mission of the latter-day Church, one that it is faithfully fulfilling before our eyes. We will discuss how the latter-day Church fulfills this mission in a later section.

The prophet Joseph Smith taught: "Zion and Jerusalem must both be built up before the coming of Christ."[1]

Elder Orson Pratt echoed the prophet's teachings on this matter when he taught:

> The Christians of all denominations expect that he will appear in the clouds of heaven with power and great glory. The Latter-day Saints expect this in common with all other Christians. But before he appears in his glory he is going to build up Zion, that is, Zion must again be built up on the earth: and *if there is not a Zion built up on the earth before he comes, or in other words, if there never is to be another Zion built up on the earth, then he never will come.*[2]

If we don't build Zion, Christ will never come? Can it be true?

I don't believe Elder Pratt is proposing that Christ won't come at all, since prophecy indicates that Zion *will* be built and He *will* return in glory. What is being emphasized by this dramatic statement is the timing of Christ's return in relation to the building of Zion. Elder Pratt is teaching us that since Christ will come to Zion when He returns, then He can't, or better stated, He won't fulfill that promise until Zion exists.

President George Q. Cannon feared that the Saints would defer the building of Zion indefinitely:

> I do fear that we will defer the redemption of Zion indefinitely through our unwillingness to do the things that God requires at our hands. I have not an earthly doubt that this revelation given in 1834 would have been fulfilled to the very letter had our people obeyed the Lord as He desired.[3]

We know from the scripture, and from statements we will quote below, that the date of the Second Coming of Christ is fixed. The date is known only to the Father (Matthew 24:36). When we speak of "delaying" the Second Coming, we mean only that in His foreknowledge of all things, the Father has fixed that date after the establishment of Zion. And since our own agency and faithfulness governs when we will get around to building Zion, we have an obvious influence upon that date.

From all this it appears that by delaying the establishment of Zion, we have also delayed the Second Coming of the Lord. If this is true, it is startling. The idea that we, through our spiritual sleepiness, could delay the return of the Lord, and thus the day of peace so long sought by the righteous of every generation, is almost horrific.

Elder McConkie said it this way:

> *Though the day of the Second Coming is fixed, the day for the redemption of Zion depends upon us.* After we as a people live the law of the celestial kingdom; after we gain the needed experience and learn our duties; after we become by faith and obedience as were our fellow saints in the days of Enoch; after we are worthy to be translated, if the purposes of the Lord should call for such a course in this day—then Zion will be redeemed, and not before.[4]

In this world of daily horror, bloodshed, and wickedness, to knowingly delay Zion further seems far less than valiant behavior.

Hugh Nibley made a similar observation:

> The Bible contains a fairly complete description of Zion, but there is one aspect of it that only the Latter-day Saints have taken to heart

(or did formerly), and it is that doctrine that sets them off most sharply from all of the other religions, namely, the belief that Zion is possible on the earth, that men possess the capacity to receive it right here and are therefore under obligation to waste no time moving in the direction of Zion. The instant one realizes that Zion is a possibility, one has no choice but to identify himself with the program that will bring about the quickest possible realization of its perfection. The call is to awake and arise, to "push many people to Zion with songs of everlasting joy upon their heads." (D&C 66:11)[5]

> Israel! Israel! Canst thou linger
> Still in error's gloomy ways?
> Mark how judgment's pointing finger
> Justifies no vain delays.
> Come to Zion, come to Zion!
> Zion's walls shall ring with praise.[6]

We look forward with great anticipation to the Lord's coming in glory. Many generations have passed with their eyes upon the eastern horizon, watching for the dawning of the great millennial day, when the Messiah will come as the rising sun in the east and will end the blood and nightmare that have always existed in this world. Yet century after century we have watched in vain. It is electrifying to think that we, not the Lord, may have delayed His coming by our not building Zion. Even to this day, Zion is a misty concept that hardly has a place in our imagination, let alone in our daily planner.

The following significant statement is attributed to the prophet Joseph Smith:

> Every saint has an equal interest in building up of the Zion of our God; for it is after the Lord has built up Zion, that he will appear in his glory. Psalms 102:16. We all look for the appearing of the great God, and our Savior Jesus Christ; *but we shall look in vain, until Zion is built;* for Zion is to be the dwelling place of our God when he comes . . .
>
> How then is the Lord to dwell in Zion, if Zion is not built up? This question we leave the saints to answer.—The salvation of the saints one and all depends on the building up of Zion; for without this there is no salvation; for deliverance in the last days is found in Zion, and in Jerusalem.[7]

As the above quote testifies, "We shall look in vain until Zion is built." We are the only ones who can build Zion. Even though Zion is an uncertain concept for most of us, truly believing that the duty, or more positively stated, the privilege, of building Zion falls upon our heads is the first step in building it. Without a firm belief that we belong in Zion, there is no motivation to find out how to build it. Later in this book we will clearly define how Zion will be established. But for the present time, we are building our personal paradigm of Zion. When we at last believe, then we will begin. Elder Wilford Woodruff taught that before Christ comes:

> I say that throughout the whole of the Scriptures—the Old and New Testament, the Book of Mormon, and the Book of Doctrine and Covenants, the Second Coming of the Lord is frequently referred to; and has the Lord promised these things without intending to fulfill them? No, he has not, they will be fulfilled. *But before Christ comes, a people have got to be prepared by being sanctified before the Lord. Temples have got to be built; Zion has got to be built up, there must be a place of safety for the people of God while his judgments are abroad in the earth, for the judgments of God will visit the earth, there is no mistake about that, the revelations are full of promises to this effect and as the Lord has declared it, he will not fail in keeping his word.*[8]

Elder John Taylor delivered the same message:

> Our course is onward; and are we going to stop? No. Zion must be built up, God has decreed it and no power can stay its progress. Do you hear that? *I prophecy that in the name of the Lord Jesus Christ. For Zion must and will be built up despite all opposition, the kingdom of God established upon the earth in accordance with the designs and purposes of God.*[9]

From this we may infer that the building of Zion is so eternally important to the timetable of the Lord that God has decreed that it *will* be built. What has not been decreed is *when* it will be built, but we do know *who* will build it—we will. Now that we have the priesthood, ordinances, and temples, when it is built is up to us. And if we never get around to it, the scriptures seem to suggest that God will take the privilege away from us and give it to someone else; perhaps our grandchildren, or even another more faithful people (3 Nephi 16:10–11; 3 Nephi 20:28–46).

The prophet Joseph left no room for question that we must build Zion before the coming of the Son of Man. He said it this way:

> Zion and Jerusalem must both be built up before the coming of Christ . . . and when these cities are built then shall the coming of the Son of man be.[10]

LDS author, Hyrum Andrus, offers this insight:

Literally thousands of people in Joseph Smith's day expected the Millennium to arrive before the middle of the nineteenth century. But in several ways the prophet differed in the position he took.

First, he claimed to receive a direct commission from God to begin preparing a people for the millennial reign, and to receive the law of the millennial system by revelation from the Lord.

Second, he taught that before Christ came, Zion had to be built as a nucleus of the millennial order, founded upon the millennial law, as the abode of the Lord. The new order would then be extended throughout the earth as the events of the last days occurred and Christ came in glory. "We all look for the appearing of the great God, and our Savior Jesus Christ," said the Bishopric at Kirtland in an epistle to the Saints; "but we shall look in vain, until Zion is built, for Zion is to be the dwelling place of our God when he comes." Joseph Smith thus proclaimed in March, 1843, as millennial fervor in America was growing to a climax of disappointment and frustration: "*Therefore hear this, O earth, the Lord will not come to reign over the righteous, in this world, in 1843, nor until everything for the bridegroom is ready.*" . . .

Fourth, though Joseph Smith exerted all his energies to build up Zion and prepare a people for the coming of Christ, he expressed a definite conviction that it would not be done in his day. Because of lack of faith and understanding in the Saints and opposition by the world, it would be reserved to a future time when the program of the last dispensation would finally be developed and God's judgments sent forth upon the wicked. Nevertheless, the law which he was given was that of Zion and of the millennial order, and when it was applied the system of universal peace and union would be introduced.[11]

Knowing *that* we must build Zion, and knowing *why* it must be built are separate truths. The first and greatest reason, as we have discussed, is that Christ will not return until Zion exists. The second most pressing reason is that we will not be able to survive the turmoil of His return without the refuge Zion offers.

Zion—A Refuge

Zion, as it will exist in its perfect state prior to the Lord's return, will be a society of people who are worthy to live in Christ's presence. When you and I rise to this pre-millennial challenge, we will be endowed with power, changed physically, endowed with gifts of knowledge that transcend the heavens, and in every way be prepared to carry out His last gathering in circumstances that would cost ordinary mortals their lives. Zion must be built as a place of refuge and safety for the righteous to endure the rigors of the cleansings prior to the Lord's return.

If Zion did not exist and He came in glory, the righteous could not survive those perilous days. Such a fierce and fiery devastation will be poured out upon the wicked, and without the attendant safety of Zion, without the powers of the fulness of the priesthood to turn aside the latter-day destructions, we would also perish.

> 5 Arise and shine forth, that thy light may be a standard for the nations;
>
> 6 and that the gathering together upon the land of Zion, and upon her stakes, may be for a defense, and for a refuge from the storm, and from wrath when it shall be poured out without mixture upon the whole earth. (D&C 115:5–6)

Elder McConkie describes it this way:

> The Holy Word also affirms that Israel gathers to Zion to escape the abomination of desolation that shall be poured out upon a wicked world in the last days. In Zion there will be safety; in the world, naught but sorrow and tribulation and desolation.[12]

More than a place, Zion is a state of being, a personal condition of absolute righteousness. We will discuss much more on this matter later on, but in short, a person becomes a member of Zion by magnifying his priesthood (if a male) and by participating in and fully honoring temple covenants.

When such a spiritual pilgrim finally arrives at the gates of Zion, they will be worthy to live in divine company and to converse with Jesus as one man speaks to another. Such a person is utterly pure in heart and a Zion individual whether the city of Zion has been built yet or not.

Becoming a member of Zion is not a result of an evolution by the Church. In fact, the Church requires no further evolution. It is functioning exactly as the Lord desires, doing exactly as is required for the building up of Zion. If something more is needed, our living prophet will make these things available exactly on schedule. It is we, the people, who must evolve into Zion worthiness. It is the result of a personal and powerful inner quest to transcend the mortal experience and take upon ourselves the stature of Zion. When there are "Saints" worthy of entering the Holy City, then when it is time, the Lord will instruct His prophet to build the actual city. Until the prophet speaks, our quest is a personal one to become Zion worthy.

Zion will be built for a defense in the times of trial and famine that will precede the advent of the Lord. Within Zion there will be the divine presence, which will guarantee our peace, safety, and joy. The Prophet Joseph said:

> Without Zion, and a place of deliverance, we must fall; because the time is near when the sun will be darkened, and the moon turn to blood, and the stars fall from heaven, and the earth reel to and fro. Then, if this is the case, and if we are not sanctified and gathered to the places God has appointed, with all our former professions and our great love for the Bible, we must fall; we cannot stand; we cannot be saved; for God will gather out His Saints from the Gentiles, and then comes desolation and destruction, and none can escape except the pure in heart who are gathered.[13]

It is little-understood that the millennial peace and prosperity will begin within the walls of Zion sometime before the Second Coming, and long before the world at large enjoys the same blessings. Outside of Zion there will be war, bloodshed, and famine. In order for the latter-day Zion to fulfill its purpose, those who dwell within must become of the same spiritual metal as Enoch's Zion. In that day the Zion of Enoch will descend from heaven, and the latter-day Zion will ascend, and they will become one, the New Jerusalem.

John Taylor wrote the following about Zion:

> Furthermore, in the latter days there is to be a Zion built up; but in these days we are told that the Lord will cut His work short in righteousness. Enoch, in his day, had his messengers go forth among the people, and when they gathered, it induced the rage of man, and great armies assembled against the Saints, but Enoch prophesied by the power of God, and the earth shook and the mountains trembled, and the enemies of the Saints in fear fled afar off. By and by when the time came for the accomplishment of the purposes of God, and before the destruction of the wicked, Enoch was caught up to heaven and his Zion with him. And we are told in latter revelation in relation to these matters that a Zion will be built up in our day; that great trouble will overtake the inhabitants of the earth; and that when the time arrives,

the [Enoch's] Zion that was caught up will descend, and the [latter-day] Zion that will be organized here will ascend, both possessed of the same spirit, their peoples having been preserved by the power of God according to His purposes and as His children, to take part in the events of the latter days. We are told that when the people of these two Zions meet, they will fall on each other's necks, and embrace and kiss each other.[14]

> Israel, Israel, God is calling,
> Calling thee from lands of woe,
> Babylon the great is falling;
> God shall all her towers o'er-throw.
> Come to Zion, come to Zion
> Ere his floods of anger flow.[15]

One of the main reasons peace and safety will be within Zion during these scenes of great destruction is that the inhabitants of Zion will be translated beings, possessing the full powers that Enoch wielded to defend his city.

Elder McConkie observes in the next quote that all those who abide (meaning to not only survive, but to thrive during) the day of the Second Coming will be translated beings:

Raphael, whom we assume to have been Enoch or someone from his dispensation, came and committed such keys as appertained to that day. No doubt these included the power to use the priesthood to translate men, as will be the state of all those who abide the day of the Second Coming.[16]

THE TEMPLE CONNECTION

If we had to pick one thing and label it "the train to Zion" we would have to pick the temple and the ordinances of the priesthood. It is priesthood ordinances that manifest the power of godliness (D&C 84:19–20) and prepare each individual for their introduction into Zion. One might say that the gospel train stops at the front steps of the temple. We must walk into the temple and from there into Zion.

We might liken the temple to an image of the world, and the Church as we know it being on one side of a bottomless canyon that is too wide and deep for any mortal to cross. On the opposite bank is Zion with all its attendant glories, including the presence of deity. Spanning this vast divide like a mighty bridge is a great latter-day temple with the entrance on our side of the chasm and its back door on the far side opening into Zion.

In this image millions of people enter the doors of the temple, participate in holy ordinances, make sacred covenants, and then return to the same door they entered to reemerge into Babylon. Figuratively speaking, the challenge of those who would become Zion in their own lives is to find the power and the knowledge offered in the temple, and instead of returning to the telestial world, to leave by the opposite door into Zion.

Catherine Thomas, a noted LDS author, highlights the power and importance of the temple in our quest for Zion:

> The temple is the narrow channel through which one must pass to reenter the Lord's presence. A mighty power pulls us through that channel, and it is the sealing power of the at-one-ment of the Lord Jesus Christ. The Savior's at-one-ment is another word for the sealing power. By the power of the at-one-ment, the Lord draws and seals his children to himself in the holy temples.
>
> In scripture we can study how the ancient great ones were drawn through that narrow channel to find their heart's desire: we find, for example, Adam, cast out, bereft of his Lord's presence, searching relentlessly in the lonely world until he finds the keys to that passage to the Lord. Abraham searches for his priesthood privileges (see Abraham 1:1) and after a diligent quest exclaims, "Thy servant has sought thee earnestly; now I have found thee" (Abraham 2:12). Moses on Horeb, Lehi at the tree, Nephi on the mountain top—all these men conducted that search which is outlined and empowered in the temple endowment, gradually increasing the hold, the seal, between themselves and their Lord.
>
> This was the very search for which they were put on earth: to rend the veil of unbelief, to yield to the pull of the Savior's sealing power, to stand in the Lord's presence, encircled about in the arms of his love (see D&C 6:20; 2 Nephi 1:15). This then is the temple endowment: having been cast out, to search diligently according to the revealed path, and at last to be clasped in the arms of Jesus (see Mormon 5:11).[17]

Because of sacred covenants, it is not possible to discuss the temple message and promises in detail. But much of what we learn in the temple is also taught in the scriptures, and from the holy writ we may teach. We do proclaim that the temple and the priesthood ordinances performed therein place into our hands the very power of godliness and the key to the *only* door into Zion. There is no other point of entry than the temple.

In the following quote, Elder Bruce R. McConkie clearly states that the purpose of the temple endowment is to enable us to see the face of the Lord. Since Zion is a society of people who dwell in the presence of Christ, and the purpose of the temple is to prepare us to enter the presence of Christ, the temple becomes the doorway into Zion. Thus, entering into the presence of the Lord is the initiatory rite of Zion, and temple ordinances are the pathway to obtaining that vast privilege.

Elder McConkie explains the purpose of the temple thus:

> "Therefore, sanctify yourselves that your minds become single to God"—and now we come to the crowning promise of the gospel—"and the days will come that you shall see him; for he will unveil his face unto you, and it shall be in his own time, and in his own way, and according to his own will." That is the Lord's promise, his great promise, his crowning promise, his last promise. What is there that can excel in importance the obtaining of that spiritual stature which enables one to see the Lord? And so the next words spoken by the Lord to his friends were: "Remember the great and last promise which I have made unto you."
>
> Then follows some counsel relative to right living, which is climaxed with these words, the full import of which is known only by those who are endowed with power from on high in holy places: "Sanctify yourselves; yea, purify your hearts, and cleanse your hands and your feet before me, that I may make you clean; That I may testify unto your Father, and your God, and my God, that you are clean from the blood of this wicked generation." Why? "That I may fulfil this promise, this great and last promise," this promise that you shall see me and that I will unveil my face, that I may fulfill this promise "which I have made unto you, when I will." (D&C 88:62–75) To those of understanding we say: *The purpose of the endowment in the house of the Lord is to prepare and sanctify his saints so they will be able to see his face, here and now, as well as to bear the glory of his presence in the eternal worlds.*[18]

Beyond membership, beyond faithfulness, beyond any and all forms of service, becoming a Zion individual is a matter of hungering and thirsting specifically for the blessings of Zion. It is a result of a lifelong pursuit of the fulfillment of temple covenants and thereby obtaining the mysteries of godliness. It is the result of an intelligent and intentional turning of the keys[19] provided by the priesthood, in the doors of eternity. The point that must be emphasized over and over is that these events must take place before the Second Coming—preferably in our lifetimes. We must become worthy of Zion so that when the prophet commands, we are prepared to go forth and build Zion. We must awaken from the slumber of Babylonian normalcy, shine forth, and rend that veil of unbelief that has separated us from our greatest privileges for over 175 years.

> 13 Come unto me, O ye Gentiles, and I will show unto you the greater things, the knowledge which is hid up because of unbelief. (Ether 4:13)

We, meaning specifically you and I, must do it. If we do not, is it possible that we may one day be partly accountable for the continuing horror of this telestial world?

When we build Zion it will be built up in obedience to the same laws, the same standards of righteousness, and the same principles of translation that Enoch and his city obeyed to enter the glory of the presence of Christ and thus become Zion.

The call and privilege of becoming like Enoch and his blessed people lies before us. To say it more plainly, it is our privilege and obligation to enter into the sacred Zion state as Enoch did, before we set out to build the center stake of Zion.

When we have become Enochonian in our lives, then, and only then will it become our right and privilege to build the City of the Living God. Brigham Young declared:

> The Lord has declared it to be his will that his people enter into covenant, even as Enoch and his people did, which of necessity must be before we shall have the privilege of building the Centre Stake of Zion, for the power and glory of God will be there, and none but the pure in heart will be able to live and enjoy it.[20]

Is it even possible for us to arrive at the same spiritual greatness as Enoch's Zion? Does a sense of hopelessness or a sense of spiritual inferiority almost make you laugh out loud at the idea of you and I becoming like Enoch? Rest assured that these grand privileges and attainments are not beyond us. At present they lie within our reach.

Spencer W. Kimball encouraged us to work as families to become like Enoch's people so that the Millennium could be ushered in:

O my beloved hearers, what a world it would be if a million families in this church were to be on their knees like this every night and morning! And what a world it would be if nearly a hundred million families in this great land and other hundreds in other lands were praying for their sons and daughters twice daily. And what a world this would be if a billion families through the world were in home evenings and church activity and were on their physical knees pouring out their souls for their children, their families, their leaders, their governments! *This kind of family life could bring us back toward the translation experience of righteous Enoch. The Millennium would be ushered in.*[21]

The Lord's stated purpose in establishing the school of the prophets in Joseph's day was to prepare us to receive the blessings of Enoch's Zion. Brigham Young noted:

The object of the School of the prophets is to train ourselves until we can receive the order of Enoch in all its Fulness.[22]

There can be little doubt as to what Brigham was referring. He understood that the Latter-day Zion was to be a translated, Enoch-like city. Even though it may seem overwhelming to contemplate building a society and city that could eventually be so worthy that Christ could walk its streets, it is not beyond us. In fact, when we have made the necessary personal preparations, nothing can stop us.

Joseph F. Smith leaves us this sublime promise:

I prophesy to you, in the name of the Lord, that when the Latter-day Saints have prepared themselves through righteousness to redeem Zion, they will accomplish that work, and God will go with them. No power will then be able to prevent them from accomplishing that work; for the Lord has said it shall be done, and it will be done in the due time of the Lord, when the people are prepared for it.[23]

For now, it seems obvious that we have a great work to accomplish. To build such a city of holiness, which is what our latter-day Zion must eventually be, we must strive to attain the same spiritual stature enjoyed by those who built the original Zion. When we are allowed to begin, which may be sometime prior to obtaining the full stature of Enoch's Zion, when the Lord instructs our living prophet to proceed, then we will begin to construct our latter-day City of Holiness. Somewhere in that progression we will obtain the requisite worthiness that will qualify us for the full presence of our Savior, and then the city we build will become Zion in all its glory. When we, by this process, at last establish the latter-day Zion, not only will it be a refuge from the destructions of those days, but it will be a beautiful, glorious habitation, one full of wonders and glory.

> Zion, Zion
> Lovely Zion;
> Beautiful Zion;
> Zion, City of our God.[24]

When at last we build Zion, all truths, everything that is beautiful and good, every grace and virtue, every exalted attribute of goodness will flourish within her glowing walls. The sciences and arts will excel, and great intelligence will produce stunning advances of technology that will forever change the future of mankind. In due time, the peace and good-will of Zion will spread to the rest of the world, initiating a 1,000-year reign of peace. Susan Easton Black explained it this way:

> As a messenger before the Lord, the society of Zion was to be a nucleus of the millennial kingdom—an opening wedge—containing the basic principles and powers through which, eventually, peace and good will could be established universally among men. The divine system was to be developed among the Saints first, and then expanded throughout the earth as the millennial kingdom of Christ was ushered in.
>
> Zion was and is to be the focus of all that is good, all that is ennobling, all that is instructive and inspirational. In Zion all things were to be gathered together in one in Christ. (Ephesians 1:10) . . . In short, "every accomplishment, every polished grace, every useful attainment in mathematics, music, in all science and art belong to the Saints." The Saints "rapidly collect the intelligence that is bestowed upon the nations, for all this intelligence belongs to Zion."[25]

The masterpiece of Zion will be the great Temple of the Living God. Hosts of angels will assist in the construction of the temple, which means the temple will be built in part by the power of God. Notice in the quote below, attributed to Wilford Woodruff, that the words of the song included the phrase, "for the Saints have overcome." This is a powerful statement considering that this temple will be raised while wars and famines still rage outside the city walls of Zion.

> I saw a short distance from the Missouri River, where I stood,

twelve men [whose] hands were uplifted while they were consecrating the ground; and later they laid the corner-stones of the house of God. I saw myriads of angels hovering over them, and above their heads there was a pillar-like cloud. I heard the most beautiful singing in the words: "Now is established the Kingdom of our God and His Christ, and He shall reign forever and forever, and the Kingdom shall never be thrown down, for the Saints have overcome." I saw people coming from the river and from distant places to help build the Temple. It seemed as though there were hosts of angels helping to bring material for the construction of that building.[26]

The temple in Zion will be unique in design, having the shape of a wagon wheel with twenty-four rooms forming a circle that is covered by a great dome. Elder Orson Pratt wrote:

We expect to build a temple different from all other temples in some respects. It will be built much larger, cover a larger area of ground, far larger than this Tabernacle covers, and this Tabernacle will accommodate from 12,000 to 15,000 people. We expect to build a temple much larger, very much larger, according to the revelation God gave to us forty years ago in regard to that temple . . . there will be 24 different compartments in the Temple that will be built in Jackson County. The names of these compartments were given to us some 45 or 46 years ago; the names we still have, and when we build these 24 rooms, in a circular form and arched over the centre, we shall give the names to all these different compartments just as the Lord specified through Joseph Smith. . . .

These buildings will be built with a special view to the different orders, or in other words the different quorums or councils of the two Priesthoods that God has ordained on the earth. That is the object of having 24 rooms so that each of these different quorums, whether they be High Priests or Seventies, or Elders, or Bishops, or lesser Priesthood, or Teachers, or Deacons, or Patriarchs, or Apostles, or High Councils, or whatever may be the duties that are assigned to them, they will have rooms in the Temple of the Most High God, adapted, set apart, constructed, and dedicated for this special purpose.[27]

When Enoch and his city return they will bring their temple with them. Monte S. Nyman made this observation:

The second reason [Enoch's] Zion is preserved is that it is the center of temple work, the work of the Millennium. Ether points out that when the city of Enoch returns to earth, it will contain "the holy sanctuary of the Lord" (Ether 13:3). Likewise, John notes that when "the holy city, new Jerusalem, [comes] down from God out of heaven . . . the tabernacle of God is with men, and he will dwell with them" (Rev. 21:2-3). Enoch saw the same thing (Moses 7:62). Elder Franklin D. Richards said he wished to speak a word in reference to the Three Nephites. They wanted to tarry until Jesus came, and that they might He took them into the heavens and endowed them with the power of translation, probably in one of Enoch's temples, and brought them back to the earth. Thus they received power to live until the coming of the Son of Man. I believe He took them to Enoch's city and gave them their endowments there. I expect that in the city of Enoch there are temples; and when Enoch and his people come back, they will come back with their city, their temples, blessings and powers.[28]

The labor of this dispensation of the gospel is to spread the gospel worldwide, and at some point to build Zion. It appears that the labor of the millennial dispensation will be to build temples and to complete the saving ordinances for all of Adam's posterity. It makes poetic sense that the focal point of the great latter-day city of Zion, that place which bridges between this present dispensation and the millennial dispensation will be the great temple there.

NOTES

1. "The Historians Corner," *BYU Studies*, 19, no. 3 (Spring 1979), 393; italics added.

2. *Journal of Discourses*, 14:348–49; italics added.

3. George Q. Cannon, in Conference Report, Oct. 1899, 50–53, as cited in *Gospel Truth: Discourses and Writings of George Q. Cannon* (Salt Lake City: Deseret Book, 1987), 42; italics added.

4. McConkie, *New Witness for the Articles of Faith*, 615; italics added.

5. Nibley, *Approaching Zion*, 28–29.

6. "Israel, Israel, God Is Calling," *Hymns of The Church of Jesus Christ of Latter-day Saints* (Salt Lake City: The Church of Jesus Christ of Latter-day Saints, 1985), no. 7.

7. *Messenger and Advocate*, 3, no. 36 (Oct. 1836–Sept. 1837), 563.

8. *Journal of Discourses*, 18:192; italics added.

9. Ibid., 23:36; italics added.

10. Ehat and Cook, *Words of Joseph Smith*, 417.

11. Andrus, *Doctrines of the Kingdom*, 4; italics added.

12. McConkie, *New Witness of the Articles of Faith*, 573.

13. Smith, *History of the Church*, 2:52.

14. John Taylor, *Journal of Discourses*, 25:305–7; bracketed comments added.

15. *Hymns*, no. 7.

16. McConkie, *The Millennial Messiah*, 119.

17. M. Catherine Thomas, "The Brother of Jared at the Veil," *Temples of the Ancient World: Ritual and Symbolism,* ed. Donald W. Parry (Salt Lake City: Deseret Book and FARMS, 1994), 388–97; italics added.

18. McConkie, *The Promised Messiah*, 582; italics added.

19. Keys, used figuratively, not referring to priesthood keys.

20. *Journal of Discourses,* 18:263.

21. Spencer W. Kimball, "The Family Influence," *Ensign*, July 1973, 15.

22. Brigham Young, *Journal of Discourses*, 210.

23. *Millennial Star,* June 18, 1894, 56:385–86.

24. *Hymns*, no. 45.

25. Susan Easton Black et al., *Doctrines for Exaltation: The 1989 Sperry Symposium on the Doctrine and Covenants* (Salt Lake City: Deseret Book, 1989), 181; italics added.

26. Matthias F. Cowley, *Wilford Woodruff: History of His Life and Labors as Recorded in His Daily Journals* (Salt Lake City: Deseret News, 1909), 505; bracketed comments added.

27. Orson Pratt, *Journal of Discourses*, 24:25–26.

28. *Journal of Discourses,* 25:236–37; see also Monte S. Nyman and Charles D. Tate Jr., eds., *Fourth Nephi through Moroni: From Zion to Destruction* (Provo: BYU Religious Studies Center, 1995), 222; bracketed comments added.

Chapter Two

THE VISION OF ZION

THE ZION PARADIGM

To clearly understand Zion is to change the paradigm of our existence, because we will begin to see who we are and how our life fits into the mosaic of the last days. Once we see who we are, we will see for the first time what our potential is, where we should be going, and how to get there. Our worldview will change. It may be surprising that understanding Zion could change someone so dramatically, because the potential to establish Zion has been with us for over 175 years. We, the people of this last dispensation, are just now beginning to understand who we are.

In physics the "unified field theory" is an attempt to unite all the forces and interactions of nature into a single theory. Einstein coined the term. His quest to define a "unified field theory" proved elusive and has remained the Holy Grail for physicists—the long sought-after theory that explains not only the nature and behavior of all things, but also how to control and manipulate them.

Beyond a unified theory of all physical things, there must be a law, an overarching truth, a "unified eternal theory," if you will, which describes all existence, including time, eternity, the existence, purposes, and power of God, and the pathway to godhood.

Without even attempting to postulate such an infinite theory with this finite mind, since the gospel is a reality in our world, we might be able to conceive a "unified gospel theory." Such a theory would bring together all other revealed truths, explaining the existence and purpose of all truths revealed in this dispensation. It would not only unify all of these truths into one concept, but also teach us in manageable terms how to fulfill and obtain them all. In as much as revealed knowledge has enlightened our minds, Zion and the quest for translation is the "unified gospel theory." This seems justified, because the principles of Zion and the proffered gifts of translation explain completely the restored gospel and every promised blessing. The gospel contains hundreds of otherwise incomprehensible promises that are clearly offered in our present day, which we mentally press beyond our present lives and into future exalted worlds to preserve our spiritual sanity.

As an example, D&C 76:52–70, which we will study in detail further on, is clearly promising blessings to those who are presently experiencing these things in the mortal world; but the blessings are so vast that we universally interpret them as being a description of the celestial kingdom.

When those glorious promises are viewed through the lens of Zion and translation, they fit with perfect alignment into the context of their own claims, which is to say that with Zion in view, the language used in these scriptures can be interpreted literally, without pushing the promises into some post-mortal fulfillment. The language clearly promises these blessings to living mortals, and when we realize these blessings have been repeatedly enjoyed by Zion dwellers, a society of translated people, then these claims are literally true in the context of their own claims. Without an understanding of Zion, the promised glories are too vast to fit our commonly held paradigm of the gospel as we know it. If the idea of Zion and the blessings it promises are not immediately in our thinking, we might incorrectly push the fulfillment of these promises into the celestial kingdom, because their vastness seems to fit better there than here.

ZION THROUGHOUT HISTORY

Throughout the entire history of the world the God of heaven has labored to elevate His people to become Zion. Zion is the ultimate potential outcome of every dispensation of the gospel. Every dispensation has either successfully established Zion, or attempted to do so.

Hugh Nibley informs us that, "In every dispensation, we are told, there has been a Zion on the earth."[1]

The prophets whom God has sent forth upon the earth have attempted to establish Zion in their own eras. The most notable of these was Enoch, who established Zion in the midst of an apostate and warlike people. He went forth among his people and preached with such power that even his enemies could not withstand him. In time he gathered his people into a great city, and Christ came and dwelt among them. Enoch's Zion thus became the prototype of Zion for all time. The scriptures inform us that Enoch built a city that was called the City of Holiness, even Zion (Moses 7:18–19).

Even though we understand that every dispensation has labored to bring forth Zion, some have gloriously succeeded, and some have not produced the full glory that Enoch's Zion did. In each case where Zion faltered, it was either because the people failed to live the laws that would have secured their place as Zion, or because it began in earnest, rose to some level of glory, and after a period of apostasy, was destroyed by the armies of evil. Such was the outcome of the Nephite Zion from A.D. 34 to A.D. 200.

In each of these attempts, whether glorious successes or partial failures, they were attempting to build an exact duplicate of Enoch's Zion, or better stated, they were attempting to build after the same pattern God gave to Enoch.

THE PROTOTYPE OF ZION

Realizing that there is only one blueprint for Zion is an important tool in seeking to understand what Zion will be like in our day. Every Zion that God brought forth was established and built using this pattern. This is the prototype of Zion, one that has been used in every dispensation, and one that will be used again to build the great and last Zion, the Heavenly City to which Jesus Christ will come in glory just prior to his taking vengeance upon a wicked world.

In order to fully understand what this prototype is, we must digress for a moment. We often repeat a rather intriguing principle of truth, but may fail to comprehend it. It is that "all truth can be circumscribed into one great whole."

President Howard W. Hunter observed:

> With God our Heavenly Father, all truth, wherever found or however apprehended, is circumscribed into one great whole. Ultimately, there are no contradictions, no quarrels, no inscrutable paradoxes, no mysteries.[2]

In other words, all truth belongs to a greater body of truth. The words "one great whole" suggests that the collective sum of all these truths is perfect. Nothing is missing. No truth is outside of this great whole. Nothing can be added. It is simply a perfect whole. It also means that there are no isolated truths floating out there that are not perfectly fitted into this greater whole. We further understand that all truth belongs to the gospel, or that all truth is encompassed by the gospel. Brigham Young noted:

> "Mormonism" embraces all truth that is revealed and that is not revealed, whether religious, political, scientific, or philosophical.[3]

Since the gospel embraces all truth, there are no truths outside of the gospel. Each dispensation of the gospel is taken from the body of all truth, and therefore the portion revealed in that dispensation is taken from the same body of truth as all other dispensations. Another way of saying this is: "There is only one gospel."

This means that when you read about God's dealings with ancient people, you are reading about *the* gospel, not some temporary set of truths crafted for that dispensation. Every truth they of old were taught belonged to the great whole from which we presently dine.

For this reason, our Zion must be built up on identical principles, priesthood, and powers that Enoch's and all other dispensations of Zion have embraced.

We understand that the Lord dispenses His gospel according to divinely ordained law, never varying from generation to generation, except according to our willingness to believe and obey Him. His course is fixed and unchanging. And, because He treats all of His children equally, He dispenses the same gospel and salvation over and over, thus His course is "one eternal round" (Alma 7:22). He is the same yesterday, today, and forever (D&C 35:3). Hence, the pattern used by Enoch to bring forth Zion was the same that was later delivered to Melchizedek. The application of the pattern would have been tailored to the times and needs of the people, but the principles, the priesthood, the promises and power would have been identical. By this I mean that God revealed the same knowledge, offered the same promises, ordained the same priesthood, and delivered the same privileges and glories equally to the righteous of both Zions. This has to be true, because God is no respecter of persons, and His course never varies.

Elder Orson Pratt stated it this way:

> The Latter-Day Zion will resemble, in most particulars, the Zion of Enoch: *it will be established upon the same celestial laws—be built upon*

the same gospel, and be guided by continued revelation. Its inhabitants, like those of the antediluvian Zion, will be the righteous gathered out from all nations: the glory of God will be seen upon it; and His power will be manifested there, even as in the Zion of old. All the blessings and grand characteristics which were exhibited in ancient Zion will be shown forth in the Latter-Day Zion. As the Zion of Enoch was caught up by the powers of heaven, so will the Latter-Day Zion be taken up into the cloud when the heavens are opened and the face of the Lord is unveiled at His Second Coming.[4]

It is true that God has at times withheld portions of His gospel when His children have not been worthy of more. But those portions which He did reveal were snug pieces from the whole, not unique, tailor-made add-ons. He didn't invent new mini-gospels. He merely revealed portions of the greater whole.

Another way to view this is that the gospel is a perfect whole. It is like a perfect sphere made of the finest material. There are no bumps, no hollow divots, and no attachments. Everything you read about the gospel in the scriptures fits within the construct of the whole.

The point here is that what happened to Enoch is an ordained part of *the* gospel. It wasn't unique to Enoch. What happened to Lehi wasn't a one-time event. What happened to the brother of Jared will happen again, and again, and again.

I am not speaking of Lehi's calling or of his prophetic labors. Fleeing Jerusalem and populating a new land may never become a prophetic calling again, but the principles, blessings, and miracles of Lehi's life have occurred many times before and will continue in every generation of time forever. I am speaking of his eternal privileges, blessings, and priesthood power. I am speaking of the gospel of Jesus Christ, which never changes. If Lehi saw visions, so may we. If Enoch was translated, so may we be, if we obey the same laws Enoch obeyed. Enoch went forth and built Zion in his day, as we have been commanded to do, and we can ultimately succeed as past dispensations gloriously have, because the pathway Enoch walked is clearly available to us.

As an example of what this means, we know that when the scriptures speak of faith, all instances of faith in prior generations are prototypical of that faith that we seek. There are no occurrences of faith in past generations that are not typical of the divine pattern. When the scriptures speak of Zion, we can go back and find every other instance of Zion. Each was patterned after the same divine blueprint. None of them were intended to be one-of-a-kind. The gospel and its impact upon men is always the same—because God is always the same. Elder Hugh B. Brown said,

> The gospel of Jesus Christ is eternal and unchangeable, its laws are inexorable and immutable.[5]

> 19 For he that diligently seeketh shall find; and the mysteries of God shall be unfolded unto them, by the power of the Holy Ghost, as well in these times as in times of old, and as well in times of old as in times to come; wherefore, the course of the Lord is one eternal round. (1 Nephi 10:19)

Joseph Smith informed us that the ordinances of the priesthood have been kept the same forever and ever:

> Therefore he set the ordinances to be the same forever and ever, and set Adam to watch over them, to reveal them from heaven to man, or to send angels to reveal them.[6]

Not all attempts to establish Zion measured up to the full glory of Enoch's Zion, but they were all seeking the same divine stature. The gospel and the blessings and privileges it bestows upon the children of men are one eternal round. In other words, it happens over and over in a never-ending pattern.

Of course there are unique callings. There was only one Joseph Smith. But the gospel Joseph understood and lived was not unique. We may not experience a first vision, because that was relevant to the opening of a dispensation and unique to Joseph Smith in becoming a prophet of a dispensation. But we can experience everything else he experienced as a priesthood holder. Every blessing, privilege, miracle, and angelic visitation is offered to us—and more. Joseph explained it this way:

> God hath not revealed anything to Joseph, but what he will make known unto the Twelve, and even the least saint may know all things as fast as he is able to bear them, for the day must come when no man need say to his neighbor, Know ye the Lord; for all shall know him . . . from the least to the greatest.[7]

THE PATTERN OF ZION

Since the gospel is attempting to achieve the same purpose and blessings in every generation, we can begin to glimpse the pattern of Zion from scriptural accounts of attempts to establish it. Even from what little we know of Zion's past, when we use what the scriptures collectively reveal, we begin to glimpse what Zion truly is and what it will be.

1) Zion generally begins with one righteous individual, a prophet, who is called to preach repentance. That prophet generally preaches with power and works miracles. The people typically reject his message and often kill him, thus ending that dispensation's opportunity to establish Zion.

2) When Zion succeeds, it exists first as a small group of individuals who believe that prophet, who obey gospel principles and ordinances, and obtain a Zion state in their souls. They are later gathered into a city or center place.

Lorenzo Snow said:

> The day will come when Latter-day Saints will be selected—all may not be called at once, but those who are worthy will be called.[8]

3) Once the city of Zion is established, it becomes exclusive, and unrighteous individuals may not enter it (Revelation 21:27, D&C 45:67). Those who are excluded fear and tremble and consider Zion both terrible and great (D&C 45:74–75).

4) Christ personally walks the streets of Zion (Moses 7:64).

5) All of the citizens of Zion must be worthy to be in Christ's presence, because He will be there in glory during the Millennium (D&C 45:59; Moses 7:64).

6) The people of Zion are worthy of a translated state, though in the beginning it is possible that not all of them are translated. When Zion has been fully perfected its citizens do not age and have no sickness, disease, disaster, or death.

7) All things are subject unto them both in heaven and on earth (D&C 50:18).

8) Zion exists in a terrestrial state, which is not subject to many of the laws of nature as we experience them. Since translated Zion remains in the telestial world, translated people are still mortal, though they

become what could be described as terrestrial mortals. The people are described as terrestrial beings living a celestial law in a telestial world (D&C 105:5).

Joseph Fielding Smith noted:

> The people of the city of Enoch, because of their integrity and faithfulness, were as pilgrims and strangers on the earth. This is due to the fact that they were living the celestial law in a telestial world, and all were of one mind, perfectly obedient to all commandments of the Lord.[9]

Monte S. Nyman and Charles Tate Jr. explained it this way:

> Joseph Smith observed that many have incorrectly supposed that translated beings are "taken immediately into the presence of God, and into eternal fulness." He explained, "Their place of habitation is that of the terrestrial order." Hence, the Three Nephites were quickened from our present telestial condition to a higher terrestrial state. What, then, will be the nature of their greater future change? The Savior had specifically told them that "when I shall come in my glory ye shall be changed in the twinkling of an eye from mortality to immortality" (3 Nephi 28:8). *In summary, we are telestial mortals, translated beings are terrestrial mortals, while exalted resurrected beings are celestial immortals.*[10]

9) Once Zion is perfected, the enemies of Zion have no power over it, but repeatedly attempt to destroy it (Moses 7:13).
10) When Zion is imperfect, or the people are not fully established in righteousness, this warfare destroys Zion, and the people are often destroyed or scattered.
11) Perfected Zion will be defended by the power of God in great glory. Zion does not fear her enemies. The people of Zion will be the only ones not at war (D&C 45:68, Moses 7:13–17).
12) The people of Zion are of one heart and one mind and are the pure in heart (D&C 97:21). The pure in heart shall see God (Matthew 5:8).
13) The righteous will be taken up to meet Christ at His return (D&C 88:95–96). As they are caught up they will be quickened in a form of translation. The effects of the "fall of Adam" will be overcome at that time. Their children will grow up without sin. Elder Orson Pratt described it this way:

> A partial change will be wrought upon them, not a change to immortality, like that which all the Saints will undergo when they are

changed in the twinkling of an eye, from mortality to immortality; but so great will be the change then wrought that the children who are born into the world will grow up without sin unto salvation. Why will this be so? Because that fallen nature, introduced by the fall, and transferred from parents to children, from generation to generation, will be, in a measure, eradicated by this change. Then the righteous will go forth, and grow up like calves of the stall; and one revelation says, their children shall grow up without sin unto salvation. Satan having no power to tempt them, these children will not sin.[11]

14) The people of Zion labor to expand Zion, to gather in the elect, and to labor with those who are "heirs of salvation" (D&C 7:5–7).

15) It is my belief that when Zion is perfected it will not be subject to the economy of Babylon and will have no need of money. Beyond enjoying a perfect economic system within Zion, translated beings have command over the elements, which suggests that wants and needs will be created by priesthood power rather than manufactured.

16) The establishment of Zion has generally preceded dramatic changes in the earth, oftentimes great cleansings or scourges, such as the flood of Noah, the destruction of the Nephites, and the final cleansing of the latter days.

17) If the people of Zion do not live the celestial law, Zion does not succeed (D&C 105:5).

18) The reason Zion does not succeed has historically been because the people are not prepared to live a celestial law that would make them worthy to enjoy the presence of the Lord. They eventually return to their telestial ways. Generally the prophet of their dispensation is killed or taken up. Such was the fate of Joseph's latter-day attempt.

19) When an attempt to establish Zion fails, the people are often driven into the wilderness to repent and to prepare to try again. This cycle may literally take hundreds to thousands of years.

20) The Latter-day Zion that we will build is the second time (in this dispensation) the Lord will set His hand to recover Israel. This time Zion will prevail and be prepared to receive her God (Jacob 6:2; 2 Nephi 6:14).

21) The latter-day Zion will dwell in peace for one thousand years (Moses 7:64–65).

From the above (admittedly incomplete) sketch of Zion, it is hard not to yearn to be a part of it in its perfect form. It is also easier to see the great task awaiting us. The God of Heaven has decreed that this latter-day Zion shall not fail. Someone will stand with the Prince of Peace upon Mount Zion, and from that holy city depart to gather in the elect. I pray to God that it will be you and me.

Speaking of Enoch's Zion, Elder Orson Pratt gave us this insight:

> They were instructed, after they assembled in one, in righteousness, for three hundred and sixty-five years; that they learned the laws of the kingdom, and concerning God and every principle of righteousness that was necessary to enable them to enter into the fullness of the glory of heaven; they were instructed to build up a city, and it was called a city of holiness, for God came down and dwelt with that people; he was in their midst, they beheld this glory, they saw his face, and he condescended to dwell among them for many long years, during which time they were instructed and taught in all of his ways, and among other things *they learned the great doctrine and principle of translation, for that is a doctrine the same as the doctrine of the resurrection of the dead, which is among the first principles of the plan of salvation; and we may also say that the doctrine of translation, which is intimately connected with that of the resurrection, is also one of the first principles of the doctrines of Christ.*[12]

The nature and prototype of Zion is that when it is fully established in righteousness, God himself will come down and dwell with His people. They will behold His glory and become familiar with His face. He will teach them all of His truths, one of which is the doctrine and principle of translation.

It is interesting here that Elder Pratt calls translation and resurrection "among the first principles of the plan of salvation" and also "the first principles of the doctrines of Christ." It isn't plain what he meant by that, but it is obvious that he did not consider translation an obscure doctrine, but one that should be understood and sought after.

Notes

1. Nibley, *Approaching Zion*, 5–6.
2. "President's Formal Charge of Responsibility," *LDS Church News,* Nov. 26, 1994.
3. Brigham Young, *Journal of Discourses,* 9:149.
4. Orson Pratt, *The Seer* 2, no. 5, 265; italics added.

5. Hugh B. Brown, *The Abundant Life* (Salt Lake City: Bookcraft, 1965), 186.

6. Smith, *Discourses of the prophet Joseph Smith,* compiled by Alma P. Burton (Salt Lake City: Deseret Book, 1977), 53.

7. Smith, *Teachings of the Prophet Joseph Smith,* 149.

8. Lorenzo Snow, in Conference Report, Apr. 1898.

9. Joseph Fielding Smith, *Church History and Modern Revelation*, 4 vols. (Salt Lake City: The Church of Jesus Christ of Latter-day Saints, 1946–49), 1:178–79.

10. Monte S. Nyman and Charles D. Tate Jr., eds., *Alma, the Testimony of the Word* (Provo: BYU Religious Studies Center, 1992), 201–2.

11. Orson Pratt, *Journal of Discourses,* 16:319–20.

12. Ibid., 17: 147; italics added.

Chapter Three

UNDERSTANDING TRANSLATION

TRANSLATION AND PRIESTHOOD SUCCESSION

To further our study of Zion and how to obtain it, let us first observe that one of the historic purposes of translation has been to perpetuate the priesthood from Adam through all the generations of mankind until the end comes. Even though there have been long periods of apostasy throughout history, we are told that there has never been a day when the priesthood has not existed upon the earth. When a righteous mortal was not found to bear the priesthood, the line of authority was perpetuated by translated beings.

Elder McConkie notes:

> Jesus and his apostles and hosts of believers in their day were all priests after this higher order, which Peter called "a royal priesthood." (1 Peter 2:5–9.) But with the martyrdom of the apostles, save John only, the keys of the kingdom were taken from mortals. The priesthood could no longer be conferred upon men, and the long night of apostate darkness fell upon the earth. *During that day, only translated beings held the priesthood, and it so continued until those arose whose right it was by lineage to claim the holy order again in the day of restoration.* (D&C 86:8–11.)[1]

TRANSLATION AND ZION

Having observed in our previous discussion that the latter-day Zion will be a society like Enoch's, the question must be asked, is it even possible for us to become a translated society? Can we even hope that such a glorious possibility is ours? Do the promises of Zion really extend to you and I?

The answer is an astonishing yes! The promises are ours to claim. We will discuss not only what these promises are, but also how to claim them. The way is clearly marked—much more clearly than one would ever imagine. A great deal has been said about translation by prophets, about who is privileged to seek it, why they would want to, and how to go about it. The scriptures hold many keys and clues regarding Zion that can be clearly understood when the underlying facts of Zion are understood by the reader. When a reader is unaware of Zion, then these statements fade into truisms rather than truths. The difference being, that truisms lack sharp meaning, they are hazy concepts that just feel true, whereas truths are facts and principles understood in a brighter light. We will discuss these points in detail as we progress.

The power of translation belongs to this priesthood. Joseph Smith simply states: "Now the doctrine of translation is a power which belongs to this Priesthood."[2]

Translation is a power integral with the priesthood in our day. Joseph further notes that these priesthood powers and associated keys are to be revealed in the latter days:

> There are many things which belong to the powers of the Priest-hood and the keys thereof, that have been kept hid from before the foundation of the world; they are hid from the wise and prudent to be revealed in the last times.[3]

Elder McConkie makes this astonishing statement:

> Raphael, whom we assume to have been Enoch or someone from his dispensation, came and committed such keys as appertained to that day. No doubt these included the power to use the priesthood to translate men, as will be the state of all those who abide the day of the Second Coming.[4]

From these statements there can be little doubt that our present priesthood embodies the power of translation.

The power of translation and the latter-day Zion are closely related. To be worthy of translation is to be a Zion-worthy individual, no matter if the command to actually build Zion has been issued in your lifetime.

When the time to build Zion actually comes, then without translation Zion cannot exist on the premillennial plane that it must. It is only a small leap to say that until we become worthy to participate in the priest-hood power of translation, we cannot completely establish Zion, nor can we be prepared to meet Christ when He comes again.

President John Taylor said:

> And then when the time comes that these calamities we read of shall overtake the earth, those that are prepared will have the power of translation, as they had in former times, and the city will be trans-lated.[5]

He also notes that it will be through this power of translation that our latter-day Zion will be able to join with Enoch's Zion when it comes.

> How perfect it was in the days of Enoch we are not told, but every-thing that they had revealed to them pertaining to the organization of the Church of God, also pertaining to doctrine and ordinances, we have had revealed to us, excepting one thing, and that is the principle and *power of translation; that, however, will in due time be restored also.* And if they in their day built a Zion, we have one to build in our day, and when this shall be done and everything is in readiness, the Zion which the people of Enoch built and which was translated, will descend from above, and the Zion of the latter days which this people will build, will ascend *by virtue of this principle and power [of translation].*[6]

In another address, President Taylor assured us:

> If there was anything associated with Enoch and his city, and the gathering together of his people, or of the translation of his city, it would be manifested in the last days. *If there was anything associated with the Melchizedek Priesthood in all its forms, powers, privileges and blessings at any time or in any part of the earth, it would be restored in the last days . . . for this is the dispensation of the fulness of times, embrac-ing all other times, all principles, all powers, all manifestations, all Priest-hoods and the powers thereof that have existed in any age, in any part of the world,* for "Those things which never have been revealed from the foundation of the world, but have been kept hid from the wise and prudent, shall be revealed unto babes and sucklings in this the dispen-sation of the fulness of times."[7]

When will the Lord at last wield the mighty sword of translation in our behalf? It will be prior to the Second Coming, prior to the establish-ment of the city of Zion, and before we build the physical buildings of Zion. In other words, translation must come before it all.

Brigham Young gave us the answer years earlier:

> How long, Latter-day Saints, before you will believe the Gospel as it is? The Lord has declared it to be his will that his people will enter into covenant, *even as Enoch and his people did, which of necessity, must be before we shall have the privilege of building the Center Stake of Zion.*[8]

We have a glorious opportunity to follow in the footsteps of Enoch, which is to enter into the perfections of Zion and the presence of God. Notice in the quotation below that President Taylor equates being "sanctified to the renewing of their bodies" with being worthy to be in the presence of God. We will discuss the oath and covenant of the priesthood in detail further on, but in short, this grand promise is making reference to translation.

> When that holy temple is built in Zion God will take away the veil from the eyes of his servants; and the day is yet to dawn when the sons of Moses and Aaron, *having become sanctified to the renewing of their bodies,* will administer in that holy house, and the veil will be taken away, and they will gaze upon the glories of that world now unseen, and upon the faces of beings now to them invisible.[9]

In the beginning of Zion it seems reasonable that not everyone will be translated. One way to view this is that many people will have become Zion worthy through the processes we will discuss as we progress through this book, but like the Nephite nine (see 3 Nephi 28:2), many will have requested some other gift than translation.

Since God is no respecter of persons and grants the same gifts for the same righteousness, it seems apparent that many people will arrive at the requisite worthiness of Zion prior to the day of actual translation being ushered in.

We know that by the time Christ suddenly comes to the temple in Zion, the people of Zion will be worthy to be in His presence.

It is the opinion of this author that translation, or an equal degree of righteousness that has not yet culminated in translation, will be required to enter Zion. The reason is that our latter-day scriptures contain numerous promises that we, the stewards of the latter days, can obtain this glorious stature.

Again, the principle of translation is inherent in and inseparable from Zion. To obtain translation is to obtain Zion.

The implications of this are vast. Since we are commanded to build Zion, we are literally being commanded to seek and obtain that degree of righteousness that will, in the due time of the Lord, qualify us to be translated.

The following quote by President John Taylor informs us that when Zion is established, it will be built by those that are prepared to be translated.

> We will build up our Zion after the pattern that God will show us, and we will be governed by His law and submit to His authority and be governed by the Holy Priesthood and by the word and will of God. And then when the time comes that these calamities we read of shall overtake the earth, *those that are prepared will have the power of translation, as they had in former times, and the city will be translated.* And Zion that is on the earth will rise, and the Zion above will descend, as we are told, and we will meet and fall on each other's necks and embrace and kiss each other. And thus the purposes of God to a certain extent will then be fulfilled.[10]

TRANSLATION DEFINED

Since it is our privilege to seek, and eventually obtain, a translated Zion stature, let us clearly define what translation is. Translation defines a state of purity and obedience which brings about an altered mortal state that rises above the physical limitations of mortality. In other words, a translated person is still mortal (see 3 Nephi 28:8) but is not subject to mortal frailty such as sickness, injury, death, or even sadness.

The scriptures inform us that eternal life is the highest outcome of our mortal experience after we depart this world, spend time in the spirit world, are resurrected, enjoy the Millennium, and finally participate in the judgment and are assigned to a kingdom.

The scriptures also quite plainly teach that translation is the highest outcome of mortality—while yet a mortal. There is no greater blessing and no greater privilege a mortal may obtain than to be translated. This truth was echoed when the Nephite three requested this superlative gift, and the Lord replied "wherefore more blessed are ye" (see 3 Nephi 28:7).

These faithful and prototypical Three Nephites were even more blessed than the nine who requested to speedily come into the Father's kingdom following their mortal labors. If you stop to analyze what the nine were actually requesting, they were asking to skip the spirit world of disembodied life, and all other events mentioned above, and speedily come into the presence of the Father, which suggests that they were requesting to be resurrected immediately and enter into eternal glory. Thus we see that translation is greater even than their fast track into eternity.

After granting the humble request of the Three Nephites, the Lord enumerated the extent of this blessing of translation and then added,

> 10 And for this cause ye shall have a fulness of joy; and ye shall sit down in the kingdom of my Father; yea, your joy shall be full, even as the Father hath given me fulness of joy; and ye shall be even as I am, and I am even as the Father; and the Father and I are one. (3 Nephi 28:10)

In matters of royalty, kings and queens sit upon thrones, and all others stand or kneel before them. Herein lies the greatness of Christ's statement that they, the three, would sit down in the Father's kingdom, meaning that they would be upon thrones.

Many others, most of whom were not translated, will also sit upon thrones. Translation is not the *only* path to exaltation, but it is the *preferred* path for mortals when it is offered in the current dispensation.

The powerful implication of the scripture above is that the blessedness of translation eclipses all other rewards, and these trailing clouds of glory will follow them into the eternities. The Lord's promises indicate that they will become even as Christ and the Father, one with Them in glory, might, and dominion. This promise is the promise of the highest possible outcome of mortality. Thus, it isn't difficult to conclude that the heightened blessedness that begins in mortality with Zion worthiness extends through all time and eternity.

This same promise is echoed in words too sacred to repeat anywhere but at that glorious moment at the veil of the temple.

Translated persons possess the power of the priesthood in great glory, and under the direction of Jesus Christ, use it in miraculous ways to further the purposes of God. The stated goal of John the Beloved was that he wanted to remain upon the earth to bring souls unto Christ (3 Nephi 28:9). This supremely righteous and Christlike desire was granted through translation. The Three Nephites were promised that they would become, and still presently are,

> 29 . . . ministers unto the scattered tribes of Israel, and unto all nations, kindreds, tongues and people, and shall bring out of them unto Jesus many souls, that their desire may be fulfilled, and also because of the convincing power of God which is in them. (3 Nephi 28:29)

The following verse expands our understanding of what John the Beloved is doing.

> 6. Yea, he has undertaken a greater work; therefore I will make him as flaming fire and a ministering angel; he shall minister for those who shall be heirs of salvation who dwell on the earth. (D&C 7:6)

Of great interest is this masterfully understated conclusion to their promised gifts that was quoted above: "because of the convincing power of God which is in them." In other words, they have the power to convince mankind in miraculous ways, or more powerfully stated, through the display of miracles. The translated become as "angels of God," able to show themselves to anyone when necessary. They become doers of "great and marvelous works," for the purpose of convincing men of the power of God, to prepare the world for the "great and coming day when all must surely stand before the judgment-seat of Christ" (3 Nephi 28:30–31).

We may wonder *where* these great ones are in our lone and dreary world. The answer is they are among us, and tragically, we "know them not" (3 Nephi 28:27). Why? We must ask ourselves this question again and again until the answer is pure and untarnished. Why don't we see them? Why aren't their works plain and obvious among us?

The obvious answer is that they have not often chosen to reveal themselves and their premillennial labors.[11] Could part of the answer also lie in the fact that we have been invited to become the citizens of Zion, the ministers of great righteousness, the translated ones we long to see? Could it be that without the faith to see this invitation we also don't have the faith to associate with those who already have?

The Nature of Translation

Translation is not a permanent state but an intermediate condition prior to resurrection. It has a specific purpose of giving individuals the power necessary to carry out express assignments that would otherwise not be possible for them to accomplish. Such an individual and mission is well known in John the Beloved, who has remained upon the earth working to prepare the world for the glorious return of the Savior. Joseph Smith explained,

> Translated bodies cannot enter into rest until they have undergone a change equivalent to death. Translated bodies are designed for future missions.[12]

These are some of the principles associated with translation:

- Translated people will not endure the "pains" of death but will be changed in the twinkling of an eye (3 Nephi 28:8).

- Translated persons will not have pain or sorrow save it be for the sins of the world (3 Nephi 28:9).

- Translated beings enjoy a "fulness of joy," and will "sit down in the kingdom of my Father" (3 Nephi 28:10).

- Translated beings are changed into an immortal state and can behold the things of God (3 Nephi 28:15).

- Prisons cannot hold them, fire can not harm them, wild beasts will not injure them (3 Nephi 28:19–22).

- Translated people can work among us and not be known (3 Nephi 28:27–28).

- They are "as the angels of God" and can show themselves to whomever it seems good to them (3 Nephi 28:30).

- They can work miracles and perform great and marvelous works (3 Nephi 28: 31–32).

- They are changed. Satan cannot tempt them or have power over them. They are sanctified in the flesh (D&C 84:33) and have power over the earth (3 Nephi 28:39). This means they are not subject to the laws of what we call nature. They can create objects they need and have mastery over all things mortal.

- Translated beings prolong their labors in the ministry.[13] Prolonging their ministry to bring souls unto Christ was the desire of the hearts of those for whom we have a detailed account of their translation.

- Translated beings are "not subject to sorrow or to disease or to death."[14]

- Translated individuals must be changed into the greater condition of resurrection before they can be exalted.

Elder McConkie Notes:

In the case of translated beings and the righteous persons who shall live during the millennial era, death and the resurrection shall take place instantaneously. They shall be changed from mortality to immortality in the twinkling of an eye, the spirit never having occasion to separate from the body, and in their cases this change is called death (D&C 63:49–52; 3 Nephi 28). But it is not death according to the most common usage of the word (D&C 101:29–31; Isaiah 65:20).[15]

Again, from Elder McConkie:

But they do pass through death and are changed from mortality to immortality, in the eternal sense, and they thus both die and are resurrected in the eternal sense. This, we might add, is why Paul wrote: "Behold, I shew you a mystery; We shall not all sleep, but we shall all be changed, In a moment, in the twinkling of an eye, at the last trump: for the trumpet shall sound, and the dead shall be raised incorruptible, and we shall be changed" (1 Corinthians 15:51–52).[16]

- This earth is a function of the telestial order. Translation belongs to the terrestrial order, and when all inhabitants of the earth are translated, the earth itself will enter a terrestrial state.[17]

- Translated people have a purpose and calling. Translation is not just a way to go downhill skiing without the possibility of injuries. Translated people belong to the Church of the Firstborn and the Church of Enoch (D&C 76:51–57). They are, among many other things, ministering angels unto many planets. They become the ministers and messengers of God, the angels of His sending to do the work of the covenants of the Father (Moroni 7:31).

The prophet Joseph taught:

Many have supposed that the doctrine of translation was a doctrine whereby men were taken immediately into the presence of God, and into an eternal fulness, but this is a mistaken idea. Their place of habitation is that of the terrestrial order, and a place prepared for such characters He held in reserve to be ministering angels unto many planets, and who as yet have not entered into as great a fulness as those who are resurrected from the dead.[18]

- The labor of translated beings has been at times to check the advance of evil when mortal men are not sufficiently righteous to do so.

Joseph Fielding Smith explained:

> Even when the great apostasy occurred following the death of the Savior's apostles, our Father in heaven held control and had duly authorized servants on the earth to direct his work and to check, to some extent at least, the ravages and corruption of the evil powers. These servants were not permitted to organize the Church nor to officiate in the ordinances of the gospel, but they did check the advances of evil as far as the Lord deemed it necessary. This truth is made manifest in the statement of the Lord in the Doctrine and Covenants wherein the following appears: Wherefore, I will that all men shall repent, for all are under sin, except those which I have reserved unto myself, holy men that ye know not of (D&C 49:8).[19]

- At least some translated beings have been assigned the ministry of bringing souls unto Christ in preparation for the return of the Lord.

Joseph Fielding Smith observed:

> We know that John the Revelator and the three Nephites were granted the privilege of remaining on the earth in the translated state, to "bring souls unto Christ." We know that this was the request of John (D&C Sec. 7) and likewise the desire of the three Nephites (3 Nephi 28:4-18).[20]

- Translated beings are not subject to what we call the "laws of nature."

Marvin J. Ballard stated:

> Although they had the ability to live in the earth among men, they had power over the elements of earth, *power over the law of gravitation*, by which they could move over the face of the earth with the speed of their own thoughts, power to reveal themselves to men; and yet power to mingle and move among men unobserved and hidden.[21]

Christ, in describing to the Three Nephites what translation would be like, left an indelible blueprint of what translated beings enjoy:

> 8. And ye shall never endure the pains of death; but when I shall come in my glory ye shall be changed in the twinkling of an eye from

mortality to immortality; and then shall ye be blessed in the kingdom of my Father.

9. And again, ye shall not have pain while ye shall dwell in the flesh, neither sorrow save it be for the sins of the world; and all this will I do because of the thing which ye have desired of me, for ye have desired that ye might bring the souls of men unto me, while the world shall stand. (3 Nephi 28:8–9)

- Translated persons are not yet resurrected. Joseph Smith observed:

This distinction is made between the doctrine of the actual resurrection and translation: translation obtains deliverance from the tortures and sufferings of the body, but their existence will prolong as to the labors and toils of the ministry, before they can enter into so great a rest and glory.[22]

- Apparently, translated beings no longer have blood flowing in their veins, but a terrestrial fluid that affects the changes of translation.

Elder McConkie states:

No longer does blood (the life-giving element of our present mortality) flow in their veins.[23]

- Translated people are immune to temptation, and have power over the earth:

39 Now this change was not equal to that which shall take place at the last day; but there was a change wrought upon them, insomuch that Satan could have no power over them, that he could not tempt them; and they were sanctified in the flesh, that they were holy, and that the powers of the earth could not hold them. (3 Nephi 28:39)

- Translated people are apparently able to see into the future.

President Taylor taught:

And the Scriptures say that when the Lord shall bring again Zion her watchmen shall see eye to eye. They shall see alike, they shall comprehend alike, they shall be under the same influence. What else shall it do? It shall show you of things to come. You shall be enabled to look through the dark vista of the unborn future, to draw aside the veil of the invisible world, and comprehend the things of God; to know your destiny and the destiny of the human family, and the events that will transpire in coming ages and times. That is what the Holy Ghost will do, and therein is the difference between that Spirit and the little portion of that Spirit which is given to every man to profit withal.[24]

TRANSLATION AND THE MILLENNIUM

A less understood concept is that a form of translation will be the millennial norm. The power of translation will begin in Zion and spread from there until it fills the whole earth. Every person living will be changed to the Zion condition. Then the whole earth will be Zion. The peace and beauty of the Millennium will flow from the beauties and perfections of Zion.

Elder McConkie states:

> During the Millennium all men will be translated, as it were; in that day "there shall be no sorrow because there is no death. In that day an infant shall not die until he is old; and his life shall be as the age of a tree; And when he dies he shall not sleep, that is to say in the earth, but shall be changed in the twinkling of an eye, and shall be caught up, and his rest shall be glorious" (D&C 101:29–31).[25]

Edersheim, an Old Testament Bible scholar, though not a member of this Church, observed:

> His [Enoch's] translation was like that of Elijah (2 Kings 2:10), and like what that of the saints shall be at the Second Coming of our blessed Lord (1 Corinthians 15:51, 52).[26]

Millennial translation will include the ability to have children. Again, from Elder McConkie:

> Millennial man will live in a state akin to translation. His body will be changed so that it is no longer subject to disease or death as we know it, although he will be changed in the twinkling of an eye to full immortality when he is a hundred years of age. He will, however, have children, and mortal life of a millennial kind will continue.[27]

Joseph Fielding Smith referred to this millennial state as a "sort of translation."

We learn now from the revelations that John the Disciple is still on the earth. He has not died. He was translated, and the inhabitants of the earth will have a sort of translation. They will be transferred to a condition of the terrestrial order, and so they will have power over disease and they will have power to live until they get a certain age and then they will die; and if a man does not keep the commandments and will not obey the Gospel, when he dies it is going to be pretty tough for him because under those conditions every man ought to receive the truth, and eventually they will, because Isaiah tells you that the time will come when the knowledge of God will cover the earth as the waters do the sea.[28]

The Millennium will begin as a world in deep chaos, with a tiny portion of the world at peace under Zion's protective dome. In fact, it appears that the millennial Zion will exist quietly at first, invisible to those who do not have ears to hear and eyes to see. It will consist of those who have privately and individually heard the call of Zion through the Holy Ghost, who have believed and walked the straighter path, kept sacred covenants, viewed the "mysteries of godliness" in inspired light, and who have become Zion themselves through an invitation into the presence of Christ.

A great missionary work among the masses is presently underway to bring people to the restored gospel. Within the gospel we find every priesthood blessing, covenant, and promise necessary to empower us to seek Zion. The evolution within the gospel into Zion worthiness is a process of private purification. When there are tens of thousands of Zion-ized souls, then there will be a convocation of Zion. When the prophet of the Lord at last commands them to gather to a center place, then Zion will take on the added beauty of sanctified geography.

Notice the personal journey to Zion Joseph F. Smith speaks of:

But when shall I be prepared to go [to Zion]? Not while I have in my heart the love of this world more than the love of God. Not while I am possessed of that selfishness and greed that would induce me to cling to the world or my possessions in it, at the sacrifice of principle or truth. But when I am ready to say, "Father, all that I have, myself included, is Thine; my time, my substance, everything that I possess is on the altar, to be used freely, agreeable to Thy holy will, and not my will, but Thine, be done," then perhaps I will be prepared to go and help to redeem Zion.[29]

Brigham Young defined the pathway to Zion as a personal quest as well.

> When we conclude to make a Zion we will make it, and this work commences in the heart of each person. When the father of a family wishes to make a Zion in his own house, he must take the lead in this good work, which it is impossible for him to do unless he himself possesses the spirit of Zion. Before he can produce the work of sanctification in his family, he must sanctify himself, and by this means God can help him to sanctify his family. . . . Then we would have Zion, for all would be pure in heart."[30]

When we, the future initiates of Zion, through the process of sanctification and the power of oaths and covenants made and realized, find our way into the company of our Redeemer, then we will become Zion in fact, not just in rhetorical symbolism. This personal victory will be the true and ultimate triumph of Zion.

Elder McConkie similarly declared that we of this generation have yet to obtain the worthiness that would let us build Zion. And while emphatically instructing us to not attempt to gather to Missouri of our own volition, he instructs us to make ourselves personally worthy of being involved in the building of Zion.

> The Lord once offered his people the chance to build that Zion from which the law shall go forth to all the world. They failed. Why? Because they were unprepared and unworthy, as is yet the case with those of us who now comprise the kingdom. When we as a people are prepared and worthy, the Lord will again command us and the work will go forward—on schedule, before the Second Coming, and at the direction of the President of the Church. Until then, none of us need take any personal steps toward gathering to Missouri or preparing for a landed-inheritance there. Let us, rather, learn the great concepts involved and make ourselves worthy for any work the Lord may lay upon us in our day and time.[31]

Elder Charles W. Penrose, an apostle of the Lord, made this profound observation. He reinforces the nature of the personal quest for Zion and suggests that those who are allowed to administer in that holy house will be translated (one possible meaning of "renewing of their bodies").

> The time will come when the servants of the living God will purify themselves before him until they will be fit to receive these blessings. When that holy temple is built in Zion God will take away the veil

from the eyes of his servants; and the day is yet to dawn when the sons of Moses and Aaron, having become sanctified to the renewing of their bodies, will administer in that holy house, and the veil will be taken away.[32]

Christ will dwell in our latter-day Zion, and as the gathering continues, Zion will increase in size and in glory. At some point Enoch's Zion will come down to join the earthly Zion, and they will combine into one holy city. The people of Enoch will be among the 144,000 and assist in the gathering and building of Zion.

From that moment on, Zion will launch a great gleaning effort to gather in the elect from across the globe and bring them to Zion. They will not be converting people to the truth, but will be gathering those who are ready to enter Zion. To what end? So that they may become translated and thus "abide" the coming of Christ.

As we have emphasized, this gathering will be of the elect, the wise virgins, those whose lamps are already full, and whose souls already sing the song of redeeming love; those for whom the exquisitely rarified environment of Zion will add to their glory, not reduce them to ash.

As the Millennium begins only a small percentage of mortals will be within Zion. There will be millions of the honorable and good of the earth who will be surviving the continuing trials. In time, perhaps a long time, everyone will be taught, lifted up, and changed into the Zion standard, and the era of perfect peace so long anticipated and yearned for by the holy men of God will finally arrive (D&C 45:11–14).

During the Millennium there will be two kinds of people. There will be living mortals who are preparing to become changed into the Zion condition, and there will be immortal beings who are either translated or resurrected.

Elder McConkie explains it this way:

> During the Millennium there will, of course, be two kinds of people on earth. There will be those who are mortal, and those who are immortal. There will be those who have been changed or quickened or transfigured or translated (words fail us to describe their state), and those who have gone through a second change, in the twinkling of an eye, so as to become eternal in nature. There will be those who are on probation, for whom earth life is a probationary estate, and who are thus working out their own salvation, and those who have already overcome the world and have entered into a fulness of eternal joy.[33]

Those who are not yet resurrected will continue to grow and serve the Lord.

> 58 And the earth shall be given unto them for an inheritance; and they shall multiply and wax strong, and their children shall grow up without sin unto salvation. (D&C 45:58)

> 20 And their generations shall inherit the earth from generation to generation, forever and ever. (D&C 56:20)

It is my opinion that during the Millennium the laws of opposition will be modified, and the earth will no longer resist the efforts of man to cultivate and beautify her. Because the people will live a translated law and will have power over all things in heaven and on earth, translated beings will thus have righteous dominion over the earth. They will dress and beautify her by the power of faith. As in the days of creation, they shall speak and all of organized nature shall obey them. They shall make her once again a fit habitation for the feet of the Savior of mankind.

I will consider the next quotation again in the course of our discussion, but it is pertinent to the subject now at hand as well. Doctrine and Covenants 76 is much-loved and oft-quoted in our day. It has powerful promises that echo those heard in holy places. Generally these verses are understood to apply to the celestial kingdom far after the Millennium. Like many things in the scriptures, these words could be true on several levels and apply to more than one fulfillment.

Another possible interpretation comes to light when they are viewed through the lens of Zion and the promise of translation. This possible understanding is almost universally overlooked as to whom the promises are being made and when they will be realized.

In this light, let us consider together for a moment verses 50 through 67 of section 76:

> 50 And again we bear record—for we saw and heard, and this is the testimony of the gospel of Christ concerning them who shall come forth in the resurrection of the just—

The time line of our present consideration is thus before the resurrection of the just, because we are speaking of those who shall participate in that mighty event. As we have established, one of the grand purposes of the latter-day Church is to establish Zion, which shall of course, immediately precede the first resurrection.

The following verses define upon whom this great blessing will be bestowed.

> 51 They are they who received the testimony of Jesus, and believed on his name and were baptized after the manner of his burial, being buried in the water in his name, and this according to the commandment which he has given—
>
> 52 That by keeping the commandments they might be washed and cleansed from all their sins, and receive the Holy Spirit by the laying on of the hands of him who is ordained and sealed unto this power;
>
> 53 And who overcome by faith, and are sealed by the Holy Spirit of promise, which the Father sheds forth upon all those who are just and true.

Let us not apply hasty meaning to eternal concepts. These are they who have been cleansed from all their sins, who have been sealed by the Holy Spirit of promise, which is to imply that they have had their calling and election made sure. They are those who are just and true. In the wise and foolish virgin metaphor, we are speaking of not all, but a few among the wise virgins who have laid hold upon all of the available blessings of the restored gospel—including having been invited into the presence of Christ.

This is the "great and last promise" that if we will

> 69 Sanctify yourselves that your minds become single to God, and the days will come that you shall see him; for he will unveil his face unto you, and it shall be in his own time, and in his own way, and according to his own will. (D&C 88:68–69)

Having thus obtained this transfigured stature (not necessarily translated, but changed as one worthy to stand in the presence of God), they become:

> 54 They are they who are the Church of the Firstborn.
>
> 55 They are they into whose hands the Father has given all things—
>
> 56 They are they who are priests and kings, who have received of his fulness, and of his glory;
>
> 57 And are priests of the Most High, after the order of Melchizedek, which was after the order of Enoch, which was after the order of the Only Begotten Son.

To receive the fulness of His glory is to be in His presence, and by that everlasting event, to become "priests and kings, priestesses and queens."

The hardest part to understand and fully integrate into our testimonies is that these people are thus blessed as mortals upon the earth, in the latter-day Zion, prior to the Second Coming. Yet, the language is unimpeachable. The promises correctly understood are Spirit-born and profound. This is the Aladdin's lamp of mortality, which we tragically esteem as little more than a pretty trinket, even while we hold it in our hands.

The holy record has more promises to bestow upon these Zionites:

58 Wherefore, as it is written, they are gods, even the sons of God—

And hence, it is the mystery of "godliness" because we obtain god-like perfections and god-like powers, yet we are still mortals, thus becoming god-ly. Many eternal generations may yet transpire before we become fully evolved gods.

Elder Orson Pratt touched upon this principle in regard to the 144,000, all of whom are sanctified Zion dwellers and translated beings though yet still mortal:

They, the one hundred and forty-four thousand, had a peculiar inscription in their foreheads. What was it? It was the Father's name. What is the Father's name? It is God—the being we worship. If, then, the one hundred and forty-four thousand are to have the name of God inscribed on their foreheads, will it be simply a plaything, a something that has no meaning? or will it mean that which the inscriptions specify?—that they are indeed Gods.[34]

John Taylor taught similarly:

John says: "And I looked, and, lo, a Lamb stood on the mount Sion, and with him an hundred forty and four thousand, having his Father's name written in their foreheads" (Revelation 14:1).

Their "Father's name," bless me! that is GOD! Well done for Mormonism; *one hundred and forty four thousand* GODS.[35]

Continuing with our quotation from section 76:

59 Wherefore, all things are theirs, whether life or death, or things present, or things to come, all are theirs and they are Christ's, and Christ is God's.

Since all things and all powers are theirs, and they know all things present and future, and they dwell in the presence of Christ, we have the millennial condition brought about, not by divine decree and by divine fire, but by the humble acquisition of god-li-ness, which is Zion.

60 And they shall overcome all things.

They *shall*, but haven't, as yet, overcome all things. That will occur after the resurrection. Notice in the following quotation how each of these promises is future, yet prior to the second coming and resurrection. They "shall" . . .

61 Wherefore, let no man glory in man, but rather let him glory in God, who shall subdue all enemies under his feet.

62 These shall dwell in the presence of God and his Christ forever and ever.

63 These are they whom he shall bring with him, when he shall come in the clouds of heaven to reign on the earth over his people.

64 These are they who shall have part in the first resurrection.

65 These are they who shall come forth in the resurrection of the just.

Now, we return to the present. These "are" . . .

66 These are they who are come unto Mount Zion, and unto the city of the living God, the heavenly place, the holiest of all.

67 These are they who have come to an innumerable company of angels, to the general assembly and church of Enoch, and of the Firstborn. (D&C 76:61–67)

Which "city of the living God, the heavenly place" and company and assembly is the capital city of Enoch's Zion, the holiest of all because Christ resides there.

Satan will have no power over the millennial Saints because of their righteousness, and the Holy One of Israel will reign upon the earth.

24 And the time cometh speedily that the righteous must be led up as calves of the stall, and the Holy One of Israel must reign in dominion, and might, and power, and great glory.

25 And he gathereth his children from the four quarters of the earth; and he numbereth his sheep, and they know him; and there shall be one fold and one shepherd; and he shall feed his sheep, and in him they shall find pasture.

26 And because of the righteousness of his people, Satan has no power; wherefore, he cannot be loosed for the space of many years; for he hath no power over the hearts of the people, for they dwell in righteousness, and the Holy One of Israel reigneth. (1 Nephi 22:24–26)

During the Millennium death will entirely lose its sting. Those who are translated, or changed into the Zion format, will still experience a type of death, which will occur in the twinkling of an eye. They will not experience pain, nor will their spirit leave their bodies, but they will be changed.

It was this translated triumph over death, the glory of the millennial hope and eventual resurrection that prompted Paul the Apostle to pen the immortal words of exultation "We shall not all sleep."

51 Behold, I shew you a mystery; We shall not all sleep, but we shall all be changed,

52 In a moment, in the twinkling of an eye, at the last trump: for the trumpet shall sound, and the dead shall be raised incorruptible, and we shall be changed.

53 For this corruptible must put on incorruption, and this mortal *must* put on immortality.

54 So when this corruptible shall have put on incorruption, and this mortal shall have put on immortality, then shall be brought to pass the saying that is written, Death is swallowed up in victory.

55 O death, where *is* thy sting? O grave, where *is* thy victory?

56 The sting of death *is* sin; and the strength of sin *is* the law.

57 But thanks be to God, which giveth us the victory through our Lord Jesus Christ. (1 Corinthians 15:51–57)

Paul's description is speaking of the final trumpet, the moment when the work will be finished and all men will be changed. He clearly separates those who will not sleep, who have not died in their time (who were translated), and the dead (those who did sleep) that will rise incorruptible through resurrection, never again subject to moral corruption.

We also know there will be an ongoing change taking place during the Millennium. Not only will there be a grand finish, a great and last call to arise, but there will also be a continual change taking place during the millennial reign that will change righteous people into translated beings and Zion people into resurrected beings, which will launch them on their immortal journey into glory.

Elder McConkie commented on it in this way:

> In the case of translated beings and the righteous persons who will live during the millennial era, death and the resurrection will take place instantaneously. They will be changed from mortality to immortality in the twinkling of an eye, the spirit never having occasion to separate from the body, and in their cases this change is called death (D&C 63:49–52; 3 Nephi 28). But it is not death according to the most common usage of the word (D&C 101:29–31; Isaiah 65:20).[36]

TRANSLATED INDIVIDUALS THROUGHOUT HISTORY

This list[37] is of people from the Old Testament that Jewish tradition records as having been translated.

Enoch	Son of Jared and builder of the Holy City
Methuselah	Son of Enoch and grandfather of Noah
Eliezer	Servant of Abraham
Serah	Daughter of Asher; is held to have been a prophetess
Bithiah	Daughter of Pharaoh; rescued Moses from the water and raised him
Moses	prophet of Israel
Phinehas	Grandson of Aaron
Jabez	Often identified with the judge Othniel
Othniel	Israelite Judge of the Scholar Class
Chileab	Son of David
Hiram	Builder of Solomon's Temple
Elijah	Israelite prophet
Jonah	Israelite prophet
Ebed-melech	Ethiopian servant of King Zedekiah; helped the prophet Jeremiah
Baruch	Scribe to the prophet Jeremiah
Hiram	King of Tyre; provided materials for Solomon's Temple
Ezra	Led a group of Jews to Jerusalem from Babylonian captivity
Three sons of Korah	Who rejected their father's wickedness
Jonadab & Descendants	The Rechabite
City of Luz	

From scripture we also learn of additional translated individuals:

Ether (possibly)	Ether 15:34
City of Enoch	Moses 17:18–21
Many Saints	between Enoch and Melchizedek, Moses 7:27; JST Genesis 14:32
City of Salem	JST Genesis 14:33–34
Melchizedek	JST Genesis 14:33–34
Alma the Younger	Alma 45:18–19
Nephi, the son of Helaman (possibly)	3 Nephi 1:3
John the Beloved, apostle of Christ	3 Nephi 28:6-8
Some Christian-era Saints	Matthew 16:28, Mark 9:1, Luke 9:27
Three Nephites	3 Nephi 28:1–40

People Promised Translation in Church History

I have included a partial list of people who were promised the gift of translation in patriarchal blessings and other events. There is no way to establish whether the following individuals realized the full power of the promises given to them in these blessings. It seems possible that one could be translated yet live and conclude what appeared to be a normal life.

The greater value of these promises is to document that our forebears in the cause of building Zion understood that translation was a normal and desirable outcome in mortality.

Most of these quotations are from *Early Patriarchal Blessings of the Church of Jesus Christ of Latter-day Saints*, compiled by H. Michael Marquardt.

Orson Pratt
1835: 29 April
Thou shalt bring many souls to the knowledge of the truth, and tarry till the Savior comes, and then thou shalt be received into the celestial kingdom of God and dwell in his presence forever. [Age, 23; scribes, Thomas B. Marsh, William E. McLellin.]
—Given by Joseph Smith, Sen.[38]

Elisha H. Groves
1835: 27 August
Thy life shall be precious in the sight of the Lord, for thou shalt live

to a good old age, and if thou wilt keep all the commandments of the Lord, and desire it with all thy heart, thou mayest be translated, that thou shalt never be brought down to the grave, but remember, that thou must become holy, like unto Enoch to obtain this great blessing—or thou mayest tarry. [Age, 37; scribe, Oliver Cowdery.]

—Given by Joseph Smith, Sen.[39]

OLIVER HARMON
1836: 8 March
I seal a blessing for thy Children & thy Childrens Children & they shall be reconed in thy covenent even in the covenent of Abraham & receive an inheritance with their brethren in Zion. Thou shalt hold them by the prayer of faith & present them spotless before God in the kingdom of the Father. Thou must Seek wisdom & Keep the Word of Wisdom, & thou Shalt live till thou art Satisfied with life, & the distroyer Shall have no power to prevail against thee, thou Shalt have power over death & the grave & not sleep in the dust, but if thou wilt seek with all thy heart thou shalt be able to translate & be with Elijah in the kingdom of heaven. & if not then God['s] will shall be done. [Age, 49; scribe, Sylvester Smith.]

—Given by Joseph Smith, Sen.[40]

ETHAN BARROWS
1836: 22 March
Thou must seek council at the hand of thy God and keep all the commandments and thou shalt receive all the power of the holy priesthood; power to raise the dead, heal the sick, cause the lame to walk, the dumb to speak. Thou shalt have power to translate thyself from land to land and from country to country, from one end of heaven to the other, and when thy work is done thou shalt translate from earth to heaven. [Age unknown; scribe, Sylvester Smith.])

—Given by Joseph Smith, Sen.[41]

OLIVE BOYNTON HALE
1836: 10 November
Thou shalt have long life, enjoy the blessings of this world and life eternal in the celestial kingdom. Thou shalt have the righteous desires of thy heart, and be thankful. Thou mayest tarry till the end of wickedness shall be accomplished; till the gathering of Israel shall be finished; till the

winding up scene of this generation; and until the Savior comes in the clouds of Heaven if thou art faithful, and if thou dost attain to that faith. [Age, 30; scribe unknown.]

   —Given by Joseph Smith, Sen.[42]

Oliver Boardman Huntington

1836: 7 December

Angels shall minister unto thee for God has prepared thee for a priest & thou shalt be filled with wisdom & intelligence from Heaven, & be able to confound the learned & the priests of this generation, thou shalt be able to exceed the youth of this generation in all wisdom & knowledge, & before thou art twenty one thou wilt be called to preach the fulness of the gospel, thou shalt have power with God even to translate thyself to Heaven, & preach to the inhabitants of the moon or planets, if it shall be expedient, if thou art faithful all these blessings will be given thee. [Age, 10; scribe, Albert Carrington.]

   —Given by Joseph Smith, Sen.[43]

Lorenzo Snow

1836: 15 December

Thou shalt have great faith, even like the brother of Jared. Thou shalt have power to translate thyself from one planet to another; and power to go to the moon if thou so desire; power to preach to the spirits in prison; power to rend the veil and see Jesus Christ at the right hand of the Father; power, like Enoch, to translate thyself to heaven.

   —Given by Joseph Smith, Sen.[44]

Willard Richards

1837: 22 February

No one shall have power to harm thee or thy posterity, if thou will put thy trust in God. Death shall have no power over thee, for thou shalt tarry and behold thy Redeemer coming in the clouds, and shall see him in the flesh; shall have power to bring thy kindred into the kingdom, who shall acknowledge thee as a man of God. [Age, 33; scribe, Frederick G. Williams.]

   —Given by Joseph Smith, Sen.[45]

FLORA JACOBS

1837: 13 June

All the righteous desires of thy heart shall be granted thee if thou hast desired to tarry in the flesh to see the winding up scene of this generation that desire shall be given thee if thou hast desired to see thy Savior it shall be granted thee. If thou will have faith in God and his promises thou mayest lay down thy life or thou mayest hold it thou mayest have thy choice. [Age, 24; scribe unknown.]

—Given by Joseph Smith, Sen.[46]

DOMINICUS CARTER

Year unknown: 18 June

You shall have power over winds and waves. You shall be cast upon a desert Island. You will feel yourself forsaken and deprived of all things but the angels of God shall administer unto you and fee[d?] you. And when you are on the ocean and your life in danger you shall have power to calm the waves and shall go and preach to the barberous people and they [shall] seek thy life. Thou shalt have power to translate thyself or call down fire from Heaven as did Elijah of old. . . . You shall have an inheritance in Zion in the due time of the Lord. . . . You shall be one of the hundred and forty-four thousand and sing that song which none but that number can sing. You shall live to see the winding up scene of this generation. [Age unknown; scribe unknown.]

—Given by Joseph Smith, Sen.[47]

SARAH HARMON

1836: 8 March

thou shalt see the desires of thy Soul & be Satisfeid if thou desire thou shalt tarry till the Redeamer comes. and thou Shalt see him in the flesh. an thy blessings shall be on the blessing of thy husband in this thing also. [Age, 49; scribe, Sylvester Smith.]

—Given by Joseph Smith, Sen.[48]

ESTHER SMITH FULLER

1836: 17 June

Thou shalt tarry with thy husband and shall see all things fulfilled which are promised him in his blessing. [Age, 25; scribe unknown.]

—Given by Joseph Smith, Sen.[49]

GEORGE MILLER

1840: 4 July

The heavens shall be opened and thou shalt behold great things and the veil shall be rent, and thou shalt be permitted to look within the veil and behold that which thou wilt not be able to utter; thy life shall be long; thou mayst tarry until the winding up scene and then be numbered with the hundred-and-forty-and-four-thousand that stand upon Mount Zion. [Age, 45; scribe unknown.]

—Given by Joseph Smith, Sen.[50]

JONATHAN CROSBY JR.

1836: 21 February

Thou shalt . . . by the power of God, Be caught up to the third heavens, and behold unspeakable things, whether in the body or out. Thou shalt see thy Redeemer in the flesh, and know that He lives. Angels shall minister unto thee, and protect thee from thine enemies, so that none shall be able to take thy life. And when thy mission is full here, thou shalt visit other worlds, and remain a Priest in Eternity. Thou shalt stand upon the earth 'till the Redeemer comes, See the end of this generation, and when the heavens rend, thou shalt rise and meet thy God in the air.

—Given by Joseph Smith, Sen.[51]

CAROLINE CROSBY

1836: 21 February

Thou shalt receive an inheritance in Zion, for thee and thy children. See the glory of God fill the house. Even the glory of the kingdom of heaven. And if thou desirest thou shalt bid the grave adieu, and never sleep in the dust, but rise to meet thy Redeemer at His coming, and shalt then be forever with the Lord. I seal these blessings upon thee in the name of Jesus. Amen. [Age, 27; scribe, Sylvester Smith.]

—Given by Joseph Smith, Sen.[52]

NOTES

1. McConkie, *New Witness of the Articles of Faith*, 311; italics added.
2. Smith, *Teachings of the Prophet Joseph Smith*, 170.
3. Ibid.

4. McConkie, *The Millennial Messiah*, 119.

5. John Taylor, *Journal of Discourses*, 21:253.

6. Ibid., 23:33; italics added.

7. Ibid, 22:299; italics and bracketed comments added.

8. Ibid., 18:263; italics added.

9. Ibid., 21:49–50; italics added.

10. Ibid., 21:253; italics added.

11. For an interesting discussion on the labors of translated beings in LDS history, please see *Life Everlasting* by Duane S. Crowther.

12. Smith, *History of the Church,* 4:425; cf. D&C 129:1–9.

13. Ibid., 4:210.

14. McConkie, *The Millennial Messiah*, 644.

15. McConkie, *Mormon Doctrine*, 185.

16. McConkie, *The Mortal Messiah,* 4:389.

17. Smith, *Teachings of the Prophet Joseph Smith,* 170–71.

18. Smith, *History of the Church,* 4:xli.

19. Joseph Fielding Smith, *Answers to Gospel Questions*, 2:45.

20. Ibid., 2:46.

21. Melvin J. Ballard, "The Path to Celestial Happiness," *Deseret News*, Oct. 31, 1925; see also N. B. Lundwall, *Masterpieces of Latter-Day Saint Leaders* (Salt Lake City: Deseret Book, 1953), 99.

22. Smith, *Teachings of the Prophet Joseph Smith,* 170.

23. McConkie, *The Millennial Messiah*, 644.

24. John Taylor, *Journal of Discourses*, 23:376.

25. McConkie, *The Mortal Messiah,* 4:389–91.

26. Alfred Edersheim, *Bible History: Old Testament* (William B. Eerdmans); bracketed comments added.

27. McConkie, *The Millennial Messiah*, 644.

28. Joseph Fielding Smith, *Signs of the Times* (Salt Lake City: Deseret Book, 1952), 39.

29. Joseph F. Smith, in *Millennial Star,* 18 June 1894, 385–86; bracketed comments added.

30. Brigham Young, *Discourses of Brigham Young* (Salt Lake City: Shadow Mountain, 1954), 118–19.

31. McConkie, *New Witness of the Articles of Faith*, 586.

32. Charles W. Penrose, *Journal of Discourses* 21:49–50.

33. McConkie, *The Millennial Messiah*, 644.

34. Orson Pratt, *Journal of Discourses* 14:243.

35. John Taylor, *The Gospel Kingdom: Selections from the Writings and Discourses of John Taylor*, selected, arranged, and edited, with an introduction by G. Homer Durham (Salt Lake City: Bookcraft, 1941), 29.

36. McConkie, *Mormon Doctrine*, 185.

37. Louis Ginzberg, *The Legends of the Jews*, 7 vols. (Philadelphia: Jewish Publication Society of America, 1938), 1:297; 2:116, 270–71; 4:30, 118, 155, 202, 253, 323; 5:95–96, 165, 263, 356–77, 435; 6:104, 187, 351, 400, 409, 412, 425, 446. Ginzberg also noted that some Christian and Muslim writers identified Jeremiah, rather than his scribe Baruch, as the one who was translated. (As quoted in an article by John A. Tvedtnes on Meridianmagazine.com, corrected and updated by Joshua Mariano.)

38. *Early Patriarchal Blessings of the Church of Jesus Christ of Latter-day Saints* comp. H. Michael Marquardt (Salt Lake City: The Smith-Pettit Foundation, 2007), 26.

39. Ibid., 40.

40. Ibid., 65.

41. Ibid., 67.

42. Ibid., 88.

43. William Phelps, Letters, 1835–36: LDS Church Archives and Published Sources, *Writings of Early Latter-day Saints*, 1.

44. *Early Patriarchal Blessings*, 94.

45. Ibid., 154.

46. Ibid., 165.

47. Ibid., 95.

48. Ibid., 65.

49. Ibid., 77.

50. Ibid., 191.

51. Ibid., 64.

52. Ibid., 64.

Chapter Four

ZION TODAY

THE MINISTRY OF ANGELS

An angel is someone sent from the presence of God to perform a task in the name of his employer. Angels can be of four types:

- Righteous souls who have not yet been born and who do not possess a body (D&C 130:5).

- Righteous souls who have lived and died and do not possess a body. These are called "Spirits of just men made perfect" (D&C 76:66–79; Hebrews 12:22–24; D&C 129).

- Righteous souls who have lived and been translated and do possess a body.[1]

- Resurrected beings (Matthew 27:52–53; Helaman 14:25; D&C 129).

It is undoubtedly true that the full purposes and functions of angels have not been fully revealed. We do know some about their mission.

Prior to the birth of Christ, God used angels to teach all mankind of the upcoming birth of His son.

22 For behold, God knowing all things, being from everlasting to everlasting, behold, he sent angels to minister unto the children of men, to make manifest concerning the coming of Christ; and in Christ there should come every good thing. . . .

25 Wherefore, by the ministering of angels, and by every word which proceeded forth out of the mouth of God, men began to exercise faith in

Christ; and thus by faith, they did lay hold upon every good thing; *and thus it was until the coming of Christ.* (Moroni 7:22, 25; italics added)

This was the ministry of angels prior to the coming of Christ. Coupled with "every word which proceeded forth out of the mouth of God," which constitutes the labors of the Holy Spirit and the conscience of mankind, angels were ministering to prepare the world for His birth in Bethlehem. Because of these angelic labors, men began to have faith and to enjoy "every good thing."

Mormon assures us that after Christ came, men were still saved by faith in his name:

26 And after that he came men also were saved by faith in his name; and by faith, they become the sons of God. And as surely as Christ liveth he spake these words unto our fathers, saying: Whatsoever thing ye shall ask the Father in my name, which is good, in faith believing that ye shall receive, behold, it shall be done unto you. (Moroni 7:26)

Then he poses this question:

27 Wherefore, my beloved brethren, have miracles ceased because Christ hath ascended into heaven, and hath sat down on the right hand of God, to claim of the Father his rights of mercy which he hath upon the children of men?

28 For he hath answered the ends of the law, and he claimeth all those who have faith in him; and they who have faith in him will cleave unto every good thing; wherefore he advocateth the cause of the children of men; and he dwelleth eternally in the heavens. (Moroni 7:26–28)

After Christ's birth, Christ ordained apostles and disciples who bore the good news of the gospel to the world. Men gained faith in Christ through their testimony, teaching, and witness (see 1 Corinthians 1:21).

The next verse asks the question: Because Christ ascended into heaven, does that mean that the ministry of angels has ended or that miracles of God have ceased?

29 And because he hath done this, [ascended into heaven] my beloved brethren, have miracles ceased? Behold I say unto you, Nay; neither have angels ceased to minister unto the children of men.

30 For behold, they are subject unto him, to minister according to the word of his command, showing themselves unto them of strong faith and a firm mind in every form of godliness. (Moroni 7:29–30)

The answer is a resounding *no*! Miracles continue as before, and the ministry of angels didn't stop at all, but changed its focus. After we have a strong faith in Christ and a firm mind (see Moroni 7:30), or true understanding of the gospel and the extraordinary promises of the priesthood, then angels can show themselves unto us as needed to fulfill the covenants of the Father. Anyone who has been within holy walls will understand the implication of this principle.

Of course much, if not most, of those angelic labors are performed without showing themselves unto mortals. What is being held forth in this verse, in the temple, and throughout all the scriptures, is the fact that angels *do* and *will* appear to us when we are prepared and if it suits the purposes of God (see 3 Nephi 28:30).

Their present mission is:

- Angels "speak by the power of the Holy Ghost" (2 Nephi 32:2–3).

- Angels "speak the words of Christ," which connects them with the functionality of the light of Christ (2 Nephi 32:3).

- The "words of Christ," and by extrapolation, angels will tell us "all things what ye should do."

- Angels reveal "things whereof he [has] appointed unto [mortals]" (Alma 12:29). In other words, they reveal those principles, doctrines, covenants, and blessings that God has ordained that we should receive in mortality.

- Angels converse with man and "cause men to behold his glory" (Alma 12:29), which is the vital process of qualifying to enter the presence of the Lord. Temple patrons will recall the involved role of angels in the process of arriving at the veil.

- Angels are subject unto Christ and minister "according to his command" (Moroni 7:30).

- Angels show themselves unto mankind when we have a "strong faith and a firm mind in every form of godliness" (Moroni 7:30), which means after we are valiant members of the kingdom of God, strong in our faith, and firm in our understanding.

- The "office of their ministry is to call men to repentance" (Moroni 7:31).

- Angels fulfill and do the "work of the covenants of the Father" (Moroni 7:31), which includes the covenants regarding Enoch, the latter-day Zion, the oath and covenant of the priesthood, eternal marriage, consecration, temple covenants, and all others that are significant to our quest for Zion.

- Angels declare the words of Christ to the "chosen vessels of the Lord that they may bear testimony of him" to the world (Moroni 7:31; bracketed comments added).

Since the coming of Christ, it appears that angels declare Christ's words to His servants, who then bear that message to the world. His servants would include all who place themselves into a state of righteousness that allows them to interact with angels, not just ordained authorities. Thus, through the ministry of angels and the labors of His servants, the Father fulfills His covenants.

> 31 And the office of their ministry is to call men unto repentance, and to fulfil and to do the work of the covenants of the Father, which he hath made unto the children of men, to prepare the way among the children of men, by declaring the word of Christ unto the chosen vessels of the Lord, that they may bear testimony of him.

> 32 And by so doing, the Lord God prepareth the way that the residue of men may have faith in Christ, that the Holy Ghost may have place in their hearts, according to the power thereof; and after this manner [the ministry of angels] bringeth to pass the Father, the covenants which he hath made unto the children of men. (Moroni 7:31–32; bracketed comments added)

And when they do appear to us, they can and will work great and marvelous miracles to prepare us for the "great and coming day" of judgment.

> 30 And they are as the angels of God, and if they shall pray unto the Father in the name of Jesus they can show themselves unto whatsoever man it seemeth them good.

> 31 Therefore, great and marvelous works shall be wrought by them, before the great and coming day when all people must surely stand before the judgment-seat of Christ. (3 Nephi 28:30–31)

Hence, miracles have not ceased unless we simply do not believe (unbelief) in the fact that angels do continue to appear, minister, and work miracles even today—especially today.

36 Or have angels ceased to appear unto the children of men? Or has he withheld the power of the Holy Ghost from them? Or will he, so long as time shall last, or the earth shall stand, or there shall be one man upon the face thereof to be saved?

37 Behold I say unto you, Nay; for it is by faith that miracles are wrought; and it is by faith that angels appear and minister unto men; wherefore, if these things have ceased wo be unto the children of men, for it is because of unbelief, and all is vain. (Moroni 7:36–37)

Even more tragic than the loss of miracles and angelic appearances such unbelief would cause is the fact that "all is vain." *Vain* means "failing to have, or unlikely to have the intended or desired result; devoid of substance or meaning."

If we ever become sullied by unbelief, not only would we miss the joy and miracles of the ministering of angels, but all else we do and believe would not have the desired result of exaltation. What portion of our lives, our faith, and our service might become "vain" due to such unbelief (if we allowed it to overtake us) is not easy to tell. Does this mean that all other parts of our faith would be without reward? Does it simply mean that the covenants of the Father wouldn't get fulfilled in this life, but maybe in the next? Does it only mean that we would live our lives without special miracles but otherwise receive the exaltation we hope for? Or is this simple phrase "all is vain" warning us that if we allow unbelief in the ministry of angels and other lofty things to obscure our view of the grand purposes of the Father's covenants in our lives, we are unavoidably allowing that same unbelief to distance ourselves from many other potential, even vital blessings in our lives, and hence, all *is* vain?

Nephi, the son of Helaman records:

26 But behold, I have seen them [the Three Nephites], and they have ministered unto me.

27 And behold they will be among the Gentiles, and the Gentiles shall know them not.

28 They will also be among the Jews, and the Jews shall know them not.

29 And it shall come to pass, when the Lord seeth fit in his wisdom that they shall minister unto all the scattered tribes of Israel, and unto all nations, kindreds, tongues and people, and shall bring out of them unto Jesus many souls, that their desire may be fulfilled, and also because of the convincing power of God which is in them.

30 And they are as the angels of God, and if they shall pray unto the Father in the name of Jesus they can show themselves unto whatsoever man it seemeth them good.

31 Therefore, great and marvelous works shall be wrought by them, before the great and coming day when all people must surely stand before the judgment-seat of Christ;

32 Yea even among the Gentiles shall there be a great and marvelous work wrought by them, before that judgment day. (3 Nephi 28:26–32; bracketed comments added)

Nephi teaches us that angels must accomplish a great and marvelous work prior to Judgment Day. Since the greatest preparatory element for Judgment Day is the building of Zion, it appears that the Three Nephites will be involved in that effort.

ZION AND THE MINISTRY OF ANGELS

A question we don't often asked is what are Enoch and his people presently doing? Elder Orson Pratt comments upon their present mission:

They have been gone, as I have already stated, about five thousand years. What have they been doing? All that we know concerning this subject is what has been revealed through the great and mighty prophet of the last days, Joseph Smith . . . that they have been ministering angels during all that time. To whom? To those of the terrestrial order, if you can understand that expression. . . . he granted to the people of Enoch their desire to become ministering spirits unto those of the terrestrial order until the earth should rest and they should again return to it.[2]

Who are the people of the terrestrial order? Since we are speaking of a time prior to the Millennium, we are not speaking of the terrestrial kingdom or of those who later qualify for it. Future terrestrial kingdom dwellers don't receive the ministry of angels to become terrestrial individuals. All that is required to enter that kingdom is to be deceived, die without law, and/or not receive the testimony of Jesus in the flesh (see D&C 76:72–74).

"Those of the terrestrial order" are a higher, more celestial class of soul. Joseph Smith described translated beings as living in a terrestrial order:

Their place of habitation is that of the terrestrial order, and a place prepared for such characters He held in reserve to be ministering angels unto many planets, and who as yet have not entered into so great a fulness as those who are resurrected from the dead.[3]

Thus, the terrestrial order is the translated state, and Enoch and his people are ministering to translated individuals, which makes sense since they, themselves, are translated. Paul the Apostle adds to their job description with the additional understanding that angels are working with those who are "heirs of salvation."

> 14 Are they not all ministering spirits, sent forth to minister for them who shall be heirs of salvation?" (Hebrews 1:14)

John the Beloved, who was translated of course, was made a ministering angel to people upon the earth who are heirs of salvation.

> 6 Yea, he has undertaken a greater work; therefore I will make him as flaming fire and a ministering angel; he shall minister for those who shall be heirs of salvation who dwell on the earth. (D&C 7:6)

If one interprets salvation as qualifying for the celestial kingdom, then there are two distinct pathways to salvation. One is the more common pathway of living the gospel in mortality, having your calling and election made sure either before or after death, experiencing the spirit world, being resurrected, judged, and assigned to glory. The less common way, but one which millions will walk, especially in the latter days, is that of being translated during mortality, skipping the spirit world, being resurrected, judged, and then assigned to celestial glory. Translation is a true form of salvation in that it not only qualifies one for the celestial kingdom but also "saves" the individual from mortal death.

"Heirs of salvation" could thus have several meanings, the most common being those people who will ultimately inherit the celestial kingdom. The other is those who will be translated during their lives. Applying this second possible meaning suggests that "heirs of salvation" includes those who are seeking a place in Zion, the terrestrial Zion state, to prepare them to eventually become translated—a process certain angels themselves experienced during their mortality.

THE COVENANTS OF GOD

When we have established ourselves with a strong faith and a firm mind in every form of godliness, the angels teach and prepare us to receive the covenants that God has established among us.

God has established several preeminent covenants with men, all of which must be fully realized to obtain the blessings of Zion (see D&C 42:67). The ones that are specific to Zion are the covenants that the Lord made with Enoch and the oath and covenant of the priesthood.

The covenant of the Lord with Enoch is little understood but impacts us significantly. Apparently when Enoch's people obtained the presence of God and their gifts of translation, they attempted but were not able to spread the gospel across the world and usher in an era of millennial righteousness. They mourned and prayed mightily with a combined voice that they might be privileged to see a day when righteousness would flood the earth and evil would not be found upon her face. Elder Orson Pratt spoke of Enoch and the covenant of the Father with Enoch in a conference address given in the old Salt Lake City Tabernacle, July 19, 1874.

> Enoch and his people prayed that a day of righteousness might be brought about during their day; they sought for it with all their hearts; they looked abroad over the face of the earth and saw the corruptions that had been introduced by the various nations, the descendants of Adam, and their hearts melted within them, and they groaned before the Lord with pain and sorrow, because of the wickedness of the children of men, and they sought for a day of rest, they sought that righteousness might be revealed, that wickedness might be swept away and that the earth might rest for a season.[4]

In response to their righteous prayers, the Lord covenanted with Enoch and his people that they would see such a day, and that He would answer their prayers, but not in that era. Accordingly, God took Enoch and his city off the face of the earth to reserve them to come back in the day when their prayers could be answered. They would return in the latter days and complete their mission, when as a result of their renewed ministry upon the mortal world, righteousness *would* sweep the earth prior to the Second Coming of Christ.

> God gave them visions, portrayed to them the future of the world, showed unto them that this earth must fulfill the measure of its creation; that generation after generation must be born and pass away, and that, after a certain period of time, the earth would rest from wickedness, that the wicked would be swept away, and the earth would be cleansed and sanctified and be prepared for a righteous people. "Until that day," saith the Lord, "you and your people shall rest, Zion shall be

taken up into my own bosom." Ancient Zion should be held in reserve until the day of rest should come, "then," said the Lord to Enoch, "thou and all thy city shall descend upon the earth, and your prayers shall be answered."[5]

This covenant with Enoch was so momentous that God placed the rainbow in the sky to remind future generations of this grand covenant, to keep it before the minds of mankind until it was fulfilled. It is intriguing that the covenant is this important, yet we hardly know of it. This is startling, because most of us have lived all of our gospel lives without realizing what the covenant associated with the rainbow actually is. Most think it has something to do with not flooding the earth ever again. In reality it is much more glorious.

The scriptures teach us:

21 And the bow shall be in the cloud; and I will look upon it, that I may remember the everlasting covenant, which I made unto thy father Enoch; that, when men should keep all my commandments, Zion should again come on the earth, the city of Enoch which I have caught up unto myself.

22 And this is mine everlasting covenant, that when thy posterity shall embrace the truth, and look upward, then shall Zion look downward, and all the heavens shall shake with gladness, and the earth shall tremble with joy;

23 And the general assembly of the Church of the Firstborn shall come down out of heaven, and possess the earth, and shall have place until the end come. And this is mine everlasting covenant, which I made with thy father Enoch. (*JST* Genesis 9:21–23)

The rainbow we see in our skies represents God's promise to Enoch that when men upon the earth "should keep all my commandments" and are righteous at last, He will fulfill their righteous prayers and bring Zion back onto the earth. This will come to pass in that era when Enoch's and our combined missionary labors will bring that righteousness which will cover the earth in the Millennial day. And, by extension, when Zion is upon the earth, Christ will come and begin His millennial reign.

In words that shake the earth, the God of heaven proclaims that when we, Enoch's posterity through the prophet Noah, embrace the truth and understand our relationship to Enoch's Zion and employ our hearts, faith, and hands in building up Zion upon the earth, Enoch and his people will look downward and all the heavens will "shake with gladness, and the earth shall tremble with joy." Enoch will descend out of heaven and rush to embrace his great and righteous posterity, and they will fall upon our necks and kiss us (see Moses 7:63). Then together with us, Enoch and his Zion will possess the earth and have a place upon it until the earth becomes the future celestial kingdom. This is the covenant, the everlasting covenant, which God made with Enoch—and since it has been renewed in our day—with us.

In the latter days the Lord reminds us of this same covenant and of the longing of holy men to see this day of righteousness.

> 11 Wherefore, hearken ye together and let me show unto you even my wisdom—the wisdom of him whom ye say is the God of Enoch, and his brethren,
>
> 12 Who were separated from the earth, and were received unto myself—a city reserved until a day of righteousness shall come—a day which was sought for by all holy men, and they found it not because of wickedness and abominations;
>
> 13 And confessed they were strangers and pilgrims on the earth;
>
> 14 But obtained a promise that they should find it and see it in their flesh. (D&C 45:11–14)

"In their flesh" means as either translated or resurrected beings. In the meantime, they are laboring as angels to prepare *us* to become Zion so we can prepare the world for *them* to return, thus fulfilling the Lord's covenant with them.

This idea of translated beings laboring among us without our being aware of them is taught in the following verses:

> 8 Wherefore, I will that all men shall repent, for all are under sin, except those which I have reserved unto myself, holy men that ye know not of. (D&C 49:8)
>
> 27 And behold they [the Three Nephites] will be among the Gentiles, and the Gentiles shall know them not.
>
> 28 They will also be among the Jews, and the Jews shall know them not. (3 Nephi 28:27–28; bracketed comments added)

The other covenant that directly impacts our efforts to become Zion today is the oath and covenant of the priesthood. This covenant of the

Father is that if we will receive and magnify the priesthood that we will be sanctified and changed into a Zion individual. We will cover this promise in greater detail in the section "The Oath and Covenant of the Priesthood."

> Israel, angels are descending
> From celestial worlds on high,
> And to man their power extending,
> That the Saints may homeward fly.
> Come to Zion, come to Zion,
> For your coming Lord is nigh.[6]

KEY TO THE MINISTERING OF ANGELS

The Aaronic Priesthood administers the initiatory ordinance of baptism. Once within the gospel embrace, we grow until we have powerful faith and an inspired understanding of the gospel. Since angels are now waiting until we have strong faith and firm mind to begin to appear to us in order to complete the covenants of the Father, one must become a member of the everlasting gospel to qualify for the ministering of angels. Thus, in the right to perform baptisms, the Aaronic Priesthood holds the *key* to their ministry. Or stated in familiar language, the Aaronic Priesthood holds the key to the ministering of angels (see Joseph Smith—History 1:69).

When we, by obedience to principles of the gospel, gain a strong faith in Christ and a "firm mind in every form of godliness" (Moroni 7:30), then the angels begin to "fulfill and to do the work of the covenants of the Father" (Moroni 7:31) even showing themselves unto us if necessary.

MOSES AND THE LATTER DAYS

There is an inescapable parallel between the exodus of Moses with the children of Israel and the latter-day exodus from Nauvoo. Moses was called to deliver the Lord's people from bondage, both political and spiritual. He went up upon the mount and received a new dispensation of the gospel which would have entitled them to seek and ultimately enter into the presence of the Lord. Speaking of the power of the priesthood to bring mankind into the presence of God in this life, the prophet Joseph wrote of Moses:

> 23 Now this [that the children of Israel could see God as Moses had] Moses plainly taught to the children of Israel in the wilderness, and sought diligently to sanctify his people that they might behold the face of God;
>
> 24 But they hardened their hearts and could not endure his presence; therefore, the Lord in his wrath, for his anger was kindled against them, swore that they should not enter into his rest while in the wilderness, which rest is the fulness of his glory.
>
> 25 Therefore, he took Moses out of their midst, and the Holy Priesthood also;
>
> 26 And the lesser priesthood continued, which priesthood holdeth the key of the ministering of angels and the preparatory gospel;
>
> 27 Which gospel is the gospel of repentance and of baptism, and the remission of sins, and the law of carnal commandments, which the Lord in his wrath caused to continue with the house of Aaron among the children of Israel until John, whom God raised up, being filled with the Holy Ghost from his mother's womb. (D&C 84:23–27; bracketed comments added)

Because the children of Israel rejected this one thing, which was God's invitation to enter into His presence and thereby establish a Zion like unto Enoch's, God withdrew both the prophet and the priesthood from their midst and gave them a law of carnal commandments. Thereafter they wandered for forty years in the wilderness until God at last gave them a homeland. For the next twenty-five hundred years, God sent them prophets who they mostly rejected. He sent them His only begotten Son, and they could not recognize Him, even as He walked their streets and taught in their synagogues.

JOSEPH SMITH AND THE LATTER-DAY ZION

When Joseph Smith, the prophet of this dispensation, went up before the Lord, he also was given a new dispensation of the gospel, which included the same blueprint of Zion that Enoch possessed and which Moses' people rejected. Christ also gave Joseph the laws, ordinances, and priesthood that would bring Joseph's people before the Lord and give them the ability to establish Zion.

To their credit, the former-day Saints truly tried to do as the Lord asked through Joseph. They did not out-of-hand reject the offer of Zion, but rather longed for and sacrificed to achieve it. They did not succeed, because as individuals they could not live the higher laws of Zion. It is evident from numerous statements (only a few of which are noted in this book) that Joseph fully understood and taught that the latter-day Zion was to be like Enoch's Zion. Joseph taught what was required of his people to bring forth Zion but often lamented that the Latter-day Saints were not living up to the standard of Zion.

Even though Joseph understood these principles, the people in general apparently did not, and thus they could not achieve a true Zion stature. So, according to the pattern, as it always occurs in the things of God relative to Zion, and like the Children of Israel, the Lord took away their prophet and drove them (meaning us) into the wilderness for a period of preparation and repentance.

But the good news, as we often say, is that by truly trying, even unsuccessfully to establish Zion, and by not rejecting God's gift, God mercifully left the priesthood in our midst, brought forth additional prophets, and promised to never take the priesthood from among us. However, as we will document in "Building of Zion Delayed," He did suspend the command to establish Zion as an actual city for the time being. It has stopped us from obtaining the blessings of actually building the city of Zion. It doesn't need to stop us from obtaining the individual worthiness and blessings of becoming a Zion individual.

After suspending the command to establish Zion as a city and Enochonian society, in a series of events that adhere to the divine pattern of Zions failed and which bear the fingerprints of Divine handling, God sent His people into the wilderness to school and prepare them to establish Zion at a later time. It does not appear that the Lord was angry with us so much as He was willing to give us a period of time to prepare our hearts and become sanctified in preparation to build Zion (see D&C 105:9–14).

In a fascinating parallel between Moses and the Latter-day Saints, we voluntarily left Nauvoo. As you recall, Moses was not driven out of Egypt but left during a lull in the oppression from Pharaoh. In the latter days it was also true that the forces of evil were combining and would have eventually slaughtered and driven them out, but they left at a moment when there were no armies attacking Nauvoo. Brigham Young simply instructed the Saints to leave.

Thereafter continuing the parallel, they endured a perilous journey that brought them across a wilderness and to a desert valley that was to be their home. The Lord instructed them to build a magnificent temple and to spread out and claim the surrounding lands. In stark parallel with Moses, they settled next to the only other large inland salt sea in the world, second largest only to the Dead Sea. Both the Dead Sea and the Great Salt Lake are fed by a river named Jordan, which comes from a freshwater lake in a similar geographical parallel.

Also intriguing is the fact that Brigham Young tried for a while to begin anew to establish Zion, but in time gave up. Since his tenure as prophet, no formal attempt has been made to establish Zion as a city. In other words, we have been living that portion of the gospel that remains after the opportunity to build Zion has been extracted. As Brigham Young states below, we are still waiting out a time of growth and preparation until the Lord again calls upon this people to establish Zion.

Brigham Young made the following observations apparently after concluding that Zion could not be built during his lifetime.

> Some may ask why we did not tarry at the centre stake of Zion when the Lord planted our feet there. We had eyes, but we did not see; we had ears, but we did not hear; we had hearts that were devoid of what the Lord required of his people; consequently, we could not abide what the Lord revealed unto us. We had to go from there to gain an experience. Can you understand this? I think there are some here who can. If we could have received the words of life and lived according to them, when we were first gathered to the centre stake of Zion, we never would have been removed from that place.[7]

> Could our brethren stay in Jackson County, Missouri? No, no. Why? They had not learned 'a' concerning Zion; and we have been traveling now forty-two years, and have we learned our a,b,c?. . . I will say, scarcely.[8]

> I never attributed the driving of the Saints from Jackson County to anything but that it was necessary to chasten them and prepare them to build up Zion.[9]

> Are we fit for Zion? . . . Could we stay in Independence? No, we could not. What is the matter with all you Latter-day Saints? Can the world see? No. Can the Saints see? No, or few of them can; and we can say that the light of the Spirit upon the hearts and understanding

of some Latter-day Saints is like the peeping of the stars through the broken shingles of the roof over our heads.[10]

Brigham Young made several attempts to establish a type of Zion through social programs, common ownership of land and goods, economic models, and legal consecration of property. But we learned that Zion cannot be built up based upon programs. Brigham Young knew that Zion could not be built when the people were not willing to live the higher laws of Zion. This realization was undoubtedly the source of the discouragement felt in the above quotes.

Zion is not a social experiment. It is a society of people who walk and talk with Christ and whose lives continue without death to prepare for the return of the Messiah.

This latter-day Zion, the New Jerusalem, will not be established by brilliant social engineering. It is not the result of a form of government or system of laws. Zion has no government but Christ, who is her king. It will not occur as a result of a group of people walking to Jackson County to build up the abandoned cities of Babylon.

Zion is a society of people who have quietly reengineered their lives to the pattern of celestial law, who have sought and found the blessings of Divine company, and while in the presence of God, have asked for the privilege of being changed to the pattern of Zion.

Zion is first and foremost a pure people who have learned to live the law of the celestial kingdom, which is the law of Zion. The latter-day Zion will be equal in power and glory to Enoch's Zion. Hyrum Andrus wrote about the striking parallel between Enoch's Zion and the latter-day Zion this way:

> A direct correlation is made in the Pearl of Great Price between the program of the Lord that was carried out before the flood and that which is designed to be accomplished in the last days. In that early day, a prophet was sent in the person of Enoch, with a special commission to fulfill the Lord's purposes; the righteous were gathered and taught the law of Zion; having been sanctified, they entered into the rest of the Lord, and their city was translated; and, finally, the wicked were destroyed. Similarly, in the latter days a prophet has been sent in the person of Joseph Smith, and through him a program of gathering the elect has been instituted. *Zion is to be built up according to the heavenly pattern and design, and in this way the Saints are to be sanctified and enter into the Lord's rest.* At the coming of Christ in glory, the latter-day Zion

is to be caught up to meet Him in the clouds. Finally, the wicked are to be destroyed, this time by an envelopment of the earth in fire—the fiery floods of glory that are then manifest.

This indicates that before Christ comes in glory in the clouds of heaven, the Saints in the latter days must attain the same standard of spiritual truth and power that Enoch and his people did. Having referred to the fact that many righteous men in former times sought, through the Gospel, to return the earth to its paradisiacal glory and failed, Joseph Smith said: "But they prophesied of a day when this glory would be revealed. Paul spoke of the dispensation of the fulness of times, when God would gather together all things in one." Not only did the righteous of the earth in subsequent ages idealize Enoch's city, but they looked forward in faith to the day when that same standard of spiritual excellence would be established upon the earth and spread over the whole sphere. That day would be in the last dispensation.[11]

With Satan's help, or in a moment of personal weakness it may seem impossible for mere mortals to rise to such a lofty stratosphere as Enoch's Zion. It is nonetheless entirely achievable. Somebody will achieve Zion; all I need to do is to decide that somebody will be myself. The Lord has placed within this latter-day gospel that we know and love the way for us to accomplish this very thing. We need not look upward and fear that we are incapable of the climb. The height of the mountain is irrelevant. The only thing that matters is that we keep climbing as the Lord directs.

If we doubt our ability to achieve a Zion state, we should also look at the celestial kingdom and wonder, or even doubt that we can evolve into someone worthy of that great kingdom, because the requirements of Zion are less stringent than for the celestial kingdom. One may enter Zion in their lifetime, with such purity as a mortal may obtain by obedience, yet still not be prepared to enter everlasting glory at that time.

But we don't doubt our appointment to celestial glory. Even with a mortal sense of inadequacy, most of us do believe that we will eventually, by some process unknown to us at present, become a celestial dweller. It is because we have schooled our beliefs and our faith to accept that we can and eventually will arrive at that stature of righteousness.

By simple deduction we may easily see that somewhere along the line of growth that will take us into the celestial kingdom, we will become worthy of Zion—which is a terrestrial state, and lower than the celestial glory we seek. The only tweak that is required to our belief system is to believe that we will arrive at that state during this life.

God does not give us impossible tasks. Sometimes we fail because of weakness, but the commandment is not beyond us. Divine law stipulates that God will always prepare a way to accomplish His commands (1 Nephi 3:7). The invitation to become a Zion individual is played out before our eyes and ears each time we attend the temple. It is within those walls that we learn of the process that brings us unto the veil that separates us from Christ. And it is at the veil that we may request our place in Zion.

WHY WE ARE WHERE WE ARE

In my opinion two things have happened that have inhibited us from establishing Zion in the latter days. First, and most important, the Lord withdrew the command to build Zion in Joseph's day.

Joseph Fielding Smith explained it this way:

> It appears from this declaration [D&C 103:16–20] that the redemption of Zion was not to come immediately, but was to be postponed to some future day.
>
> Moreover, that day would not come until the members of the Church were willing to keep their covenants and walk unitedly, for until the members of the Church learn to walk in full accord and in obedience with all of the commandments, this day cannot come. It may be necessary in order to bring this to pass for the Lord to use drastic measures and cleanse the Church from everything that offends. This he has promised to do when he is ready to redeem Zion.[12]

The second inhibiting factor seems to be that even though the opportunity to build the actual city of Zion has been temporarily suspended, the command to become a Zion individual was not withdrawn, but it did become veiled, difficult to see and feel, because we were driven from Zion. With the limited worldview of Zion as a physical place now beyond our reach and not a spiritual state of being, it appears we lost the motivation to continue to build a Zion society when we lost ownership of the real estate of Zion.

When the call of Zion lifts our minds from the geography of a lost city to achievable spiritual realities directly before us, we suddenly realize that we may become a Zion individual, full of the promise and blessings and privileges of Zion. We may become a Zion family, a Zion ward or stake, and on and on. The command to build the actual city of Zion will, in my opinion, be renewed by our living prophet with a shout of angelic acclamation when there are once again Zion people to heed the call.

A time of awakening seems to be upon us, a time when the beauties of Zion are once again warming hearts and souls, and the pathway leading there is appearing beneath the snows of forgetfulness. The sun of Zion appears to be rising directly overhead, lighting our minds and reawakening within us the promised glories awaiting us in Zion.

ZION IN THE LATTER DAYS

The term *Zion* is like many other gospel truths in that it is has meaning on many levels. It is correct to refer to the latter-day Church as Zion, since God referred to this Church by that name when it was founded and sent forth to establish the millennial Zion. God named Enoch's city Zion. We will call the city and society we will build prior to the Millennium Zion as well.

Even though we often refer to the latter-day Church as Zion when speaking rhetorically, it is clear from the statements of early Church authorities that the Church, as it is presently constituted, is not that Zion which will exist to greet Christ when He comes in glory. In other words, a new millennial Zion must be built.

Hugh Nibley notes:

> Brigham Young admonished the people who came to the Valley lest they "go into error when they expect to see that Zion here which they have seen in vision." The Zion in the vision was the real one. It must always be kept in mind, not as a present reality, but as the goal toward which all the labor of the Church is a preparation.[13]

Elder McConkie stated it this way:

> But we are of Israel and have already gathered to a pre-Millennial Zion, a Zion that is a forerunner, an Elias, as it were, of the Zion that is yet to be. . . . Ours is a day of beginnings, a day of slight and partial fulfillment of the divine word. The great day for the Lord's people lies ahead.[14]

It is startling that Elder McConkie characterizes our day as constituting a "slight and partial fulfillment" of the promises of Zion. The role of the latter-day Church is to build that millennial Zion—a task that we have partially begun, but not yet completed. So, in waiting for the Lord to return in glory we find ourselves in the awkward position of waiting for the doorbell to ring on a house we have not yet built.

In other words, the latter-day Church is sent forth to establish the millennial Zion (D&C 6:6) but is not (in its present state) that Zion which will receive Christ in glory.

Elder Bruce R. McConkie further describes our condition of seeking to become Zion as opposed to actually being Zion:

> We have yet to gain that full knowledge and understanding of the doctrines of salvation and the mysteries of the kingdom that were possessed by many of the ancient Saints. O that we knew what Enoch and his people knew! Or that we had the sealed portion of the Book of Mormon, as did certain of the Jaredites and Nephites! How can we ever gain these added truths until we believe in full what the Lord has already given us in the Book of Mormon, in the Doctrine and Covenants, and in the inspired changes made by Joseph Smith in the Bible? . . . .
>
> We have yet to attain that degree of obedience and personal righteousness which will give us faith like the ancients: faith to multiply miracles, move mountains, and put at defiance the armies of nations; faith to quench the violence of fire, divide seas and stop the mouths of lions; faith to break every band and to stand in the presence of God. Faith comes in degrees. Until we gain faith to heal the sick, how can we ever expect to move mountains and divide seas?
>
> We have yet to receive such an outpouring of the Spirit of the Lord in our lives that we shall all see eye to eye in all things, that every man will esteem his brother as himself, that there will be no poor among us. . . . As long as we disagree as to the simple and easy doctrines of salvation, how can we ever have unity on the complex and endless truths yet to be revealed?
>
> We have yet to perfect our souls, by obedience to the laws and ordinances of the gospel, and to walk in the light as God is in the light, so that if this were a day of translation we would be prepared to join Enoch and his city in heavenly realms. How many among us are now prepared to entertain angels, to see the face of the Lord, to go where God and Christ are and be like them? . . .
>
> We have yet to prepare a people for the Second Coming. . . .
>
> Shall we not now, as a Church and as a people and as the Saints of latter days, build on the foundations of the past and go forward in gospel glory until the great Jehovah shall say: "The work is done; come ye, enter the joy of your Lord; sit down with me on my throne; thou art now one with me and my Father."

President Brigham Young also observed that, in general, the Saints are not prepared for the blessings that the Lord anticipates bestowing on them: "Jesus has been upon the earth a great many more times than you are aware of. When Jesus makes his next appearance upon the earth, but few of this Church and kingdom will be prepared to receive him and see him face to face and converse with him.[15]

The latter-day Church holds somewhat the same relative position to the millennial Zion as Zion holds to the Millennium. They are key and integral to one another, but they are not the same thing; the former flowing into and becoming the latter. When the millennial Zion is established, the latter-day Church of God will in time become the kingdom of God. It is conceivable that the name will even change, since it will no longer be the "latter day" but the "millennial day."

There will come a time prior to the advent of Christ when Zion exists in full purity, and yet the world all around Zion will be unredeemed and excluded from Zion, indeed largely unaware of what Zion is. During that transitory time it is likely that the Church as we know it will perform a parallel role by maintaining its commission in the world at large, sending out missionaries, building buildings, and collecting tithing even while a portion of that same organization has become Zion, perfected and glorious, where missionaries will be translated beings, and buildings will be constructed by the creative power of God.

The prophet Joseph Smith repeatedly taught:

> We ought to have the building up of Zion as our greatest object. When wars come, we shall have to flee to Zion. The cry is to make haste.[16]

Joseph Smith wrote in 1839:

> It has been the plan of the devil to hamper and distress me from the beginning, to keep me from explaining myself to them, and I never have had opportunity to give them the plan that God has revealed to me.[17]

This plan that the prophet wanted to reveal was the same that had existed in the days of Enoch. How do we know this? Because Joseph had the building of Zion as his greatest objective, and there is only one "plan" for building Zion.

Notice the past tense "was going to" lamentation Joseph penned in March 1842:

> The Lord was going to make of the Church of Jesus Christ a kingdom of Priests, a holy people, a chosen generation, as in Enoch's day,

having all the gifts as illustrated to the Church in Paul's epistles and teachings to the Churches in his day.[18]

A little later Joseph wrote:

> The Church is not fully organized, in its proper order, and cannot be, until the Temple is completed, where places will be provided for the administration of the ordinances of the Priesthood.[19]

Joseph was killed before the Nauvoo Temple was completed, but he had performed the ordinances mentioned above for Brigham Young and others of the Twelve. Between that time and their expulsion from Nauvoo, the temple was used night and day to perform the exalting ordinances of the priesthood.

The startling fact is that the Church was thus not fully organized until just shortly before it was driven from Nauvoo, and the command to build Zion was withdrawn by the Lord. The only conclusion we can draw is that the Church is presently fully organized, but the opportunity to build Zion was postponed. When we have prepared ourselves to build Zion, and the Lord gives the command for this last great Zion to begin, those of us who have laid hold upon these lofty blessings will be ready as individuals, and in time as a holy city, to receive the coming Christ.

Building of Zion Delayed

Joseph realized at some point that Zion would not be perfected and redeemed during his lifetime. He drew this conclusion from the fact that his people manifestly could not live the celestial laws of Zion. Much of the content of the Doctrine and Covenants is exhortation and warnings regarding our failure to build Zion.

Joseph F. Smith explained in 1894 why Zion was not built in Joseph's day.

> But they did not redeem Zion, because the Saints were not prepared. Consequently, the day for the redemption of Zion was postponed, until the time should come when the people, through the experiences they would be called to pass through, should be prepared for the redemption of Zion and for the building of the House of God at the center stake thereof. And the day was not yet come; and no man, so far as I know, can foretell the day to the hour, the month or the year when the people of God are prepared to go back, and not before. Whether

it be in this generation or in the next generation, it matters not; it will only be when the people have prepared themselves to do it by their faithfulness and obedience to the commands of God. I prophesy to you, in the name of the Lord, that when the Latter-day Saints have prepared themselves through righteousness to redeem Zion, they will accomplish that work, and God will go with them. No power will then be able to prevent them from accomplishing that work; for the Lord has said it shall be done, and it will be done in the due time of the Lord, when the people are prepared for it.[20]

Because the Saints of Joseph's era were unprepared to establish Zion, the Lord withdrew the command to redeem Zion for "a little season." Elder McConkie notes:

Therefore, in consequence of the transgressions of my people, it is expedient in me that mine elders should wait for a little season for the redemption of Zion—that they themselves may be prepared, and that my people may be taught more perfectly, and have experience, and know more perfectly concerning their duty, and the things which I require at their hands." A little season—how long will it last? Will it be two hundred years? or three hundred? Though the day of the Second Coming is fixed, the day for the redemption of Zion depends upon us. *After we as a people live the law of the celestial kingdom; after we gain the needed experience and learn our duties; after we become by faith and obedience as were our fellow saints in the days of Enoch; after we are worthy to be translated, if the purposes of the Lord should call for such a course in this day—then Zion will be redeemed, and not before.*

This cannot be brought to pass until mine elders are endowed with power from on high. For behold, I have prepared a great endowment and blessing to be poured out upon them inasmuch as they are faithful and continue in humility before me." As of this time the ordinances of the house of the Lord had not been revealed, and the endowment of power from on high received through them was needed in the heavenly work that lay ahead. "Therefore it is expedient in me that mine elders should wait for a little season, for the redemption of Zion." (D&C 105:1-13) And so we wait, wondering the while how long the "little season" is destined to last. As to its length, we cannot say. This much only do we know: the "little season" is the appointed period of preparation for the Latter-day Saints. *In it we must attain the same spiritual stature enjoyed by those who built the original Zion. Then and then only will we build our latter-day City of Holiness.*[21]

We have been granted the "little season" to prepare ourselves to build up Zion. This preparatory period is by the grace of God, and due to His love and patience. If He had not granted it, our chance to establish Zion would have passed from our hands in the days of Joseph and into the hands of another people.

> 10 And thus commandeth the Father that I should say unto you: At that day when the Gentiles shall sin against my gospel, and shall reject the fulness of my gospel, and shall be lifted up in the pride of their hearts above all nations, and above all the people of the whole earth, and shall be filled with all manner of lyings, and of deceits, and of mischiefs, and all manner of hypocrisy, and murders, and priest-crafts, and whoredoms, and of secret abominations; and if they shall do all those things, and shall reject the fulness of my gospel, behold, saith the Father, I will bring the fulness of my gospel from among them.
>
> 11 And then will I remember my covenant which I have made unto my people, O house of Israel, and I will bring my gospel unto them. (3 Nephi 16:10–11)

As Elder McConkie ponders above, how long will the patience of the Lord await our awakening while the world tortures itself into mindless self-destruction?

The latter-day Church seems to be quietly marching toward Zion without placing visible emphasis upon building Zion. The reason for this is simple—this is how the Lord has directed the present progress of the Church, and in the challenge of building Zion, it is the perfect approach simply because it is what the Lord directs for our present day.

After the people of Joseph's era failed to bring forth Zion, the Lord withdrew the opportunity and the command to build Zion, took Joseph from their midst through martyrdom, and drove them into the wilderness to prepare for the future day when the call of Zion would again be sounded from the heavens. Heber J. Grant noted in his dairy:

> It came to us as a Revelation from God, in the same manner as the one to the prophet Joseph regarding the building of Center Stake of Zion and the Temple in Jackson Co., Missouri. The people failed to carry out the Order of Enoch and God gave a command to suspend the law.[22]

We have already discussed the condemnation resting upon the children of Zion because of vanity and unbelief. Consider the following verses.

54 And your minds in times past have been darkened because of unbelief, and because you have treated lightly the things you have received—

55 Which vanity and unbelief have brought the whole church under condemnation.

56 And this condemnation resteth upon the children of Zion, even all.

57 And they shall remain under this condemnation until they repent and remember the new covenant, even the Book of Mormon and the former commandments which I have given them, not only to say, but to do according to that which I have written—

58 That they may bring forth fruit meet for their Father's kingdom; otherwise there remaineth a scourge and judgment to be poured out upon the children of Zion.

59 For shall the children of the kingdom pollute my holy land? Verily, I say unto you, Nay. (D&C 84:54–59)

If we do not do according as the Lord has commanded, and speaking historically we did not, there remains a scourge and judgment to be poured out. The Lord then asked with the voice of thunder, "Shall the children of the kingdom pollute my holy land?" And the answer, "Verily, I say unto you, Nay!" And, as history records, the children of the kingdom were removed to a place where they could grow until they were at last ready to redeem Zion.

It is fascinating that the Lord apparently considers it acceptable for non-believers to "pollute" the holy land. But it is not acceptable for those who should be Zion pure to occupy the holy land in an impure state. Orson Pratt taught:

We find, therefore, that the Lord drove out this people because we were unworthy to receive our inheritances by consecration. As a people, we did not strictly comply with that which the Lord required. . . . The Lord said concerning them that they should be delivered over to the buffetings of Satan in this world, as well as be punished in the world to come. . . .

I will repeat the words—"Let those commandments which I have given concerning Zion and her law, be executed and fulfilled after her redemption." Here you perceive that, for the salvation of this people and of the nations of the earth among the Gentiles, God saw proper to revoke this commandment and to lay it over for a future period, or until after the redemption of Zion.[23]

What is important to note here is that the immediate command to build Zion was suspended, but the overarching command was not. In other words, Zion must still be built before the Lord can come again; we just don't have the immediate command to start stacking bricks.

As noted earlier, if we don't build it, the Lord will find someone else who will.

> 10 And thus commandeth the Father that I should say unto you: At that day when the Gentiles shall sin against my gospel, and shall reject the fulness of my gospel, and shall be lifted up in the pride of their hearts above all nations, and above all the people of the whole earth, and shall be filled with all manner of lyings, and of deceits, and of mischiefs, and all manner of hypocrisy, and murders, and priestcrafts, and whoredoms, and of secret abominations; and if they shall do all those things, and shall reject the fulness of my gospel, behold, saith the Father, I will bring the fulness of my gospel from among them. (3 Nephi 16:10)

THE CALL OF ZION

Before we as a people, or as an individual, can rise to the glorious challenge of building our latter-day Zion, the "call of Zion" must be heard once again. Every entrant into that holy city will have heard its mighty tolling in their hearts and made sweeping personal preparations to be worthy of Zion, or Zion will be invisible to them.

By referring to the call of Zion, nothing special or unusual is being suggested. All truths are obtained this way. One might coin the phrase "the call of the Book of Mormon" to define the feelings, the interest, the urging that precedes a revealed testimony of the Book of Mormon. It is this "call" by the Holy Spirit that motivates the first curious look, the first turned pages, the scattered reading, and finally a heartfelt prayer of inquiry. Chapters could be written on the process. Suffice it to say that most revealed truths grow in this way.

If the latter-day Zion is truth, if we must be the dispensation that builds it, if the time ever arrives that we must obtain a profound and personal part in Zion—then the God of Salvation will send forth a quiet call via the Holy

Spirit that will whisper within the souls of all whose ears are divinely tuned to such things, and that tinkling truth will be "the call of Zion."

In its infancy, the call of Zion is a quiet urging, a hunger of sorts that will not be filled by anything less than a glory your spirit knows awaits, but which you cannot yet define.[24]

In its childhood, the call is a commitment to a belief that stretches the mortal mind; to faith beyond the tensile strength of mortal logic. It is an emerging belief in things which eye hath not seen, nor ear heard, neither have entered into the heart of man (see 1 Corinthians 2:9).

In its adulthood, the call is an invitation to obedience to covenants already made, to finally understand glorious gifts promised in holy places; to approach the veil; to knock, ask, and receive; to at last enter into the divine presence. This is our personal call that will culminate in the triumph of Zion, and it is being heard and heeded anew.

It strikes this seeker as an irony of sorts, a curious actuality of the human/divine interface, that the fact that a reader has picked up this book and persisted in reading this far, most probably is an indicator that he or she has already heard that precious, Spirit-born call and is now looking for a place for their feet upon the path. Without this spiritual urging, one most probably should have lost interest many pages ago.

PURITY FIRST, REAL ESTATE SECOND

When the Lord commands, both by His living oracles and by His living voice, those righteous souls who have heeded the call of Zion will gather and build a central city, and their dwelling place will then be called Zion.

In other words, the first step in establishing Zion is to create a Zion people, or people who have been sanctified through the Atonement of Christ and who are worthy to live in Zion. The second, and far less weighty step, is to actually construct a city.

Brigham Young noted:

> When we conclude to make a Zion, we will make it, and this work commences in the heart of each person.[25]

This is the way Zion has been built in every instance that it has succeeded. First, the people are sanctified, changed, and in many cases translated. Then they are gathered, and at last they build their Zion of brick and mortar.

Brigham Young spoke often on this principle:

> Then do not be too anxious for the Lord to hasten his work. Let our anxiety be centered upon this one thing, the sanctification of our own hearts, the purifying of our own affections, the preparing of ourselves for the approach of events that are hastening upon us. This should be our concern, this should be our study, this should be our daily prayer, and not be in a hurry to see the overthrow of the wicked.[26]

In those instances where Zion has not triumphed, including the attempt in Joseph's day, they worked to sanctify themselves, but when that process faltered somewhat, they nevertheless proceeded with building a city.

In fact, building a righteous citizenry first is the only way Zion can be successfully established. It isn't possible to buy real estate, build a city, and then start inviting the best of the best to move in. What you create with this model is a social experiment or just a nice neighborhood. Zion must first blossom in the souls of a people; then when those souls are called to gather, the physical environs they inhabit become Zion because of their righteous presence.

It is the people that sanctify the habitation. When they are commanded to build a city, it becomes a City of Holiness, because they are holy. And when Zion is at last established, it will steadily spread to fill the whole earth. Zion will become the last and greatest step that Daniel saw wherein the kingdom of God will be cut out of the mount without hands and roll forth to fill the whole earth (see Daniel 2:34–45).

That promise to Daniel so long ago has been specifically restated in this day, and the promise is ours. These words are from the prayer offered at the dedication of the Kirtland temple, Ohio, March 27, 1836. It is a prayer that has yet to be fulfilled. Individually and collectively, we must be adorned as a bride for the day when the Bridegroom will come.

> 72 Remember all thy church, O Lord, with all their families, and all their immediate connections, with all their sick and afflicted ones, with all the poor and meek of the earth; that the kingdom, which thou hast set up without hands, may become a great mountain and fill the whole earth;
>
> 73 That thy church may come forth out of the wilderness of darkness, and shine forth fair as the moon, clear as the sun, and terrible as an army with banners;

74 And be adorned as a bride for that day when thou shalt unveil the heavens, and cause the mountains to flow down at thy presence, and the valleys to be exalted, the rough places made smooth; that thy glory may fill the earth;

75 That when the trump shall sound for the dead, we shall be caught up in the cloud to meet thee, that we may ever be with the Lord;

76 That our garments may be pure, that we may be clothed upon with robes of righteousness, with palms in our hands, and crowns of glory upon our heads, and reap eternal joy for all our sufferings. (D&C 109:72–76)

Notice the deep connection between the establishment of "the kingdom" and the return of the Lord. When our garments are pure and we are clothed with robes of righteousness, with crowns of glory upon our heads, then and only then will we take our place in Zion. When we as a people shine forth and take our correct position in the eternal scheme of things, and the Lord, through His prophet at last commands us to build Zion, then Christ will be unveiled in the heavens.

President Benson noted the same principle in this way:

Only a Zion people can bring in a Zion society. And as the Zion people increase, so we will be able to incorporate more of the principles of Zion until we have a people prepared to receive the Lord.[27]

Later in this book we will explore the process of individually bringing forth Zion. It is a process that will titillate your soul, because it has been before you all your life. It isn't new, but chances are you did not realize that it was leading you to a place within the City of the Living God. When your soul expands to encompass these things, you will have heard the call of Zion.

In time, the divine trumpet will sound, and all those who have personally obtained the sanctification of a Zion person will be gathered into the city which will then be known as Mount Zion, the New Jerusalem, the City of the Living God, the holiest of all, even Zion.

Those who have not founded Zion in their own lives will not hear the call and will not be gathered. It is even possible that they may be unaware of the existence of Zion until the more dramatic signs of the times begin. For those who ultimately end up outside of Zion, they will look upon Zion as great and terrible. (See D&C 97:18–19; D&C 45:66–72.)

She will be great because she will be glorious and beautiful, powerful and unassailable. Her enemies will try and fail to distress her. She will glow with the power of God day and night and will set at defiance the armies of nations, defending herself even by fire from heaven. She will be beautiful because there will be no struggle within her walls, no pain or illness, neither sorrow nor death. And within her sacred environs the Son of God will dwell (see 2 Nephi 27:2–3; Moses 7:63–64).

She will be terrible because her enemies will be consumed by the fiery power of God. She may also seem terrible because she will not admit those who are not prepared to dwell in the presence of their Savior. To people who are hungry, terrified, and dying, especially those who then realize they had a chance to be inside of Zion, this may seem terrible indeed.

Thereafter the Lord will send forth from Zion the largest body of missionaries ever assembled to teach, heal, and gather in the elect.[28] In process of time, as the elect become Zion worthy, these great and last teachers of Christ will bear their converts upon their shoulders, and they will speedily come to Zion.

PARALLELS WITH CHRIST'S TIME

It strikes most studious observers that we are today somewhat like the Jews in the days of Christ's nativity. In the days of Christ's birth the Jewish Church, though apostate in many ways, had been "the true Church" for many generations. They held the true (Aaronic) priesthood, had a true form of temple worship, and for thousands of years were His favored and covenant people. They knew of the Messiah's coming in glory and yearned and prayed for it with tears and sacrifices. No matter how adrift their theology and ideology had become, they were still the only true Church upon the earth at that time.

Yet, their scriptures spoke of a quiet and lowly coming of Christ that they refused to countenance. They killed the prophets who taught of a Messiah who would be anything other than a conquering hero. The following quotation is by President Joseph F. Smith.

> His advent was contemplated with longing by the people of God and was a theme on which the prophets of old delighted to dwell. The great results of His earthly mission and the glory of His coming filled their minds to the exclusion of the thought of His being poor and of humble birth; yet Isaiah in his prophecy, sometimes called the fifth Gospel, depicts with a few masterstrokes the Redeemer's meek and

lowly sojourn and the great purpose of His coming. The prophet makes this almost as clear as either of the eye witnesses who wrote the story of His life. *The people, however, were looking for a Messiah who should deliver them from the foreign yoke under which they were groaning. Their spiritual bondage and captivity did not seem to concern them; and when the Lord of lords came to take captivity captive they rejected him.*[29]

The prophet Lehi was merely mocked for calling his contemporaries to repentance during his ministry. They didn't like him accusing them of sin, but they weren't murderous in their rejection. However, when he began to speak of a Christ who would be lowly born and who would die for the sins of the world, they sought to kill him as they had the prophets before him.

> 19 And it came to pass that the Jews did mock him because of the things which he testified of them; for he truly testified of their wickedness and their abominations; and he testified that the things which he saw and heard, and also the things which he read in the book, manifested plainly of the coming of a Messiah, and also the redemption of the world.

> 20 And when the Jews heard these things [concerning the Messiah] they were angry with him; yea, even as with the prophets of old, whom they had cast out, and stoned, and slain; and they also sought his life, that they might take it away. (1 Nephi 1:19–20, comment added.)

Why did they hate the idea of an atoning Messiah so vehemently that they were willing to kill him? We may never entirely know what the ancient Israelites were thinking. But clearly they were incensed by Lehi's teaching of the redeeming Messiah. In their theology they had apparently concluded that there could only be one coming of their Messiah. Since the scriptures testified of both a lowly and a triumphant coming, they decided to throw their vote behind the triumphant coming. It appears that they were not yearning for salvation and the remission of sins so much as a powerful political kingdom over which they envisioned themselves as kings and rulers. There was no place of power for them in a lowly coming of their Messiah. Richard D. Draper writes,

> To Nicodemus and most of the Jews, the Messiah would come as a conquering warrior to put an end to their oppressors. The concept of a Messiah who would die to save all men—Greeks, Romans, and Samaritans included—was foreign to them. He was not coming as a condemning Messiah but as one who saved.[30]

The testimonies of the prophets as recorded in the brass plates all testified of Christ (see Mosiah 13:33; 1 Nephi 19:21–22; 2 Nephi 11:4). However, our version of the same prophecies in the Old Testament contain little about the birth of Christ, indicating that sometime after the brass plates were written, the plain and precious references to Christ's lowly birth were modified or removed, leaving only the veiled references.

> 10 And I said unto him: Believest thou the scriptures? And he said, Yea.
>
> 11 And I said unto him: Then ye do not understand them; for they truly testify of Christ. Behold, I say unto you that none of the prophets have written, nor prophesied, save they have spoken concerning this Christ. (Jacob 7:10–11)

One is left to speculate that the idea of a lowly Christ seemingly threatened their seat of power and negated their hope of a glorious kingdom and unrivaled power. When Lehi and others began to teach of the lowly birth (as opposed to the conquering advent) of the Messiah, they thought it politically justifiable to kill him.

Their fixation upon a conquering Messiah was so powerful that even after His resurrection, as He was just minutes from ascending into heaven, the burden of Christ's disciples fears was still, "When are you going to throw off the Roman yoke and establish the kingdom?"

> 6 When they therefore were come together, they asked of him, saying, Lord, wilt thou at this time restore again the kingdom to Israel? (Acts 1:6)

Minutes later Christ ascended into heaven.

In the latter-day Church we have been taught of two comings of Christ as well. We yearn for the conquering and glorious Second Coming and wait with anxious souls for the day. We store food and water and hope the scourges don't take longer than our food storage lasts. We wonder about the timing of His coming, count the days, and hope the prophet gives us enough warning to prepare. Somewhat like our ancient counterparts, we have become fixated upon the distant, glorious return of our Messiah.

Yet we also know of another coming, though it figures lightly in our minds. It is the coming that all of the prophets record, which the brother of Jared experienced, and which the temple prefigures at the veil. It is the Second Comforter. It is a personal and private coming with no devouring fire or conquering of the wicked. And since it is based upon personal worthiness and purity of heart (for the pure in heart shall see God), we think it beyond ourselves. So we look again to the eastern sky for signs of the glorious coming. In this light, it is startling that we may possibly be falling into a similar trap as our ancient brethren.

We can't know when the glorious coming will be. But we do have control over our own lives, and we do know that if we seek we will find, if we ask we will receive, and if we righteously knock it shall be opened unto us—and we know that it can occur within our lifetime. The promises are before us, and the evidence is voluminous.

Just as Christ had to be born in Bethlehem prior to His coming in Glory, we must receive Christ in our private chambers before we can expect to receive Him at His Coming. The reason this is true is because Zion must be built before the glorious Second Coming can occur. Since Zion is established among men and women as they receive Christ in their private chambers and in their souls, this clearly means that we must attune ourselves to righteousness and bring to pass the personal coming before the Second Coming can occur.

NOTES

1. Smith, *Teachings of the Prophet Joseph Smith*, 170.

2. Orson Pratt, *Journal of Discourses*, 17:148–49.

3. Smith, *Teachings of the Prophet Joseph Smith*, 170.

4. Orson Pratt, *Journal of Discourse*, 17:148.

5. Ibid.

6. *Hymns*, no. 7.

7. *Journal of Discourses*, 11:103.

8. Ibid., 15:4–5.

9. Ibid., 13:148.

10. Ibid., 15:4.

11. Andrus, *Doctrinal Commentary*, 335; italics added.

12. Joseph Fielding Smith, *Church History and Modern Revelation*, 3:16; bracketed comment added.

13. Nibley, *Approaching Zion*, 25–26.

14. McConkie, *New Witness of Articles of Faith*, 582.

15. McConkie, "This Final Glorious Gospel Dispensation," *Ensign*, May 1986, 4; as quoted in *Selected Writings of M. Catherine Thomas*, Deseret Book, 47)

16. Smith, *History of the Church*, 3:390–91.

17. Ibid., 3:285–86.

18. Ibid., 4:570.

19. Ibid., 4:603.

20. *Latter-day prophets and the Doctrine and Covenants,* comp. Roy W. Doxey (Salt Lake City: Deseret Book, 1978), 3:458–59.

21. McConkie, *New Witness of Articles of Faith,* 615–16; italics added.

22. Diary Excerpts of Heber J. Grant, 1887–99.

23. Pratt, *Journal of Discourses,* 15:358–59.

24. And with this inner disquiet lies a certain danger: a person might erroneously conclude that the satisfaction of their unnamed hunger might be found outside of the restored gospel, rather than by laying hold of the greater blessings—unseen and unclaimed but nonetheless immediately before us.

25. Brigham Young, *Journal of Discourses,* 9:283.

26. Young, *Journal of Discourses,* 9:3.

27. Ezra Taft Benson, *The Teachings of Ezra Taft Benson* (Salt Lake City: Bookcraft, 1988), 123–24.

28. *History of the Church,* 6:365

29. *Messages of the First Presidency of The Church of Jesus Christ of Latter-day Saints,* 6 vols., comp. James R. Clark, (Salt Lake City: Bookcraft, 1965–75), 4:28.

30. Richard D. Draper, ed., *A Witness of Jesus Christ: The 1989 Sperry Symposium on the Old Testament* (Salt Lake City: Deseret Book, 1990), 278.

Chapter Five

SEEK THE FACE OF THE LORD

As has been noted, the process of obtaining a place in Zion is that of seeking and obtaining an audience with Christ. It is during that divine interview that we may ask for any righteous endowment, including the greater gift of translation, and thus become a Zion individual. It is also worth observing that it is not necessarily the pathway of every individual to be translated—especially in days prior to the actual establishment of Zion. In these days the greater request may be many other things. But the fact remains that to be in Christ's presence is to become Zion, no matter what we may request of Him.

One of the great privileges of the gospel that has existed in many dispensations is the privilege of obtaining a personal visitation of the Lord. The scriptures are replete with accounts of those who have sought and obtained this great gift. A notable few of those who have obtained the privilege of conversing with the God of heaven face to face include Adam (and most of his contemporaries), Enoch and his whole city, Noah, Melchizedek and his city, Abraham, Isaac, Joseph (of Egypt), Moses, Aaron and seventy of the elders of Israel, Elijah, Elisha, Ezekiel, Isaiah, Peter, James, John, Paul, Lehi, Nephi, Jacob, the brother of Jared, Alma, Moroni, Helaman, Nephi (III), the Nephite twelve, thousands during Christ's appearance at Bountiful, and Joseph Smith with many of his contemporaries. It is also undoubtedly true that countless others, whose names are unknown to history, also obtained this consummate gift in mortality. In our own time, apostles have the same privilege of being personal witnesses of Christ to bear testimony that they have seen Him face-to-face.

Oliver Cowdery explained it this way:

> You have been indebted to other men, in the first instance, for
> evidence; on that you have acted; but it is necessary that you receive a
> testimony from heaven for yourselves; so that you can bear testimony
> to the truth of the Book of Mormon, and that you have seen the face
> of God. That is more than the testimony of an angel. When the proper
> time arrives, you shall be able to bear this testimony to the world.
> When you bear testimony that you have seen God, this testimony God
> will never suffer to fall, but will bear you out; although many will not
> give heed, yet others will. You will therefore see the necessity of getting
> this testimony from heaven.
>
> Never cease striving until you have seen God face to face.
> Strengthen your faith; cast off you doubts, your sins, and all your unbe-
> lief; and nothing can prevent you from coming to God. Your ordina-
> tion is not full and complete till God has laid His hand upon you. We
> require as much to qualify us as did those who have gone before us;
> God is the same. If the Savior in former days laid His hands upon His
> disciples, why not in latter days?[1]

It is worth observing that even during times of spiritual decline and
darkness, many faithful sought and obtained this grand blessing. Many
of the Old Testament prophets prevailed with the Lord while all around
them wickedness reigned.

So sublime is this visitation, and so vast the blessings it bestows, that
it is literally impossible to overstate its attendant blessings. In the following pages we will examine these blessings, as well as the requirements laid
upon those who would be so bold as to seek the face of God. Let us begin
by observing that we are literally commanded to seek His face.

> 38 And seek the face of the Lord always, that in patience ye may possess
> your souls, and ye shall have eternal life. (D&C 101:38)

Moses sought to bring his people out of spiritual darkness into the
full light of the glory of God. He sought to prepare them that they might
do as he had done, ascend the Holy Mount and see the face of God. He
labored diligently to prepare them to enter within the veil.

> 19 And this greater priesthood administereth the gospel and holdeth
> the key of the mysteries of the kingdom, even the key of the knowledge
> of God.
>
> 20 Therefore, in the ordinances thereof, the power of godliness is mani-
> fest.

21 And without the ordinances thereof, and the authority of the priesthood, the power of godliness is not manifest unto men in the flesh;

22 For without this [the power of godliness] no man can see the face of God, even the Father, and live.

23 Now this Moses plainly taught to the children of Israel in the wilderness, and sought diligently to sanctify his people that they might behold the face of God;

24 But they hardened their hearts and could not endure his presence; therefore, the Lord in his wrath, for his anger was kindled against them, swore that they should not enter into his rest while in the wilderness, which rest is the fulness of his glory. (D&C 84:19–24; bracketed comments added)

Please observe that verse 22 clearly defines "the power of godliness" as that which makes it possible to see the face of God, to be in His presence, and to enter into His rest, which is the fulness of His glory.

It seems no more tragic for the children of Israel to reject the invitation to enter into the fulness of God's glory, than for us to likewise reject the same invitation through failure to realize it is being offered to us, or even worse, to fail to believe we are capable of seeing the Lord.

23 If a man love me, he will keep my words: and my Father will love him, and we will come unto him, and make our abode with him. (John 14:23)

It requires monumental faith to translate a promise given to all mankind into a personal belief as seemingly audacious as "I can seek and obtain a personal audience with my Savior." It almost seems irreverent to so believe, as if one is leapfrogging an entire paradigm of mortality—which is that God only appears to prophets, period. The internalization of a belief that you, or I, can and must find ourselves on the other side of the veil in this life is almost superhuman.

Mortal frailty notwithstanding, the promise has stood through time, sounding a divine invitation to awake and behold.

Beyond human unbelief, the enemy of our souls does not want us to believe such lofty things and carefully steals the precious seeds of veil-rending belief before they even touch the rich soils of our soul.

Still, the promise stands, and all mankind is invited to enter in.

Elder McConkie declared: "Seeing the Lord is not a matter of lineage or rank or position or place of precedence."[2]

Joseph Smith said:

> God hath not revealed anything to Joseph, but what he will make known unto the Twelve, and even the least saint may know all things as fast as he is able to bear them, for the day must come when no man need say to his neighbor, Know ye the Lord; for all shall know him . . . from the least to the greatest.[3]

We who, largely inaccurately, consider ourselves the "least Saint" can take great hope from the foregoing promise. The reason this promise is extended to all is that God will lead us to the veil as fast as we are able, or perhaps better stated, as fast as we are willing to bear it.

The process to approach the veil is clearly defined in scripture:

> 1 Verily, thus saith the Lord: It shall come to pass that every soul who forsaketh his sins and cometh unto me, and calleth on my name, and obeyeth my voice, and keepeth my commandments, shall see my face and know that I am. (D&C 93:1)

Chapters could be written on this divine formula. The power of what it tells us is that *every* soul who follows this process may partake of the divine gift—not just the anointed few, but *every* soul. The process is thus defined:

1. "Forsake your sins." Though this process must include repentance, it reaches much farther than simply repenting faster than one sins. It is a state of forsaking, walking away from sin, abandoning it, and living life as sinlessly as mortals may. To do so is to drink from the divine river of grace. It is to qualify, through obedience to law, for a retooling of the soul that makes sinless living far more than merely possible, but joyful. No mortal can forsake sin so completely without the power of Christ's grace. However, when obedience, fueled by unconquerable desire, taps into the power of the Atonement, all things are possible—all spiritual refinements, including forsaking all sin, becomes not just possible, but sweetly distills upon our souls as the dews from heaven. We become pure in heart, not by our own discipleship, but by the discipline of obedience and the upgrading of the soul by God. (Mosiah 5:1–5)

2. "Come unto me." How can one come unto Christ unless one perceives where Christ is? Faith, repentance, and baptism bring the seeker to Christ a significant distance, but much more remains to be done to truly come unto Christ.

To come unto Christ, one must hear His voice and turn toward the sound thereof with faith-born desire. We must struggle if necessary, walk when able, and eventually run toward the sound thereof.

> 20 Behold, I stand at the door, and knock: if any man hear my voice, and open the door, I will come in to him, and will sup with him, and he with me. (Revelation 3:20)

If any man hears my voice, and opens the door, I will come in to him! Notice though, that we are the ones who must open the door!

What a marvelous promise. Christ's voice is light and truth and spirit (D&C 84:45). To walk with His voice is to walk in the light, surround by truth, guided by His Spirit. To walk without His voice is to walk in darkness, lies, and confusion. Throughout scripture the Lord laments that man is walking in darkness at noon day (D&C 95:6). Christ laments over and over that He is a light shining in darkness, and the darkness does not perceive the light (D&C 6:21, 10:58, 34:2, 39:2, 45:7, 88:49).

More than in any other way, we come unto Christ by hearkening to His voice. Every other criteria follows as naturally as day follows the night: Ordinances, ordination, covenants, contracts, promises, perfections, visions, visitations, and glories unspeakable all flow from this one obedience and in no other way. It is not possible that someone unwilling to follow His voice would stumble into these glories, no matter how many outward ordinances they wiggle themselves into.

3. "Call on my name." The language here is interesting and powerful. These words can't imply calling upon Him in prayer, since we have been instructed to pray not to Christ, but to the Father. Why then instruct us to call *on* His name? What use must we make of His name?

The answer lies in the fact that, as fallen mortals, we are not invited to pray unto the Father in our own right. Since we must petition the Father for all blessings, this is an obstacle of eternal proportions. Since no unclean thing (including voices) can come into the presence of the Father, as mortals we simply are not worthy to petition the Father in our own behalf to ask for blessings—let alone to petition for forgiveness, intercession, insight, visions, miracles, or visitations and a fulness of His glory.

It may be easier to consider the audacity of asking for an interview with an earthly king. Even if our cause is just or our need overwhelming, we commoners would have no privilege to ask for relief from the king. Most kings shroud themselves in bureaucracy to avoid just such contact with the masses. We would be stopped at the outer gate long before reaching his ear. We have no personal claim upon his time or upon his power.

However, continuing the analogy, if the master whom we obeyed and served, and who loved us and championed our needs, was the favored son of the king and heir to the throne, we might prevail upon him to intercede with his father, the king. Factor in that we were not mere servants but adopted sons and daughters, and in this setting we could rightly petition our master and adoptive father to intercede with the king.

The actual interview might go something like this: We would stand outside of the throne room while our intercessor goes before the king. He might well say: "O king, I, your beloved son, am here to intercede for my faithful sons and daughters, whom I love, and who love and serve me. In my behalf, please hear their request." At this point the Father is acceding to his worthy son and can invite us into his presence. We then humbly plead our cause "in the name of Jesus Christ."

To call upon His name is to invoke our covenant relationship with Christ when calling upon the Father. It is to stand not behind Christ, but upon His Atonement in our behalf, which makes us able to make righteous requests of the Father. Christ thus implores the Father in our behalf. We do not pray through Christ, nor does He relay our prayers, but we pray to the Father in the name of Christ.

> 4 I am the same which have taken the Zion of Enoch into mine own bosom; and verily, I say, even as many as have believed in my name, for I am Christ, and in mine own name, by the virtue of the blood which I have spilt, have I pleaded before the Father for them. (D&C 38:4)

We might well imagine the futility of asking Jesus Christ to intercede for us when we have not been faithful, or have not, through obedience to His voice, made Him our master and the speaker of our words and doer of our deeds. In such a case it may be in fact unlawful for Him to bring our cause to the Father.

Since we are considering the principles of Zion in this book, how does calling upon the name of Christ relate to our topic? It is because of the quotation above. Christ's intercession for us is not limited to answering our prayers in times of need. When we believe in His name as profoundly as Enoch did, then Christ will plead before the Father in our behalf to let us become a member of Zion. This is the hidden virtue of the above reference.

To whom is this great blessing of becoming a Zion individual promised? Who has actually been translated? According to the words of Christ above, everyone who believes on His name in this degree of righteousness has become a Zion soul. "Even as many as have believed in my name." Such a statement almost makes the mind spin. The burning question that arises is "what does it mean to believe in His name?" We will explore this principle later on, but for now, to believe in His name is to simply believe without reservation that through the Atonement all things are possible to them that believe. In the cause of establishing Zion, its a firm belief that I can become a Zion individual and quite literally be translated if that is my righteous desire.

Our relationship with the Father, our hope of divine intervention in our lives, our salvation, our hope of redemption, our hope of Zion and eternal glory thereafter, is all in the name of Christ.

Hence, we must call upon His name.

4. "Obey my voice." This is a topic upon which much has been written of late and many general authorities have taught. Everywhere in scripture the injunction is the same. Those who obey His voice will be exalted—those who do not, will not. More than obedience to the commandments, more than obedience to law, more than obedience to any doctrine or principle, obedience to the voice of the Lord is listed as the dividing line between righteousness and wickedness (D&C 84:44–50).

Christ's voice begins as the voice of our conscience. This means that conscience is the most rudimentary manifestation of Christ's voice. Other purer manifestations follow as greater obedience to this tiny voice of truth calls them forth. Promptings, insights, bursts of understanding, doctrine distilling upon our souls, revelations, visions, conversations, angelic visitations, and even the Divine Presence are increasingly more pure manifestations of revelation. One cannot evolve to the greater forms without first perfecting the lesser.

Most mortals vastly underestimate the power of obedience to Christ's counsels, which are promptings from the Holy Spirit. Most journeys back into the kingdom will consist of millions of small obediences, rather than a few huge ones. Rendering service when it is not deserved, saying a kind word to unkind people, being friendly to the unfriendly and humble before the proud, dispensing grace when we know it is right, being helpful only because the thought quietly surfaced amid the jumble of the day, saying family prayers when it is right but inconvenient. These and a billion other small things are what bring us to Christ.

Why? It is because each act of right-doing comes to our understanding through revelation from the voice of Christ. We draw nearer and nearer to Him by the small things that quietly add up to eternal glory. These principles, and the blessed results of learning to obey Christ's voice, are vast. A few of them are:

- Promptings constitute the voice of Christ (D&C 84:43–45).
- Promptings communicate the will of Christ.
- We are obeying Christ when we obey promptings.
- Promptings constitute our primary means of knowing the will of Christ.
- Knowing what is right constitutes revelation, no matter how it came to us; a feeling, a thought or understanding (D&C 8:2–3; Moroni 7:15–16).
- Wickedness is defined as hardening one's heart and failing to listen to the voice of Christ (D&C 38:6; D&C 93:31–32, 39).
- We come unto Christ by hearkening to His voice (D&C 29:2).
- We become Christlike by *always* doing His will.
- Christ gives us His "grace for [our] grace" as we serve others according to His direction (D&C 93:20).
- His grace is the only means of becoming perfect. We grow from grace to grace (D&C 93:13).
- Hence, we receive His grace by obeying His voice.
- Obedience is the first law of heaven[4]

5. "Keep my commandments." Last, having done all other things, the penitent must keep the commandments—all of them.

So much has been written and said to encourage us to keep the commandments that literally nothing can be added to clarify what is meant and what we should be doing. What may yet remain to be said is this, that obedience for the sake of obedience, or mere obligation, is a formula for frustration and spiritual burnout. There are simply too many commandments for us to have them all in our minds, let alone upon our lips and hands. The classic harried laborer in the Church who runs exhausted from home to church to home to church with a tired smile that resembles a grimace more than a grin is the prototype of this phenomenon.

However, the Lord has provided a perfect way for us to keep the commandments almost without noticing it. It is so precious and soul-saving that anyone who applies it will succeed. It is rare to hear it spoken of. Those who learn this great secret do so in the process of their personal quest and rarely step back to analyze what they have done or to smith it into words they can share.

It works like this: You live your life in obedience to the still small voice. If you are aware of its presence, you will hear it. It will constitute many promptings to do something, or perhaps, to not do something. The key is to do exactly as it guides you without hesitation.

This is the process.

Does it sound like an oversimplification? Does it sound as if there should be something more profound, more flashy, more physical and down-to-earth in the description, like fasting once a week, or paying double fast offerings? The fact is that this is all there is to it. Those who learn to hear and obey the voice of the Lord are exalted (see Helaman 12:23). Those who do not, are not (see Moses 4:4).

Let us not confuse simple with easy. It is conceptually simple because even a child can understand and begin to apply it. It is not easy, because the opposition and opportunity to turn away from the straight way is intense. Every element of mortality is designed to distract and dissuade us. Most everything we take in through our five senses tells us of a more entertaining, popular, exciting, alluring, or economically rewarding way.

To paraphrase Alma, do not let us be slothful because of the easiness of the way (see Alma 37:46). In practical terms, it is the pursuit of a lifetime to develop flawless obedience to the voice of revelation.

Not only does this process work, but it is the only form of obedience that does work. Have you ever done some service with good intent and had it blow up in your face? You meant to be encouraging but were accused of criticizing. You meant to be supportive, but instead you inadvertently offended someone. You used certain language in a conversation or lesson but a misunderstanding hurt some tender soul's feelings. You meant to bless but were criticized for your efforts. These things often happen because we have acted with real intent but without real inspiration. They can also happen because the recipient of our intended good works was uninspired in embracing our gift.

The Holy Spirit is never mistaken in what will work—never. So, in yielding to the Holy Spirit, joy always distills upon the obedient, even when other people's agency allows them to reject or criticize our labors. When we act in obedience, peace descends no matter how harried the world spins around us. The reason it works is because when one is obedient to the voice of revelation in their lives, they simply are obedient to all aspects of the gospel, including the commandments.

No longer must we pick among the lesser of evils, trying to decide which commandment to keep at the moment. No longer is there a war between doing our church duties and serving our families fully. No longer must we determine whether to prepare our Sunday School lesson or cook dinner. You just listen. The Holy Spirit will guide you, and in time your soul delights in obedience, because joy always follows. And right in the midst of the joy, the realization brightly dawns that you have almost effortlessly aligned your soul with every commandment.

In the mundane affairs of life the Spirit does not always intercede. Often we are left to choose our course when matters of right and wrong are not present. This is a natural and important process of maturation and growth. What is being suggested isn't that we must receive revelation to guide us in every detail of our lives, or that we should become paralyzed when revelation is not evident, but that when revelation *is* provided, and we recognize it as such, we follow it without debate, doubt, or delay.

Moroni left us with timeless counsel when he taught us that just as the devil fights against God continually and invites and entices to commit sin continually, so does "that which is of God" invite and entice us continually to do good and to serve God (Moroni 7:12–13). The challenge may well be to identify that which is of God from all other elements of our lives so that we can yield ourselves to obedience. Moroni gives us the grand key. He proclaims that we may tell the difference between good and evil (both of which influence us continually) as clearly as we can tell the daylight from the dark night.

> 15 For behold, my brethren, it is given unto you to judge, that ye may know good from evil; and the way to judge is as plain, that ye may know with a perfect knowledge, as the daylight is from the dark night.
>
> 16 For behold, the Spirit of Christ is given to every man, that he may know good from evil; wherefore, I show unto you the way to judge; for

every thing which inviteth to do good, and to persuade to believe in Christ, is sent forth by the power and gift of Christ; wherefore ye may know with a perfect knowledge it is of God. (Moroni 7:15–16)

Accordingly, everything which entices or invites mankind to do good, to believe in Christ, to be kind or loving or forgiving, to help and support and encourage, to show forth increased love, to serve and support and sustain—all of these things come to us through the pipeline of revelation directly from God. To lay hold upon each one of these is to lay hold upon "every good thing" (see Moroni 7:20–28).

6. "See My Face and Know That I Am." Then, having complied with these five requirements, this last and greatest promise follows—that we will be privileged to see His face and know that He is. Then faith turns to knowledge, and knowledge to power, and power to privilege. These six steps define a pathway to the presence of God. They are the same that every faithful man and woman has trod to enter the divine presence. They will, in the timetable of the Lord, bring us to the same spiritual stature as the Brother of Jared. Elder McConkie's grand summation of these matters is this:

> If and when we obtain the spiritual stature of this man Moriancumer, then we shall see what he saw and know what he knew.[5]

Elder McConkie records the following sweet and encouraging insight. Commenting upon Doctrine and Covenants 88:62–63, "Call upon me while I am near—Draw near unto me and I will draw near unto you; seek me diligently and ye shall find me; ask, and ye shall receive; knock, and it shall be opened unto you." McConkie exults:

> Surely, this is what we must do if we ever expect to see his face. He is there waiting our call, anxious to have us seek his face, awaiting our importuning pleas to rend the veil so that we can see the things of the Spirit.[6]

These words bring about powerful stirrings in the soul. It is so precious to envision our Lord anxiously awaiting our call, delighting in our importuning pleas to rend the veil. The prophet Joseph asked:

> How do men obtain a knowledge of the glory of God, his perfections and attributes? By devoting themselves to his service, through prayer and supplication incessantly strengthening their faith in him, until, like Enoch, the brother of Jared, and Moses, they obtain a manifestation of God to themselves.[7]

A manifestation of God isn't just a vision of heavenly things; it is when God manifests Himself—when we are at last in His presence.

It appears that what some of us have lacked all along is a Spirit-born testimony, or understanding if you will, that they are being offered to us—to you and me. From the following scripture we learn that to obtain such a belief, and thereafter purify ourselves before Him, qualifies us for this most high and holy privilege.

> 116 Neither is man capable to make them known, for they are only to be seen and understood by the power of the Holy Spirit, which God bestows on those who love him, and purify themselves before him;
>
> 117 To whom he grants this privilege of seeing and knowing for themselves;
>
> 118 That through the power and manifestation of the Spirit, while in the flesh, they may be able to bear his presence in the world of glory. (D&C 76:116–18)

Joseph says that if we love Him and purify ourselves before Him (for the pure in heart shall see God), He will grant us the privilege of seeing God and knowing these glorious things for ourselves. When? While in the flesh! In this life! We are invited to seek and obtain the power of the Spirit to change us so that, as a mortal, we may enter His presence in the world of glory.

Do you hear the sweet echoes of the temple?

Regarding the availability of these blessings to all the faithful, Elder McConkie penned these timeless words:

> After the true saints receive and enjoy the gift of the Holy Ghost; after they know how to attune themselves to the voice of the Spirit; after they mature spiritually so that they see visions, work miracles, and entertain angels; after they make their calling and election sure and prove themselves worthy of every trust—after all this and more—it becomes their right and privilege to see the Lord and commune with him face to face. Revelations, visions, angelic visitations, the rending of the heavens, and appearances among men of the Lord himself—all these things are for all of the faithful. They are not reserved for apostles and prophets only. God is no respecter of persons. They are not reserved for one age only, or for a select lineage or people. We are all our Father's children. All men are welcome.[8]

Elder McConkie continues with this astonishing promise:

> The attainment of such a state of righteousness and perfection is

the object and end toward which all of the Lord's people are striving. We seek to see the face of the Lord while we yet dwell in mortality, and we seek to dwell with him everlastingly in the eternal kingdoms that are prepared.[9]

While we are yet mortal!

Commenting upon the other comforter mentioned in the book of John, the prophet Joseph taught us:

> Now what is this other Comforter? It is no more nor less than the Lord Jesus Christ Himself; and this is the sum and substance of the whole matter; that when any man obtains this last Comforter, he will have the personage of Jesus Christ to attend him, or appear unto him from time to time, and even he will manifest the Father unto him, and they will take up their abode with him, and the visions of the heavens will be opened unto him, and the Lord will teach him face to face, and he may have a perfect knowledge of the mysteries of the Kingdom of God; and this is the state and place the ancient saints arrived at when they had such glorious visions—Isaiah, Ezekiel, John upon the Isle of Patmos, St. Paul in the three heavens, and all the saints who held communion with the general assembly and Church of the Firstborn.[10]

The following quote by Elder McConkie is under the heading of "The righteous see him while in the flesh."

> We must not wrest the scriptures and suppose that the promises of seeing the Lord refer to some future day, either a Millennial or a celestial day, days in which, as we all know, the Lord will be present. The promises apply to this mortal sphere in which we now live. This is clearly set forth in the Vision of the Degrees of Glory. After Joseph Smith and Sidney Rigdon had seen the Father and the Son, concourses of angels, and the wonders of each kingdom of glory, and after they had written the account thereof, their continuing language says: "Great and marvelous are the works of the Lord, and the mysteries of his kingdom which he showed unto us, which surpass all understanding in glory, and in might, and in dominion; which he commanded us we should not write while we were yet in the Spirit, and are not lawful for man to utter; neither is man capable to make them known, for they are only to be seen and understood by the power of the Holy Spirit, which God bestows on those who love him, and purify themselves before him; to whom he grants this privilege of seeing and knowing for themselves; that through the power and manifestation of the Spirit, while in the flesh, they may be able to bear his presence in the world of glory"

(D&C 76:114-118). While in the flesh! For those who "purify themselves before him," this is the time and the day and the hour when they have power to see their God![11]

"Seeing" is perhaps a weak verb for what happens when someone is admitted into the glorious presence of Christ. It is like describing inheriting a fortune unexpectedly as "seeing" someone hand you a billion dollar check. There is much more to that event than mere sight.

It is true that we will see Him, but it is more important that great blessings flow from that event, including being given the opportunity to request some great endowment from the Lord. It is my opinion that this privilege of asking for some astronomical gift from the Lord is what has brought down upon the heads of every great person of righteousness those extraordinary powers and gifts for which they are known in the scriptures.

This great personal interview with Christ is also the ultimate form of receiving Christ in mortality. To receive Him in this way is to claim the greatest blessings of mortality and eternity.

> 21 Verily, verily, I say unto you, except ye abide my law ye cannot attain to this glory.

> 22 For strait is the gate, and narrow the way that leadeth unto the exaltation and continuation of the lives, and few there be that find it, because ye receive me not in the world neither do ye know me.

> 23 But if ye receive me in the world, then shall ye know me, and shall receive your exaltation; that where I am ye shall be also.

> 24 This is eternal lives—to know the only wise and true God, and Jesus Christ, whom he hath sent. I am he. Receive ye, therefore, my law. (D&C 132:21–24)

The reason few obtain these great blessings is that they do not receive Christ in the world, which the inspired word proclaims is a result of our not knowing Him. Of course, "in the world" refers to mortality. Many people receive Christ in their hearts, in their testimonies, and in their faith, which are all glorious mortal blessings. But the above verse proclaims "few there be that find it." In other words, it is a rare and exalted privilege that occurs to those who receive Christ in this way. Viewed from another perspective, the vast majority of us won't ascend to this privilege because we do not reach beyond the norm and "receive" Christ in the way this verse is suggesting.

PRIESTHOOD AND SEEING THE LORD

Commenting upon Doctrine and Covenants 131:5, which states, "The more sure word of prophecy means a man's knowing that he is sealed up unto eternal life, by revelation and the spirit of prophecy, through the power of the holy priesthood," Elder McConkie instructs:

> *It follows that the priesthood is the power, authority, and means that prepares men to see their Lord; also,* that in the priesthood is found everything that is needed to bring this consummation to pass. Accordingly, it is written: "The power and authority of the higher, or Melchizedek Priesthood, is to hold the keys of all the spiritual blessings of the Church—To have the privilege of receiving the mysteries of the kingdom of heaven, to have the heavens opened unto them, to commune with the general assembly and church of the Firstborn, and to enjoy the communion and presence of God the Father, and Jesus the mediator of the new covenant."[12]

This profound connection between the restored priesthood and seeing the God of Heaven is not obscure doctrine, nor is it new. This has never varied dispensation after dispensation. Each dispensation of the gospel through the eons of time has included this great and last gift. What has varied is our ability to perceive and believe this great promise. Some dispensations rejected the invitation to stand in the presence of God outright. This occurred with Moses and the children of Israel. Other dispensations obtained and enjoyed the divine presence, such as Adam, Enoch, Melchizedek, and the post-advent Nephites, as well as others.

Seeing God isn't just an attendant privilege of the priesthood or limited to those of high office—it is the highest blessing of the priesthood in this life. Though we may enjoy many other blessings through the priesthood, the overarching and accumulative effect of all other priesthood blessings is that they prepare us to enter the presence of God.

Elder McConkie notes that when the priesthood operates fully in any life, we will have this grand privilege:

> Thus, through the priesthood the door may be opened and the way provided for men to see the Father and the Son. From all of this it follows, automatically and axiomatically, that if and when the holy priesthood operates to the full in the life of any man, [or woman, they] will receive its great and full blessings, which are that rending of the heavens and that parting of the veil of which we now speak.[13]

It is important to note here that most blessings of the priesthood do not flow to the holder of that priesthood. No one has ever baptized himself or ordained himself to an office. Even Christ, the greatest priesthood authority of all eternity, asked John, an Aaronic Priesthood holder, to baptize Him. Thus, these stated blessings and privileges are not the birthright of men, they are the birthright of mankind. All blessings that flow *from* the priesthood, all privileges, every right and promise is held out equally to women and to men.

The caveat is that the priesthood isn't a train track that ends at the veil. You don't just get on the priesthood train and snooze until you arrive at the "Presence of God" station. The priesthood takes us to whatever destination we *desire* to achieve. Such is also true of our faith and every other blessing of the gospel, and even life in general—we achieve what we desire, and nothing more. Alma said it this way:

> 4 I ought not to harrow up in my desires . . . for I know that he granteth unto men according to their desire, whether it be unto death or unto life; yea, I know that he allotteth unto men, yea, decreeth unto them decrees which are unalterable, according to their wills, whether they be unto salvation or unto destruction. (Alma 29:4)

Our desires produce unalterable decrees, which have eternal impact whether unto salvation or destruction. Faith tells us that any righteous desire, even one that stretches our faith and belief beyond its inherent strength as we reach for the grand and glorious promises, will produce an unalterable decree that we will obtain.

In order for the greatest priesthood blessing of standing in the presence of God to manifest fully in our lives, we must desire it more than anything else. But before we can desire such an audacious thing, we must first believe that it is in fact our privilege and right to seek such a glorious blessing. Following belief and desire, we must thereafter be willing to pay any price required of us to so obtain. We must seek it with all our might, mind, and strength.

To believe all the rest of the gospel and yet not believe we have the privilege of seeing God is to only believe a lesser portion of the gospel (Alma 12:10–11). When we at last "believe all things" (thirteenth article of faith), then the priesthood can operate to the full and all the blessings ultimately will be bestowed, including the rending of the heavens and the appearance of the Father and the Son.

An individual whose faith or belief never includes this great privilege will never enjoy the Father's and Son's divine presence in this life. Of course, as we grow in righteousness, the Spirit strives to instill these truths in our souls and to prepare us with belief, desire, and unconquerable faith sufficient to part the veil of heaven.

At some point we must cease looking at the scriptures as an inspired history book of the lives of the ancient faithful and begin to look at it more as a divine mail order catalog.

With such an inspired belief, desire will blossom with insistence and faith will soon follow, as will the necessary purity, and in time the heavens will open to our view and to our eternal reward.

> 10 And again, verily I say unto you that it is your privilege, and a promise I give unto you that have been ordained unto this ministry, that inasmuch as you strip yourselves from jealousies and fears, and humble yourselves before me, for ye are not sufficiently humble, the veil shall be rent and you shall see me and know that I am—not with the carnal neither natural mind, but with the spiritual. . . .

> 14 Let not your minds turn back; and when ye are worthy, in mine own due time, ye shall see and know that which was conferred upon you by the hands of my servant Joseph Smith, Jun. Amen. (D&C 67:10, 14)

President Lorenzo Snow penned this charming picture of Zion and how the Lord's presence would affect us then:

> I can tell you what I think: Many of you will be living in Jackson County, and there you will be assisting in building the temple; and if you will not have seen the Lord Jesus at that time you may expect Him very soon, to see Him, to eat and drink with Him, to shake hands with Him and to invite Him to your houses as He was invited when He was here before. I am saying things to you now of which I know something of the truth of them.[14]

PRIESTHOOD ORDINANCES AND MYSTERIES OF GODLINESS

All gospel blessings, especially those related to entering the presence of the Lord, flow from priesthood ordinances. The power of godliness lies in the right that the priesthood gives us to righteously perform binding ordinances. Thus, being a priesthood holder does not give us a greater privilege in obtaining these promised blessings. The power of the priesthood is in the ordinances, not in the offices. It is in the fulfillment of the promised blessings held forth by those ordinances that the mysteries of the kingdom are revealed, even the key of the knowledge of God.

> 19 And this greater priesthood administereth the gospel and holdeth the key of the mysteries of the kingdom, even the key of the knowledge of God.
>
> 20 Therefore, in the ordinances thereof, the power of godliness is manifest.
>
> 21 And without the ordinances thereof, and the authority of the priesthood, the power of godliness is not manifest unto men in the flesh;
>
> 22 For without this no man can see the face of God, even the Father, and live.
>
> 23 Now this Moses plainly taught to the children of Israel in the wilderness, and sought diligently to sanctify his people that they might behold the face of God;
>
> 24 But they hardened their hearts and could not endure his presence; therefore, the Lord in his wrath, for his anger was kindled against them, swore that they should not enter into his rest while in the wilderness, which rest is the fulness of his glory. (D&C 84:19–24)

You noticed that the desire of Moses' heart was to sanctify his people that they might behold the face of God. Not only was this his desire, but he plainly taught it to them and sought diligently to bring them into God's presence. This was more than a fatherly desire for his flock to experience the same wonderful things he had. This *is* the gospel! This is the greatest possible outcome of the gospel in any dispensation, that we may enter into the presence of God and there partake of the incomparable blessings described in the last verse as entering into God's rest and partaking of the fulness of His glory. Moses understood the majestic power of what God was offering his people, and he labored diligently to lead them into full reception of the promises.

But they could not endure His presence. It is interesting that their rebellion is described in this way. The children of Israel seem to have understood what they were rejecting, otherwise God's ire would have been unjustified. They apparently did not want the responsibility and the obligations of entering God's presence. They wanted Moses to interface with God and to let them dwell in the semi-darkness of wickedness and indulgence. Even with a plain understanding of the glorious blessings being offered, they rejected not just Moses' offer, but also God's invitation. For this reason God's wrath was, and apparently still is, upon them (D&C 84:24).

In our day, we have likewise been offered these blessings in plainness. There can be no misunderstanding that we have the fulness of the gospel, the greater priesthood, and the temple-taught invitation to come into the presence of God.

The higher priesthood holds the "key" to all the spiritual blessings of the kingdom, specifically that which invites us into the presence of God. It is interesting that there is only one key—not keys.

The word *key* used in the verse above is not speaking of priesthood keys, but of the priesthood offering us the means (key) to obtain the mysteries and knowledge of God. Only the prophet and those whom he designates have priesthood keys. The key referenced above and the opportunity it represents flows from priesthood ordinances and is available to all mankind according to their faith.

This key, when received and fully utilized, gives us the ability to open the doors and enter into the covenant relationships that ultimately distill into what the above verse describes as the "fulness of his glory." The key should not be confused with the door itself. Once in possession of the key, one must still learn how to use it. Possessing the key is not to automatically know how or even be worthy to open the door.

The object of our journey, the hope of our souls, the yearning desire of our faith is beyond the door. It would be foolish to acquire the key and then hang it in a place of honor upon our wall and revere it as the manifestation of life's mission accomplished. The purpose of the gospel, the purpose of the priesthood, the purpose of ordinances, and the key it hands us is to open the door—nothing less.

What lies beyond the door? As the above-quoted scripture attests—it is the very presence of God.

Let us not siphon the virtue from this glorious promise by assuming that this divine audience with deity is the inevitable day when we will all kneel before Him to be judged, or some automatic event at death.

Moses sought to bring his people—his very much mortal and living people—into the presence of God. Such is the nature of the keys the ordinances offer us. Such is the invitation before us.

Between that glorious audience with God and where we are today lies a vast array of divinely ordained mysteries which must be obtained and understood in crystalline clarity. These mysteries, when stripped of their mystery through personal revelation and inspired understanding, are revealed to be those glorious truths which then give us the ability to apply the key and open the door into the presence of the Lord.

Much could be said about the mysteries of godliness. Suffice it to say that the mysteries are glorious, wholesome, and vitally necessary. They are suggested many times in scripture, but the process of learning them and claiming them for ourselves is intentionally obscure, otherwise they wouldn't be mysteries.

A better way to look at the relationship of the scriptures and the great mysteries is to compare them to a cookbook of wonderful desserts that shows page after page of mouth-watering pictures but has no recipes. We must pay a price and purchase each recipe individually. In this metaphor, the recipes for the mysteries of God are learned by revelation and no other way. The scriptures show us that the greater blessings exist and that many people have obtained them. Each of us must obtain our personal recipe through righteousness and personal revelation. The price we pay is flawless obedience.

No book adequately describes the mysteries because it is not possible to communicate such things by words to readers—inspired or otherwise. Each person must obtain these truths through personal effort and personal righteousness. The best literary description of the mysteries is the scriptures themselves, and yet few people pierce the veil of mystery and obtain those promised glories for themselves, those things which are described as faithfully and correctly as inspired mortal pens may set to word.

Once we obtain a great mystery for ourselves, we may well find that the holy word described it and how to obtain it as clearly as words may. We just could not understand until the Holy Ghost distilled the doctrine upon our soul "as the dews from heaven" (D&C 121:45). Once a mystery is understood, it becomes obvious and evident throughout the scriptures. When our eyes are at last opened to a mystery, we "see" it everywhere.

Because of the multiple layering of the scriptures wherein many things are true on many levels, it is possible to read a scripture many times and not recognize the mystery described therein until revelation lifts it off the page and transports it into our souls. Such distillations of the doctrine of the priesthood are, in fact, the mysteries of godliness being made manifest in our lives.

It requires a high degree of faith and spiritual acuity to translate the blessings recorded in scripture into a personal invitation to partake of the glories of the heavens for ourselves.

Through the scriptures we are allowed to view the powerful effect of these gifts and mysteries in the lives of the ancient faithful. Most all of us believe in their blessings. What we often can't see is the invitation to step forth and partake for ourselves.

Where in the scriptures are the mysteries to be found? They're actually easy to find. Read until you come to a passage or phrase you don't understand, or to which you have an indistinct, warm-fuzzy understanding. Most probably it is an oft-repeated phrase. Mysteries cause the true seeker to ponder and wonder how the ancient righteous obtained that particular privilege. You've just found a mystery. There are hundreds of them.

These precious pearls remain mysteries until revealed through personal revelation. Once a seeker has learned a mystery, mortal language is not able to make it known to another. No combination of words, no matter how powerful or inspired, can transport it into the soul of another. Each person must acquire it through personally revealed truth.

18 The power and authority of the higher, or Melchizedek Priesthood, is to hold the keys of all the spiritual blessings of the Church—

19 *To have the privilege of receiving the mysteries of the kingdom of heaven,* to have the heavens opened unto them, to commune with the general assembly and church of the Firstborn, and to enjoy the communion and presence of God the Father, and Jesus the mediator of the new covenant. (D&C 107:18–19; italics added)

The mysteries are those principles of the gospel which must be received and understood through the Holy Ghost. There is a huge divide between seeking the mysterious, and seeking the mysteries. The mysterious are just things that are not revealed in scripture. One of these mysterious things is the true nature of our Heavenly Mother. It is not revealed in scripture, and for that reason is not a subject we can speculate about. If Heavenly Father wants someone to know more about His companion, He will reveal it. Until then, in my opinion, it is not on the menu of things we should speculate about. There are many such things that are not offered to us.

The mysteries of godliness that are offered to us are highlighted in scripture in the lives of others. We know they are available because they have been obtained by the ancient faithful. The mysteries of godliness are not to be shunned, but rather, appropriately sought under the guidance of the Spirit. It is the mysteries which give us the key to the knowledge of God, and in time, the actual knowledge of God—which is life eternal (John 17:3).

10 It is your privilege, and a promise I give unto you that have been ordained unto this ministry, that inasmuch as you strip yourselves from jealousies and fears, and humble yourselves before me, for ye are not sufficiently humble, the veil shall be rent and you shall see me and know that I am—not with the carnal neither natural mind, but with the spiritual.

11 For no man has seen God at any time in the flesh, except quickened by the Spirit of God.

12 Neither can any natural man abide the presence of God, neither after the carnal mind.

13 Ye are not able to abide the presence of God now, neither the ministering of angels; wherefore, continue in patience until ye are perfected.

14 Let not your minds turn back; and when ye are worthy in mine own due time, ye shall see and know that which is conferred upon you by the hands of my servant Joseph Smith, Jun. (D&C 67:10–14)

So, when does it become appropriate to diligently seek a particular mystery of godliness? This is a worthwhile question. The answer lies in the vantage point of the spiritual pilgrim. In other words, if through the Holy Spirit a person recognizes a gift and has a desire to enjoy the same, then the mere fact that the Holy Spirit has opened it to your view means that not only can you seek it, but also that you should. It means you will eventually obtain it. In other words, if the Holy Spirit opens it to your view, it is yours to pursue.

As a reality check, let us firmly note that the Holy Spirit does not speak in opposition to the seated mouthpiece of the Lord. We have three sources of truth for a reason. The living prophet, the scriptures, and the Holy Spirit always agree. If we obtain any prompting that is divergent with one of these other witnesses, then we should return to the Lord for further light and truth.

Even among the elect there are those who yet lack the belief that would fire their souls with a vision of the greater blessings promised. Elder McConkie wrote:

There are, of course, those whose callings and election have been made sure who have never exercised the faith nor exhibited the righteousness which would enable them to commune with the Lord on the promised basis. There are even those who neither believe nor know that it is possible to see the Lord in this day, and they therefore are without the personal incentive that would urge them onward in the pursuit of this consummation so devoutly desired by those with spiritual insight.[15]

The next question is, "How can I obtain these lofty things?"

Some of these gifts are so glorious that it may actually seem presumptuous to view yourself as a participant in them.

Herein lies the first step. Through the ministrations of the Holy Spirit one must come to a belief pattern that includes themselves in these incredible gifts; a belief that removes every shadow of presumption, audaciousness, or even overconfidence, and simply goes boldly unto the throne of grace (Hebrews 4:16). Without a belief that these blessings are meant for one personally, that person could not seek them with sufficient faith to lay hold upon them.

Perhaps the next question would be: "If I don't yet have this belief, how can I obtain the foundation of belief that I lack?"

The answer lies in desire.

> 27 But behold, if ye will awake and arouse your faculties, even to an experiment upon my words, and exercise a particle of faith, yea, even if ye can no more than desire to believe, let this desire work in you, even until ye believe in a manner that ye can give place for a portion of my words. (Alma 32:27)

Alma taught that even if we can no more than desire to believe, this will work in us until we can believe in our own invitation to enter into these blessings. We then take that desire to the Lord and lay it before Him and plead for that which we lack. In a short time we will find our belief growing if we don't smother it with unbelief or separate ourselves from the flow of light through sin. Along with this increase in belief will come an adornment of our faith in the things we are being led to believe. As our faith matures, we begin to understand the recipe to making this delectable pastry. The next step is to actually combine the ingredients.

In summary, the process looks like this:

- Recognize that the gift is being offered.
- Pray for and obtain a firm belief that God desires you to partake of the gift.
- Exercise your faith in learning what God desires of you in

order to obtain the blessing. This is the law upon which that blessing is predicated for you personally (D&C 130:21).

- Obey the law forevermore.
- Obtain the blessing.

This principle is actually well known. What may not have been obvious is that this formula can also pull down great blessings upon our heads. To obtain the mysteries of the kingdom we can seek them with a firm belief that they are available, have faith that we can and will qualify for them, and be willing to happily pay whatever price the Lord places upon them.

Notes

1. Oliver Cowdery, *History of the Church*, 2:195.
2. McConkie, *The Promised Messiah*, 569.
3. Smith, *Teachings of the Prophet Joseph Smith*, 149.
4. Joseph F. Smith, *Journal of Discourses,* 16:248.
5. McConkie, *The Promised Messiah*, 582.
6. Ibid., 582.
7. Smith, *Lectures on Faith,* 2:55.
8. McConkie, *The Promised Messiah*, 575.
9. Ibid., 578.
10. Smith, *Teachings of the Prophet Joseph Smith*, 149–51.
11. McConkie, *New Witness for the Articles of Faith*, 495.
12. McConkie, *The Promised Messiah*, 587; italics added.
13. Ibid., 588; bracketed comment added.
14. Lorenzo Snow, *The Teachings of Lorenzo Snow*, ed. by Clyde J. Williams (Salt Lake City: Bookcraft, 1984), 186.
15. McConkie, *The Promised Messiah*, 586.

Chapter Six

The Oath and Covenant of the Priesthood

Since all blessings flow from the priesthood, Zion also flows from the priesthood. When we receive the full blessings of Zion they will come because of this oath and covenant which the Father has established. Therefore, to understand the oath and covenant of the priesthood, what it is, what it promises, and where it is taking us, is to understand our full potential in the gospel, including the establishment of Zion!

To fully receive the promised blessings of the oath and covenant of the priesthood is to become a Zion soul. The two are inseparably connected. It is not possible as an individual or as a church to fulfill our covenants and fully receive the blessings of the priesthood without becoming Zion.

Many years ago, when I was being interviewed to receive the Melchizedek Priesthood in preparation for going on a mission, my stake president asked me to explain the oath and covenant of the priesthood. My reply was appropriately superficial for a nineteen-year-old. When it became obvious that I didn't really understand it, he instructed me to read the 84th section of the Doctrine and Covenants.

I promised I would but asked him to explain it to me. I don't remember his exact words, but the flavor of his response has vividly remained in my mind all these years. His explanation was not much more detailed than my own. I realized that he didn't feel he understood it himself. His response energized my curiosity. When I got home I anxiously read through the 84th section. When I closed the book I understood both his and my general lack of clarity on the subject. The oath and covenant of the priesthood is couched in language not easily understood. Let us carefully examine the language of the covenant to see what it is promising us.

The oath and covenant of the priesthood is laid out in verses 33 to 40 of the 84th section of the Doctrine and Covenants. The first half of the first sentence describes what we must do to fulfill our obligation in this covenant:

> 33 For whoso is faithful unto the obtaining these two priesthoods of which I have spoken, and the magnifying their calling, . . .

Everything that follows describes the blessings associated with its fulfillment:

> . . . are sanctified by the Spirit unto the renewing of their bodies.

> 34 They become the sons of Moses and of Aaron and the seed of Abraham, and the Church and kingdom, and the elect of God.

> 35 And also all they who receive this priesthood receive me, saith the Lord;

> 36 For he that receiveth my servants receiveth me;

> 37 And he that receiveth me receiveth my Father;

> 38 And he that receiveth my Father receiveth my Father's kingdom; therefore all that my Father hath shall be given unto him.

> 39 And this is according to the oath and covenant which belongeth to the priesthood.

> 40 Therefore, all those who receive the priesthood, receive this oath and covenant of my Father, which he cannot break, neither can it be moved. (D&C 84:33–40)

It is significant to note that this oath and covenant was established by the Father. It exists because the Father of us all ordained a process whereby we could obtain the blessings listed above. It is a covenant that the Father always establishes between Himself and His righteous posterity. And whoso is faithful unto obtaining these priesthoods and magnifying their calling will invariably receive the promised rewards because the covenant cannot be broken or moved.

The blessings received by obedience to the Holy Spirit (the Light of Christ) are preliminary and preparatory to this greater covenant offered by the Father.

> 45 For the word of the Lord is truth, and whatsoever is truth is light, and whatsoever is light is Spirit, even the Spirit of Jesus Christ.

46 And the Spirit giveth light to every man that cometh into the world; and the Spirit enlighteneth every man through the world, that hearkeneth to the voice of the Spirit.

47 *And every one that hearkeneth to the voice of the Spirit cometh unto God, even the Father.*

48 And the Father teacheth him of the covenant which he [the Father] has renewed and confirmed upon you, which is confirmed upon you for your sakes, and not for your sakes only, but for the sake of the whole world. (D&C 84:45–48; italics and bracketed comment added)

In other words, Christ sends forth His Spirit into the hearts of all who come into the world to lead them to this greater covenant of the Father. This Christ does freely, and without any requirement that we ask for it, or even accept it. There is only the associated promise that if we choose to hearken to the voice of the Spirit, we will come unto the Father and this greater covenant.

And, what is the covenant which the Father has confirmed upon you? There are several such covenants, but the one most relevant to Zion is the oath and covenant of the priesthood that He has established for the sake of the whole world—indeed, the whole of creation.

In simpler terms, obedience to the voice of the Holy Spirit brings the spiritual pilgrim to the receipt of all gospel blessings, including priesthood ordinances and ordinations. When such a person righteously participates in priesthood ordinances, they come unto Christ in a very real way. Having thus righteously begun that lifelong journey, the Father confirms upon them a promise given by His oath and covenant, that if they will magnify their calling, He will pour out an additional blessing that is so great and grand that many of us Latter-day Saints have yet to even glimpse what that blessing is. These are the blessings leading us to the veil, which are promised in the temple, in scripture and in the revealed mysteries of Godliness. These are the blessings wherein Zion is nested.

Please note that these blessings are not just for our sake; they are for the sake of the whole world. Why? Because without our obtaining these two priesthoods and thereby eternally sealing past righteous generations to ourselves in the temples, the earth would be utterly wasted at Christ's glorious return.

1 Behold, I will reveal unto you the Priesthood, by the hand of Elijah the prophet, before the coming of the great and dreadful day of the Lord.

2 And he shall plant in the hearts of the children the promises made to the fathers, and the hearts of the children shall turn to their fathers.

3 If it were not so, the whole earth would be utterly wasted at his coming. (D&C 2:1–3)

47 The prophet Elijah was to plant in the hearts of the children the promises made to their fathers,

48 Foreshadowing the great work to be done in the temples of the Lord in the dispensation of the fulness of times, for the redemption of the dead, and the sealing of the children to their parents, lest the whole earth be smitten with a curse and utterly wasted at his coming. (D&C 138:47–48)

The river of divine blessings that flows from the priesthood does not end there, but includes the promises and privileges that will enable us to establish Zion.

The oath and covenant of the priesthood bears a precious truth regarding Zion. Buried within it is a promise so glorious that it defies mortal thinking and stretches the fabric of faith, and thus easily falls prey to unbelief. Herein lies a "mystery of godliness"—a grand key to the establishment of Zion and those things which "eye hath not seen, nor ear heard, nor yet entered into the heart of man" (1 Corinthians 2:9).

OBTAINING THESE TWO PRIESTHOODS

The journey to obtaining these two priesthoods began millennia prior to our birth. In that premortal life I believe we viewed the day of mortality as a glorious and perhaps even frightening final exam of our long journey to become like our Heavenly Father. I believe obtaining these precious priesthoods was one of the most wonderful obtainments of mortality, a reason to press onward into that final exam no matter the cost then or the cost in mortality. Such an understanding would be a powerful motivation to walk the straight path through the towering flames of opposition, and eloquent, but dissident, voices that attempted to dissuade us from entering mortality.

Why did it seem so glorious to us then? Because in that long day of our spiritual nativity we understood what the priesthood meant to our eternal hopes. Alma 13 establishes that we were taught about the priesthood in premortality; we chose good over evil, exercised exceedingly great faith, and as a result were called with a holy calling and ordained to the priesthood in that world. All this was accomplished in and through the Atonement of Christ.

We lived in the presence of God the Father and could behold with our eyes what He was like, which vision would have caused us to yearn to be like Him. We wanted to be like Him because we loved Him, and for a more pragmatic reason—we wanted the life He possessed. The glory that we saw with our eyes, the very glory that made His countenance shine like the sun, that made everything subject to His creative power and responsive to His perfect will, that made His life not just everlasting but eternally filled with honor, glory, and unmatchable happiness were the visible manifestation of His priesthood.

In simplest terms, we wanted the same priesthood and its associated earthly blessings so we could become like Him and thus claim the same blessings for ourselves.

In that life we were undoubtedly taught how His priesthood had brought Him the life we saw Him enjoying. We understood it then but have since forgotten most of what we once knew and believed. In mortality our premortal life is a mystery and one of considerable opacity.

Having now arrived in mortality, happily oblivious to the perilous journey that brought us so far to get here, many of us are only marginally aware of the glorious possibilities of the priesthood, for which we were then willing to risk so much to obtain. Many of us take our gifts for granted. This is evident in the fact that "many are called but few are chosen" (D&C 121:40). Some of us possess the priesthood with little more thought than owning a driver's license. We lose our true identity in the clatter, clutter, glamour, and gore of mortality.

According to D&C 84:33 quoted above, for those who, by the grace of God, have come to possess the priesthood, the key to all these greater blessings now lies in magnifying their calling.

Magnifying Our Calling

Many times we have heard discussions on magnifying our calling. The question isn't how to magnify our calling, but what it is that we are to magnify. The issue is—what actually constitutes our calling? Once we know what our calling is, we can be led by the Holy Spirit to magnify it. Until then, we may be magnifying the wrong thing.

There are two possible ways to look at one's calling. The first is that our calling is those labors we are asked to perform. The second is that our calling is the eventual outcome of those labors. In other words, we are "called" (or ordained) to specific priesthood responsibilities, but our greater ordination, our greater calling, is to become like God.

One example might be that we were called to be a mother or father in mortality, and conditioned upon righteous fulfillment of that responsibility, we have also been called to be an eternal parent.

In other words, a calling is both what we are asked to do in the here-and-now and what we are called to become as a result of those labors.

As priesthood holders we are called to do home teaching, man offices, perform ordinances, and other services. Faithful sisters have equally worthy callings both in and outside of the home. We must be faithful to our duties, but these labors are only the mortal part of our calling. There is an eternal outcome, an eventual reward to which we are called, to which we are to be elected upon righteous accomplishment of those labors.

It would be nearsighted of us to only view the calling of the priesthood as a series of duties to perform. Our greater priesthood calling is almost too amazing for mortals to comprehend (and hence, to believe). It is that we may eventually become like God.

A large part of what we are called upon to do may be home teaching and other earth-bound services, but our calling, that thing which we are to magnify through those earthly labors, is not earth-bound but is vast and eternal. We are not magnifying home teaching—we are magnifying our call to divinity by home teaching and other righteous labors.

Along the same reasoning, it is difficult to rationalize how one may, through their labors, magnify one's office within the priesthood. Even the idea of doing such an inspired job that others glorify God and view the priesthood we hold in greater reverence lacks some element of logic. How can finite man actually do anything to magnify an infinite priesthood office through mortal works? The priesthood is perfect, and all offices derive their greatness from God, not from the office holder. If this were not so, then it would also be possible for an unholy officer to diminish his office, even rendering it unusable, which thing is unthinkable. Judas, an apostle, betrayed the Christ, but he did not diminish the priesthood nor the office of apostle. Only the man is diminished; the priesthood remains impervious to man's ability to either add or detract. Elder McConkie notes, "The priesthood is greater than any of its offices. No office adds any power, dignity, or authority to the priesthood. All offices derive their rights, virtues, authorities, and prerogatives from the priesthood."[1]

On the same note, it is easy to understand that by the same inspired service we are magnifying and enlarging our personal, and much greater eternal calling, bringing us closer and closer to the perfect day.

Many are Called

The challenge we face is to evolve from the world of unsanctified mortals, to the world of sanctified beings, which is to become a true part of Zion.

> 34 Behold, there are many called, but few are chosen. And why are they not chosen?
>
> 35 Because their hearts are set so much upon the things of this world, and aspire to the honors of men, that they do not learn this one lesson—
>
> 36 That the rights of the priesthood are inseparably connected with the powers of heaven, and that the powers of heaven cannot be controlled nor handled only upon the principles of righteousness. (D&C 121:34–36)

Many are called, that is, in the premortal world many were called and ordained to both hold the priesthood and to reap the eternal blessings thereof, both male and female. This calling to hold the priesthood and receive its promised blessings must occur twice in our journey.

We received our first calling in a premortal "calling" to future blessings in mortality and beyond. The second part of our calling occurs in mortality after we align ourselves with the restored gospel and receive our priesthood blessings as a mortal. Then, upon righteous magnifying of that calling, we will be "elected" or chosen, to receive the full weight of eternal glory associated with that calling. When these blessings are fully realized in mortality we will find our "calling and election" made sure. Elder McConkie explained it this way:

> Actually, if the full blessings of salvation are to follow, the doctrine of election must operate twice. First, righteous spirits are elected or chosen to come to mortality as heirs of special blessings. Then, they must be called and elected again in this life, an occurrence which takes place when they join the true Church (D&C 53:1). Finally, in order to

reap eternal salvation, they must press forward in obedient devotion to the truth until they make their "calling and election sure" (2 Peter 1), that is, they are "sealed up unto eternal life." (D&C 131:5)[2]

Still, with so lofty an advantage in this life, with blessings purchased at great cost in premortality (Alma 13:3) through eons of righteous choices despite towering flames of opposition (Revelation 12:7), still there are apparently few people (D&C 121:34) who ultimately magnify their callings so that they are "elected" to actually receive the promised rewards.

To be elected is to receive the promise of the fullest blessings that priesthood has to offer; it is to fully and completely magnify our calling. As Elder McConkie notes above, we are thus "sealed up unto eternal life" (D&C 131:5). Few cross that bridge into glory. Why? Because as the scripture above proclaims, among other things, their hearts are so set upon the things of this world.

Every time we hear this accusation we allow ourselves to imagine it points its accusing finger at someone who perhaps bears the priesthood with hypocrisy or mediocrity, or who does it to be seen or to enjoy worldly acclaim or positions and power.

One might be tempted to say, "Well, yes, I know a few priesthood holders who are still caught up in the world and who aspire to the honors of men." Or, "Yes, brother so-and-so still won't do his home teaching." Yet, this verse doesn't say only a few of us are caught in the trap, it says most of us are. "Few are chosen" means that the vast majority of us are caught up in whatever this worldly trap is.

Since almost all of us are caught in this snare, we can logically conclude that most of us have our hearts set upon the things of this world.

How could that be? What are most of us doing? We're going about our duties, working as best we can to get them done, and to do it so that it blesses our brothers and sisters. So, how could this constitute having our hearts set upon the world? It doesn't seem to make sense.

Yet it does. If our hearts are focused upon any worldly accomplishment, no matter how worthy, then our hearts are set upon that worldly thing. If we labor day by day with all of our hearts to fulfill a duty, then our hearts are set upon that earthly duty and not upon the eternal outcome. In other words, we have focused upon our mortal calling as opposed to our eternal calling.

As verse 35 suggests, we who have our hearts set upon these worldly accomplishments "aspire to the honors of men." This could simply mean we do our home teaching because we enjoy the rapport we gain with that family; they honor and respect us. They call upon us in their needs and rely on us for spiritual input and fellowship. We enjoy reporting that we have done a full and complete job and relish the honor and praise of priesthood leaders. We like looking in the mirror and feeling good about ourselves.

These aren't bad things, they're just myopically devoting ourselves to our worldly duties with little or no view of the divine calling of the priesthood. In other words, we're magnifying only part of our calling—the mortal part, and hence, our hearts are set upon the things of this world.

One who is truly magnifying his eternal calling in the priesthood will still be a great home teacher but will have his eye upon the greater rights and privileges that flow therefrom. His motivation for service will be to serve Christ by magnifying a far greater calling. Otherwise, he is magnifying things of mortality rather than things of eternity.

Such performances done for worldly reasons take on a life of their own. They become a lifestyle, having a form of godliness. Those outward acts become our reason for other works that outwardly appear righteous yet still fail the divine test of eternal purpose. When done for the right reasons—eternal reasons—such acts become a small part of a divinely-orchestrated straight and narrow path that leads unto immortality and eternal life.

One might wonder, isn't doing a good work or a good service simply good—no matter why the work is done? And, since we are here to serve one another, what is wrong with focusing upon and magnifying the earthly portion of our callings? Won't the eternal blessings follow this type of service?

It seems evident that doing any good for any reason has merit. However, the sum of all such acts does not have the full saving power we seek. Mortal acts may in fact be where everyone starts to serve, and mortal services fulfill a marvelous purpose in the kingdom. However, service for service's sake is not exalting. Nowhere in the scriptures are we promised that if we just do enough good works we will be exalted (Ephesians 2:8–9). We are always admonished to come unto Christ, obey His voice, and be perfected in Him, and thus partake of the salvation He offers (Moroni 10:32–33). Coming unto Christ and being perfected in Him is far different from being perfected through a series of good works and lifelong service.

Good works for any reason are important, but not sufficient to bring us to the greater blessings of the priesthood and of Zion. These greater things, these "mysteries of godliness," are what bring us to the full purposes of the priesthood and into the realms of Zion.

The lesser, non-mystery, visible-to-all portion of the gospel requires only rudimentary faith to embrace. The programs and practices are plain to see, the benefits evident to all. We can be content with our testimony and working hard at the tasks at hand and before our eyes. Such a life is a life of goodness and is upon the straight path. Everyone starts here. However, the scriptures teach of greater blessings, a greater priesthood calling, and of a personal interview with Christ, which we are admonished to seek. Without a specific desire and an unyielding intent to so seek and so obtain, good works can never cross the divide between the lesser and the greater portion of the eternal blessings of Christ's gifts to us.

It seems apparent that to focus upon one's lesser mortal calling without a view of one's vastly greater potential both here and in eternity is to remain under the condemnation of unbelief and outside of the full function and blessing of the priesthood.

To recognize and focus upon the greater portion of the gospel is to pierce the heavens, align ourselves with divine providence, and to become like Enoch, Melchizedek, and all those who dedicated their lives to a cause far greater than any single good work, and who in so doing had their names written forever in the book of the Lamb of God.

We understand that each of us has a calling that we received in the premortal world, which we must accomplish in order to receive eternal life (Abraham 3:22–26). We can only learn what that calling is for each of us by watching it unfold line-by-line as we live lives of righteousness. As Elder McConkie noted in the previous quote, the principle of election operates both in the premortal world and in this world. When a person so lives their life that they eternally set a righteous course from which they will never deviate, the heavens open and the voice of God declares that person's calling and election made sure—even though years of righteous service remain to be accomplished. In effect, what occurs is to have the judgment day advanced and to be told what the glorious outcome of that event will be. In a very real and literal sense, that person's exaltation is made sure. The words we commonly use are to have your "calling and election made sure." Those who receive such a lofty privilege become the elect of God.

THE ELECT OF GOD

To become the elect of God is to have the full blessings of the priesthood unconditionally promised but not yet bestowed. To become the elect of God is to be "elected" unto eternal life, to have the unconditional promise of eternal glory made known but not yet received.

> 33 For whoso is faithful unto the obtaining these two priesthoods of which I have spoken, and the magnifying their calling, are sanctified by the Spirit unto the renewing of their bodies.
>
> 34 They become the sons of Moses and of Aaron and the seed of Abraham, and the Church and kingdom, and the elect of God." (D&C 84:33–34)

Elder Marion G. Romney taught:

> The prophet Joseph Smith used to repeatedly urge the brethren to make their calling and election sure. There is no way to do this except by receiving the priesthood and magnifying it.[3]

Obtaining the priesthood and magnifying our callings has the ultimate effect of making us the elect of God, which is to say that one's calling and election has been made sure. Consider the words of Elder McConkie on the eternal effect of this blessing:

> What is meant by having one's calling and election made sure? To have one's calling and election made sure is to be sealed up unto eternal life; it is to have the unconditional guarantee of exaltation in the highest heaven of the celestial world; it is to receive the assurance of godhood; *it is, in effect, to have the day of judgment advanced*, so that an inheritance of all the glory and honor of the Father's kingdom is assured prior to the day when the faithful actually enter into the divine presence to sit with Christ in his throne, even as he is "set down" with his "Father in his throne." (Revelation 3:21, italics added)
>
> But when the ratifying seal of approval is placed upon someone whose calling and election is thereby made sure—because there are no more conditions to be met by the obedient person—this act of being sealed up unto eternal life is of such transcendent import that of itself it is called being sealed by the Holy Spirit of Promise, which means that in this crowning sense, being so sealed is the same as having one's calling and election made sure.[4]

In having our election made sure we become a member of the heavenly kingdom of God. Our place in that eternal kingdom is made sure such that it can only be lost on a very grievous transgression.

Those so blessed are told by revelatory voice from the heavens that their place is made sure. This revelation may take the form of a quiet surety that comes upon one without an actual voice, or it may include spoken words, visions, angelic visitation, or other profound and astonishing heavenly manifestations. Whatever form it takes for you, it will be greater and more easily recognized than any previous revelation you may have received. This added profundity is echoed in the following scripture.

> 5 The more sure word of prophecy means a man's knowing that he is sealed up unto eternal life, by revelation and the spirit of prophecy, through the power of the Holy Priesthood. (D&C 131:5)

"The more sure word" suggests that this prophecy does not spring from faith alone, or mere belief, or even a profound hope, but from revealed knowledge: *knowing*, not merely believing, that you are sealed up unto eternal life. Such a revelatory voice will not be easily mistaken, though it is possible that it may not be correctly understood at the time it occurs.

A search of the scriptures reveals multiple ways whereby this message is delivered and a different language for each circumstance. It may be that every individual hears a unique message suited to their circumstance and understanding. The language is immaterial. The message is everlasting.

Hyrum Andrus made these observations regarding this sacred subject:

> There are several examples in latter-day scripture of individuals who obtained a guarantee from the Lord that they would receive eternal life. To Alma the elder the Lord said: "Thou art my servant; and I covenant with thee that thou shalt have eternal life." Enos, another Nephite prophet, apparently received such a guarantee, for he wrote:
> . . . I soon go to the place of my rest, which is with my Redeemer; for *I know that in him I shall rest.* And I rejoice in the day when my mortal shall put on immortality, and shall stand before him; then shall I see his face with pleasure, and he will say unto me: Come unto me, ye blessed, *there is a place prepared for you in the mansions of my Father.*
> To the Twelve whom Jesus chose to administer the affairs of His church in the Western hemisphere after His resurrection, He promised: "After that ye are seventy and two years old ye shall come unto me in

my kingdom; and with me ye shall find rest." And as Moroni labored abridging the record of the Jaredites, he received from the Lord this assurance: "Thou hast been faithful; wherefore, thy garments shall be made clean. And because thou hast seen thy weakness thou shalt be made strong, even unto the sitting down in the place which I have prepared in the mansions of my Father."[5]

The Lord Himself can pronounce one's calling and election to be sure. The prophet Joseph taught,

> After a person has faith in Christ, repents of his sins, and is baptized for the remission of his sins and receives the Holy Ghost (by the laying on of hands), which is the first Comforter, then let him continue to humble himself before God, hungering and thirsting after righteousness, and living by every word of God, and the Lord will soon say unto him, Son, thou shalt be exalted.[6]

This statement making one's calling and election sure can also be issued by the living prophet under the direction of Heavenly Father.

> 12 And of as many as the Father shall bear record, to you shall be given power to seal them up unto eternal life. Amen. (D&C 68:12)

> 7 And verily I say unto you, that the conditions of this law are these: All covenants, contracts, bonds, obligations, oaths, vows, performances, connections, associations, or expectations, that are not made and entered into and sealed by the Holy Spirit of promise, *of him who is anointed, both as well for time and for all eternity, and that too most holy, by revelation and commandment through the medium of mine anointed, whom I have appointed on the earth to hold this power* (and I have appointed unto my servant Joseph to hold this power in the last days, and there is never but one on the earth at a time on whom this power and the keys of this priesthood are conferred), are of no efficacy, virtue, or force in and after the resurrection from the dead; for all contracts that are not made unto this end have an end when men are dead. (D&C 132:7; italics added)

And since we are now contemplating Zion, we must consider the eternal connection between one's calling and election being made sure, becoming the elect of God, and becoming a part of the Church of the Firstborn, which is the society of Zion.

> 3 Wherefore, I now send upon you another Comforter, even upon you my friends, that it may abide in your hearts, even the Holy Spirit of

promise; which other Comforter is the same that I promised unto my disciples, as is recorded in the testimony of John.

4 This Comforter is the promise which I give unto you of eternal life, even the glory of the celestial kingdom;

5 Which glory is that of the Church of the Firstborn, even of God, the holiest of all, through Jesus Christ his Son— (D&C 88:3–5)

Notice in verse 4 that the Holy Spirit of Promise literally constitutes "the promise . . . of eternal life" which we know to be having one's calling and election made sure. Verse 5 equates that same promise with being the glory of the Church of the Firstborn, which we previously established as being the Enochonian society of those who have been in the presence of Christ, "even of God, the holiest of all." As we have discussed several times so far, entering into the presence of God is the doorway into Zion.

It is important to remember that this is a promise of these things, not the actual receipt of them. We aren't being admitted into the presence of Christ at that moment, but being promised that our journey *will* arrive there. We are being assured that we will ultimately be invited into the presence of God, into the Church of the Firstborn, and by extension, into Zion. This is a matchless "Comforter" indeed. Perhaps no knowledge could be of greater comfort in this life. Only in that glorious day when the heavens open, the veil parts, and we fully realize the complete fulfillment of those promises will we luxuriate in greater peace.

Notice that Comforter is capitalized, thus rendering it a proper noun. It is in fact referring to the Holy Ghost, a member of the Godhead, and the means whereby this great knowledge of the promised outcome of our lives is transmitted to the aspirant's soul, and whereby it is sustained day by day. This is the fulfillment of the ordinance of the laying on of hands at baptismal water's edge. It is the moment when the blessed soul begins to have the constant companionship of the Holy Ghost, and if he or she proceeds faithfully through the remainder of their lives, they will retain the constant companionship always.

Of course there is only one individual who accomplished the mortal journey without sin, and that was our Savior. We, on the other hand, suffer a series of ups and downs, of error and repentance, that may inhibit the constant nature of that gift from time to time. However, the gift will return as soon as the heart is again pure and the eye single to the glory of God.

Elder McConkie assures us that those who have their calling and election made sure may in time see God and talk with Him face to face. This appearance of Jesus Christ himself is called the Second Comforter.

> It is the privilege of all those who have made their calling and election sure to see God; to talk with him face to face; to commune with him on a personal basis from time to time. These are the ones upon whom the Lord sends the Second Comforter. Their inheritance of exaltation and eternal life is assured, and so it becomes with them here and now in this life as it will be with all exalted beings in the life to come. They become the friends of God and converse with him on a friendly basis as one man speaks to another.[7]

The prophet Joseph described calling and election as prerequisite to enjoying the Second Comforter, which, as we have already discussed, is the personal interview with Christ.

> When the Lord has thoroughly proved him, and finds that the man is determined to serve Him at all hazards, then the man will find his calling and his election made sure, then it will be his privilege to receive the other Comforter, which the Lord hath promised the saints. . . .
>
> Now what is this other Comforter? It is no more nor less than the Lord Jesus Christ Himself; and this is the sum and substance of the whole matter; that when any man obtains this last Comforter, he will have the personage of Jesus Christ to attend him, or appear unto him from time to time, and even he will manifest the Father unto him, and they will take up their abode with him, and the visions of the heavens will be opened unto him, and the Lord will teach him face to face, and he may have a perfect knowledge of the mysteries of the Kingdom of God; and this is the state and place the ancient saints arrived at when they had such glorious visions—Isaiah, Ezekiel, John upon the Isle of Patmos, St. Paul in the three heavens, and all the saints who held communion with the general assembly and Church of the Firstborn.[8]

Now that we have discussed the importance of believing all things and of making your calling and election sure, let us consider what these "Mysteries of Godliness" are. These are the mysteries which unbelief will not allow us to even view in concept, let alone in fact. Quite literally, unbelief is the very reason they are mysteries.

THE MYSTERIES

Doctrine and Covenants 121:36 proclaims that those whose hearts are set upon the things of this world do not learn this one lesson:

> 36 That the rights of the priesthood are inseparably connected with the powers of heaven, and that the powers of heaven cannot be controlled nor handled only upon the principles of righteousness.

What are the rights of the priesthood? Notice that it says rights, not rites. A rite is an ordinance, like baptism. A right is a privilege one obtains through obedience to law. Righteous priesthood acts give us certain rights which are inseparably connected with the powers of heaven.

The powers of heaven are vast—the power to create, the power to heal, the power to know all truth, and the power to enter the presence of God are among them. And these powers are inseparably connected with the rights of the priesthood. Inseparably means that they cannot be separated, that they can't exist apart. Like breath and life, if you take away breath, life ceases. If you take away life, breath ends.

So, since they are inseparable, if we are not experiencing the powers of heaven, then we are not participating in the rights of the priesthood! Think about it. If one observes an absence in one's life of true priesthood power—of revelations, healings, visions, visitations, miracles, raising the dead, and restoring withered limbs, to name a scant few—then that individual has not yet enjoyed the full rights of the priesthood and the inseparably connected powers of heaven.

By that definition most of us are *not* enjoying the rights of the priesthood, and those who are probably aren't enjoying them to their fullest. In other words, it is a bleak and observable truth that many are called, but few are chosen.

Why? The answer is stated in verse 35—because our hearts are so set upon the things of this world. Even the good things of this world are not the ultimate calling of the priesthood. By so myopically setting our vision upon these earthly functions of priesthood service, we are failing to magnify our true, eternal callings. How can this be? Again, the answer seems obvious. We have yet to understand and believe how vast our calling is. We still think its home teaching and similar earth-bound services.

The Lord gives us a grand definition of what both the duties and the rights of the priesthood are.

19 And this greater priesthood administereth the gospel and holdeth the key of the mysteries of the kingdom, even the key of the knowledge of God. (D&C 84:19)

Our mortal duties are to administer the gospel. These labors we perform are the mortal component of our calling. These include every service we perform, office we hold, and ordinance in which we officiate. This is the earth-bound portion of our calling.

The eternal portion of our calling is described as the "key of the mysteries of the kingdom, even the key of the knowledge of God." The mysteries of the kingdom are specifically designed to unveil the "rights" of the priesthood as we become ready to receive them. These rights and privileges are the eternal element of the calling of the priesthood! These rights are the glorious blessing of receiving the powers of heaven, which we are meant to enjoy during mortality, including those powers we justly call miracles. Such blessings will be commonplace in Zion.

They are mysteries for now because one must pass a rigorous process of preparation before the greater light of the gospel is even visible to the mortal eye. The fact that they are mysteries in the beginning is the divine order of growth. But they must not forever remain a mystery. The door must open and the light of revealed glory must be fully received in this life.

We have at times heard that we should leave the mysteries alone. Yet, such a statement is not scriptural. The scriptures specifically instruct us to seek the mysteries and promise that these are the very truths which bring eternal life. In fact, eternal life comes in no other way. This isn't *a* way to immortal glory, it is *the* way.

Consider these scriptures:

7 Seek not for riches but for wisdom, and behold, the mysteries of God shall be unfolded unto you, and then shall you be made rich. Behold, he that hath eternal life is rich. (D&C 6:7)

11 And if thou wilt inquire, thou shalt know mysteries which are great and marvelous; therefore thou shalt exercise thy gift, that thou mayest find out mysteries, that thou mayest bring many to the knowledge of the truth, yea, convince them of the error of their ways. (D&C 6:11)

5 For thus saith the Lord—I, the Lord, am merciful and gracious unto those who fear me, and delight to honor those who serve me in righteousness and in truth unto the end.

6 Great shall be their reward and eternal shall be their glory.

7 And to them will I reveal all mysteries, yea, all the hidden mysteries of my kingdom from days of old, and for ages to come, will I make known unto them the good pleasure of my will concerning all things pertaining to my kingdom.

8 Yea, even the wonders of eternity shall they know, and things to come will I show them, even the things of many generations.

9 And their wisdom shall be great, and their understanding reach to heaven; and before them the wisdom of the wise shall perish, and the understanding of the prudent shall come to naught.

10 For by my Spirit will I enlighten them, and by my power will I make known unto them the secrets of my will—yea, even those things which eye has not seen, nor ear heard, nor yet entered into the heart of man. (D&C 76:5–10)

61 If thou shalt ask, thou shalt receive revelation upon revelation, knowledge upon knowledge, that thou mayest know the mysteries and peaceable things—that which bringeth joy, that which bringeth life eternal. (D&C 42:61)

10 And he said, Unto you it is given to know the mysteries of the kingdom of God: but to others in parables; that seeing they might not see, and hearing they might not understand. (Luke 8:10)

9 And now Alma began to expound these things unto him, saying: It is given unto many to know the mysteries of God; nevertheless they are laid under a strict command that they shall not impart only according to the portion of his word which he doth grant unto the children of men, according to the heed and diligence which they give unto him. (Alma 12:9)

THE LESSER PORTION

To those who harden their hearts, which is another way of saying, to those whose minds are darkened by unbelief (see D&C 84:53), God gives the "lesser portion of the word."

10 And therefore, he that will harden his heart, the same receiveth the lesser portion of the word; and he that will not harden his heart, to him

is given the greater portion of the word, until it is given unto him to know the mysteries of God until he know them in full.

11 And they that will harden their hearts, to them is given the lesser portion of the word until they know nothing concerning his mysteries; and then they are taken captive by the devil, and led by his will down to destruction. Now this is what is meant by the chains of hell. (Alma 12:10–11)

Notice that the "greater portion" is enshrined within the mysteries, and the lesser portion is to know nothing of the mysteries. This is not to say those individuals know nothing of the truth, or nothing of the gospel, or do not have a testimony; it is merely to know nothing beyond that. The grand dividing line is that those with the greater portion have not hardened their hearts. Those who harden their hearts eventually know nothing of the mysteries until they are in fact "taken captive by the devil, and led by his will down to destruction," after which they find themselves bound by "the chains of hell" (Alma 12:9–12).

The scriptures inform us that there is one great hallmark of those who harden their hearts, which is that they shut out the voice of the Master.

7 And ye are called to bring to pass the gathering of mine elect; for mine elect hear my voice and harden not their hearts. (D&C 29:7)

6 And even so will I cause the wicked to be kept, that will not hear my voice but harden their hearts, and wo, wo, wo, is their doom. (D&C 38:6)

Anyone who inhibits the revelatory voice, or even filters it through incorrect beliefs, is by definition "hardening their hearts." In this condition they cannot even see, much less understand, the exalting mysteries of godliness. They who are caught in this hardened condition, who do not repent, cannot become the "elect of God." They will never learn the exalting mysteries, reach their fullest potential, or become a part of the latter-day Zion.

These unfortunate folks are left with the non-mysterious, the saving but less-exalting, the commonly known, the oft-spoken and commonly understood "portion of the word." All of us begin there but must not remain there throughout our lives. As a matter of divine law, the "lesser portion of the word" is the only portion that is spoken out loud; it is the portion which God grants "unto the children of men, according to the heed and diligence which they give unto him" (Alma 12:9). This is the gospel portion that we have been taught all of our lives. Very little of the "greater portion" has entered our ears, and if it did, we most probably were unprepared to comprehend it.

There must be an evolution toward spiritual maturity and the promised blessings flowing from the "greater portion" of the gospel. We all start as spiritual babes, performing our labors and services for service's sake. We naturally believe what we see and feel and enjoy the fellowship and rewards of membership. These are glorious things, true things, saving things! Nothing being observed here is meant to denigrate or lessen the power of these things. However, it is not the purpose of the gospel that we should remain in an infant state. We are to become god-like men and women, to company with angels, to have miracles and visions and godly powers commonplace among us. Clearly, we must catch the vision of who we can truly become—the vision of Zion—and pray with all fervency that we can evolve beyond the "lesser portion of the word," or we will ever remain outside of the embrace of the vast blessings.

As the latter-day holy scriptures describe, our minds are (not were—are) darkened by unbelief (which means, among other things, that we have not yet begun to believe in our greater potential), and hence, we are not seeking and finding the greater portion of the word, which is to say, the mysteries of Godliness.

When these mysteries begin to be revealed great blessings flow, miracles are received, the heavens open, and angels descend. The higher ordinances and promises are clearly viewed and the full light of revealed truth distills upon our souls.

NOTES

1. McConkie, *The Promised Messiah*, 594.

2. McConkie, *Mormon Doctrine*, 216.

3. Marion G. Romney, in Conference Report, Oct. 1960, 73.

4. McConkie, *Doctrinal New Testament Commentary*, 331.

5. Hyrum L. Andrus, *Principles of Perfection* (Salt Lake City: Bookcraft, 1970), 334.

6. Joseph Smith, *Teachings of the Prophet Joseph Smith*, 149–51.

7. McConkie, *The Promised Messiah*, 584.

8. McConkie, *The Promised Messiah*, 584.

Chapter Seven

THE GREATER PORTION
OF THE WORD

THE GREATER PORTION

To those who will not harden their hearts, to them is given the "greater portion of the word," until they know the mysteries in full. This greater portion of the word constitutes those things which are vast and true but which must be obtained by direct and personal revelation. As a point of fact, when someone obtains a mystery for themselves by obedience and revelation, they are generally not permitted to openly discuss what they have learned.

> 9 And now Alma began to expound these things unto him, saying: It is given unto many to know the mysteries of God; nevertheless they are laid under a strict command that they shall not impart only according to the portion of his word which he doth grant unto the children of men, according to the heed and diligence which they give unto him. (Alma 12:9)

These are not just interesting principles and doctrines we receive during some divine bonus round; these are the very truths which have catapulted the righteous of every dispensation into the great blessings that they record in the scriptures.

These mysteries unveil the "rights of the priesthood" in the sense that they open our view to the greater blessings and privileges that flow from the priesthood. These rights, as we observed earlier, are "inseparably connected with the powers of heaven" (D&C 121:36). In other words, the fulness of the rights of the priesthood are only to be found within the "greater portion of the word," which are called "mysteries" because so "few are chosen" (D&C 121:34) to receive them. It may be more accurate to say, because so few choose to receive them.

Additionally, the mysteries are those things that "bringeth joy, that which bringeth life eternal" (D&C 42:61). For those who obtain these "hidden mysteries of my kingdom" in full, their "wisdom shall be great, and their understanding reach to heaven."

> 7 And to them will I reveal all mysteries, yea, all the hidden mysteries of my kingdom from days of old, and for ages to come, will I make known unto them the good pleasure of my will concerning all things pertaining to my kingdom.
>
> 8 Yea, even the wonders of eternity shall they know, and things to come will I show them, even the things of many generations.
>
> 9 And their wisdom shall be great, and their understanding reach to heaven; and before them the wisdom of the wise shall perish, and the understanding of the prudent shall come to naught.
>
> 10 For by my Spirit will I enlighten them, and by my power will I make known unto them the secrets of my will—yea, even those things which eye has not seen, nor ear heard, nor yet entered into the heart of man. (D&C 76:7–10)

Why will their understanding reach to heaven? Because they will literally see into heaven. "The wonders of eternity shall they know, and things to come will I show them, even the things of many generations" (v. 8). These mysteries are by definition the "greater portion of the word" (Alma 12:10). These are the things of the Spirit and cannot be known any other way than by revelation. For he or she who does not reach beyond sight into faith and into the grand mysteries, the mysteries of godliness remain those things which "eye hath not seen, nor ear heard, neither have entered into the heart of man, the things which God hath prepared for them that love him" (v. 10).

Apparently, this defines the vast majority of us—we whose hearts are so set upon our worldly labors. But should we even be trying to rise above the norm? Isn't the revealed portion that we all love and embrace enough? Why press into something that isn't commonly known? Isn't that shooting beyond the mark? Aren't we supposed to adhere to the basics and leave the mysteries alone?

Elder McConkie had this to say:

> There is a true doctrine on these points, a doctrine unknown to many and unbelieved by more, a doctrine that is spelled out as specifically and extensively in the revealed word as are any of the other great revealed truths. There is no need for uncertainty or misunderstanding; and surely, if the Lord reveals a doctrine, we should seek to learn its principles and strive to apply them in our lives. This doctrine is that mortal man, while in the flesh, has it in his power to see the Lord, to stand in his presence, to feel the nail marks in his hands and feet, and to receive from him such blessings as are reserved for those only who keep all his commandments and who are qualified for that eternal life which includes being in his presence forever.[1]

Alma describes having only the lesser portion of the word and knowing nothing of the mysteries as being "taken captive by the devil, and [being] led by his will down to destruction."

> 11 And they that will harden their hearts, to them is given the lesser portion of the word until they know nothing concerning his mysteries; and then they are taken captive by the devil, and led by his will down to destruction. Now this is what is meant by the chains of hell. (Alma 12:11)

Since the greater portion of the word and the powers of heaven that are being offered us bring us closer to the blessings of establishing Zion, and since Zion in our day is ultimately to become a translated city, let us consider another great mystery: the doctrine of translation.

TRANSLATION

Joseph Smith taught that translation is an outgrowth of the highest blessing of the priesthood. However, in the last 175 years, we have not forgotten exactly, but deemphasized that perspective. Perhaps the reason it has been deemphasized is that the time to build Zion had temporarily passed. Andrew F. Ehat, the compiler of the important book *The Words of Joseph Smith*, noted:

> "Much evidence suggests that Joseph Smith considered the doctrine of translation to be an outgrowth of the highest blessings of the priesthood. For example, JST Genesis 14:25–36 is a clear statement of the relationship of the highest powers of the priesthood and the blessing of 'translation.' "[2]

The Melchizedek Priesthood possesses all of the same powers in this day as in the days of Melchizedek, the great high priest himself. During his ministry he established Zion after the order of Enoch.

> 27 And thus, having been approved of God, he was ordained an high priest after the order of the covenant which God made with Enoch,
>
> 34 And his people wrought righteousness, and obtained heaven, and sought for the city of Enoch which God had before taken, separating it from the earth, having reserved it unto the latter days, or the end of the world;
>
> 35 And hath said, and sworn with an oath, that the heavens and the earth should come together; and the sons of God should be tried so as by fire.
>
> 36 And this Melchizedek, having thus established righteousness, was called the king of heaven by his people, or, in other words, the King of peace. (JST Genesis 14:27, 34–36)

Our Melchizedek Priesthood, the one we presently hold, is "after the order of Enoch," whose name has become a key word signifying translation and Zion. Inherent (albeit in our day latent) within the priesthood is the power of translation.

Elder Orson Pratt explained it this way:

> Thus this greater Priesthood had place on the earth from Adam till Moses; and each successive Priest proclaimed the same salvation, administered the same gospel, with all its ordinances and blessings, that were preached and received after Christ. In and through the ordinances of the Priesthood, the power of Godliness was manifest, and by it, holy men were enabled to converse with God face to face; *and also through the Priesthood many obtained sufficient faith and power to be translated; by the power of the Priesthood Enoch and his city were taken up into heaven, and reserved until a day of righteousness shall come, when they will come again on earth and have place until the end.*[3]

In the ordinances of the priesthood the powers of godliness are manifest. The term *manifest* means "to reveal plainly and clearly." *Manifest* can also mean to cause to appear or to take place. One possible meaning is that the "powers of godliness" are being made manifest to our understanding, not necessarily the actual receipt of them. In other words, we are being allowed to view these blessings and develop our belief and desire to obtain them. This seems reasonable in the sense that few priesthood ordinances produce an immediate display of the "power of godliness" in the classic sense. Clearly, much more is necessary than mere ordination to obtain these dramatic powers. The ordinances *reveal* the powers of godliness, and we thereafter pursue a course to obtain them such that they are fully "manifest" in our lives.

THE PRINCIPLE OF GODLINESS

Even the term "godliness" is fascinating. It is a dynamic of language that must be pondered somewhat to be understood. The term implies that the individual who possesses or exhibits godliness possesses qualities and attributes or even powers of God but is not actually a god. The root word is god, with the suffix "-ly" adding the idea of likeness or resembling in characteristics. Therefore godly means to be like God with the additional suffix "-ness," implying a state of being or condition. Godliness therefore becomes a state of being like God, without actually being a god.

As an example, if you were referring to a mother, you would not correctly refer to her as being motherly. The title "mother" bears with it all the qualities of motherhood. Just as one would never call Jehovah a godly God, calling someone a motherly mother does not add to the known qualities of that person. The term motherliness is therefore more commonly used to describe someone who is *like* a mother in attributes, but who is not actually a mother. A babysitter, a doting aunt, even an older sister could all exude motherliness without actually being a mother.

A mortal who possesses godliness is someone who possesses the attributes of God in part, but who is not themselves a god. By this definition, godliness, as a gift from God, is the power bestowed upon a mortal to be like God and to do some portion of the things He does prior to actually becoming a god. Clearly, no mortal, except Jesus Christ himself, has received the full power of God while yet a mortal. We have no record of someone creating a world, or decreeing everlasting laws, or populating worlds while in the mortal state. "Godliness" is thus deemed to include just those powers which the Father grants to mortals, the same which the scriptures detail in the lives of the spiritually noble.

Perhaps it is hard to imagine godliness in this context. It would include having power over life and death, power over the elements of the earth, having a perfect knowledge of things and an understanding of all truth—while still being a mortal. Such a person could move mountains, walk upon the water, raise the dead—and in short, do all things that Christ did during His mortality.

Does it sound impossible?

In fact, such a state has occurred in the economy of God's dealings with mankind many times. Each time He translates an individual they are recipients of the power of God, and still being mortals, they thereafter possess the powers and attributes of godliness. God, in fact, gives them power over all things in heaven and on the earth and makes them the greatest of all, even though they are the servants of all.

> 26 He that is ordained of God and sent forth, the same is appointed to be the greatest, notwithstanding he is the least and the servant of all.
>
> 27 Wherefore, he is possessor of all things; for all things are subject unto him, both in heaven and on the earth, the life and the light, the Spirit and the power, sent forth by the will of the Father through Jesus Christ, his Son. (D&C 50:26–27)

He or she that is ordained of God has, of course, been in the presence of God. This person is still mortal, yet vastly changed to possess the powers of God. They are by pure definition godly, and thus possess the attributes and powers of godliness. These powers are inseparably connected with the ordinances of the priesthood.

If we accept that the fulfillment of these promises is to occur during this mortal sojourn, then the above verse cannot be understood in any other context than translation.

> 20 Therefore, in the ordinances thereof, the power of godliness is manifest.
>
> 21 And without the ordinances thereof, and the authority of the priesthood, the power of godliness is not manifest unto men in the flesh;
>
> 22 For without this no man can see the face of God, even the Father, and live. (D&C 84:20–22)

Another way to say the same thing is that in the ordinances of the priesthood, the power to become like God *is* revealed while still in the flesh (see verse 21).

In words too powerful and plain to mistake, the Lord proclaims that through the ordinances—which include all of them, such as temple ordinances—the power of godliness is made manifest unto men in the flesh. The next two verses tell us what happens without the authority of the priesthood: The power of godliness is not manifest, and no man can see God and live.

The language of verses 21 and 22 contains double negatives, which produces the same logical meaning as when both negative tenses are removed. Rewording them in affirmative language proclaims, "*With* the ordinances thereof, and the authority of the priesthood, the power of godliness *is* made manifest unto men in the flesh; for with this, men *can* see the face of God, even the Father, and live."

When stated in the negative, as verses 21 and 22 are, it sounds as if men who see God without the priesthood will die. Yet simple logic suggests it is not possible to see God in an unrighteous state. Except for the judgment day, such may be in fact impossible. When these verses are stated in the positive, they say that we can see God and live! In other words, we can see God and thereafter live a life that does not end in death. This is the prototype. This is one of the transcendent outcomes of full priesthood blessings.

We know that Enoch was translated and that his order of the priesthood was that of a translated society. We also know that Melchizedek and his city were translated (see JST Genesis 14:32–34).

In our day when the Lord gave Joseph the description of those who will receive the full celestial outcome of mortality, He described them as being:

> 57 Priests of the Most High, after the order of Melchizedek, which was after the order of Enoch, which was after the order of the Only Begotten Son (D&C 76:57).

This verse means that there is inherent within the restored Melchizedek Priesthood the same holy order, patterned after the order of the Only Begotten Son, which Enoch and his whole city exercised, which resulted in their translation and ascension into Heaven. This holy order and all of its attendant blessings is fully embodied within our priesthood. Joseph received them fully and passed them on to the Twelve, where they have remained ever since. Wilford Woodruff explained it this way:

> Brother Joseph received the Patriarchal or Melchisedek Priesthood from under the hands of Peter, James, and John. From those Apostles Joseph received every power, blessing, and privilege of the highest authority of the Melchisedek Priesthood ever committed to man on the earth. . . . Joseph Smith gave unto me and my brethren, the Twelve,

all the priesthood, power, and authority which he held, and those are powers which belong to the Apostleship.[4]

We have the same privileges as Enoch and Melchizedek, though we have not yet availed ourselves fully of them.

Speaking of Melchizedek's holy order, the author of Genesis continues:

> 28 It being after the order of the son of God; which order came, not by man, nor the will of man; neither by father nor mother; neither by beginning of days nor end of years; but of God; (JST Genesis 14:28)

This is merely to say that this grand order of Enoch is patterned after and derived from the order of the Son of God, which is eternal and everlasting. It is not patriarchal in nature; it doesn't flow from father to son, nor from mother to daughter. Anyone, without regard to a chosen race or favored genealogy, may seek and obtain it. It predates the earth and will endure long past the numbering of years. It has been a part of the divine order of creating and exalting divine offspring forever and exists because God has ordained it to be so.

> 29 And it was delivered unto men by the calling of his own voice, according to his own will, unto as many as believed on his name. (JST Genesis 14:29)

Again, the grand prototype is viewed. This is what every man and woman of holiness has experienced. They are called up into a high or holy place, and the voice of God calls them to an extraordinary calling and ultra-mortal life that in notable cases included becoming immune to death. This is the reason that D&C 50:26 describes them as being "ordained of God," because God personally administers the ordinance.

Furthermore, verse 29 describes this calling as being according to His perfect will and purpose to bless His children alike and gloriously, unto as many as believed on His (Christ's) name.

The next verse tells us why these things exist. It isn't because man requested it or because we even merited it. It is because God ordained it with an "oath by himself." In other words, it is a process of eternity that continues in God's works because God ordains it. The fact that it is by oath implies that it is immutable and cannot be abridged, even by God.

> 30 For God having sworn unto Enoch and unto his seed with an oath by himself; that every one being ordained after this order [of Enoch]

and calling [of translation] should have power, by faith, to break mountains, to divide the seas, to dry up waters, to turn them out of their course. (JST Genesis 14:30, bracketed comment added)

The almost unthinkable result of being ordained to this high and holy Enochonian office is to receive power, by faith, to command the mountains and seas and earth to defy the armies of nations, to stand in the presence of God, and thereafter to go forth and do all things as Christ directs. It is to escape every form of captivity, even to defy armies and subdue principalities and powers according to the will of God.

Read this beautiful scripture with new eyes:

31 To put at defiance the armies of nations, to divide the earth, to break every band, to stand in the presence of God; to do all things according to his will, according to his command, subdue principalities and powers; and this by the will of the Son of God which was from before the foundation of the world. (JST Genesis 14:31)

Whenever any mortal has this faith they come up unto this order of God. *Any* mortal! Every righteous soul, not just the chosen few, not just the unique and blessed notables, but every soul, in every dispensation, who obtains this same faith, will come up unto this same order. They will then have the same privilege of asking to be translated and taken up into heaven or to ask for some other gift according to the inspiration that is upon them.

32 And men having this faith, coming up unto this order of God, were translated and taken up into heaven. (*JST* Genesis 14:32)

33 For this Melchizedek was ordained a priest after the order of the Son of God, which order was without father, without mother, without descent, having neither beginning of days, nor end of life. And all those who are ordained unto this priesthood are made like unto the Son of God, abiding a priest continually. (JST Hebrews 7:33)

This holy order of the Son of God is "without father, without mother," which seems to imply that it is extra-mortal, or that it is not received by genetic inheritance, but directly from God. Further, it is "without descent," which implies that your children won't inherit it from you. It has no "beginning of days," which seems to suggest that this holy order has been an institution prior to the creation of the earth, and it has no "end of life," which is that it does not terminate in death as we understand it.

It is wonderful to contemplate what it might mean to be made "like unto the Son of God." Clearly, it refers back to our original discussion of godliness—that we may become like unto Christ, even prior to becoming gods ourselves. The term "like unto" suggests that we have acquired some likeness, approaching some of His perfections, but not them all.

In simpler terms, when a mortal thus enters into a state of godliness, they have entered the translated state. We have no indication that Christ was translated Himself, but being made perfect, he would have possessed greater powers and greater gifts than translation. Hence, we become "like unto the Son of God."

These are glorious promises—so much so that it requires astronomical faith to compress these infinite promises into the finite space within our personal paradigm. Yet the promises exist, and they are reiterated and renewed before our eyes, in our hearing, and in our lives with unmistakable clarity.

In clarification, let us remember that translation is not the ultimate blessing we seek. It is the highest and most desirable outcome of mortal righteousness while we are yet mortal. But it is not the only pathway to exaltation; it is just the preferred pathway when it is available. Far more souls will be exalted who were not translated while mortal than those who were. Having made this observation, it is even more important to note that translation exists, not for our blessing alone, but to prepare the world for the return of Christ. It is indispensable to the whole winding-up scene of the earth, the establishment of Zion, the protection of the Saints during that time, the gathering of the elect, and the final triumph of righteousness. Even though it is not required for personal exaltation, it is absolutely essential to the completion and fulfillment of our dispensation of the gospel.

Once our service as a translated being ends, then resurrection and vastly greater blessings than translation await the faithful. Thus, translation is not *the* goal; it is an intermediate accomplishment, one that extends and promises vast blessings upon ourselves and upon our posterity, but it is not the end objective of everything we do.

In Christ's day these great blessings were extended, and some availed themselves of them, most notably John the Beloved. But there were undoubtedly others. Luke 9:27, quoted below, says there are some who will not taste of death, which of course implies that more than just John were translated. This we can also surmise because when the heavens bestow this blessing into the midst of a gospel dispensation, the promises are extended to all the faithful. In some cases, nobody but the prophet of that dispensation achieves Zion stature. In a few cases there were entire cities.

In this light, two thousand years ago Christ made the next few statements about living forever and never dying. They are impossible to understand in any other light than translation. They cannot be dismissed. Either they are true, or Christ misspoke. And if He misspoke, then He was not divine. Only in the light of glorious latter-day revealed truth does the significance of these statements distill upon our souls.

> 47 Verily, verily, I say unto you, He that believeth on me hath everlasting life.
>
> 48 I am that bread of life.
>
> 49 Your fathers did eat manna in the wilderness, and are dead.
>
> 50 This is the bread which cometh down from heaven, that a man may eat thereof, *and not die.*
>
> 51 I am the living bread which came down from heaven: if any man eat of this bread, *he shall live for ever.* (John 6:47–51, italics added)

Notice that Christ uses "everlasting life" and "living forever" synonymously. So many times He promised His disciples everlasting life. Could it be that at least in some of these statements, what they (and we) are being promised is far more immediate than eternal life in the hereafter? Consider these startling scriptures in this light:

> 51 Verily, verily, I say unto you, If a man keep my saying, *he shall never see death.* (John 8:51)
>
> 25 Jesus said unto her, I am the resurrection, and the life: he that believeth in me, though he were dead, yet shall he live:
>
> 26 And whosoever liveth and believeth in me *shall never die.* (John 11:25–26)
>
> 27 Verily, I tell you of a truth, there are some standing here who *shall not taste of death,* until they see the kingdom of God coming in power. (Luke 9:27)

This then is the true and greater calling of the priesthood: to see the face of God the Father—and live! Not just live, as in not being consumed by the presence of God, but LIVE, as in never die. This is the glorious calling that we hardly realize exists because our minds are darkened by unbelief. Or, perhaps they've been darkened because we were not taught these things in our childhood. So we just don't believe it! We weren't taught it in childhood because it is a mystery of godliness. Even if our fathers understood it, they may not have been allowed to teach it to us (Alma 12:9). This blinding truth is one of the greater mysteries of godliness, and as the very nature of a mystery imposes, we can hardly see it. Yet, the evidences are everywhere.

A Mystery of Godliness

A ponderable question might be, is it appropriate for an author to proclaim something as being a mystery of godliness? The fact is that it is the scriptures that make the claim.

> 51 Behold, I shew you a mystery; We shall not all sleep . . . (1 Corinthians 15:51)

Beyond Paul's words, which plainly refer to everyone not experiencing death, the fact that the connection between the priesthood and translation is almost universally not understood firmly establishes it as a mystery. The license for this claim arises from the definition of the term godliness discussed above. By that definition, translation is a form of godliness. Hence, translation is a mystery of godliness: A play on words if you wish; a shaft of sunlight in a dark place, if you prefer.

Renewing of Their Bodies

When our souls realign to magnify this grand calling, then the remainder of our original quotation on the oath and covenant of the priesthood makes exciting, glorious, life-altering sense.

> 33 For whoso is faithful unto the obtaining these two priesthoods of which I have spoken, and the magnifying their calling, are sanctified by the Spirit unto the renewing of their bodies. (D&C 84:33)

Verse 33 above is speaking of a beginning and an eventual glorious outcome, all in the same sentence. The Lord speaks of obtaining the priesthood and magnifying our callings. Then, in a masterful over-simplification, He sweeps forward in time to the grand fulfillment of that whole process and proclaims that we will be sanctified unto the renewing of our bodies.

Elder Orson Pratt described this promised renewing of bodies in verse 33. He makes this statement about all of the sons of Moses and Aaron, whom he describes as holders of the Melchizedek and Aaronic Priesthood:

> [All] who are pure in heart will behold the face of the Lord and that too before he comes in his glory in the clouds of heaven, for he will suddenly come to his Temple, and he will purify the sons of Moses and of Aaron, until they shall be prepared to offer in that Temple an offering that shall be acceptable in the sight of the Lord. [Mal. 3:1-4.] In doing this, he will purify not only the minds of the Priesthood in that Temple, but he will purify their bodies until they shall be quickened, renewed and strengthened, and they will be partially changed, not to immortality, but changed in part that they can be filled with the power of God, and they can stand in the presence of Jesus, and behold his face in the midst of that Temple.
>
> This will prepare them for further ministrations among the nations of the earth, it will prepare them to go forth in the days of tribulation and vengeance upon the nations of the wicked, when God will smite them with pestilence, plague and earthquake, such as former generations never knew. [Sec. 29:14-21; 45:28-42; Rev. 9.] Then the servants of God will need to be armed with the power of God, *they will need to have that sealing blessing pronounced upon their foreheads that they can stand forth in the midst of these desolations and plagues and not be overcome by them.*[5]

Without using the term "translation," Elder Pratt clearly describes the translated state. Translated people are still mortals, and thus not "immortal" as he notes. He also notes that they can endure the presence of Christ and behold His face, which is also the means whereby one is allowed to request this supreme blessing.

To understand what the Lord meant by "sanctified by the Spirit unto the renewing of our bodies" we need to examine for a moment what sanctification means.

SANCTIFICATION

There are many degrees of sanctification. The first noticeable experience with the power of the Holy Ghost to make saintly (sanctify) is when a person first accepts that Jesus is the Christ and decides to make life changes for that knowledge. Such a change often occurs prior to baptism. Many Christians refer to this change as being born again; and so it is, in a real but rudimentary way. In the LDS vernacular, we often refer to this as "being converted," which means to be changed or upgraded. John 3:3 suggests that being born again is to "see" the kingdom of God.

> 3 Jesus answered and said unto him, Verily, verily, I say unto thee, Except a man be born again, he cannot see the kingdom of God.
>
> 4 Nicodemus saith unto him, How can a man be born when he is old? can he enter the second time into his mother's womb, and be born?
>
> 5 Jesus answered, Verily, verily, I say unto thee, Except a man be born of water and of the Spirit, he cannot enter into the kingdom of God. (John 3:3–5)

In other words, at this initial rebirth of the soul mentioned in verse 3, the believer can begin to see himself obtaining the future glories of eternal life, and thus begins to seek after them. Their conversion gives them faith in Jesus Christ, a testimony of His Atonement, and a strong desire to lay hold upon the promises of Christ.

It is not necessary to be baptized into the true Church to experience this marvelous but rudimentary change. Millions upon millions in the Christian community enjoy this gift from our merciful Savior and have great faith in Him because of it. It uplifts and prepares for a journey that may actually be unfathomable until much later in one's growth.

Moroni calls this stage of sanctification "hope" (Ether 12:28; Moroni 10:20–21). It is a revealed "hope" born of the Spirit (the Light of Christ), which gives a hope that there will be a place in eternity for the spiritual pilgrim. They can now see with an eye of faith as suggested in verse 3.

The greater rebirth mentioned in John 3:5 follows being born of the water (baptism) and of the Spirit (the Gift of the Holy Ghost) and makes one able to *enter* the kingdom of God. Obviously, one must be baptized by authority to enjoy this incrementally greater sanctification.

This further sanctification to enter into the kingdom is when one receives the Holy Ghost and is upgraded by the grace of the Atonement to become Christlike, which makes them willing and anxious to sacrifice and consecrate all that they have to enter the kingdom of God. At this time the person is changed, upgraded by the Atonement of Christ, filled with righteous desire, and changed from fallen man to a saintly man or woman. Such a change is prefigured in Mosiah 3:19.

> 19 For the natural man is an enemy to God, and has been from the fall of Adam, and will be, forever and ever, unless he yields to the enticings of the Holy Spirit, and putteth off the natural man and becometh a saint through the Atonement of Christ the Lord, and becometh as a child, submissive, meek, humble, patient, full of love, willing to submit to all things which the Lord seeth fit to inflict upon him, even as a child doth submit to his father. (Mosiah 3:19)

This degree of sanctification is generally referred to in the LDS community as being born again. As the verse above indicates, this change is accompanied by sweeping upgrades to the soul. The qualities of becoming like a child, submissive, meek, humble, and so on, are enhancements to the soul brought about by the Holy Ghost at this marvelous change.

There is further sanctification and a greater change when one is so blessed to receive an assurance in mortality that they have a guaranteed place in the eternal kingdom. This change is often referred to as making one's calling and election sure. Joseph spoke of this change. These gifts are part of the enabling aspect of the atonement, and are received as gifts, we simply become these things.

> The other Comforter spoken of is a subject of great interest, and perhaps understood by few of this generation. After a person has faith in Christ, repents of his sins, and is baptized for the remission of his sins and receives the Holy Ghost, (by the laying on of hands), which is the first Comforter, then let him continue to humble himself before God, hungering and thirsting after righteousness, and living by every word of God, and the Lord will soon say unto him, Son, thou shalt be exalted. When the Lord has thoroughly proved him, and finds that the man is determined to serve Him at all hazards, then the man will find his calling and his election made sure.[6]

The following quote is when Joseph Smith experienced his own calling and election being made sure.

> 3 Wherefore, I now send upon you another Comforter, even upon you my friends, that it may abide in your hearts, even the Holy Spirit of promise; which other Comforter is the same that I promised unto my disciples, as is recorded in the testimony of John.

4 This Comforter is the promise which I give unto you of eternal life, even the glory of the celestial kingdom;

5 Which glory is that of the Church of the Firstborn, even of God, the holiest of all, through Jesus Christ his Son—(D&C 88:3–5)

As we noted earlier, this is the "promise" of those blessings, not the actual receipt of them. It is a promise of eventual eternal life in the celestial kingdom, and a promise that we may enjoy the glory of the Church of the Firstborn, a subject we will touch upon later. This grand experience bestows upon the humble soul further degrees of sanctification that greatly expand the previously obtained perfections of the rebirth.

Even beyond these glorious steps on the upward reaches of sanctification is the far greater blessing of at last entering into the presence of Christ and there being changed and made able to endure His presence. We call this glorious gift the Second Comforter. This degree of sanctification and the blessings it bestows upon the body and soul of righteous men and women is supernal.

Once a person qualifies himself to be in the presence of God in this life, there are blessings that may be requested as part of one's "endowment." One of these is the renewing of their bodies mentioned above. It is this glorious and powerful blessing of sanctification unto the renewing of their bodies that Doctrine and Covenants 84:33 is describing. It is not referring to resurrection, because these people have not yet died, and all mankind will be resurrected. This renewing is wholly conditioned upon magnifying priesthood callings and being purified through priesthood ordinances. Renewal implies taking something worn out and repairing it. Resurrection is not a renewal since the body has died and decayed into dust. Resurrection is a re-creation of the body, a return of life, not a renewal of the existing one.

Other grand truths here are less obvious. One is that if our bodies are being sanctified and renewed, then this whole process can and must take place while we yet have a body, while we are still mortal. This grand outcome of righteous priesthood is to occur in this life.

RENEWAL OF THE BODY

The question that arises is: What does it mean to have our bodies renewed?

As was stated earlier, there is only one gospel. The faith our fathers obtained to rend the heavens and raise the dead is that same faith which we presently employ as we reach into the eternities. When we speak of a renewing of our bodies, a search of the scriptures for instances when bodies were renewed will bring to us what the Lord has always done and what He continues to do when we follow His divine pattern.

As is true in many gospel principles, renewing of one's body can have many meanings. There is the undeniable effect of this blessing in prolonging the lives of righteous men and women. This blessing has been testified to by several prophets in regard to themselves and fellow servants. President Hugh B. Brown testified that President David O. McKay had been sanctified by the Spirit unto the renewing of his body.[7] On a more lofty application of this blessing we also have the glorious renewal of the body that translation offers, and which is clearly an outcome of the priesthood and an essential part of the latter-day scene.

In the cases where we have a detailed account of people who were translated, it occurred during their personal interview with Christ. The Lord asked each of them what they desired from Him after He returned to the Father. The account of the Three Nephites is the most detailed.

> 4 And when he had spoken unto them, he turned himself unto the three, and said unto them: What will ye that I should do unto you, when I am gone unto the Father?
>
> 5 And they sorrowed in their hearts, for they durst not speak unto him the thing which they desired.
>
> 6 And he said unto them: Behold, I know your thoughts, and ye have desired the thing which John, my beloved, who was with me in my ministry, before that I was lifted up by the Jews, desired of me.
>
> 7 Therefore, more blessed are ye, for ye shall never taste of death; but ye shall live to behold all the doings of the Father unto the children of men, even until all things shall be fulfilled according to the will of the Father, when I shall come in my glory with the powers of heaven. (3 Nephi 28:4–7)

Does it seem unthinkable that the oath and covenant of the priesthood, our priesthood, in this day, could be pointing us to translation? Bearing in mind that Doctrine and Covenants 84:33 is speaking in superlative terms of the ultimate blessings of the priesthood, it isn't preposterous at all. In fact, it has to be true that if the outcome of Enoch's priesthood was to eventually be translated and walk and talk with God, then our priesthood, in this the fulness of times, must offer us the same.

Do we have claim upon these glorious promises in this day? Yes!

18 The power and authority of the higher, or Melchizedek Priesthood, is to hold the keys of all the spiritual blessings of the Church—

ALL the spiritual blessings!

19 To have the privilege of receiving the mysteries of the kingdom of heaven, to have the heavens opened unto them, to commune with the general assembly and church of the Firstborn, and to enjoy the communion and presence of God the Father, and Jesus the mediator of the new covenant. (D&C 107:18–19)

The above reference promises that when we receive the mysteries of the kingdom of heaven, we will be blessed to be able to commune with the general assembly and Church of the Firstborn. Let us discover then what that great congregation is.

THE CHURCH OF THE FIRSTBORN

Notice in Doctrine and Covenants 107:18–19, quoted above, that becoming a member of the Church of the Firstborn is made synonymous with enjoying the presence of God the Father and Jesus Christ. Since the gospel is unchanging, any time one enters into the presence of deity in this life, the same privilege offered to the Three Nephites is offered to everyone. In other words, those who belong to the Church of the Firstborn are often translated beings.

I say often because we have record of many people who during their personal interview with God asked for gifts other than translation. In fact, the record seems to indicate that most ask for a gift other than translation. The Nephite nine asked to speedily go into the kingdom of God.

The pattern is that members of the Church of the Firstborn have had this personal interview. They have been in the presence of Christ, who *is* "the Firstborn." They have seen the divine personage as they are seen (without a veil), and they know God as they are known (in perfect clarity and truth). They have received of the fulness of God's glory, which means they have been in His presence and have fully partaken of His Grace, which implies the fullest application of priesthood promises.

Following the divine pattern of such things, they have thus had the opportunity to request translation, which would be to request a place in Zion, or they have requested some other gift.

> 94 They who dwell in his presence are the Church of the Firstborn; and they see as they are seen, and know as they are known, having received of his fulness and of his grace; (D&C 76:94)

> 21 And now, verily I say unto you, I was in the beginning with the Father, and am the Firstborn;

> 22 And all those who are begotten through me are partakers of the glory of the same [ie, Father and the Son], and are the Church of the Firstborn. (D&C 93:21–22, bracketed comment added)

Notice again the connection between receiving of the fulness of God's glory and being a member of the Church of the Firstborn. Those who enter into the presence of God become members of this exclusive assemblage.

This is salient to our study of Zion because it is in the presence of God that we may request a place in Zion.

> 22 But ye are come unto mount Sion, and unto the city of the living God, the heavenly Jerusalem, and to an innumerable company of angels,

> 23 To the general assembly and church of the Firstborn, which are written in heaven, and to God the Judge of all, and to the spirits of just men made perfect. (Hebrews 12:22–23)

The general assembly and Church of the Firstborn are those who have completed the full gospel course with valiant obedience and through ordinances have come unto the city of the living God to live in the presence of Christ. The "City of the Living God" is another name for Enoch's capital city. Notice the following quote in this regard. The Lord refers to this organization as the Church of Enoch and of the Firstborn. In other words, these two churches, at least during the time referenced here, will be one. Just prior to the coming of our Lord in glory, the Church of the Firstborn, as it exists among men, will be joined by the Church of Enoch, and they will be one (Moses 7:63).

Thus, membership in one qualifies you for membership in the other. The requirements to enter either are the same, and the glories and blessings flowing from them are the same.

What then is the Church of Enoch? Hugh Nibley describes it thus:

But it's in the last days that the fulfillment will really get under-way with the restoration and the steps approaching the establishment of Zion. In every age, though, as the Doctrine and Covenants tells us, the saints are "they who are come unto Mount Zion, and unto the city of the living God, the heavenly place, the holiest of all, . . . the general assembly and church of Enoch, and of the First-born" (D&C 76:66–67). *That is the eternal order of Zion, and the saints have been at work for many years, supposedly preparing to receive it.*[8]

Over and over we see the connection between those who are worthy to fully participate in the resurrection of the just, which includes those who have been in the presence of deity, those who dwell in Enoch's Zion or the city of the living God, and those who are members of the Church of Enoch or the Church of the Firstborn. The connection is that those who qualify themselves for the one are qualified for all the blessings of the others. Any list of these blessings is too short, because they encompass all the Father has.

65 These are they who shall come forth in the resurrection of the just.

66 These are they who are come unto Mount Zion, and unto the city of the living God, the heavenly place, the holiest of all.

67 These are they who have come to an innumerable company of angels, to the general assembly and church of Enoch, and of the Firstborn. (D&C 76:65–67)

All these blessings flow from that priesthood which we now possess. Why is it so difficult to believe that we have the right to lay claim to these blessings—here, now, in this life?

18 The power and authority of the higher, or Melchizedek Priesthood, is to hold the keys of all the spiritual blessings of the Church—

19 To have the privilege of receiving the mysteries of the kingdom of heaven, to have the heavens opened unto them, to commune with the general assembly and church of the Firstborn, and to enjoy the communion and presence of God the Father, and Jesus the mediator of the new covenant. (D&C 107:18–19)

Perhaps the reason we have difficulty believing these blessings apply to us is that, spiritually speaking, we are yet little children, and we struggle with small obediences and lesser commandments. It is possible to content ourselves with warm feelings and spiritual testimonies of true things without catching the vision of what all those baby steps are toddling us toward. Nevertheless, the Lord has promised to lead us as a child and bestow these blessings upon us when we are worthy to receive them. And though His tender mercies are all around us, He has been leading us as children now for 175 years. The time must shortly come when we set aside our spiritual pacifiers and actually build Zion.

> 17 Verily, verily, I say unto you, ye are little children, and ye have not as yet understood how great blessings the Father hath in his own hands and prepared for you;
>
> 18 And ye cannot bear all things now; nevertheless, be of good cheer, for I will lead you along. The kingdom is yours and the blessings thereof are yours, and the riches of eternity are yours.
>
> 19 And he who receiveth all things with thankfulness shall be made glorious; and the things of this earth shall be added unto him, even an hundred fold, yea, more.
>
> 20 Wherefore, do the things which I have commanded you, saith your Redeemer, even the Son Ahman, who prepareth all things before he taketh you;
>
> 21 For ye are the Church of the Firstborn, and he will take you up in a cloud, and appoint every man his portion. (D&C 78:17–21)

THE CHURCH OF THE FIRSTBORN AND THE LATTER-DAY CHURCH

The question naturally arises in the faithful heart, what is the difference between the true and living latter-day Church and this Church of the Firstborn?

Joseph Fielding Smith gave us this insight:

> What is the difference, if there is a difference between the Church of the Firstborn and The Church of Jesus Christ of Latter-day Saints, or of any day saints? Well, the members of the Church of the Firstborn are members of the Church of Jesus Christ, but not all those who are members of the Church of Jesus Christ become members of the Church of the Firstborn, for they are they unto whom the Lord has given all things. They are priests and kings. They are they who have received the exaltation, they who are made equal in power, and in might, and in dominion, who attain to the fulness and become the sons, and for the sisters, the daughters of God.[9]

In other words, all members of the Church of the Firstborn are Latter-day Saints. But not all LDS are qualified for membership in the Church of the Firstborn. The latter-day Church is a stepping stone into the Church of the Firstborn. Another way to view this is that the Church of the Firstborn is a gathering of the uniquely righteous from among the general latter-day Church. They receive "all that the Father hath," which is the fullest attainment and outcome of membership in Christ's true Church.

It may be important to note that the Church of the Firstborn is not an earthly organization. It does not own buildings or land and hold conference every six months. This is a sacred society whose highest officer is Jesus Christ and whose members are those who have been ushered into His presence and there received the endowment of Zion, and thus, membership in this august body.

As we previously noted, all of the blessings of Zion flow from the priesthood. Just as there is a holy society of those who overcome by faith and lay claim upon the blessings of the Church of the Firstborn (which is to say, of Zion), there is a holy order of the priesthood that presides over Zion and possesses the greater powers the ancients employed to command the elements, divide the seas, and move mountains. All of these blessings and promises are ours to claim when we become Zion.

They who dwell in the presence of God are the Church of the Firstborn. Since Christ will dwell in the latter-day Zion, those who live in Zion become the Church of the Firstborn by virtue of that divine company.

The Church of the Firstborn is populated by many people: Mortals who have achieved a Zion stature, spirits of righteous men and women of prior ages who met the qualifications of Zion during mortality but were not translated, translated beings (such as Enoch and his people), resurrected beings, and since Jesus Christ is there, divine beings.

Only members of the Church of the Firstborn receive the fullest promises of exaltation. Elder McConkie, speaking of the eternal outcome of those so blessed, offers this grand summation:

> It [eternal life] is "the greatest of all the gifts of God" (D&C 14:7), for it is the kind, status, type, and quality of life that God himself enjoys. Thus those who gain eternal life receive exaltation; they are sons of God, joint-heirs with Christ, *members of the Church of the Firstborn*; they overcome all things, have all power, and receive the fulness of the Father. They are gods."[10]

Our latter-day scripture attests to the same eternal glory of those who achieve membership in the Church of the Firstborn:

> 92 And thus we saw the glory of the celestial, which excels in all things—where God, even the Father, reigns upon his throne forever and ever;
>
> 93 Before whose throne all things bow in humble reverence, and give him glory forever and ever.
>
> 94 *They who dwell in his presence are the Church of the Firstborn*; and they see as they are seen, and know as they are known, having received of his fulness and of his grace;
>
> 95 And he makes them equal in power, and in might, and in dominion. (D&C 76:92–95: italics added)

Notes

1. McConkie, *New Witness for the Articles of Faith*, 492.
2. Ehat and Cook, *Words of Joseph Smith*, 52.
3. Orson Pratt, *The Seer* 1, no. 10, 149.
4. Wilford Woodruff, *Wilford Woodruff, His Life and Labors*, comp. Matthias F. Cowley (Salt Lake City: Deseret News, 1916), 319–20.
5. Orson Pratt, *Journal of Discourses*, 15:366; bracketed comments and quotations added.
6. Smith, *Teachings of the Prophet Joseph Smith*, 150.
7. Carlos E. Asay, "The oath and covenant of the Priesthood," *Ensign*, Nov. 1985, 44.
8. Nibley, *Approaching Zion*, 6; italics and bracketed comments added.
9. Joseph Fielding Smith, *Seek Ye Earnestly* (Salt Lake City: Deseret Book, 1970), 62–63.
10. McConkie, *Mormon Doctrine*, 237; italics added.

Chapter Eight

THE HOLY ORDER

Those who become members of the holy order are called "priests of the Most High." They are after the order of Melchizedek, who was translated (JST Genesis 14:25–40), which is after the order of Enoch, who was also translated, which is after the order of the Only Begotten Son, who possesses all powers of the priesthood, including those of translation of course.

This holy order of the priesthood spoken of above arises from the Melchizedek Priesthood commonly received by ordination in the latter-day Church. However, entering or obtaining this holy order includes a further endowment of the full power of godliness.

Richard O. Cowan made this observation:

> Joseph Smith's translation of Genesis 14 indicates how Melchizedek was "after the order of Enoch." Verse 34 indicates that Melchizedek followed Enoch's example, leading a Zion-like community that obtained a place in heaven. The Lord further explained that both Melchizedek and Enoch were "after the order of the Only Begotten Son" (D&C 76:57). This relationship was reflected in the original name of the higher priesthood (see D&C 107:3).[1]

The promises and privileges we potentially enjoy in this dispensation are enormous, even that they have no peer in any previous dispensation. Our blessings are intended to be the most glorious ever offered to a people or a time.

> 9 Having made known unto us the mystery of his will, according to his good pleasure which he hath purposed in himself;

10 That in the dispensation of the fulness of times he might gather together in one all things in Christ, both which are in heaven, and which are on earth; even in him;

11 In whom also we have obtained an inheritance. (JST Ephesians 1:9–11.)

One of those glorious "things" which will be brought together from heaven and earth are Enoch's (former-day) Zion from the heavens and Joseph's (latter-day) Zion from the mortal earth. They will be combined in the dispensation wherein we live, and as verse 11 attests, we have obtained an inheritance through Christ within those holy walls of Zion.

Then there will begin a glorious day of righteousness which all holy men saw in vision and longed to share but could not because it was reserved for this last great dispensation.

11 Wherefore, hearken ye together and let me show unto you even my wisdom—the wisdom of him whom ye say is the God of Enoch, and his brethren,

12 Who were separated from the earth, and were received unto myself—a city reserved until a day of righteousness shall come—a day which was sought for by all holy men, and they found it not because of wickedness and abominations; (D&C 45:11–12)

They did not find Zion at that time because it was reserved until the latter days, a time when wickedness and abominations would be swept away by the closing scenes of all time. In their day, the world wasn't ready. There were many generations left to come to the earth, and much work to be done—including the birth and Atonement of Christ.

In order to build Zion we are instructed to become the priests of the Most High, after the order of Enoch, which will then usher in this last great dispensation of peace. Consider this following quotation:

53 And who overcome by faith, and are sealed by the Holy Spirit of promise, which the Father sheds forth upon all those who are just and true.

54 They are they who are the Church of the Firstborn.

55 They are they into whose hands the Father has given all things—

56 They are they who are priests and kings, who have received of his fulness, and of his glory;

57 And are priests of the Most High, after the order of Melchizedek,

which was after the order of Enoch, which was after the order of the Only Begotten Son. (D&C 76:53–57)

There is power in these words we don't dare misread. When one becomes a member of an order, one assumes the attributes and abilities of all other members of that order. This is the reason it is called an order, because all the members are alike in the attributes that define the order.

Thus, to be a member of the order of Enoch is to possess the priesthood of Enoch and the powers Enoch possessed, including the powers of translation and his unmatched command of the earth and her elements. To be after the order of Melchizedek is to possess all of Melchizedek's gifts, which includes translation. To be after the order of the Only Begotten Son is to possess all the powers of heaven, which is what the Father covenants to bestow upon us as noted in verse 55 above.

Observe that those who are sealed by the Holy Spirit of promise are the Church of the Firstborn. Furthermore, when the referenced time comes for this verse to be fulfilled, then they have (not shall have at some future date, but *have*) received all things, and are priests (which is an ecclesiastical office) and are kings (which is a secular role) of the Most High.

PRIESTS AND KINGS

There are clearly two offices being referenced here: a priesthood of kings, and a priesthood of priests. We have often heard these terms without stopping to separate them or to realize that there are actually two "holy offices" within the same priesthood. Speaking of these priesthood offices, Apostle Orson Pratt said:

> The Kingly authority is not separate and distinct from the Priesthood, but merely a branch or portion of the same. The Priestly authority is universal, having power over all things; the Kingly authority until perfected is limited to the kingdoms placed under its jurisdiction: the former appoints and ordains the latter; but the latter never appoints and ordains the former: the first controls the laws of nature, and exercises jurisdiction over the elements, as well as over men; the last controls men only, and administers just and righteous laws for their government. Where the two are combined and the individual perfected, he has almighty power both as a King and as a Priest; both offices are then merged in one.[2]

This holy order of priests and kings is specifically the order of those who have realized all of the sacred promises of the temple, and thus have obtained the blessings of Zion. The priestly authority is the authority to control the laws of nature, the elements of the natural world—and the authority to ordain kings. Enoch manifested this authority when he moved mountains, rivers, and defended his city with the power of God. Melchizedek manifested the kingly aspect of this office when he became the king of Salem and was called the "King of Peace" by his people (JST Genesis 14:36).

The priestly priesthood embodies the fulness of the priesthood, which we may obtain by living and obtaining a Zion stature, which places this attainment near the beginning of the Millennium. The priestly priesthood will then ordain "kings" to rule in righteousness across the millennial earth.

FULNESS OF THE PRIESTHOOD

Joseph Smith, in the reference below, associates obtaining a fulness of the priesthood as a prerequisite to becoming part of the 144,000. Since the 144,000 depart from Zion to gather in the elect, the fulness of the priesthood thus appears necessary to become a member of Zion:

> [Joseph] indicated that the conferral of the fulness of the priesthood was a "sealing . . . on top of the head," of which the phrase "sealed in their foreheads" was symbolic. Furthermore, Joseph Smith here taught that it was through the ordinance of conferral of the fulness of the priesthood that men could be qualified to be a part of the special missionary force of the last days which would number 144,000 high priests.[3]

Brigham Young taught that nobody he was aware of in his time had received a fulness of the priesthood:

> Brigham Young demonstrated that the prophet made clear to those who had received the endowment and patriarchal marriage ordinances, that they had not as yet received the fulness of the priesthood. On 6 August 1843, Brigham Young said, "If any in the Church [have] the fulness of the Melchizedek Priesthood [I do] not know it. For any person to have the fulness of that priesthood, he must be a king and priest."[4]

Continuing the same discourse, Brigham referred to the fulness of the priesthood as the "third order of priesthood blessings" (the endowment being first and eternal marriage second). He taught:

> Based on his understanding from Joseph the prophet, Brigham Young said of this third order of priesthood blessings, "Those who . . . come in here [the Nauvoo Temple] and *have received* their washing & anointing *will* [later, if faithful], be ordained Kings & Priests, and will then have received the fulness of the Priesthood, all that can be given on earth. For Brother Joseph said he had given us all that could be given to man on the earth."[5]

Orson Hyde, an apostle and contemporary of Joseph Smith taught:

> The chosen vessels unto God are the kings and priests that are placed at the head of these kingdoms. These have received their washings and anointings in the temple of God on this earth; they have been chosen, ordained, and anointed kings and priests, to reign as such in the resurrection of the just. Such as have not received the fulness of the priesthood, (for the fulness of the priesthood includes the authority of both king and priest).[6]

Joseph referred to receiving the fulness of the priesthood as being the highest blessings available to man. Since this holy order is the order of Zion, we begin to glimpse that obtaining fulness of the priesthood (and consequently Zion) in our lifetime is the greatest blessing available to man while in mortality. Joseph Smith noted:

> That is, when Abraham offered up Isaac (Genesis 22), as repulsive a request as this was, Abraham went ahead and proved his integrity and faith. Consequently God bestowed upon him the highest blessing available to man, the fulness of the priesthood.[7]

We may thus say that eternal life is the greatest outcome *of* mortality, and receiving the fulness of the priesthood, being translated and obtaining Zion, is the greatest outcome *in* mortality.

We may aspire to this kingly priesthood and holy order because it was restored by Elijah to Joseph Smith.

Joseph Smith taught us that "Elijah restored the authority of the fulness of the priesthood." (See D&C 110:12-16.)[8]

> Now for Elijah, the spirit power & calling of Elijah is that ye have power to hold the keys of the revelations ordinances, oricles powers &

endowments of the fulness of the Melchezedek Priesthood.[9]

Elijah restored the sealing powers to Joseph Smith. Inherent in that sealing power is this grand "fulness of the Melchizedek Priesthood."

The promise is that all who become a part of Zion, and of the Church of the Firstborn, are those who are sealed by the Holy Spirit of Promise, and thus obtain the fulness of the priesthood.

> 53 And who overcome by faith, and are sealed by the Holy Spirit of promise, which the Father sheds forth upon all those who are just and true.
>
> 54 They are they who are the Church of the Firstborn.
>
> 55 They are they into whose hands the Father has given all things— (D&C 76:53–55)

It appears then that the following terms are nearly synonymous, and while different in many ways, a person who obtains any one of them potentially obtains them all.

- Sealed by the Holy Spirit of Promise
- Church of the Firstborn
- Fulness of the priesthood
- Zion

Thus we see that obtaining the fulness of the priesthood is not an optional accomplishment. It isn't something that we must do only if we are seeking the advanced blessings of Zion.

If we ever arrive at godhood, and have power over the elements— power to create, to give life, and to act in all the duties that godhood bestows—we will do so by the power of the fulness of the priesthood. At some point in our journey we will ultimately have to climb this mountain. Joseph Fielding Smith authoritatively proclaimed: "There is no exaltation in the kingdom of God without the fulness of the priesthood."[10]

Climbing it in the next life and obtaining the promised power will make us gods! Climbing it in this life will give us the "power of godliness" and make us Zion (D&C 84:19–24)!

Once again, let us note that the term "the holy order" has been appropriately applied in many ways over the years. Often our leaders have referred to the Melchizedek Priesthood itself as this holy order. Yet, in the verses that follow we find that there is also a holy order that eclipses any other definition, in that it bestows a fulness of priesthood power, and cannot be gifted from one human to another, but most come from God himself.

This holy order of the priesthood promises to bestow the same powers Christ manifested during His ministry. These are the powers Enoch displayed during his ministry. Melchizedek obtained this same holy order, and in time established Zion, and his people were translated.

> 26 Now Melchizedek was a man of faith, who wrought righteousness; and when a child he feared God, and stopped the mouths of lions, and quenched the violence of fire.
>
> 27 And thus, having been approved of God, he was ordained an high priest after the order of the covenant which God made with Enoch,
>
> 28 It being after the order of the son of God; which order came, not by man, nor the will of man; neither by father nor mother; neither by beginning of days nor end of years; but of God;
>
> 29 And it was delivered unto men by the calling of his own voice, according to his own will, unto as many as believed on his name. (JST Genesis 14:26–29)

Notice that verse 28 says this holy order does not come by man, or by the will of man, but by God. In other words, mankind and our estimation of when we are ready, our timetable, our desires, our will, is not the determining force governing when these things happen. It is God who decides when we enter this holy order, and it comes by the calling of His own voice, not by a mortal speaking in His name. Furthermore, the holy order cannot be transferred from one man to another. It only comes by direct and personal contact with deity.

Further and glorious indeed, is the promise of the Father, the oath of the God of Heaven, that every one who is ordained unto this same order will have these same glorious powers. And as verse 29 above states, this promise is unto even as many as believe on His name. These are not just glorious accounts of God's unique dealings with unusually righteous men in the dim antiquities of history. These are promises that are repeatedly offered to you and me.

It gives one a moment's pause to ponder the idea that these gifts come to as many as believe on His name. Since these powers are not manifestly evident in our lives and ministries, we must sadly wonder if any of us truly "believe on His name" to the degree being referenced here. One cannot doubt that we do believe; undeniably and with joy do we have great faith in our Christ, but apparently we do not believe in the way that would bring us these great blessings. The great canyon separating us from receipt of these blessings is the very definition of belief. Just a casual glance around informs us that we receive all that we do believe in—including miracles, healings, and great blessings of many kinds. What we have yet to begin to believe in are these blessings now under our microscope—and all of them lead us to Zion.

So, how do we obtain the fulness of the priesthood? The Lord has left us a road map, one with which we are familiar. The process begins in the temple, where we receive and make covenants which when fully realized will bestow upon us this great privilege.

Joseph Smith noted:

> If a man gets the fulness of the priesthood of God, he has to get it the same way that Jesus Christ obtained it, and that was by keeping the commandments and by obeying all the ordinances of the house of the Lord.[11]

Joseph Fielding Smith taught the same principle, adding that it did not matter what office you held in the Church, only that we receive and keep the temple covenants.

> Let me put this in a little different way. I do not care what office you hold in the Church—you may be an apostle, you may be a patriarch, a high priest, or anything else—but you cannot receive the fulness of the priesthood and the fulness of eternal reward unless you receive the ordinances of the house of the Lord; and when you receive these ordinances, the door is then open so you can obtain all the blessings which any man can gain.
>
> *Do not think because someone has a higher office in the Church than you have that you are barred from receiving the fulness of the Lord's blessings. You can have them sealed upon you as an elder, if you are faithful; and when you receive them, and live faithfully and keep these covenants, you then have all that any man can get.*[12]

Joseph Fielding Smith also noted that any righteous priesthood holder could obtain this great blessing of the fulness of the priesthood.

> To obtain the fulness of the priesthood does not mean that a man must become President of the Church. Every man who is faithful and will receive these ordinances and blessings obtains a fulness of the priesthood, and the Lord has said that "he makes them equal in power,

and in might, and in dominion." Only one man at a time on the earth holds the keys of the priesthood; only one man at a time has the power to receive revelations for the Church; but the Lord has made it possible for every man in this Church, through his obedience, to receive the fulness of the priesthood through the ordinances of the temple of the Lord. This cannot be received anywhere else.[13]

An indispensable part of the prophet Joseph Smith's mission was to restore the fulness of the priesthood, which was to enable the full operation of latter-day temples. Without this sealing power, the ordinances of the temple could not function with power.

Ehat and Cook have this to say regarding the restoration of the sealing power:

> One of the major milestones, if not the major milestone, of the Latter-day work was to be the restoration of the fulness of the priesthood (D&C 124:28). The prophet's "mission . . . [was to] firmly [establish] the dispensation of the fulness of the priesthood in the last days, that all the powers of earth and hell [could] never prevail against it" (*History of the Church*, 5:140, or *Teachings*, p. 258). What was this fulness of the priesthood? The most concise but inclusive definition of the authority of the fulness of the priesthood was given by Joseph Smith in his 10 March 1844 discourse when he said, "Now for Elijah; the spirit, power and calling of Elijah is that ye have power to hold the keys of the revelations, ordinances, oracles, powers and endowments of the fulness of the Melchizedek Priesthood and of the Kingdom of God on the Earth and to receive, obtain and perform all the ordinances belonging to the kingdom of God . . . [to] have power to seal on earth and in heaven." However, the prophet had not as yet administered the ordinances that made men kings and priests. Brigham Young said three weeks before this discourse that no one yet in the Church had the fulness of the Melchizedek Priesthood.[14]

Joseph's greatest anxiety prior to his death was to finish the Nauvoo Temple and there transfer the ordinances necessary to obtain a fulness of the priesthood to the Twelve. This is also from Ehat and Cook:

> Previous to his death, the prophet Joseph manifested great anxiety to see the temple completed, as most of you who were with the Church during his day, well know. "Hurry up the work, brethren," he used to say, "let us finish the temple; the Lord has a great endowment in store for you, and I am anxious that the brethren should have their endowments and

receive the fulness of the Priesthood. . . . Then," said he, "the Kingdom will be established, and I do not care what shall become of me."[15]

Does it seem overwhelming? Does it seem impossible that one as lowly as we often know ourselves to be could accomplish such an eternal thing? The only reason one might feel that way is because of the principle discussed in the proceeding chapters—which is that we don't yet believe in our own place in Zion. When someone doesn't believe they can, or even that they *should* do something, it always seems impossible. Yet, when the Holy Spirit distills the faith, personal belief, and peace that is "the call of Zion" into a soul, then the process becomes imminently possible—even when we can't possibly see how.

Joseph was addressing similarly overwhelmed Saints when he wrote:

22 Brethren, shall we not go on in so great a cause? Go forward and not backward. Courage, brethren; and on and on to victory. Let your hearts rejoice and be exceedingly glad. (D&C 128:22)

THE HOLY ORDER AND THE LATTER-DAY CHURCH

As a matter of record, we are to this day laboring under a divinely imposed condemnation for taking lightly the things which we have received.

54 And your minds in times past have been darkened because of unbelief, and because you have treated lightly the things you have received—

55 Which vanity and unbelief have brought the whole church under condemnation.

56 And this condemnation resteth upon the children of Zion, even all.

57 And they shall remain under this condemnation until they repent and remember the new covenant, even the Book of Mormon and the former commandments which I have given them, not only to say, but to do according to that which I have written—(D&C 84:54–57)

Even though this condemnation will remain until we remember the Book of Mormon, the solution isn't in reading the divine word within, but as verse 57 notes, in doing "according to that which I have written." The Book of Mormon's opening pages records Lehi having a personal visitation with God and receiving his commission to call the people of

Jerusalem to repentance. The next big account is of his son Nephi having a similar experience. The Book of Mormon is a graphic witness to the vastness of our privileges in the priesthood, of seeking the face of God, and obtaining these grand blessings, from page one onward. So, if we do as "I have written" in the Book of Mormon, we should be seeking the face of God.

In this light, could it be that our chief failure is that we have not yet taken the offered blessings of the priesthood and these profound privileges of the "greater portion of the word" seriously? And in so doing, we have yet to find ourselves within the holy order and Zion?

Why could our inability to become a Zion people be a part of this condemnation? It is because Zion was to be our greatest accomplishment as a people—and thus has the potential to become our greatest failure. As the language aptly defines, we haven't built Zion because our predecessors ("in times past") for whatever reason, failed to do so, and we in this generation are continuing to take lightly our privilege of building it. We have received the priesthood and the promises, and yet we continue in the wilderness, even while myopically proclaiming our exile habitation to be the very Zion which we were expelled from for not building.

Once again, only the living prophet can command the construction of the city and society of Zion. I completely believe that when we are ready as individuals, and when the timetable of the Lord has matured, then the Lord will speak, and only then will we build the New Jerusalem. Until then, we are only speaking of the personal quest of building Zion within our own hearts. Becoming a Zion people can only open the doors and hasten the time when the actual city will be built.

Even to the careful observer, it appears to have been thousands of years since anyone has divided the seas or performed any of these greater miracles of Enoch-like power. Since obtaining a fulness of the priesthood, Zion and the holy order are closely associated, when the holy order is at last populated, the Enochonian miracles will be plainly manifest (JST Genesis 14:30–32).

Please don't misunderstand. This is not any type of criticism of the Church. The Lord has offered us these privileges, and the ordinances necessary to claim them are performed daily. If there is any fault at all, it lies with us, the rank and file priesthood bearers and priesthood users, for not recognizing and claiming the vast privileges of the priesthood we bear.

Having said the above, it also is true that the commandment to build

Zion was withdrawn approximately 160 years ago. It is obvious that the Lord's prior anointed in this cause understood well what Zion was to be. But without the immediate command to build Zion's cities, apparently the impetus, the motivation, and perhaps even the inspiration to understand Zion has quietly slipped from our spiritual paradigm.

The hopeful theme of this whole book is that "the call of Zion" is beginning to sound again in our ears. Why believe such an astonishing idea? It is because Zion must be built before Christ will return and because we are the designated builders of Zion. Another reason for this belief is that we have all of the tools to become Zion, even though we may not realize what they are for. Still, we plainly possess them, and the order of God's House does not leave a clutter of doctrine past its expiration date—unobtainable blessings and antiquated promises—lying around.

Once again, let us carefully observe that the Church stands in its correct posture regarding Zion. Among many other things in preparation for the future building of Zion, it perpetuates the priesthood, builds the temples, and administers the holy ordinances specifically designed to bring us to Zion. All this is being done. As an organization, the Church will not begin to build the actual cities of Zion until the Lord instructs His prophet to do so. It is improbable that the Lord will instruct His prophet to build a city until a city-sized group of people are worthy to enter it. Thus, building Zion, if it is hindered in our day, would be because it is high-centered upon our own unbelief, not upon some theological or ecclesiastical misstep of the Church.

In that light, it seems quite astonishing but true that the Church has, for the moment, reached its full potential regarding Zion. What remains to be done is for a million members to awaken and claim the blessings being offered. That isn't something the Church can control or even influence more profoundly than it presently is. When we are ready and sanctified, then the Church will have something more to do regarding Zion.

Perhaps another observation needs to be made here, which is that there may already be 90 percent of the necessary sanctified souls presently prepared and worthy to enter Zion. This author has no special insight into this process or into how many are upon the highway that ends in Zion. An observation that Zion can't exist until there are worthy souls to inhabit her is not meant as a criticism of our collective righteousness, but rather as an analysis of why Zion does not presently exist. We may be almost there, or we may be almost ready to start. That insight can only be clearly seen in one's mirror.

An even larger question may be: Do we, as individuals, have the authority to pursue a personal place in Zion? For nearly two centuries most of us have left the future of Zion in the hands of the latter-day Church with no sense of personal responsibility other than faithful membership. Is it even appropriate for us to adopt a personal quest to obtain a Zion stature when the Church says little about this aspect of the latter-day Zion? Even if it is within our reach, is it within our calling and our privilege to do this? Can we just march up to the veil and purchase a seat on a bus that the Lord apparently mothballed some 160 years ago?

I believe the answer to all of these questions is a resounding yes! The first reason is that the bus to Zion was not mothballed, it was merely given a more personal destination. The second reason for so believing is that the Lord is no respecter of persons. Anyone who obeys the laws of Zion must, by divine justice, be given the blessings of Zion—"even to as many as believe on my name" (JST Genesis 14:29)—regardless of whether it is time for Zion to exist as a city or not.

But beyond any Zion-specific reasoning about our personal rights and privileges is the simple truth that all spiritual attainments, blessings and rights, are totally and completely personal. Even the most rudimentary testimony, or a bedrock belief in the existence of God, is a personal triumph. Every prophet, every priest, every righteous man or woman who obtained any blessing, whether it was in or outside of a Zion past, so obtained as a result of a personal quest.

Another reason is that even if Zion was at this very moment glowing in the millennial night, only those who have been in the presence of the Lord—which is the ultimate mortal triumph—will be allowed to enter.

The scriptures are full of examples of righteous souls who obtained their blessings of (if not in) Zion while surrounded by utter corruption, among a people to whom the Lord had certainly withdrawn the option of building Zion. Yet, they obeyed laws invisible to everyone but themselves, and in the privacy of their own quest, they obtained Zion.

Also, there is the fact that if any person comes to recognize Zion as a true principle, then that truth has distilled upon their soul by the power of the Holy Ghost. All truth comes from God. The mere fact that it *is* true and that the Holy Ghost *has* borne witness to you is prima-facie (obvious at first glance) evidence that the time of Zion has come for you personally, because divine law stipulates that the Holy Ghost cannot set you upon a path that is unobtainable (see 1 Nephi 3:7).

Beyond that, far beyond in fact, is the truth that the revealed word assures us that Zion will be built before the Messiah returns—and that we (meaning this dispensation) will build it. That alone releases the nuclear fuel in the reactor of our faith and makes Zion fully within our grasp. The revealed word pointedly promises that the pure in heart of any and all generations shall see God (Matthew 5:8) and that same class of believer is Zion (D&C 97:21).

Entering the Holy Order

JST Genesis 14:31 quoted below includes "stand in the presence of God" as a power that belongs to this higher priesthood order.

> 31 To put at defiance the armies of nations, to divide the earth, to break every band, to stand in the presence of God; to do all things according to his will, according to his command, subdue principalities and powers; and this by the will of the Son of God which was from before the foundation of the world.

Enjoying the presence of God is elsewhere clearly defined as a potential blessing that is a part of the Melchizedek Priesthood common among us today.

> 18 The power and authority of the higher, or Melchizedek Priesthood, is to hold the keys of all the spiritual blessings of the Church—
>
> 19 To have the privilege of receiving the mysteries of the kingdom of heaven, to have the heavens opened unto them, to commune with the general assembly and church of the Firstborn, and to enjoy the communion and presence of God the Father, and Jesus the mediator of the new covenant." (D&C 107:18–19)

Thus, our present Melchizedek Priesthood is the doorway to entering the holy order. Our present priesthood gives us the right and the ability to seek the presence of deity, and the holy order is a society of those who have thus obtained.

Obtaining the Melchizedek Priesthood is an ordinance performed by the laying on of mortal hands, and as we have discussed previously, entering the holy order is an ordination performed by God himself.

We have discussed the following verse at some length previously, but let us look at it again in a new light. The promise of this verse is that we may become ordained *of* God—which is viewed in this context as being an ordination by God, under His hands, and by the calling of His own voice (see JST Genesis 14:29).

> 26 He that is *ordained of God* and sent forth, the same is appointed to be the greatest, notwithstanding he is the least and the servant of all.
>
> 27 Wherefore, he is possessor of all things; for all things are subject unto him, both in heaven and on the earth, the life and the light, the Spirit and the power, sent forth by the will of the Father through Jesus Christ, his Son. (D&C 50:26–27; italics added)

By this ordination "of God," we become possessors of all things, because all things are subject unto us. The Lord personally ordained Noah and Enoch this same way, and they both possessed miraculous priesthood power.

> 19 And the Lord ordained Noah after his own order, and commanded him that he should go forth and declare his Gospel unto the children of men, even as it was given unto Enoch. (Moses 8:19)

Elder Oliver Cowdery made this powerful statement to the early apostles:

> Never cease striving until you have seen God face to face. Strengthen your faith; cast off your doubts, your sins, and all your unbelief; and nothing can prevent you from coming to God. Your ordination is not full and complete till God has laid his hand upon you. We require as much to qualify us as did those who have gone before us; God is the same. If the Savior in former days laid his hands upon his disciples, why not in latter days?[16]

Commenting upon Elder Cowdery's statement, Elder Bruce R. McConkie wrote:

> Few faithful people will stumble or feel disbelief at the doctrine here presented that the Lord's apostolic witnesses are entitled and expected to see his face, and that each one individually is obligated to "call upon him in faith in mighty prayer" until he prevails. But the Twelve are only a dozen in number. There are seldom more than fifteen men on earth at a time who have been ordained to the holy apostleship, which brings us to another statement made by Elder Cowdery in his apostolic charge: "God does not love you better or more than

others." That is, apostles and prophets do not gain precedence with the Lord unless they earn it by personal righteousness. The Lord loves people, not office holders. *Every elder is entitled to the same blessings and privileges offered the apostles. . . .* All of the elders in the kingdom are expected to live the law as strictly as do the members of the Council of the Twelve, and if they do so live, *the same blessings will come to them that flow to apostles and prophets.*[17]

This is the Second Comforter, the great personal appearance of Christ to those who enter the holy order. While in His glorious company, He will lay His hands upon our heads and ordain us to the new and grand order.

How can mortal men and women arise to an accomplishment which is so wonderful that it can only reside in the human psyche by virtue of powerfully revealed truth? The answer is supremely simple:

Begin where you are. Take the Holy Spirit for your guide. Be faithful in all things. Be as fearless and constant in obedience as you are able, constantly moving toward the light. Do this, and you will, in the due time of the Lord, arrive in His presence.

> 24 That which is of God is light; and he that receiveth light, and continueth in God, receiveth more light; and that light groweth brighter and brighter until the perfect day. (D&C 50:24)

The "perfect day" will dawn when we become perfect by the continual reception of light, which grows brighter and brighter within us until we are like unto God, purified and worthy. Then, all darkness will depart, and the pure in heart will see God. The next verse states:

> 25 And again, verily I say unto you, and I say it that you may know the truth, that you may chase darkness from among you; (D&C 50:25)

And in that purified and rarified atmosphere of light and total absence of darkness, we will be:

> 26 . . . ordained of God and sent forth, the same is appointed to be the greatest, notwithstanding he is the least and the servant of all.

> 27 Wherefore, he is possessor of all things; for all things are subject unto him, both in heaven and on the earth, the life and the light, the Spirit and the power, sent forth by the will of the Father through Jesus Christ, his Son. (D&C 50:26–27)

Such a powerful and incredible outcome to mortality! We will be changed into the Christ pattern (which is godliness), be ordained to the holy order (of Enoch and Zion), and be sent forth by the will of the Father, through Jesus Christ, His Son, to become and to build Zion.

Then in the next verse the promise of power in the priesthood is given. We shall ask whatsoever we will in the name of Jesus and it shall be done!

> 28 But no man is possessor of all things except he be purified and cleansed from all sin.
>
> 29 And if ye are purified and cleansed from all sin, ye shall ask whatsoever you will in the name of Jesus and it shall be done. (D&C 50:28–29)

And in that state of righteousness, with our hearts and souls, mind and might dedicated to Christ, with the fulness of priesthood power, as members of the holy order, as citizens and practitioners of Zion, we shall not ask amiss because we shall know the will of Christ with perfect clarity:

> 30 But know this, it shall be given you what you shall ask. (D&C 50:30)

Then, we shall have this greater priesthood power that Moses exhibited when he divided the Red Sea, which Enoch employed to move mountains and protect his people; which Christ used to walk upon the water and raise the dead, and which all the righteous of every dispensation have enjoyed when they climbed the mountain of unbelief and arrived at the face of God.

Those who do surmount this one grand priesthood precipice will become a member of an eternally elite and exclusive order of those who have been ordained under the hands of God in mortality. They will be members of the holy order after the Son of God.

Elder McConkie noted:

> It follows that the priesthood is the power, authority, and means that prepares men to see their Lord; also, that in the priesthood is found everything that is needed to bring this consummation to pass. Accordingly, it is written: "The power and authority of the higher, or Melchizedek Priesthood, is to hold the keys of all the spiritual blessings of the Church—*To have the privilege of receiving the mysteries of the kingdom of heaven, to have the heavens opened unto them, to commune with the general assembly and church of the Firstborn, and to enjoy the communion and presence of God the Father, and Jesus the mediator of the new covenant.*" (D&C 107:18-19)[18]

The holy order thus becomes a grand effect, a glorious outcome of the priesthood we presently hold, which we may seek and obtain!

> 10 And again, verily I say unto you that it is your privilege, and a prom-ise I give unto you that have been ordained unto this ministry, that inasmuch as you strip yourselves from jealousies and fears, and humble yourselves before me, for ye are not sufficiently humble, the veil shall be rent and you shall see me and know that I am—not with the carnal neither natural mind, but with the spiritual. (D&C 67:10)

The bridge between these two priesthood orders is entering into the presence of God.

Thus, all these promised blessings are but many manifestations of the same grand blessing of becoming a Zion individual. As we have detailed in the proceeding pages, these blessings are:

1) Being sealed by the Holy Spirit of Promise
2) The Second Comforter and entering the presence of God
3) Translation or some other "endowment"
4) Entering the holy order
5) Receiving fulness of the priesthood
6) Receive all the Father has
7) Membership in Zion
8) Membership in the Church of the Firstborn
9) Membership in the Church of Enoch and Order of Enoch
10) Becoming priests and kings of the Most High

Such are the unfathomable blessings of our priesthood.

This glorious transition from our present calling in the kingdom into the holy order is much more deliberate and demanding than the transition from elder to high priest might be presently perceived. It is not a natural progression that one simply waits until maturity or some other natural trigger moves us on. Obtaining ordination under the hands of God into the holy order is a blessing that we must actually be holy to obtain.

Obtaining the holy order is not the by-product of long and faith-ful service alone. It is the result of specifically seeing this grand promise through the lens of revealed truth as the destiny and promise of your life, and in a series of inspired strides that never waver, to allow the Master Sculpture to reshape our lives into purity and holiness. Obtaining the holy order is a result of an inspired decision, of a diamond-hard determi-nation to lay anything and everything that is required upon the altar.

It bears being said that such a pursuit will not be the desire of every heart nor the ordained pathway for every soul. It is not normally required of mankind to be a member of the holy order, Zion, or to be translated to enter the celestial kingdom, or to receive the highest exaltation available to mortals. We must, however, obtain the fulness of the priesthood in this life or the next in order to be exalted. Joseph Fielding Smith taught: "There is no exaltation in the kingdom of God without the fulness of priesthood."[19]

Since the fulness of the priesthood, the holy order, and Zion are closely associated, it becomes obvious that we will at some point pass through this degree of worthiness on our way to the celestial kingdom. The question is whether we do it in this life, thus obtaining the blessings of Zion, or wait until the next, and miss being a part of these glorious mortal privileges and being a builder of Zion.

As a people these blessings are required to enable us to build Zion. If as an individual it is our foreordained duty to be a part of the latter-day Zion, then we cannot expect to be exalted without accomplishing this great labor. It is a grand personal epiphany when one hears the voice of revelation issue the call of Zion and to thereafter know that they are ordained to be a part of the building of Zion. But not every righteous soul is ordained to this path, and not every celestial soul will hear the call.

Blessed are you if your ordained pathway crosses other thorny ground or ends in some other real estate than Zion. But in my humble opinion, far more blessed are those whose feet fall upon the holy soil of Zion and whose destiny it is to engage and conquer in this, the greatest endeavor mankind will ever undertake; to build the City of the Living God, end the telestial world, receive the conquering Christ at His return, and invite the millennial era of peace to begin.

It is also worth observing that entering the divine presence is a right belonging to the priesthood we hold, and it is a privilege that will amplify our blessings, add to our exaltation hereafter, and most probably gain us eternal blessings and divine advantages that will bless us forever.

> 18 Whatever principle of intelligence we attain unto in this life, it will rise with us in the resurrection.
>
> 19 And if a person gains more knowledge and intelligence in this life through his diligence and obedience than another, he will have so much the advantage in the world to come. (D&C 130:18–19)

Even though entire cities have been ushered into the presence of Christ and hundreds of years have passed where translation was the rule rather than the exception within them, it is probably a true statement that relatively few people have, in the history of the world, obtained this grand outcome in their lives. But it is also undeniable that God has placed upon our shoulders, the stewards of the latter-days, the requirement to build Zion before Christ will return in glory; and Zion will consist of literally hundreds of thousands of men and women who have seen God and entered His holy order. From their midst 144,000 missionaries will depart. We can only assume this missionary army will not be the entire citizenry of Zion but a mere fraction of it.

None of us can look around with clear vision and not see the horror and depravity of our world, nor can we mistake the signs that define the times in which we live. Nobody can say with certainty when the end will come, but we can say with absolute certainty that there have never been greater signs than today, and that they will continue to escalate in gut-wrenching intensity until we humble ourselves, build Zion, and receive our Messiah.

THE RIGHTS OF THE PRIESTHOOD AND ZION

Verses 33 and 34 of section 84, which we have considered thus far, constitute the oath and covenant of the priesthood in its entirety. Beginning in verse 35 we read a description of the blessings that flow therefrom.

35 And also all they who receive this priesthood receive me, saith the Lord;

36 For he that receiveth my servants receiveth me;

37 And he that receiveth me receiveth my Father;

38 And he that receiveth my Father receiveth my Father's kingdom; therefore all that my Father hath shall be given unto him. (D&C 84:35–38)

Now we come to the truly grand promises and the glorious "rights" of the priesthood, that through the oath and covenant of the priesthood we may have free association with the Son, receive the Father, receive His kingdom, and ultimately receive all that the Father has.

Let us not twist the meaning of this diadem of truth by mentally inserting death or resurrection into the timetable. We are not discussing the eternities nor the events after this life. The grand endowment of the oath and covenant of the priesthood is to be enjoyed in this life.

It is also undeniably true that these blessings do come to righteous people in the eternal worlds. But the language of these promises clearly makes them presently and powerfully available now, to be enjoyed in the day of mortality.

In all the passages of scripture wherein men and women are promised that they can see the Lord, nowhere is it even hinted that we must first die to do so. In fact, every instance in the scriptures I can recall of man having an interview with God occurred to a mortal person. We have no record of a post-mortal visitation of this type. Why would there be? The scriptures are written for the benefit and guidance of mortals. Whatever occurs after death requires no warning, no instruction from scriptures. It just happens however it happens. Our preparations for that event are the life we live here, and no further instruction is given or needed. The scriptures are largely silent on what we must do following death. It details some things that will occur, but says little or nothing of what we must do in that world. The sacred word is instruction for the living in mortality.

What we must prepare to accomplish is this grand promise in mortality. This is the focus of the scriptures, the burden of the teachings of the prophets, and the nexus (the center or focal point; that which connects all other points of the entire gospel) to which all other doctrines point. It is the zenith, the highest obtainable outcome of our faith in God, the pattern of the temple, and the greatest possible outcome in mortality.

It boggles the mind, then, that this principle is so obscure in our minds, and yet it is plainly manifest in the scriptures. The scriptures everywhere attest to this one grand thing—that mortal men and women can be, have been, and are invited into the presence of deity. We just read the associated statements and exclude ourselves by a trick of the mind (unbelief). We mentally insert some fine print that ultimately excludes us personally. We may confuse ourselves by thinking it applies to an event after this life when all mankind will see God to be judged of Him. We may conclude that it isn't something we personally can obtain in this life, or that we even should. We may silently conclude we've already sinned too much to even hope for such a thing. Or—far worse—we may simply not believe, no matter how voluminous the evidence, because it just stretches the fabric of our belief beyond its inherent strength.

Perhaps we just don't prayerfully study the scriptures where these lofty truths are enshrined, relying instead upon well-meaning teachers who themselves may not fully understand this message within the holy word. Or, it may be that when a teacher comes to understand these truths, they are not permitted by the Holy Spirit to speak them aloud with much clarity because such truths are only to be known via personal revelation.

Alma taught:

> 19 And now Alma began to expound these things unto him, saying: It is given unto many to know the mysteries of God; nevertheless they are laid under a strict command that they shall not impart only according to the portion of his word which he doth grant unto the children of men, according to the heed and diligence which they give unto him. (Alma 12:9)

Another issue stopping us could be that we're content with the lifestyle of the priesthood and the palpable blessings that flow from Church membership and are not aware of anything greater offered to us. We feel secure in what we "know" and content with where we are. Such an attitude is in fact a form of damnation, meaning that it stops our progress.

> 21 And others will he pacify, and lull them away into carnal security, that they will say: All is well in Zion; yea, Zion prospereth, all is well—and thus the devil cheateth their souls, and leadeth them away carefully down to hell. (2 Nephi 28:21)

ALL IS WELL IN ZION

It is stunning that this prophecy states that we will say, "All is well in Zion; yea, Zion prospereth," because Zion in its pre-millennial format does not actually exist at this time. We refer to ourselves as Zion when speaking rhetorically, because we hope to become so; but we must never forget that, even though we have begun the preparatory work of Zion, the society of Zion—the city of the Living God—does not exist in this day.

If this truly were Zion, then all *would* be well, and no cheating of souls could occur. However, mistaking our present society for Zion, contenting ourselves with believing there is nothing further to accomplish, and thinking all is well while living under that error, truly would lead us away carefully down to hell.

Church membership for the purpose of enjoying the society of the

Saints and participating in the works and ways of Church might be likened to the student who enrolls in college, signs up for a heavy load, and proceeds with the process of education with determination. He does so simply because he believes in college yet has never glimpsed the purpose of his education, which is that eventually he must graduate from his classes, declare a life profession, and use his education as a springboard into a real life. Without a concept of what the greater purpose of college is, the process of education becomes a purpose unto itself. The process, society, and fellowship of college life becomes life rather than a gateway to something far greater.

As odd as it may sound, Church membership could devolve into something like this. It could become a way of life, with no concept in our hearts of where it is designed to take us.

The purpose of the priesthood isn't just possession of the priesthood. The purpose of the priesthood isn't even the ordinances and offices and ordinations we perform. These are the *processes* of the priesthood. The purpose of the priesthood is to prepare mankind to see God—in this life! Everything we labor to accomplish is done to that end, even when we don't have that objective in mind.

It bears remembering that there is only one gospel in operation. It has taken different forms in different dispensations because of our worthiness, or lack thereof, but it is the same gospel. We know by study of others who have been so privileged to be invited into divine company that several things always happen. This is the pattern recorded in scripture.

The Pattern of Seeing God

When the prophets of old were ushered into the presence of God they were also shown a vision of all the workmanship of the Lord's hands. This vision often includes the grand events of earth's history. Moses saw this vision and penned the book of Genesis. Every prophet who records his personal experience with the Lord in any detail includes seeing a sweeping vision of his future ministry, and quite often, of the entire history of the world, sometimes of the whole workmanship of God's hands. Many of the Old Testament prophets saw this grand vision: Isaiah, Jeremiah, Abraham and Enoch, to name a few. John the Beloved recorded a portion of his vision in the book of Revelation. Lehi saw and mentioned his vision. Nephi, inspired by his father's account, saw and recorded parts of his vision in First Nephi. The brother of Jared saw the vision and wrote what is now the sealed portion of the Book of Mormon, purportedly the greatest literary work ever written. Mormon saw our day. Moroni wrote to us with prophetic vision because he saw and knew us intimately. Joseph Smith recorded parts of his vision in Section 76.

This vision is typified in today's temple experience. Since the actual endowment event begins with a vision of the creation of the earth, the temple ordinance prefiguring that same event also begins in this way.

Another consistent element of this divine interview is that we are taught and spiritually edified, given knowledge that always eclipses what can be known by common man. Such knowledge was given to many notables, such as Adam, Abraham, Moses, Daniel, Elijah, and John the Baptist. In fact, since there is only one gospel—we may safely surmise that it was given to all of the great patriarchs who entered the divine presence.

This grand vision is prefigured in this promise:

> 7 And to them will I reveal all mysteries, yea, all the hidden mysteries of my kingdom from days of old, and for ages to come, will I make known unto them the good pleasure of my will concerning all things pertaining to my kingdom.

> 8 Yea, even the wonders of eternity shall they know, and things to come will I show them, even the things of many generations.

> 9 And their wisdom shall be great, and their understanding reach to heaven; and before them the wisdom of the wise shall perish, and the understanding of the prudent shall come to naught.

> 10 For by my Spirit will I enlighten them, and by my power will I make known unto them the secrets of my will—yea, even those things which eye has not seen, nor ear heard, nor yet entered into the heart of man. (D&C 76:7–10)

During our interview with Christ we will be offered the chance to request some divine gift, which is our actual endowment. Even though the temple ordinance is called the endowment, it would be more correct to say it is a temple ordinance that teaches of, instructs in the laws governing, and prefigures this actual endowment. The actual endowment is a gift received from the Lord.

In some cases we are told what the righteous have requested of the Lord. In other cases we can surmise by the events of their lives what they requested. The pattern is that once the request is made, the Lord grants it and often much more.

The Three Nephites experienced it this way:

4 And when he had spoken unto them, he turned himself unto the three, and said unto them: What will ye that I should do unto you, when I am gone unto the Father?

5 And they sorrowed in their hearts, for they durst not speak unto him the thing which they desired.

6 And he said unto them: Behold, I know your thoughts, and ye have desired the thing which John, my beloved, who was with me in my ministry, before that I was lifted up by the Jews, desired of me.

7 Therefore, more blessed are ye, for ye shall never taste of death; but ye shall live to behold all the doings of the Father unto the children of men, even until all things shall be fulfilled according to the will of the Father, when I shall come in my glory with the powers of heaven. . . .

10 And for this cause ye shall have fulness of joy; and ye shall sit down in the kingdom of my Father; yea, your joy shall be full, even as the Father hath given me fulness of joy; and ye shall be even as I am, and I am even as the Father; and the Father and I are one; (3 Nephi 28:4–7, 10)

Last, during our divine audience, we are ordained of God and sent forth on a task of eternal consequence. All of the great spiritual giants in history obtained their divine commission in this way. If it is our inspired wish to become like Enoch, then we need but sanctify ourselves to enter the divine presence, and ask.

29 Therefore, ask, and ye shall receive; knock, and it shall be opened unto you; for he that asketh, receiveth; and unto him that knocketh, it shall be opened. (3 Nephi 27:29)

Those who have experienced the temple will hear sweet harmonies in the above quote.

We thus receive the greater gifts, which may include translation, the power to create, power over the elements, power to walk upon the waters, to calm the seas, raise the dead, restore lost limbs and sight. We receive whatever we righteously request, and power over all things in heaven and on earth. We will be sent forth by the will of the Father, through Jesus Christ, His Son.

When the glorious day comes that you and I stand in the presence of the Lord, this same divinely ordained and orchestrated event will again unfold.

Consider the following verse in this light.

26 He that is ordained of God and sent forth, the same is appointed to be the greatest, notwithstanding he is the least and the servant of all.

27 Wherefore, he is possessor of all things; for all things are subject unto him, both in heaven and on the earth, the life and the light, the Spirit and the power, sent forth by the will of the Father through Jesus Christ, his Son.

28 But no man is possessor of all things except he be purified and cleansed from all sin.

29 And if ye are purified and cleansed from all sin, ye shall ask whatsoever you will in the name of Jesus and it shall be done. (D&C 50:26–29)

These words in Section 50 are a true mystery of godliness and are only understandable in the light of this grand outcome of righteous priesthood. Read them carefully and see in them the translated gifts that are promised. Note that in this life we are ordained by men with authority from God. But the only way to be ordained of God is to be in the presence of God. The preposition *of* is used in this setting to indicate the person performing the action.

If we incorrectly interpret this verse to mean those who are ordained of God to be the priesthood ordinations under the hands of authorized mortals, we create a logical conundrum of titanic proportions. If this is a mortal ordination being referenced above, then those so ordained must be possessors of all things, with all things being subject unto them in heaven and on earth. We don't appear to be exhibiting this degree of priesthood power, and since the Church *is* true, it can't be referring to the ordinations which we all experience in the course of the gospel today.

However, when understood as described above, that this ordination is under the hands of God Himself, then there is vast evidence for this statement being true throughout history. These gloriously blessed souls did possess the stated powers, did work mighty miracles, and did have authority in heaven and on the earth.

Our challenge, our privilege, is to rise to the same "rights" our fore-bearers in the priesthood rose to in their lives.

In the following quotation we again find the same grand promises of the priesthood as in Section 50. Notice the tense of the verbs. Promised blessings in mortality are described as: "These are they who are. . ."—present tense. Each time the scripture says "are," this incredible promise applies to this life! The future promises of eternal glory read "These shall . . ."

> 52 That by keeping the commandments they might be washed and cleansed from all their sins, and receive the Holy Spirit by the laying on of the hands of him who is ordained and sealed unto this power. (D&C 76:52)

Notice that verse 52 is speaking of being cleansed from all their sins, the same as in 50:29. We are speaking of a full application of the Atonement, of being made pure and worthy to enter into the presence of God.

> 53 And who overcome by faith, and are sealed by the Holy Spirit of promise, which the Father sheds forth upon all those who are just and true.
>
> 54 They are they who are the Church of the Firstborn.
>
> 55 They are they into whose hands the Father has given all things—

Note the similarity to Section 50:27 quoted above. Recall that to become a member of the Church of the Firstborn, one must enter the Divine Presence. They are they whom the "Father *has* given all things."

> 56 They are they who are priests and kings, who have received of his fulness, and of his glory;

As we already discussed, being a priest and being a king are two different callings. The sublime message is that they have been in His presence and received of God's fulness and glory.

> 57 And are priests of the Most High, after the order of Melchizedek, which was after the order of Enoch, which was after the order of the Only Begotten Son.

The divine order of this priesthood is after the order of Christ, Enoch and Melchizedek, and possesses the power and privileges of translation.

> 58 Wherefore, as it is written, they are gods, even the sons of God—
>
> 59 Wherefore, all things are theirs, whether life or death, or things present, or things to come, all are theirs and they are Christ's, and Christ is God's. (D&C 76:58–59)

They are gods! Notice the small "g." They are gods, possessing "godliness," yet they are not Gods. We are speaking of a state of godliness, as may be achieved prior to the eternal world, in this life. This suggests vast powers and "rights." All things are theirs. Consider the possibility that if one has the power to create anything one needs or righteously desires, you truly have "all things" at your fingertips. The power to see into the past and the future is ours, and we are Christ's, for it is by Him and His Atonement that all this flows to us.

Notice now that the next few verses speak of future blessings.

60 And they shall overcome all things.

In other words, they have not *yet* overcome all things, including death. Death is only postponed with translation. It is overcome by resurrection. Verse 60 is placing the receipt of these godlike blessings once again prior to mortal death and the resurrection.

Now we enumerate the future blessings these specially endowed ones "shall" enjoy in the future.

61 Wherefore, let no man glory in man, but rather let him glory in God, who shall subdue all enemies under his feet.

62 These shall dwell in the presence of God and his Christ forever and ever.

63 These are they whom he shall bring with him, when he shall come in the clouds of heaven to reign on the earth over his people.

These promised Zion-like blessings precede the glorious Second Coming, because he shall bring them with Him when he returns to reign over the earth. There can be no misinterpreting of the timetable here.

64 These are they who shall have part in the first resurrection.

65 These are they who shall come forth in the resurrection of the just.

And, as we read above, these blessings all precede the resurrection.

Now we return to the present blessings. Mount Zion is the city of the Living God. It is a place where Zion-dwellers may come and go, the heavenly place, the holiest of all. Mount Zion in the pre-millennial day will be the city of Zion. Prior to the construction of that city, Mount Zion is the city and Church of Enoch, as verse 67 suggests.

66 These are they who are come unto Mount Zion, and unto the city of the living God, the heavenly place, the holiest of all.

67 These are they who have come to an innumerable company of angels, to the general assembly and church of Enoch, and of the Firstborn.

Verse 67 is a description of the types of beings in the city of the living God. The angels are those without bodies, either unborn or the righteous dead. The Church of Enoch is the grand assembly of those who are translated, and the Church of the Firstborn are those for whom the blood of Christ has wrought its fullest blessings—those who have washed their garments in the blood of the lamb and become pure and holy, and entered into His presence—in mortality! In other words, the "city of the living God" is in part, populated by mortals.

68 These are they whose names are written in heaven, where God and Christ are the judge of all.

Again—present day blessings.

69 These are they who are just men [mortals] made perfect [translated to godliness] through Jesus the mediator of the new covenant, who wrought out this perfect Atonement through the shedding of his own blood.

70 These are they whose bodies are [not will be, but are] celestial, whose glory is that of the sun, even the glory of God, the highest of all, whose glory the sun of the firmament is written of as being typical. (D&C 76:52–70; bracketed comments added)

Please note again that these events are pre-resurrection. So, we are not speaking here of resurrected bodies. Yet, we are taught that their bodies are celestial, meaning that they have been changed in mortality to be able to endure the divine presence. These verses can't be speaking of the celestial kingdom, because these things happen before the Millennium. They appear to be calling translated bodies "celestial" since they have been in the fulness of Christ's glory and can from that time on endure the glory and presence of God.

Also observe how powerfully this next oft-quoted verse dovetails with the power of the promises of the oath and covenant of the priesthood:

59 That by reason of transgression cometh the fall, which fall bringeth death, and inasmuch as ye were born into the world by water, and blood, and the spirit, which I have made, and so became of dust a living soul, even so ye must be born again into the kingdom of heaven, of water, and of the Spirit, and be cleansed by blood, even the blood of

mine Only Begotten; that ye might be sanctified from all sin, and enjoy the words of eternal life in this world, and eternal life in the world to come, even immortal glory. (Moses 6:59)

So, we are to be sanctified from all sin and enjoy the words of eternal life *in this world*. It is my opinion that the words of eternal life are when the Father utters the more sure word of prophecy and gives notice that our place in the kingdom is made sure. Along with this earthly promise comes the assurance of eternal life, even immortal glory.

> 60 For by the water ye keep the commandment; by the Spirit ye are justified, and by the blood ye are sanctified. (Moses 6:60)

Baptism in water is an unalterable commandment. The Spirit justifies and delivers promised blessings when the applicant is finally ready, perhaps even many years after the ordinance. The blood of Christ is the agent of purification and sanctification. However, this verse is saying far more than the obvious.

It is easiest to understand the meaning of verse 60 by examining verse 61. The fact that further explanation is being offered for being justified by the Spirit and sanctified by the blood in the next verse is indicated by "therefore," which informs us that because we have been sanctified, now these additional things are also ours to claim:

> 61. Therefore it is given to abide in you; the record of heaven; the Comforter; the peaceable things of immortal glory; the truth of all things; that which quickeneth all things, which maketh alive all things; that which knoweth all things, and hath all power according to wisdom, mercy, truth, justice, and judgment. (Moses 6:61)

Verse 61 is describing the effect of verse 60. All of these descriptions add to our understanding of what happened when we were "sanctified." What is being described is a series of events that flow from the glorious but not uncommon events of baptism, justification, and sanctification.

The record of heaven refers to having your name written in heaven as one entitled to enter after your labors are completed. It is to have your calling and election made sure. It is also described in D&C 88:2–4, quoted below as being "another comforter . . . even the Holy Spirit of promise." This comforter is the promise of eternal life, which from that time onward abides in you, or becomes your constant companion.

2 Behold, this is pleasing unto your Lord, and the angels rejoice over you; the alms of your prayers have come up into the ears of the Lord of Sabaoth, and are recorded in the book of the names of the sanctified, even them of the celestial world.

3 Wherefore, I now send upon you *another Comforter,* even upon you my friends, that it may abide in your hearts, even the Holy Spirit of promise; which other Comforter is the same that I promised unto my disciples, as is recorded in the testimony of John.

4 *This Comforter is the promise which I give unto you of eternal life, even the glory of the celestial kingdom.*

Then, back to Moses 6, where verse 61 informs us that additionally we receive "the peaceable things of immortal glory." Bearing in mind that these glorious gifts occur in this life, while we are mortals, then this phrase refers to immortal glory during mortality. D&C 76:58 described this condition as being gods—with a small "g." In other words, through these promised gifts we enter into a state of peace and immortal glory (since we can't die we are immortal), yet we continue to dwell in mortality. This is the very definition of the translated state. These scriptural gems are only understandable when viewed through the lens of translation. There is ample evidence that this promise of peace is part of the divine pattern and is often referred to as "entering into the rest of the Lord."

ENTERING INTO THE REST OF THE LORD

12 Now they, after being sanctified by the Holy Ghost, having their garments made white, being pure and spotless before God, could not look upon sin save it were with abhorrence; and there were many, exceedingly great many, who were made pure and entered into the rest of the Lord their God. (Alma 13:12)

Notice how the above reference combines being sanctified and becoming pure and spotless with entering into the "rest of the Lord"? Again and again we must remind ourselves that there is only one gospel. The result of being sanctified is always the same, even when slightly different language emphasizes different points.

There is a grand connection between entering into the rest of the Lord and the establishment of Zion, both as a personal triumph and as a city. Zion will be built upon laws that supersede the laws of opposition and will literally be "the rest of the Lord."

Hyrum Andrus described it this way:

> A direct correlation is made in the Pearl of Great Price between the program of the Lord that was carried out before the flood and that which is designed to be accomplished in the last days. In that early day, a prophet was sent in the person of Enoch, with a special commission to fulfill the Lord's purposes; *the righteous were gathered and taught the law of Zion; having been sanctified, they entered into the rest of the Lord,* and their city was translated; and, finally, the wicked were destroyed. Similarly, in the latter days a prophet has been sent in the person of Joseph Smith, and through him a program of gathering the elect has been instituted. *Zion is to be built up according to the heavenly pattern and design, and in this way the Saints are to be sanctified and enter into the Lord's rest.* At the coming of Christ in glory, the latter-day Zion is to be caught up to meet Him in the clouds. Finally, the wicked are to be destroyed, this time by an envelopment of the earth in fire—the fiery floods of glory that are then manifest.
>
> This indicates that before Christ comes in glory in the clouds of heaven, the Saints in the latter days must attain the same standard of spiritual truth and power that Enoch and his people did. Having referred to the fact that many righteous men in former times sought, through the Gospel, to return the earth to its paradisiacal glory and failed, Joseph Smith said: "But they prophesied of a day when this glory would be revealed. Paul spoke of the dispensation of the fulness of times, when God would gather together all things in one." Not only did the righteous of the earth in subsequent ages idealize Enoch's city, but *they looked forward in faith to the day when that same standard of spiritual excellence would be established upon the earth and spread over the whole sphere. That day would be in the last dispensation.*[20]

There is only one gospel, so if the gospel Enoch loved took him to a state of perfect peace and safety, and in fact, of "rest" in the presence of the Lord, then that is where our gospel is taking us if we allow it. The confluence, or the point at which these two principles of personal revelation and the godly mysteries merge, is receiving the peaceable things (entering into the rest of the Lord), for nothing brings greater peace in this life.

> 62 If thou shalt ask, thou shalt receive revelation upon revelation, knowledge upon knowledge, that thou mayest know the mysteries and peaceable things—that which bringeth joy, that which bringeth life eternal. (D&C 42:61)

Now combine this peace, this entering into the rest of the Lord with the words "peaceable things of immortal glory," and again the unspeakable promise of translation whispers in our souls almost unnoticed and unsung.

What peace might distill upon your soul when you suddenly realize that the laws of mortality no longer bind you, that temptation no longer reaches you, that death, pain, sickness, and even sadness cannot afflict you; that by your inspired word illness is healed, death is rebuked, that all elements of mortality must obey your words, and you have become the greatest among ordinary mortals and the servant of all? Such peace surely would be entering into a state of rest that surpasses the ability of mortal man to comprehend.

Alma indelibly placed entering into the rest of the Lord with the promised blessings of righteous priesthood when he concluded:

> 13 And now, my brethren, I would that ye should humble yourselves before God, and bring forth fruit meet for repentance, that ye may also enter into that rest. (Alma 13:13)

THE TRUTH OF ALL THINGS

The last great gift in Moses 6:61 is "the truth of all things." There is only one source of all truth. Christ describes himself as "the Spirit of truth."

> 11 And I, John, bear record that I beheld his glory, as the glory of the Only Begotten of the Father, full of grace and truth, even the Spirit of truth, which came and dwelt in the flesh, and dwelt among us. (D&C 93:11)

What follows in Moses 6:61 is further description of what the Lord means by "the truth of all things." He further describes it as "that which quickeneth all things, which maketh alive all things; that which knoweth all things, and hath all power according to wisdom, mercy, truth, justice, and judgment." Even though this may appear to be a description of the Holy Ghost, it is not.

This is a description of Jesus Christ himself. What this verse promises is that which will come and abide in us is Jesus Christ himself. It is Christ that quickeneth all things and makes all things alive. Christ knows all things and is the perfect embodiment of wisdom, mercy, truth, and judgment. Furthermore, it is Christ and He alone who will judge all mankind.

But can Christ actually abide in us? Listen with new ears to the promises of Christ as recorded by John.

20 Neither pray I for these alone, but for them also which shall believe on me through their word;

21 That they all may be one; as thou, Father, art in me, and I in thee, *that they also may be one in us*: that the world may believe that thou hast sent me.

22 And the glory which thou gavest me I have given them; that they may be one, even as we are one:

23 *I in them*, and thou in me, that they may be made perfect in one; and that the world may know that thou hast sent me, and hast loved them, as thou hast loved me.

24 Father, I will that they also, whom thou hast given me, be with me where I am; that they may behold my glory, which thou hast given me. (John 17:20–24; italics added)

When someone becomes one with Christ, the Master comes and abides in us. We become one as Christ and His Father are one, and in so doing, we inherit all the Father has. This fulfills the promises of Moses 6:61, which is, among other things, that we will know "all things, and [have] all power according to wisdom, mercy, truth, justice, and judgment."

We become one with Christ in the same process whereby Christ became one with His Father. Christ obeyed His Father in all things, even to laying down His life. Through this process the Father began to dwell *in* Him, and Christ partook of the perfections of the Father, thus making him perfect. In a similar process, we hear Christ's voice and do all that revelation sends us to do and say and be. In becoming one with Christ, we become like Christ and take upon ourselves His perfections, His grace, and His love. Christ's will becomes our will and, perhaps more difficult to understand, our will becomes Christ's. We become one with Him, filled with His love, not overpowered and dominated by Him. We become consumed in Christ, not by Him.

Elder F. Enzio Busche described it this way:

This is the place where we suddenly see the heavens open as we feel the full impact of the love of our Heavenly Father, which fills us with indescribable joy. With this fulfillment of love in our hearts, we will never be happy anymore just by being ourselves or living our own lives. We will not be satisfied until we have surrendered our lives into the arms of the loving Christ, and until He has become the doer of all our deeds and He has become the speaker of all our words.[21]

A few verses previous to the ones we have been considering in Moses 6, we find the Lord promising all these blessings to Adam if he would turn unto Christ and hearken to His voice.

> 52 And he also said unto him: If thou wilt turn unto me, and hearken unto my voice, and believe, and repent of all thy transgressions, and be baptized, even in water, in the name of mine Only Begotten Son, who is full of grace and truth, which is Jesus Christ, the only name which shall be given under heaven, whereby salvation shall come unto the children of men, ye shall receive the gift of the Holy Ghost, asking all things in his name, and whatsoever ye shall ask, it shall be given you. (Moses 6:52)

That same promise is renewed in our day.

> 6 And even so will I gather mine elect from the four quarters of the earth, even as many as will believe in me, and hearken unto my voice. (D&C 33:6)

Of course, the "elect" are those who will inherit all the promised blessings of the priesthood.

So, returning to Moses 6:60–61, the promise is that through justification by the Spirit and sanctification by the blood of Christ, we may:

1) Have the constant companionship of the Holy Ghost
2) Have our calling and election made sure
3) Have a personal appearance and companionship of the Lord Jesus Christ
4) Be translated or some other gift
5) We may enter into the "rest of the Lord," which is the fulness of His glory
6) And, as a direct result of these glorious gifts being "given to abide in you," we will become one with Christ,
7) And because He dwells in us, we will possess the truth of all things
8) Have power to quicken and make alive all things (power over life and death)

9) Have knowledge of all things
10) Have all power as governed by wisdom, mercy, truth, justice and judgment

We can add to this list of marvelous gifts these additional glories listed earlier:

11) Sealed by the Holy Spirit of promise
12) The Second Comforter and enter into the presence of God
13) Translation
14) Enter the holy order
15) Receive full power in the priesthood
16) Receive all the Father has
17) Membership in Zion
18) Membership in the Church of the Firstborn
19) Membership in the Church of Enoch
20) Become Priests and Kings of the Most High

Notice how fitly joined this list is with D&C 76:52–70 and D&C 50:26, which we have quoted above.

Not only is this the promise we enjoy, but as verse 62 so beautifully states below, it is also the plan of salvation unto all mankind, in all ages. There is only one gospel and it is unchanging. It is the pattern that Adam followed to his exaltation, and thus may all become the sons and daughters of God.

> 62 And now, behold, I say unto you: This is the plan of salvation unto all men, through the blood of mine Only Begotten, who shall come in the meridian of time.
>
> 65 And thus he [Adam] was baptized, and the Spirit of God descended upon him, and thus he was born of the Spirit, and became quickened in the inner man.
>
> 66 And he heard a voice out of heaven, saying: Thou art baptized with fire, and with the Holy Ghost. This is the record of the Father, and the Son, from henceforth and forever;
>
> 67 And thou art after the order of him who was without beginning of days or end of years, from all eternity to all eternity.
>
> 68 Behold, thou art one in me, a son of God; and thus may all become my sons. Amen. (Moses 6:62, 65–68; bracketed comment added)

Why Should I Even Try?

It is understandable that a deep discussion of the oath and covenant of the priesthood, Zion, translation, or any other lofty principle will give rise to more questions that it answers. Most of these questions will of necessity be answered to each individual by the Holy Spirit as they seek and find their place in the grand plan of the eternities.

One question worth considering together is, "Why?" Why should we move ourselves into such a pursuit, such a life-altering and potentially life-disturbing quest?

The answer is that the price for eternal glory is fixed. The pathway is one, not many. Abraham paid a certain price, and we will pay the same price, though tailored for our needs and our mission in life. If we expect to emerge through the flames into glory, we will sooner or later find ourselves at last upon that path, not some other. As observed earlier, Zion worthiness is but a stepping stone to celestial worthiness. At some point, either in this life or the next, we will be worthy of all things associated with Zion on our way to the higher requirements of celestial reward. Thus it becomes a matter of common sense that sooner is better—better because we never know how long our lives may be, or when we may be called to circumstances of life that may make this, the greatest quest, harder or impossible. Sooner is better because we arrive at the unthinkably grand blessings in this life instead of delaying them into the next where certain mortal blessings (like teaching our children and grandchildren, translation, and helping build Zion) cannot be bestowed even when we have arrived at the requisite righteousness.

And, sooner is better because we—you and I—are the designated dispensation to bring forth Zion. There is no other. Joseph Smith proclaimed:

> The building up of Zion is a cause that has interested the people of God in every age; it is a theme upon which prophets, priests and kings have dwelt with peculiar delight; they have looked forward with joyful anticipation to the day in which we live; and fired with heavenly and joyful anticipations they have sung and written and prophesied of this our day; but they died without the sight.
>
> *We are the favored people that God has made choice of to bring about the Latter-day glory*; it is left for us to see, participate in and help to roll forward the Latter-day glory, "the dispensation of the fulness of times,

when God will gather together all things that are in heaven, and all things that are upon the earth," even in one.[22]

And last, if we don't do it—it will not be done in this dispensation. If we fail to bring forth Zion, God has decreed that He will take the fulness of His gospel away and give it to another.

> 16 And thus commandeth the Father that I should say unto you: At that day when the Gentiles shall sin against my gospel, and shall reject the fulness of my gospel, and shall be lifted up in the pride of their hearts above all nations, and above all the people of the whole earth, and shall be filled with all manner of lyings, and of deceits, and of mischiefs, and all manner of hypocrisy, and murders, and priestcrafts, and whoredoms, and of secret abominations; and if they shall do all those things, and shall reject the fulness of my gospel, behold, saith the Father, I will bring the fulness of my gospel from among them. (3 Nephi 16:10)

One may question whether this unrighteous group of people is actually Church members or just people in general. The Church has always existed among evil people who do the things listed above, yet as long as His people were faithful, God did not threaten to limit their access to the greater blessings. Only when His people became corrupt did He withdraw blessings. It is unthinkable that the general wickedness of mankind could cause God to take the fulness of the gospel away when within the Church sweeping righteousness prevails.

A flawed argument would propose that these Gentiles referenced above are Christians at large, not members of the restored gospel. The error in that thinking is that our friends in the cause of Christ can only see that portion of the gospel which is visible to the world, and therefore cannot intelligently reject a "fullness" of which they are unaware. We "gentiles," however, possess the fullness of the gospel whether we are aware of its true nature or not. We are the only people on earth who could actually reject the fullness, whether it be by innocent ignorance, through fear, or reluctance.

As we have observed before, the rejection isn't of the whole gospel plan, it is of the "fulness of my gospel." In other words, even though we do embrace a portion of the word, we must not reject the fulness, which would bring us into the presence of the Master and enable us to at last build Zion.

FULNESS OF THE GOSPEL

The "fulness of the gospel" is a phrase found in scripture. Since the warning is that if we, "the gentiles," reject the fulness of the gospel it shall be taken away from us, let us consider what the phrase means.

Joseph Smith taught that the Book of Mormon contains the fulness of the gospel (D&C 20:9, 27:5, 35:12 and 17, 42:12). Yet, there are many principles that we presently believe and practice that are not taught in the Book of Mormon. Among these are temple covenants, baptism for the dead, salvation for the dead, eternal marriage, the three degrees of glory, and several others. Clearly, the "fulness of the gospel" can exist without these apparently missing doctrines.

Elder McConkie makes this observation:

> The fulness of the gospel consists in those laws, doctrines, ordinances, powers, and authorities needed to enable men to gain the fulness of salvation. Those who have the gospel fulness do not necessarily enjoy the fulness of gospel knowledge or understand all of the doctrines of the plan of salvation. But they do have the fulness of the priesthood and sealing power by which men can be sealed up unto eternal life. The fulness of the gospel grows out of the fulness of the sealing power and not out of the fulness of gospel knowledge.[23]

The fulness does not flow from knowledge of gospel principles, thus explaining how the Nephite faithful could have the fulness, yet apparently not understand, or at least record their understanding of the principles noted above. The fulness of the gospel grows out of the "fulness of the sealing power."

Here is another term to ponder: the "fulness of the sealing power." We understand what the sealing powers are that Elijah restored to Joseph Smith in April of 1836 (D&C 110). They include the following:

- Sealing power[24]
- Power to perform temple ordinances[25]
- Power to perform eternal marriage[26]
- Keys necessary to perform work for the dead[27]
- Authority of the "fulness of the priesthood"[28] (see D&C 110:12–16)

- Keys of the revelations, ordinances, oracles, powers, and endowments of the fulness of the Melchizedek Priesthood.[29]
- Operation and availability of Holy Spirit of Promise

While not directly restored by Elijah, the Holy Spirit of Promise flows from the covenants of the priesthood that Elijah did restore. The Holy Spirit of Promise seals and ratifies those ordinances in this life and the next. Elder McConkie described it this way:

> To seal, in the scriptural sense, is to ratify, to justify, and to approve. Any act that is approved by the Lord, any act that is ratified by the Holy Ghost, any act that is justified by the Spirit, is one upon which the Holy Spirit of Promise places a divine seal. "All covenants, contracts, bonds, obligations, oaths, vows, performances, connections, associations, or expectations"—in short, all things—must be sealed by the Holy Spirit of Promise, if they are to have "efficacy, virtue, or force in and after the resurrection from the dead." (D&C 132:7.) All that falls short of this divine approval passes away and has no eternal virtue. Among other things, this provision prevents anyone from gaining an unearned blessing.[30]

When a person receives the full sealing and ratification of all the ordinances of the gospel, then that person will have experienced the "fulness of the sealing power." When a person is thus blessed, they will have received every blessing possible for a mortal to receive, including the blessings associated with Zion, and if appropriate to their life mission, translation.

The phrase "fulness of the gospel" clearly suggests that there is also a lesser portion of the gospel that God dispenses among righteous people, with those doctrines and principles which constitute the "fulness" being added when worthiness allows. We have already discussed the principle of the lesser and greater portion of the word. The lesser portion constitutes those doctrines and principles which bring a person through the preparatory gospel of Jesus Christ and prepares them to seek and obtain the greater blessings. Those principles which constitute the greater portion are not often taught openly, but (at least in our dispensation) remain "mysteries of godliness" which must be found in a personal quest through righteousness and personal revelation.

Hyrum Andrus makes this observation about the fulness of the gospel.

The fulness of the everlasting gospel, on the other hand, is the higher program of salvation which is concerned with developing in man the divine truths, powers, gifts, and blessings of the Holy Spirit until he is able to partake of the divine nature, or glory, of God and make his calling and election sure to a fulness of glory in the resurrection. . . . The earthly program of this higher phase of the plan of life and salvation is consummated when man receives the fulness of the sealing power of the priesthood.[31]

Notice that Andrus defines the fulness of the gospel as beginning with partaking of the divine nature, or glory of God, making your calling and election sure, and qualifying for a full glory in the resurrection. He then makes the observation that all these higher and "greater portion" blessings flow from the "fulness of the sealing power."

We may, from all these various principles quoted above, draw this tentative portrait of what constitutes the "fulness of the gospel." It is that man may seek and obtain every promised blessing that any mortal has ever received by obedience to law, partaking of the full glory and power of the priesthood, enjoying the fulfillment of every covenant, and thus "partake of the divine nature" and seek and obtain the supernal promise of having their calling and election made sure and thereafter obtain a personal audience with their Savior.

This is the gateway into Zion.

NOTES

1. Richard O. Cowan, *Answers to Your Questions about the Doctrine and Covenants* (Salt Lake City: Deseret Book, 1996), 89.
2. Pratt, *The Seer* (October 1853): 145, as quoted in Andrus, *Doctrines of the Kingdom,* 405–6.
3. Ehat and Cook, *Words of Joseph Smith,* 297; bracketed comment added.
4. Ibid., 304.
5. Heber C. Kimball Journal, kept by William Clayton, 26 December 1845, Church Archives; italics added. As quoted in Ehat and Cook, *Words of Joseph Smith,* 304; bracketed comment in original.
6. Orson Hyde, "A Diagram of the Kingdom of God," *Millennial Star* 9 (15 January 1847): 23–24; parenthetical comment in original.
7. Ehat and Cook, *Words of Joseph Smith,* 302.

8. Ibid., 303.

9. Ibid., 305–6.

10. Joseph Fielding Smith, in Conference Report, Apr. 1970, 58.

11. Smith, *Teachings of the Prophet Joseph Smith*, 308.

12. Joseph Fielding Smith, in Conference Report, Apr. 1970, 58; italics added.

13. Joseph Fielding Smith, *Doctrines of Salvation* 3 vols., ed. Bruce R. McConkie (Salt Lake City: Bookcraft, 1956), 3:132.

14. Ehat and Cook, *Words of Joseph Smith*, 306; bracketed comments in original.

15. Ibid., 302.

16. Oliver Cowdery, *History of the Church*, 2:195–96.

17. McConkie, *The Promised Messiah*, 594; italics added.

18. Ibid., 587; italics added.

19. Joseph Fielding Smith, *Doctrines of Salvation*, 3:132.

20. Andrus, *Doctrinal Commentary*, 335; italics added.

21. F. Enzio Busche, "Truth is the Issue," *Ensign*, Nov. 1993, 25.

22. *History of the Church*, 4:609–10

23. McConkie, *Mormon Doctrine*, 333.

24. Smith, *Teachings of the Prophet Joseph Smith*, 330.

25. Ibid.

26. Ibid.

27. Ibid.

28. Ehat and Cook, *Words of Joseph Smith*, 303.

29. Ibid., 305–6.

30. McConkie, *New Witness for the Articles of Faith*, 273.

31. Hyrum L. Andrus, *Principles of Perfection* (Salt Lake City: Bookcraft, 1970), 17.

Chapter Nine

THE FINAL SCENE

PRIESTHOOD AND THE SISTERS OF ZION

The scriptures are largely written in the masculine case, making promises that seem to be primarily to priesthood holders, with blessings flowing to the sisters by inference more than reference. I'm not sure what cultural or traditional realities created this, but it seems unfortunate, and our wives and sisters often yearn for a clear declaration of their claim upon these promises themselves.

We need only sit through one temple session to learn every answer regarding a woman's place in these glorious things. Every promise, every gift, every ordination, every visitation and privilege is shared equally by our wives and daughters. There is only one place in the temple where there is a greater privilege, and it is the sisters who have the favored, protected position.

The process of exaltation and of obtaining Zion stature is taught in couched terms and in visible symbolism in the temple. The entire object of approaching the veil in this life and making requests of the Lord is symbolized within those holy walls. As we have said so many times—there is only one gospel. When you and I approach the veil, it will follow the pattern of Enoch and the brother of Jared, which is undeviating in the blessings offered there. We learn in the temple that priesthood holders have no more elevated privilege at the veil than do the sisters.

Joseph Smith, the great champion of womanhood, wrote:

> Females, if they are pure and innocent, can come in the presence of God; for what is more pleasing to God than innocence; you must be

innocent, or you cannot come up before God; if we would come before God, we must keep ourselves pure, as He is pure.[1]

Elder McConkie affirms that all blessings are held forth to righteous womanhood as they are to any priesthood holder.

> An elect lady is a female member of the Church who has already received, or who through obedience is qualified to receive, the fulness of gospel blessings. This includes temple endowments, celestial marriage, and the fulness of the sealing power. She is one who has been elected or chosen by faithfulness as a daughter of God in this life, an heir of God, a member of his household. Her position is comparable to that of the elders who magnify their callings in the priesthood and thereby receive all that the Father hath.[2]

After speaking on righteous brethren receiving a fulness of the priesthood, Elder Mark E. Peterson makes this comment about righteous women:

> Women cannot receive their higher blessings anywhere else either, for those blessings are conferred upon men and women jointly as they kneel at the marriage altar. All of course is conditioned upon faithfulness.
>
> We read in D&C 131 of the Doctrine and Covenants: "In the celestial glory there are three heavens or degrees; and in order to obtain the highest, a man must enter into this order of the priesthood [meaning the new and everlasting covenant of marriage]; and if he does not, he cannot obtain it."
>
> It is the same for women as for men. The man is not without the woman, neither is the woman without the man in the Lord.[3]

President Joseph Fielding Smith also spoke of women and the fulness of the priesthood:

> There is no exaltation in the kingdom of God without the fulness of priesthood. How could a man be an heir in that kingdom without priesthood? While the sisters do not hold the priesthood, they share in the fulness of its blessings in the celestial kingdom with their husbands. These blessings are obtained through obedience to the ordinances and covenants of the house of the Lord.[4]

Our Zion Equal to Enoch's Zion

When our Zion, the New Jerusalem, is established upon the earth prior to the return of Christ, it will be a city of the pure in heart, equivalent in righteousness to Enoch's city. In the divine order of things, when we have at last built that great city, then Enoch's Zion will return to the earth and join with our New Jerusalem. We will be enabled to join them because we have risen to the stature of Zion. Together these two great cities will be called Zion.

> 62 And righteousness will I send down out of heaven; and truth will I send forth out of the earth, to bear testimony of mine Only Begotten; his resurrection from the dead; yea, and also the resurrection of all men; and righteousness and truth will I cause to sweep the earth as with a flood, to gather out mine elect from the four quarters of the earth, unto a place which I shall prepare, an Holy City, that my people may gird up their loins, and be looking forth for the time of my coming; for there shall be my tabernacle, and it shall be called Zion, a New Jerusalem.
>
> 63 And the Lord said unto Enoch: Then shalt thou and all thy city meet them there, and we [Christ and Enoch] will receive them into our bosom, and they shall see us; and we will fall upon their necks, and they shall fall upon our necks, and we will kiss each other. (Moses 7:62–63; bracketed comment added)

The salient point here is that our Zion, the New Jerusalem, must be equal to Enoch's Zion in order to be worthy to join with it. Christ walks the streets of Enoch's Zion (Moses 7:16). Notice that the plurality of pronouns "us" and "we" in verse 63 refers to Enoch and Christ. How shall Christ embrace us if His presence consumes us? The laws of worthiness that separate us from Christ and His angels will still be in full force. When Enoch's city joins ours it will be because we have become like them—a Holy City, a habitation of the "elect" of God. We will be as they are—even as Christ is.

This combined city of the righteous of many generations has been given many names, among them Zion, and the City of the Living God, the heavenly place, the holiest of all (D&C 76:66), "the sons of Moses and of Aaron and the seed of Abraham, and the Church and kingdom, and the elect of God" (D&C 84:34) and "the general assembly and Church of the First-born" (D&C 107:19). Those who dwell there are described as being a "possessor of all things; for all things are subject unto [them], both in heaven and on the earth, the life and the light, the Spirit and the power, sent forth by the will of the Father through Jesus Christ, his Son" (D&C 50:27).

But the greatest description of that combined city of Zion is from Doctrine and Covenants 76. We have considered this scripture already in this document. Please study it again, for it is also precious in describing the Latter-day Zion. Most interpret this as a description of the celestial kingdom, even though verses 63–65 clearly place the time as prior to the Second Coming and the Millennium, and consequently, prior to the establishment of the celestial kingdom which shall be this earth in its sanctified state following the Millennium. These words describe living people, people who *are*. Pay special attention to the tenses of the verbs.

54 They are they who *are* the Church of the Firstborn. [Which tells us that they belong to the society of Enoch.]

55 They are they into whose hands the Father *has* given all things—

56 They are they who *are* priests and kings, who *have* received of his fulness, and of his glory; [They have been in the presence of Christ.]

57 And *are* priests of the Most High, after the order of Melchizedek, which was after the order of Enoch, which was after the order of the Only Begotten Son. [The "order of Enoch" suggests that they are translated.]

58 Wherefore, as it is written, they *are* gods, even the sons of God— [The power of godliness is theirs.]

59 Wherefore, all things *are* theirs, whether life or death, or things present, or things to come, all are theirs and they are Christ's, and Christ is God's. [They possess the translated powers over life and death and all elements of mortality. They can see into the future, and they are the fruits of Christ's ministry. They are Christ's at His coming.]

Now we come to blessings that will occur in the future. Notice in verse 60 that these people *shall* overcome all things. If this were the celestial kingdom, they would have already overcome all things.

60 And they *shall* overcome all things. [Indicating that at the time under consideration they have not yet overcome all things.]

61 Wherefore, let no man glory in man, but rather let him glory in God, who *shall* subdue all enemies under his feet.

62 These *shall* dwell in the presence of God and his Christ forever and ever. [They shall continue to dwell with Christ and the Father forever in the celestial kingdom, but haven't accomplished such yet.]

63 These are they whom he *shall* bring with him, when he shall come in the clouds of heaven to reign on the earth over his people. [Obviously, placing this prior to the Second Coming.]

64 These are they who *shall* have part in the first resurrection. [Prior to the Resurrection.]

65 These are they who *shall* come forth in the resurrection of the just.

And back to present blessings regarding Zion:

66 These are they who *are* come unto Mount Zion, and unto the city of the living God, the heavenly place, the holiest of all. [The combined cities of Zion.]

67 These are they who *have* come to an innumerable company of angels, to the general assembly and church of Enoch, and of the Firstborn.

68 These are they whose names *are* written in heaven, where God and Christ are the judge of all.

69 These are they who *are* just men made perfect through Jesus the mediator of the new covenant, who wrought out this perfect Atonement through the shedding of his own blood.

70 These are they whose bodies *are* celestial, whose glory *is* that of the sun, even the glory of God, the highest of all, whose glory the sun of the firmament is written of as being typical. [They have already obtained a celestial glory prior to being resurrected. Such is the description of those who inherit Zion.] (D&C 76:54–70, bracketed comments added.)

It is interesting that in verse 66 Mount Zion is described as being the city of the living God, "the heavenly place." Clearly this is not heaven but a place like heaven, the holiest of all. The holiest of all what? It will be the holiest of all places on earth. In other words, there are places around it that are less holy or perhaps not holy at all. During the pre-millennial day, a day when corruption still reigns upon the earth, this will be a heavenly place, the holiest place on earth.

THE 144,000

From that combined city an elite missionary force of 144,000 will be sent forth to gather in the elect of the earth. This will be the greatest missionary effort of all time. I suggest they will be translated men *and women*. Why do I say there will be men and women? Because these great missionaries will all be translated, and the gift of translation is being offered equally to all worthy people—men and women alike. We are taught in the temple that the approach to the veil and the blessings beyond, including translation, are offered to all the children of Adam. The natural conclusion is that when a daughter of God becomes worthy of Zion, she is also worthy of serving as one of the 144,000. Once again, the same worthiness must bring forth the same blessings, otherwise God is not just. We can't say definitively that translated women will be part of that great missionary force, but we can say that it feels true.

They will be ordained by the angels to bring "the elect" (JST Matthew 1:36–37) to the Church of the Firstborn, which will be the combined cities of Enoch and the New Jerusalem.

> Q. What are we to understand by sealing the one hundred and forty-four thousand, out of all the tribes of Israel—twelve thousand out of every tribe?
>
> A. We are to understand that those who are sealed are high priests, ordained unto the holy order of God, to administer the everlasting gospel; for they are they who are ordained out of every nation, kindred, tongue, and people, by the angels to whom is given power over the nations of the earth, to bring as many as will come to the Church of the Firstborn. (D&C 77:11)

Notice, these missionaries are members of the holy order, a subject we have discussed. It is also instructive that they will "administer" the everlasting gospel, not preach it. This suggests that they aren't missionaries in the classic sense. They aren't sifting and convincing and proselyting people. These words suggest that they are going forth to administer the ordinances (necessary to become Zion) to people who are already worthy but who lack some essential elements of their preparation.

It is also interesting that they will be ordained "by the angels to whom is given power over the nations of the earth." It appears that this will not be a calling originating with the Church as we understand it. Since by that time Enoch's Zion will have descended from heaven to join with our earthly Zion, it is possible that these "angels" will be citizens of Enoch's Zion.

Orson Pratt made this observation:

> They [the saints] will dwell in Zion a good while, and during that time, there will be twelve thousand chosen out of each of these ten tribes, besides twelve thousand that will be chosen from Judah, Joseph, and the remaining tribes, one hundred and forty-four thousand in all [see Revelation 7:4-8; D&C 77:11]. Chosen for what? To be sealed in their foreheads. For what purpose? So that the power of death and

pestilence and plague that will go forth in those days sweeping over the nations of the earth will have no power over them. These parties who are sealed in their foreheads will go forth among all people, nations and tongues, and gather up and hunt out the house of Israel, wherever they are scattered, and bring as many as they possibly can into the Church of the firstborn, preparatory to the great day of the coming of the Lord. One hundred and forty-four thousand missionaries! Quite a host. All this has got to take place.[5]

And after these last great missionaries have completed their administrations, where will they bring their converts? They will bring them back to Zion, to the Church of the Firstborn—the city of Enoch and Zion.

Notice that the Matthew reference below is referring to the same gathering. He refers to those who will do the gathering as "his angels," whom he will send with the great sound of a trumpet. "His angels" refer to the 144,000, giving light to the status and stature of those last missionaries. What that trumpet will sound like is unknown, but it is apparently going to be heard primarily by the elect, who will then be gathered from the whole earth into Zion. It is also worth observing that these things take place after the tribulation of "those days," which immediately precede the Lord's coming.

> 36 And, as I said before, after the tribulation of those days, and the powers of the heavens shall be shaken, then shall appear the sign of the Son of Man in heaven, and then shall all the tribes of the earth mourn; and they shall see the Son of Man coming in the clouds of heaven, with power and great glory;
>
> 37 And whoso treasureth up my word, shall not be deceived, for the Son of Man shall come, and he shall send his angels before him with the great sound of a trumpet, and they shall gather together the remainder of his elect from the four winds, from one end of heaven to the other. (JST Matthew 1:36–37)

It is often true in the scriptures that different scriptural writers, who are from divergent backgrounds, use different words or metaphors to describe the same thing. Even though the Matthew reference does not mention the 144,000, there will only be one gathering of the elect prior to the Lord's coming. Therefore these are one and the same event.

These translated missionaries will go forth with true power, miracles, and undeniable witnesses to gather the elect. They will snatch the elect from the jaws of destruction, defy armies, move mountains, and deliver by the power of God. They will travel by the power of God into all the world and gather one of a city, two of a family, showing forth miracles and bringing them to Zion, the throne of the Lord.

These are the 144,000 that publish these good tidings and publish salvation. They will say unto those to whom they are sent that God dwells and reigns in Zion, which news of the existence of Zion may be unknown to them until that moment. The people they rescue will be living in a world of terror and darkness until the light is suddenly revealed. It will be great tidings of joy to those who hear.

> 8 Thy watchmen shall lift up the voice; with the voice together shall they sing: for they shall see eye to eye, when the LORD shall bring again Zion. (Isaiah 52:8)

They shall sing songs of joy because they see the Lord eye to eye—which means without the veil, when the Lord again brings forth Zion.

> 9 Break forth into joy, sing together, ye waste places of Jerusalem: for the LORD hath comforted his people, he hath redeemed Jerusalem. (Isaiah 52:9)

Not only has the Lord redeemed Zion, the New Jerusalem, but he has also redeemed Old Jerusalem and comforted His ancient people who suffer no more from their rejection of their God.

> 10 The LORD hath made bare his holy arm in the eyes of all the nations; and all the ends of the earth shall see the salvation of our God. (Isaiah 52:10)

At that time the work of God will roll forth without apology, without shame, and without hiding from the eyes of the unbelievers. All the ends of the earth shall see the gathering and will quake, wonder, and fear.

And unto those to whom the 144,000 minister, their urgent message shall be depart ye, depart ye from Babylon. Go ye out of the midst of her, be ye clean and come serve the Lord in His temple.

> 11 Depart ye, depart ye, go ye out from thence, touch no unclean *thing*; go ye out of the midst of her; be ye clean, that bear the vessels of the LORD. (Isaiah 52:11)

Because they are protected by the power of God and their translated status makes them immune to the terrors falling upon the worldly, they will not be in a hurry. Their gathering shall be a peaceful and glorious exercise in salvation.

12 For ye shall not go out with haste, nor go by flight: for the LORD will go before you; and the God of Israel *will be* your rereward. (Isaiah 52:12)

Jeremiah spoke of this great gathering to Zion:

14 Turn, O backsliding children, saith the LORD; for I am married unto you: and I will take you one of a city, and two of a family, and I will bring you to Zion. (Jeremiah 3:14)

I am inclined to interpret "one of a city and two of a family" as meaning this great missionary effort will be directed at individuals who either are, or must shortly become, the elect of God. The miracles they perform will be the power of salvation to those with eyes of faith anxiously watching and waiting to be gathered in.

The following quote is from Joseph Fielding Smith. Notice that he alludes to the fact that this great missionary force will be like John the Beloved and the Three Nephites in their desires to bring souls unto Christ. He concludes by observing what a wonderful blessing it will be to be part of the 144,000.

> This certainly is a great honor to be one of the 144 thousand who are specially called by the power of "the angels to whom is given power over the nations of the earth," to bring souls unto Christ. John the Apostle had the great desire to bring souls to Christ. The three Nephite Disciples likewise sought this great honor, and it was granted to them. It is one of the noblest desires that a man can have. It will be a wonderful blessing to those who are called in this great group.[6]

Orson Pratt, an apostle and friend of the prophet Joseph, made this fascinating explanation regarding why this missionary force needs to be translated beings.

> When the Temple is built [in the New Jerusalem] the sons of the two Priesthoods [Melchizedek and Aaronic] . . . will enter into that Temple . . . and all of them who are pure in heart will behold the face of the Lord and that too before he comes in his glory in the clouds of heaven, for he will suddenly come to his Temple, and he will purify the sons of Moses and of Aaron, until they shall be prepared to offer in that Temple an offering that shall be acceptable in the sight of the Lord. In doing this, he will purify not only the minds of the Priesthood in that Temple, *but he will purify their bodies until they shall be quickened,*

and renewed and strengthened, and they will be partially changed, not to immortality, but changed in part that they can be filled with the power of God, and they can stand in the presence of Jesus, and behold his face in the midst of that Temple.[7]

Astonishingly, Elder Pratt is describing a purification process that will render us worthy of making an unspecified offering in the temple. Since there is only one gospel and one temple and we have the fulness of both, all temple-goers know what those offerings are. We symbolically make them by way of covenant every time we attend. The scriptures and Elder Pratt attest that when we at last make them in *righteousness*, not just symbolically or as a matter of ceremony, but in truth and righteousness—then the God of heaven will translate us!

Does the fact that they will *eventually* make an offering in righteousness mean that our temple offerings at this time are lacking some element of righteousness? As with all things spiritual, truths—even temple truths—are layered, the more exalted truths becoming apparent as we grow to understand their full import and potential impact. We perform temple ordinances primarily to bless the dead, which is a wonderful and important work—but it is not the only purpose of those ordinances.

Could this statement have something to do with the fact that these temple "offerings" are or should be pointing us to Zion? Could it be that no matter how pure our intent may be in doing work for the dead, until we understand the added significance of translation and Zion, we cannot make these offerings in such righteousness as is required to bring forth these astronomical blessings of Zion? Can it be that until we reorder our faith, belief, and desires, our offerings cannot yield the fullest blessings for which they were designed?

Continuing the quote from above:

This [being translated] will prepare them for further ministrations among the nations of the earth, it will prepare them to go forth in the days of tribulation and vengeance upon the nations of the wicked, when God will smite them with pestilence, plague and earthquake, such as former generations never knew. Then the servants of God will need to be armed with the power of God, *they will need to have that sealing blessing pronounced upon their foreheads that they can stand forth in the midst of these desolations and plagues and not be overcome by them.*[8]

In other words, we will need to be translated just to physically survive being sent forth to gather the elect out of the world. Elder Pratt continues:

> When John the Revelator describes this scene he says he saw four angels sent forth, ready to hold the four winds that should blow from the four quarters of heaven. Another angel ascended from the east and cried to the four angels, and said, "Smite not the earth now, but wait a little while." "How long?" "Until the servants of our God are sealed in their foreheads." What for? *To prepare them to stand forth in the midst of these desolations and plagues, and not be overcome. When they are prepared, when they have received a renewal of their bodies in the Lord's temple, and have been filled with the Holy Ghost and purified as gold and silver in a furnace of fire, then they will be prepared to stand before the nations of the earth and preach glad tidings of salvation in the midst of judgments that are to come like a whirlwind upon the wicked.*[9]

If Elder Pratt is right, and I deeply believe he is, then one of the grand purposes of the temple we will build in the New Jerusalem is to bestow upon us the privilege of translation, which is the same thing as saying, to make us a part of Zion. But as he notes above, the angels are holding back from cleansing the earth until we, the people of this dispensation, are sealed in our foreheads, which Elder Pratt equates with translation. In this sealing we will become sanctified and ready to take our place in Zion and among the 144,000.

Even though the New Jerusalem temple is apparently the place where translation will take place, it is feasible that in that day our other temples, or even holy places of the Lord's choosing, may be used for the same purpose. It is certainly the case that all of our temples perform the necessary preparatory ordinances that can bring us to these great blessings.

The angels are waiting until we are prepared by having our bodies renewed in the temples to stand before the nations of the earth in the midst of swirling judgments and gather out the elect and bring them to Zion.

As discussed earlier, we often trouble ourselves with the timing of the Second Coming by looking for signs and obediently storing food, which we will apparently need if we remain outside of Zion. But can food be our salvation? Isn't there a far safer salvation inside of Zion?

We do not know with any degree of precision when Christ will come. But we do know that He will come when there is a Zion to receive Him. As noted above by Joseph Fielding Smith (quoting from Revelation 7:1–3), the Lord has instructed His angels to wait a little while before destroying the earth.

Why? To give the servants of God time to be sealed in their foreheads.

Notice in the following quote that Joseph taught that being sealed "on top of the head" resulted in a person being translated and becoming one of the 144,000. This idea is interesting when you consider it with the one above about waiting for the sealing to occur before cleansing the earth. We find that what the angels are waiting for is for the 144,000 to be identified, called, and translated. Why? Because the 144,000 must gather up all of the elect before the earth is cleansed by fire. If the elect weren't gathered but were destroyed with the wicked, the whole earth would indeed be utterly wasted. From Ehat and Cook:

> [Joseph] indicated that the conferral of the fulness of the priesthood was a "sealing . . . on top of the head," of which the phrase "sealed in their foreheads" was symbolic. Furthermore, Joseph Smith here taught that it was through the ordinance of conferral of the fulness of the priesthood that men could be qualified to be a part of the special missionary force of the last days which would number 144,000 high priests.[10]

Since the angels are waiting upon us in a roundabout way, the timing of His coming is actually up to us. When we are ready, when we are sealed in our foreheads, when we have the fulness of the priesthood and enough of us have become translated, when we have established Zion—He will come.

Thus, we find ourselves in an awkward position of waiting for the doorbell to ring on a house we have yet to build.

THE FINAL SCENE

If history is any teacher, there is one thing which evil cannot abide, will not endure, and upon which it unleashes all its fury to destroy. That thing is Zion. Every time God has brought forth Zion in any degree, the armies of evil have combined against it. This is the pattern. It occurred to Adam (in Cain's rebellion and subsequent wars), to Enoch (in the wars of nations), to Melchizedek (in wars and bloodshed), to Christ (in crucifixion, war, and apostasy), to the Nephites (in wars and annihilation) and to Joseph Smith (in mob warfare, martyrdom, and expulsion).

When the New Jerusalem—the Latter-day Zion—is established, the pattern will again occur. Since this is the last and greatest Zion, all the nations of the earth will combine to wage the greatest war any Zion has endured. This warfare will constitute the great destructions every prophet has seen and foretold regarding the latter days.

Of course, as Wilford Woodruff proclaims, their warfare against Zion will result in their own destruction:

> Woe to that nation, kindred, tongue and people under the whole heavens who war against Zion in the latter-days; every weapon shall be broken that is formed against her, and that nation that will not serve her shall be utterly wasted away saith the Lord of hosts. These things are true, and I would warn Jew and Gentile, Saint and sinner and all the world to be careful what they do as touching them.[11]

The long-foreseen scenes of destruction, plague, and pure evil will begin—not because evil has triumphed at last—but because Zion has triumphed at last! The point being that this is warfare against Zion, which of course can't begin until Zion exists. The question is—where shall we stand? In Zion's safety, or in the war-torn world looking through bitter tears at the unscalable walls of Zion?

Shall we be among the 144,000, or desperately hoping our name is on the list of those they will deliver and bring to Zion? Shall we be among those terrified souls yearning to be saved, or shall we be their saviors? The promise of the oath and covenant of the priesthood is a call to glory:

> 33 For whoso is faithful unto the obtaining these two priesthoods of which I have spoken, and the magnifying their calling, are sanctified by the Spirit unto the renewing of their bodies.
>
> 34 They become the sons of Moses and of Aaron and the seed of Abraham, and the Church and kingdom, and the elect of God.
>
> 35 And also all they who receive this priesthood receive me, saith the Lord;
>
> 36 For he that receiveth my servants receiveth me;
>
> 37 And he that receiveth me receiveth my Father;
>
> 38 And he that receiveth my Father receiveth my Father's kingdom; therefore all that my Father hath shall be given unto him.
>
> 39 And this is according to the oath and covenant which belongeth to the priesthood.
>
> 40 Therefore, all those who receive the priesthood, receive this oath and covenant of my Father, which he cannot break, neither can it be moved. (D&C 84:33–40)

Forgive me if I take a little literary license with the same verses to summarize our discussion.

- For whoso is faithful unto the obtaining of these two priesthoods, and magnify their eternal callings, shall be sanctified by the Spirit unto the renewing of their bodies through translation.

- They shall become the inheritors of the promises given to Moses, Aaron, and Abraham, and will become the Church and kingdom, and will have their calling and election made sure.

- And also all they who receive this priesthood, I will personally visit them, saith the Lord;

- All who receive my servants (which includes the ministering angels [see Moroni 7 29–31]), I will visit them.

- All whom I visit, the Father will visit;

- And all whom the Father visits, will receive my Father's kingdom; therefore all that my Father hath shall be given unto him.

- And these blessings are according to the oath and covenant which belongs to the priesthood.

- Therefore, all who receive this priesthood in its fulness will receive every blessing associated with the oath and covenant of my Father, which He always honors, which can never be altered.

If Zion is to exist in our dispensation, then we alone bear the burden of its establishment. The quest for Zion is not yet a universal phenomenon, but a private one. When there is one Enochonian soul, there will soon be two, then four, then forty, then a hundred and forty-four thousand, until the call comes to gather, and by the power of God a city will glisten in the spiritual night. We will do our part in bringing forth Zion by becoming Zion in the privacy of our own quest.

NOTES

1. Smith, *Teachings of the Prophet Joseph Smith*, 226.
2. McConkie, *Mormon Doctrine*, 217.
3. Mark E. Petersen, *The Way to Peace* (Salt Lake City: Bookcraft, 1969), 264; bracketed comment in original.
4. Smith, *Doctrines of Salvation*, 3:132.

5. Orson Pratt, *Journal of Discourses*, 18:25; bracketed comments added.

6. Joseph Fielding Smith, *Church History and Modern Revelation,* 4 vols. (Salt Lake City: The Church of Jesus Christ of Latter-day Saints, 1946–49), 2: 71–72.

7. Orson Pratt, *Journal of Discourses*, 15:365–66; italics and bracketed comments added.

8. Ibid.

9. Ibid.

10. Ehat and Cook, *Words of Joseph Smith*, 297.

11. Wilford Woodruff, *Journal of Discourses*, 16:272.

Chapter Ten

OBTAINING ZION

THE PERFECT PATHWAY TO ZION

It is understandable that this lofty view of Zion as a translated society is intimidating, even perhaps a bit discouraging. To accept and truly believe that you and I have a responsibility to prepare to be worthy to enter Zion might be a steeper climb than it may be for an atheist to accept the existence of God and join His true Church. We have spent generation after generation with the belief that we *are* Zion, not that we must become Zion—let alone a Zion that includes perfect righteousness and sanctification sufficient to bring us into the realms of Enoch's Zion and translation.

Let us not faint at the thought, but rather rejoice that we are the chosen dispensation, that we are the ones who are empowered to build Zion, and that it is within our ability to do so. Faith and correct believing can provide us with the understanding that God has never given a commandment that could not be obeyed. We *can* become Zion, and there is a perfect pathway to arrive within her glorious walls.

This is how Joseph Fielding Smith viewed the pathway to establishing Zion in our day:

> The Lord has established all things in order and has given us a perfect system. We cannot improve upon it. If we would carry out that which the Lord has revealed, as he has revealed it, then all things would be perfect; for the organization is a perfect organization: the theory of it, the plan of it, is without flaw. If we followed all the orders that have been given to us in the priesthood and otherwise; if we would put into

practice the great doctrines which have been revealed in the revelations contained in the holy scriptures, *it would only be a matter of a very short time until this great people would be in the same condition, absolutely, as were the people in the city of Enoch. We would be able to walk with God, we would be able to behold his face, because then faith would abound in the hearts of the people to the extent that it would be impossible for the Lord to withhold himself, and he would reveal himself unto us as he has done in times past.*[1]

As President Smith beautifully proclaimed, the Lord has given us a perfect system for creating Zion. That system is the latter-day gospel of Jesus Christ as we presently have it. Nothing further is needed. No additional revelation is needed. No additional ordinances, powers, or keys are required. Everything is present and before us. And when we lay our hands upon what already belongs to us and fully avail ourselves of these privileges, we will become Zion worthy.

Zion is not outside or apart from the Church; it is a blossoming of the very gospel we presently have. It is the fullest and most complete outcome of every gospel principle, covenant and promise, and the final destination of the Church's long journey that was started April 6, 1830.

The pathway to Zion would not be perfect if it were impossible, or if it were feasible only for the strongest of the strong and greatest of the great. Zion will be populated by possibly hundreds of thousands before He comes again, which means it can't be overwhelming to accomplish.

As we have already discussed, translation will become the normal state of existence during the Millennium. From the small nucleus of the Zion we will establish by our sacrifices and our faith, the true doctrine of Christ will spread from Zion until all the world is, in time, completely translated. Then the promises of the Millennium—no death, disease, suffering or war—will be realized through translation or a form of translation. If the whole world is to eventually become translated, it can't be impossible.

Let us therefore take this perfect system that God has established and break it into manageable steps that lead toward Zion. It isn't necessary that the process be frightening or intimidating. Such emotions do not flow from the Holy Spirit. Peace, love, and joy fill the souls of those correctly seeking Zion. Fear and hopeless inadequacy are messages of lying voices. God has placed us here, in this time period, and charged us with building Zion because we are capable of doing so. Zion is not an impossible goal. It is not beyond us. We are the founders and architects and excavators of Zion. Others will show up to build the temples, towers, and golden streets upon the foundation we lay.

The process I am about to outline will sound familiar to you. As you ponder this pathway to Zion, you will quickly realize you have been on it all your life. What you may not have realized is where it was taking you and the power that has always been within your grasp.

The Lord's perfect pathway to Zion begins at birth. When a soul enters mortality and is endowed with the gift of the Spirit of Christ, they have begun their journey to Zion.

> 46 And the Spirit giveth light to every man that cometh into the world; and the Spirit enlighteneth every man through the world, that hearkeneth to the voice of the Spirit. (D&C 84:46)

HOLY GHOST AND THE HOLY SPIRIT

The scriptures, and most latter-day Saints, do not use distinctly different names for the Spirit of Christ and that member of the Godhead we know as the Holy Ghost. Only for the purpose of clarity, whenever this book uses the term the Holy Spirit, we are speaking of the Spirit of Christ. Whenever we speak of the Holy Ghost, we are referring to the third member of the Godhead.

The Holy Ghost operates quite differently than the Spirit of Christ or the Holy Spirit. The Holy Ghost is an actual personage of spirit, a member of the Godhead, whose function is to bear witness of the Father and the Son. When we hear a message from the Holy Ghost it is generally unmistakable. These messages enter our souls with force and leave behind a witness that can't easily be missed. Such messages include all of those things which constitute our testimony, such as Jesus is the Christ, God lives and loves me, Joseph Smith was a true prophet, and the Church is true. All such powerful enhancements to our spiritual understanding come to us through the Holy Ghost acting in His primary role as revelator and testator.

Whenever we are blessed to receive a greater manifestation such as a vision, an angelic visitation, or the very opening of the heavens, all such things come to us by the power of the Holy Ghost.

Another difference between the Holy Ghost and the Holy Spirit is that we only receive the Holy Ghost when we are worthy of the intended message. The Holy Ghost will not testify to unworthy ears. All such messages from the Holy Ghost are obtained by obedience to a specific law.

When we obey that law, the Holy Ghost bears record, and if we receive it, our souls expand.

Truth that comes from the Holy Ghost does not become a permanent fixture of our souls but is sustained by the continued presence of the Holy Ghost. Thus, a testimony of Christ lasts only as long as we remain within the revelatory light that is transmitting that truth into our being. When we sever our contact with the Holy Ghost through sin or disobedience, the light dims and the truths begin to fade. In time all we have is a memory that we once knew something was true, but we no longer feel the same way. This is the reason that someone can have a profound testimony at one point in their lives, and after transgression or apostasy can lose that testimony in a short period of time.

The Holy Spirit, on the other hand, comes to us prepaid, as it were, by the Atonement of Christ. Thus everyone, regardless of their initial standing, hears its messages. The Holy Spirit is persistent, and though it can be offended and even silenced by repeated disobedience, it will return again and again throughout our lives to attempt to lead us back into the embrace of truth.

While the Holy Ghost primarily reveals larger, specific elements of our faith, such as the knowledge that Jesus is the Christ, the Holy Spirit functions in the minute, bearing witness of all things that are right or wrong, truth or error, righteous or wicked. As an example, the Holy Ghost will not comment upon our tone of voice with our children, but the Holy Spirit always will, if we're not too angry to hear it. The Holy Ghost will have no opinion on where we drop our dirty laundry, but the Holy Spirit will consistently urge us to do everything that is right, and kind, and loving.

While we carefully draw a distinction between these two voices of truth, it is nonetheless true that even though we are blessed with both voices, all communication we have with deity comes through the ministry of the Holy Ghost. The difference is merely this: When Christ delivers the message to us as the Spirit of Truth, by virtue of His Atonement, the Holy Ghost speaks in a still small voice. When we receive a message from the Father, the Holy Ghost speaks with authority and power that cannot easily be mistaken.

The Holy Ghost is a messenger. He does not speak of himself. The content and power of His messages vary depending upon the source of the message.

Another rather paradoxical difference in the operation of the Holy Spirit and the Holy Ghost is that all of the spiritual gifts we receive in this life come to us through the Spirit of Christ rather than from the Holy Ghost directly. This is due to the mercy of the Atonement, which makes it possible to deliver a spiritual gift when we are less than worthy, which elevates and brings us toward perfection. The Holy Ghost would only be able to bestow these gifts *after* we had fully earned them. The Holy Spirit bestows them when we need them, when we ask for them, or when we qualify for them by obedience to law, with less regard for worthiness.

Elder McConkie offers this explanation:

> Moroni says that the gifts of God come from Christ, by the power of the Holy Ghost and by the Spirit of Christ (Moroni 10). In other words, the gifts come by the power of that Spirit who is the Holy Ghost, but the Spirit of Christ (or light of Christ) is the agency through which the Holy Ghost operates.[2]

According to this, all gifts of the Spirit—which include love, joy, peace, longsuffering, gentleness, goodness, faith, meekness, temperance (Galatians 5:23), testimony, wisdom, knowledge, faith to be healed, faith to heal, miracles, prophecy, discerning of spirits, speaking in tongues, and the interpretation of tongues (D&C 46:15–25), childlike obedience, humility, meekness, being full of love (Mosiah 3:19)—all these gifts and thousands more, come to us as a gift from Christ through the Spirit of Christ.

These gifts of the Spirit are too vast and miraculous for us to earn. Christ's Atonement makes it possible for us to qualify for things which we otherwise could never merit in our lives. This is the grace of Christ; when He pays the price we could never meet and then allows us to qualify for those gifts by obedience to laws that are well within our mortal abilities.

One may ask, since both the voice of the Spirit of Christ, and the more powerful voice of the Holy Ghost come through that same member of the Godhead we call the Holy Ghost, why draw the distinction between the two at all?

The answer lies in the fact that the scriptures define the difference, and we should strive to understand the sacred word. The larger reason is that the giver of the gifts of the Holy Spirit paid with His life, His body, and His precious blood to provide them to us, and we must understand this to properly honor His sacrifice, and to properly worship Him.

After speaking extensively on the Light of Christ, the scripture asks:

33 For what doth it profit a man if a gift is bestowed upon him, and he receive not the gift? Behold, he rejoices not in that which is given unto him, neither rejoices in him who is the giver of the gift. (D&C 88:33)

Quite often the scriptures speak of the Spirit of Christ, which can easily be confused with the Holy Ghost.

The Spirit of Christ

The Spirit of Christ manifests itself in our lives in many ways, but the most easily recognized is that it is our conscience. The conscience is also called the "still small voice" because of its ability to communicate through impressions, thoughts, and feelings, rather than as an internally audible voice. In those who have received the "gift of the Holy Ghost," conscience sometimes includes the whisperings of the Holy Ghost. Elder McConkie says it this way:

> For the generality of mankind, conscience consists in the pleading, striving, and enlightening promptings which come from the Light of Christ. But where the Saints of God are concerned, those favored few who have the gift of the Holy Ghost, conscience sometimes includes the whisperings of the Spirit, the still small voice that comes from the Holy Ghost.[3]

Another way of saying this is that as we grow nearer and nearer to perfection, the operation of the Light of Christ and that of the Holy Ghost becomes nearly the same.

The whisperings of the conscience will persist year after year even when we ignore them. The gifts of the Spirit are generally received without requesting them or without even qualifying for them. People are just born with certain gifts, such as great faith, the ability to see visions, or the gift of discernment. We are invited to seek earnestly the best gifts (D&C 46:8), which suggests that we can acquire gifts of the Spirit through righteous request.

As Doctrine and Covenants 84:46 quoted above suggests, the still small voice, which is the voice of the Spirit of Christ, only blesses and enlightens us when we hearken to it, which means to hear and obey.

The enlightenment offered to us by the Spirit of Christ brings us from the darkness and confusion of this world into the light of truth and begins us on the pathway that is designed to ultimately take us to Zion. We all begin our journey in mortality as natural men and women. We come into this world as flesh and blood beings, driven largely by the need to satisfy the demands of the flesh. But our true self is not flesh and blood. That which animates, thinks, learns, and grows comes from God, does not have physical needs or lusts, and yearns only to become like God. Our spirit, our primal intelligence, is our primary identity only after we conquer the flesh. Until then, the natural man is an eternal being whose identity has been greatly overshadowed by the identity of the flesh.

When that spirit within us silences the voice of the flesh and yields to the enticings of the Holy Spirit, he or she becomes a spiritual being, directed by the voice of Christ and sanctified through His Atonement.

Perhaps you have seen the clever analogy of a glove representing the mortal flesh and a hand which represents the primal intelligence, or spirit within us, placed inside that glove to give apparent life and animation to the glove. While this illustration is true in many ways, it would actually be more illuminating if the glove were jointed steel, robotic in nature, and had life and movement of its own, with desires, lusts, and needs that obscured the movements of the living hand inside and made movement extremely difficult at times, even dulling the sensation of the hand in favor of the senses of the robotic glove.

We primarily think of "me" as our body, and somewhere buried out of sight deep within is a spirit we can hardly feel or communicate with. When we at last are like God and have overcome the world through Christ, we will be first and foremost a being of spirit, eternal and perfect, and our bodies will be a component of our perfection, housed within the greater framework of our spirit. In fact, the body will become eternal only after it is changed by the processes of sanctification to become like our spirits.

In this world we are pulled both by the body of flesh with its weakness to be enticed by earthly needs, lusts, and temptation, and by the Holy Spirit, which speaks quietly to the spirit within us. Whether we hearken to the flesh, which is the voice of the world heavily influenced by evil, or to the Holy Spirit, which is the voice of Christ, is the dividing line between being an enemy to God and becoming a Saint through the Atonement of Christ.

> 19 For the natural man is an enemy to God, and has been from the fall
> of Adam, and will be, forever and ever, *unless he yields to the enticings*
> *of the Holy Spirit, and putteth off the natural man and becometh a saint*

through the Atonement *of Christ the Lord,* and becometh as a child, submissive, meek, humble, patient, full of love, willing to submit to all things which the Lord seeth fit to inflict upon him, even as a child doth submit to his father. (Mosiah 3:19; italics added)

The way to begin our journey into Zion, and the perfect system that is ordained to bring us there, is to yield to the enticings of the Holy Spirit. The list of attributes above is not a list of requirements that we must discipline into our souls, but is rather a list of gifts that distill upon our souls. We simply become all these wonderful things, childlike, submissive, meek, humble, patient, full of love, and willing to submit, by virtue of the ability of the Holy Spirit to upgrade and sanctify, and because of the Atonement's supreme ability to cleanse and perfect. The most important thing we may understand about the enticings of the Holy Spirit is that they are the voice of Christ to our souls: "The truths communicated to you by your conscience come from Jesus Christ, are administered by the Holy Ghost, and are revelation."[4]

The following verses give us a great insight into from whence the Holy Spirit enters our souls—it proceeds forth from the mouth of God.

43 And I now give unto you a commandment to beware concerning yourselves, to give diligent heed to the words of eternal life.

44 For you shall live by every word that proceedeth forth from the mouth of God.

45 For the word of the Lord is truth, and whatsoever is truth is light, and whatsoever is light is Spirit, even the Spirit of Jesus Christ. (D&C 84:43–45)

Notice that this is a commandment—that we must give diligent heed to every word that proceeds forth from the mouth of God. This is not optional. We are commanded to obey.

In explanation, verse 45 describes the word of the Lord as being truth, light, and the Spirit of Jesus Christ. When used in this context, these terms are synonymous. This divine property is so powerful that it has many names, probably because of the many different ways it affects us. But the end effect is that it has the ability to lead us back to the Father.

46 And the Spirit giveth light to every man that cometh into the world; and the Spirit enlighteneth every man through the world, that hearkeneth to the voice of the Spirit.

47 And every one that hearkeneth to the voice of the Spirit cometh unto God, even the Father. (D&C 84:46–47)

The purpose of the voice of Christ in our souls is to initiate and conclude a lifelong process that will ultimately bring us to the Father. To say it more simply then, the ordained means—the only means whereby we may return to the presence of the Father is by hearkening to the voice of the Spirit of Christ. For what purpose does it bring us to the Father?

48 And the Father teacheth [them] of the covenant which he has renewed and confirmed upon you, which is confirmed upon you for your sakes, and not for your sakes only, but for the sake of the whole world. (D&C 84:48; bracketed comment added)

Which covenant is this verse referring to? There are many covenants that have been renewed in this dispensation, including the new and everlasting covenant of marriage. As discussed earlier, there are two great covenants regarding Zion: The covenant made with Enoch, which is symbolized by the rainbow, and the oath and covenant of the priesthood, which we have discussed throughout this book. The oath and covenant is the key to establishing Zion. The fact that the covenant being referred to is "for the sake of the whole world," leads one to conclude that it is referring to all the blessings that flow from the priesthood. Preeminent for our dispensation are the blessings of Zion, for without these covenants "the whole earth would be utterly wasted at His coming" (D&C 2:1–3).

Then, the scripture pointedly proclaims:

49 And the whole world lieth in sin, and groaneth under darkness and under the bondage of sin.

50 And by this [that they do not hear my voice] you may know they are under the bondage of sin, because they come not unto me [Christ]. (D&C 84:49–50; bracketed comment added)

The dividing line between righteousness and wickedness is not just whether we attend church, pay tithing, or even if we commit murder or adultery, but the far less flashy sin of whether or not we hear and hearken to the voice of Christ. This may seem easier to fathom in the light that nobody ever committed murder without first, and many, many sins ago, shutting out the voice of Christ.

By this definition someone could be doing a lot of things right, serving in the Church, even working hard to complete their assignments, yet be guilty of a form of wickedness merely because they do it all themselves, without first seeking the direction of the voice of Christ and walking in His light. Inconceivable? Perhaps not when compared with the rather stark assessment that many are called and few are chosen, because their hearts are so set upon the things (meaning performances and acts) of this world.

Does it seem harsh to define anyone who doesn't hear and obey their conscience as wicked? It makes greater sense when we consider that the Holy Spirit is not just *a* voice of truth and light and righteousness, it is *the* voice of truth. There is no other. The Lord considers anyone wicked who will not hear his voice.

> 5 But behold, the residue of the wicked have I kept in chains of darkness until the judgment of the great day, which shall come at the end of the earth;
>
> 6 And even so will I cause the wicked to be kept, *that will not hear my voice but harden their hearts*, and wo, wo, wo, is their doom. (D&C 38:5–6; italics added)

If a person understands any truth, whether it be a gospel truth or something personal, that truth has come either directly or indirectly from the Spirit of Christ. Any enlightenment that enters this world comes from Christ.

Truth leads unto truth. In illustration, one cannot fathom internal combustion engines without a working knowledge of fuel and fire. One cannot understand Zion and the glories of translated life if one does not acknowledge the existence of God. All truth is sequentially gained. Therefore, a whispering of the tiniest truth is a stepping stone that must be embraced and obeyed to elevate ourselves to receive the next saving truth.

Conversely, if a person stifles the voice of the Holy Spirit by repeated disobedience and abuse of its still small voice, that person in time loses the ability to distinguish truth and eventually cannot differentiate between right and wrong. In time such a person becomes unable to distinguish between love or lust, good or bad, or even kindness and murder. Only the needs of the flesh sound in their ears; "right" becomes answering those lusts, and "wrong" becomes denying them.

Therefore, wickedness is defined as anyone who does not hearken to the voice of the Spirit of Christ—regardless of the works of our hands. The most rudimentary manifestation of the Spirit of Christ is the conscience of man.

The Conscience

As we have discussed, the conscience we all begin life with is the first step on our perfect pathway to Zion. But the conscience is not a destination; it is a beginning.

Although the conscience is the first and most elementary manifestation of the Holy Spirit, the Spirit of Jesus Christ in our lives, it is not intended to remain our only contact with God. It has a specific purpose, which is to teach us right from wrong. If obeyed, it will ultimately lead to the gospel of Jesus Christ, which then leads us to the ordinances of the priesthood, and on and on until we are redeemed from the fall and return to the presence of God.

The challenge of the conscience is that it is a still small voice. It can be hard to recognize, and hard at times to distinguish from the other noise that the world pounds into our heads.

Elder Faust made this observation:

> The Adversary tries to smother this voice [of the Holy Spirit] with a multitude of loud, persistent, persuasive, and appealing voices: murmuring voices that conjure up perceived injustices, whining voices that abhor challenge and work, seductive voices offering sensual enticements, soothing voices that lull us into carnal security, intellectual voices that profess sophistication and superiority, proud voices that rely on the arm of the flesh, flattering voices that puff us up with pride, cynical voices that destroy hope, entertaining voices that promote pleasure seeking, commercial voices that temp us to "spend money for that which is of no worth" and our "labor for that which cannot satisfy" . . . and delirious voices that spawn the desire for a "high." . . . [which is] death-defying experiences for nothing more than a thrill.[5]

There are three main sources of "voice" in a healthy human mind.

The Voice of the Mind

The first voice we hear is our own mind. We hear ourselves think. We discuss life with ourselves, argue, debate, and analyze. This voice is easy to recognize because it is unsure. It rarely states things in the absolute. It might say, "I wonder if I should call family prayers." Whereas, the Holy Spirit would simply command, "Call family prayers." The voice of the mind often takes the personal case. It will say "I'm hungry." "I'm not sure." "I think I'll go to bed now."

The voice of our own mind often debates with the other voices. It is unsure and seeks understanding. "Why did that happen?" or "What should I do?" would be easily recognized as commentary from our own mind.

THE VOICE OF EVIL

The second voice we hear is the voice of opposition. This voice originates with Satan or his minions and is intelligent and malicious. A book I previously authored gives some details about this voice:

> The second voice comes from Satan's realm. It is unlikely that we receive much attention from the king of that kingdom personally. Rather, we deal with his minions, his messengers, and tempters. These beings have been in the business of tempting mankind as long as the earth has existed, perhaps longer. They are undoubtedly very skilled and highly motivated. They have probably each tempted thousands or more people like ourselves. Even though they have never possessed a body of their own, they have spent thousands of years of intimate contact with mortals. They have much more experience with tempting mortals to sin than we could possibly have in resisting it. They know the subtleties and tricks necessary to entice and trick us into failing. They undoubtedly specialize in their work, meaning that certain of them specialize in anger, marital infidelity, family disharmony, murder, drugs, illness, depression, hate, or a million other maladies, sins and vices. Once successful, they linger year after year with those they afflict.[6]

Their dark motivations are not entirely known to mortals. Suffice it to say that hearkening to the voice of evil has the specific effect of strangling our contact with the Holy Spirit. While their motive may appear to be to get us to commit sin, their larger goal is to separate us from God entirely. This cannot happen until after we sever our link with Christ. This must happen before anyone will perform damning acts. Any sinful act was proceeded by many, perhaps thousands of internal acts of defying and silencing the voice of our conscience. For this reason, the way Satan leads us away from God and into sin is through silencing the voice of the Holy Spirit.

Thus, muffling the voice of the Holy Spirit is our enemy's primary labor, even though their overall objective is to lead us away from God and bring us into subjection to the master of darkness and to themselves.

For reasons we won't discuss, they see our demise as their salvation. They hate us with unimaginable fury and rejoice in our destruction. These messages from the darkness will generally appeal to the flesh. They will seem sensually or sexually enticing, enjoyable or alluring. They will titillate the flesh, inflame the senses, bloat the ego, and urge domination of others. Anything that severs us from the Spirit of Christ will be used against us, including memories of past offenses.

We can distinguish this voice because it is always negative, generally emphatically stated, and often reactionary. To say it more plainly, the voice of temptation often follows a prompting to do something good—it reacts to the voice of truth. We may hear a prompting to call our family for family prayers. Immediately thereafter, the voice of opposition fights against it. "It's too late. Everyone is ready for bed. You're tired and need to get up early. Everyone will resist coming. It will just create discord. Just do it tomorrow night."

One of the weaknesses of the opposition is that they can rarely just voice one objection but seem to prefer to rant.

The main conduit they use to gain access to us is the natural body and the lusts of the flesh. Note how Nephi puts it:

> 28 And now, my sons, I would that ye should look to the great Mediator, and hearken unto his great commandments; and be faithful unto his words, and choose eternal life, according to the will of his Holy Spirit;
>
> 29 And not choose eternal death, according to the will of the flesh and the evil which is therein, which giveth the spirit of the devil power to captivate, to bring you down to hell, that he may reign over you in his own kingdom. (2 Nephi 2:28–29)

This is how I described it in a previous book:

> These [negative] promptings will always lead us away from the truth. They prompt us to disobey, to not pray, to abandon church assignments, to commit sin and to walk in forbidden paths. They do not limit themselves to voices alone. They can draw from the trash stored in our minds to harrow up memories which will either lure us away from purity and virtue, or keep our minds harrowed up with vivid memories of our sins—even after we have repented of them.[7]

THE VOICE OF THE HOLY SPIRIT

The last and greatest voice we hear is the voice of Christ, which we often call the Holy Spirit. It is the easiest to recognize because it is always right and always prompts us to do good, to love God, and to serve our fellowman. It never errs. It never leads us to harm. Happiness, in fact eternal life, is the outcome of obedience to this voice. Everything that invites us to do good and persuades us to believe in Christ is sent forth by the voice of Christ (Moroni 7:16).

When humans hear this voice it enters their minds as a still small voice. Presumably, when a rock or tree hears the voice of Christ, it sounds no louder. The difference is that the rocks and trees obey, and mankind filters it through their lusts. Thus, this light is the power of God and the law by which all things are governed (see D&C 88:13). But to be governed is not to be controlled, and because of their agency, God's highest creations most often do not obey His voice.

When we hear a prompting from our conscience we may, and actually must, identify it as the voice of Christ. More than any other thing, our conscience is revelation directly from our Savior.

The voice of the Holy Spirit is our conscience in the positive mode. Most folks are familiar with their conscience telling them to *not* do something. This negative mode is generally the first recognizable revelation mortals receive, telling them to stop or not do something evil. When that same voice speaks positively or instructs us to *do* something as opposed to *not* do something, very few people can recognize the message as revelation. They feel free to ignore such messages. Learning to hear and recognize such positive communications from the Holy Spirit is the first major step toward righteousness.

All good that occurs in this mortal world occurs because someone heard and hearkened to a positive *to do* message from the divine through the Holy Spirit. The voice of the Holy Spirit never uses "I" and is never unsure. Rather than "I think I should go to church," the Holy Spirit would just say, "Go to church."

Another hallmark of the Holy Spirit is that it is not verbose. It generally speaks only once. It will almost never repeat itself or debate. It is not reactionary in that it doesn't compete with the other voices and can be smothered by the voices of the world. Loud music, especially uninspired music, loud noises, and even loud entertainment can drown out the voice of the Spirit.

This voice of the Holy Spirit is easily offended and will depart when we enter spiritual darkness or expose ourselves to evil people, places, sounds, raucous laughter, anger, argumentation, violence, pornography, illicit sexuality, uninspired music, dark ideas, embraced temptations, or even uninspired thoughts, teachings, or philosophy.

Besides being easy to offend, the Holy Spirit can be driven from our lives through repeated abuse, and will in time be silenced. The scriptures refer to the process of turning off the voice of the Holy Spirit as "hardening your heart." A hard heart is made steely by self-will, inflated ego, and a compelling urge to answer the lusts of the body at any cost. Such a body-captivated person smothers the voice of the Holy Spirit through the hardening of their heart. When the voice of truth is actually silenced, the scriptures refer to this terrible state as the "chains of hell" because it is so difficult to escape. To such a soul the light is no longer visible, and thus there is no motivation to deny the flesh anything, no matter the cost—especially when the cost is invisible.

> 11 And they that will harden their hearts, to them is given the lesser portion of the word until they know nothing concerning his mysteries; and then they are taken captive by the devil, and led by his will down to destruction. Now this is what is meant by the chains of hell. (Alma 12:11)

> 6 And even so will I cause the wicked to be kept, that will not hear my voice but harden their hearts, and wo, wo, wo, is their doom. (D&C 38:6)

There is one somewhat paradoxical aspect of the Holy Spirit given that it is so easily offended, and this is that it is actually quite persistent. Even after we drive it off in certain areas of our lives, it will return time and again to attempt to lead us into the light in other areas. Even the darkest of minds receive urgings to repent and show mercy in other areas. Even when parts of our minds are dead to truth, others may yield to the Holy Spirit. For example, we are told that one of Hitler's worst butchers was ironically a loving and doting grandfather.

As we choose to obey its urgings, the Holy Spirit quickly abandons the negative mode of "don't steal the candy bar" level of warning and elevates to a voice of revelation and truth that blesses our lives powerfully. And, even though it never grows beyond a whisper, its messages grow in power and import as we obey. When we disobey, the content and power of this voice quickly degrades and can in time disappear altogether.

We are privileged to receive the Holy Spirit because of the Atonement of Christ. A great deal of what Christ endured in Gethsemane was to give Him a perfect understanding about all aspects of mortality necessary to become the "light of truth."

> 6 He that ascended up on high, as also he descended below all things, in that he comprehended all things, that he might be in all and through all things, the light of truth. (D&C 88:6)

The impact of this principle is that we enjoy this gift of the Holy Spirit because of those things that Christ suffered in Gethsemane. He descended below all things so that he could comprehend all things, including those things which are awful and horrifying, so that when we, His spiritual offspring, look to Him for guidance, relief or comfort, He can be for us an unfailing "light of truth." The outcome of all this is that we take part in His Atonement every time the Holy Spirit whispers to us. We honor his sacrifice when we obey and become one of the mockers and disobedient when we knowingly reject His voice.

THE PURPOSE OF THE CONSCIENCE

The voice of the Holy Spirit has a specific initial goal, which is to bring us to the gospel of Christ and the ordinances of the priesthood. Any person who learns to consistently hearken to the voice of their conscience will eventually end up within the embrace of the restored gospel. Not every journey accomplishes this in this life, and some journeys are of necessity designed to be outside of the latter-day Church. This process is obvious in the many righteous souls that do the vast preparatory work that yields a fertile field from which our latter-day missionaries harvest. Some complete their journey in the next life, but obedience to the voice of truth will ultimately yield this divinely ordained outcome every time.

When such a person learns to obey their conscience, they will quickly discover that happiness always follows obedience. They will begin to value their inner voice and will in time identify it as their primary connection with God, no matter how society defines God in their time. They will discover that peace, joy, and safety are the maxim, or general rule, of their lives when they obey.

In our day when a missionary of the latter-day gospel rings a conscience-obeying soul's doorbell and they open their door, no matter what they have been conditioned to believe by the world, that same voice will urge them to listen and embrace. They may struggle with their decision, and it may take multiple opportunities to respond obediently, but they will ultimately be taught the gospel and will feel a sweet urging to join themselves with the Church of God. Every true conversion and baptism from the beginning of time to the end of eternity will be among that tiny subset of society that has learned to listen to their conscience prior to the missionaries arriving at their door.

Considering the flip side makes this process more understandable. A person devoid of the ability to discern spiritual truth will always see the missionaries and their message as foolishness. The fact that statistically a missionary has to knock on about 5000 doors to experience one baptism tells a great deal about the condition of the world in general.

Thus, the perfect pathway to Zion continues. Obedient souls develop faith as they are taught by the missionaries. Their souls are fed by the Holy Ghost as it bears witness to the words of the missionaries. They begin a lifelong process of repentance and at last find themselves standing in the waters of baptism.

After they emerge from the cleansing waters of baptism, they will have hands placed upon their heads, and the authority of the priesthood will give them the gift of the Holy Ghost.

For this important reason, learning to obey the Holy Spirit is the first cobblestone in the perfect pathway to Zion. Since obeying the voice of the Spirit is the first step on our journey to Zion, understanding the sacrament and how it affects our contact with the Holy Spirit is important.

THE SACRAMENT

Each Sunday we partake of the sacrament, which draws us into a covenantal obligation to always remember Christ and His great sacrifice that was wrought in our behalf. We witness that we are willing to take upon ourselves His name, to always remember him, and to keep His commandments.

> 77 O God, the Eternal Father, we ask thee in the name of thy Son, Jesus Christ, to bless and sanctify this bread to the souls of all those who partake of it, that they may eat in remembrance of the body of thy Son, and witness unto thee, O God, the Eternal Father, that they are willing to take upon them the name of thy Son, and always remember him and keep his commandments which he has given them; that they may always have his Spirit to be with them. Amen. (D&C 20:77)

But why? Why make this covenant over and over, week after week, year after year? It is for this one glorious reason as stated in the sacramental prayer itself: that by doing these things we may *always* have His (meaning Christ's) Spirit to be with us.

We are not petitioning for the Holy Ghost to be with us. Receipt of that gift is governed by other laws. In making the sacramental covenants we are seeking Christ's Spirit—the Holy Spirit, the Light of Christ, the Voice of Christ, the Spirit of God—to be with us, because this is our continuing and unfaltering link with the Divine. This is how we know all things that are good. This is how we discern all truth, all light, and all goodness. Without this light we would be unable to tell the difference between good and evil, love and lust, tenderness and tyranny. All things which satisfied our natural lusts would seem good.

Thus, in renewing this covenant through always remembering Christ, taking upon ourselves His name, and obeying His commandments, we seek for a greater endowment of Christ's voice. This is the grand purpose of the sacrament. Moroni 7 holds a precious revelation on the blessings that flow from the Holy Spirit in our lives. Since all good things come from Christ, whether it be spiritual or material, laying hold upon all good things becomes a by-product of drawing nearer and nearer to unfailing obedience to His voice.

The process of thus coming unto Christ requires faith, because when the voice of Christ speaks, we cannot know beforehand what the result of obeying may be. We can only have faith that it will be for our vast betterment. Mormon urges us to search diligently within that inner voice, the light of Christ, to determine all that is good, and promises us that if we will lay hold upon every good thing, which is to say all truth, all revelation to us, and all material good the Holy Spirit identifies for us, that we will become a child of Christ.

> 19 Wherefore, I beseech of you, brethren, that ye should search diligently in the light of Christ that ye may know good from evil; and if ye will lay hold upon every good thing, and condemn it not, ye certainly will be a child of Christ. (Moroni 7:19)

Then, apparently acknowledging the human tendency to doubt the immediate and long-term benefits of obedience, Mormon asks:

> 20 And now, my brethren, how is it possible that ye can lay hold upon every good thing? (Moroni 7:20)

He then answers his own question this way:

> 21 And now I come to that faith, of which I said I would speak; and
> I will tell you the way whereby ye may lay hold on every good thing.
> (Moroni 7:21)

He then proceeds to tell us how Christ knows all things past, present, and future, and reminds us that every prophet accomplished their great works by first having faith in Christ, which faith enabled them to do the great works that enshrine their names in sacred history. Mormon concludes with this rather concise summation:

> 28 For he hath answered the ends of the law, and he claimeth all those
> who have faith in him; and they who have faith in him will cleave unto
> every good thing; wherefore he advocateth the cause of the children of
> men; and he dwelleth eternally in the heavens. (Moroni 7:28)

Christ provided for mercy and forgiveness (which answer the ends of the laws of justice) by instilling His voice in our hearts. If—or better stated, when—through faith we lay hold upon everything Christ communicates through this magnificent gift, then we will be laying hold upon every good thing, and will thus come to dwell eternally with Him in the heavens.

As has been observed earlier, there is a rather paradoxical relationship between faith and belief, in that we can have great faith that something is true, both in the past and for other people, yet not believe that it is true for us. Thus, our beliefs, or "unbelief" as it were, robs us of the fruits of our faith. Let us consider for a moment what unbelief is and how to overcome it.

UNBELIEF

Since childhood we have rehearsed the thirteenth article of faith, which contains these words: "We believe all things." In stark contrast, the brother of Jared, in prophetic commentary on our time declared of the latter-day Gentiles:

> 13 Come unto me, O ye Gentiles, and I will show unto you the greater
> things, the knowledge which is hid up because of unbelief. (Ether
> 4:13)

It is intriguing that we emphatically profess as an article of our faith that we believe all things, and yet the Lord considers us, as a people, to be living under a veil of unbelief. What are the "greater things" which the Lord is willing, even anxious, to show unto us, but which we exclude from our paradigm through unbelief? We will examine this concept further on, but no matter what else these hidden greater things may include, one of them is obviously the truth about Zion, what it really is, and how to establish it. I say it seems obvious because these are the things which we have yet to do, and for which we yet dwell under a divinely imposed sanction.

No people can rise above their beliefs, and in the present dispensation we have underwhelmed ourselves by taking our commission to build Zion lightly, bringing down upon our heads a stern condemnation.

> 54 And your minds in times past have been darkened because of unbelief, and because you have treated lightly the things you have received—
>
> 55 Which vanity and unbelief have brought the whole church under condemnation.
>
> 56 And this condemnation resteth upon the children of Zion, even all. (D&C 84:54–56)

Unbelief in what? How can we be stumbling over disbelief? Isn't this the true Church? Don't we have the fulness of the gospel?

Of course it is, and of course we do! But there is at least one thing that we don't yet believe, because the whole Church is still under condemnation for unbelief. In my opinion, the term "the whole Church" isn't referring to the Church organization, it's referring to us, the people, the "children of Zion." The Church organization is doing exactly as the Lord directs it to do. The Church as an institution can't struggle with unbelief, because an institution is incapable of either belief or unbelief. The unbelief lies with the citizens of that noble institution. We have allowed unbelief to trick us into treating lightly the things we have received, because we don't even realize we presently have them.

By the sheer actuality that we were commanded to build Zion 175 plus years ago, and were told we eventually must and that we ultimately would when we had prepared ourselves, it is an unassailable fact that one of the things we have failed to truly accept is our role in establishing Zion. Why? As the above verse attests, it is because we simply don't believe it. We don't believe we have anything else to do, or perhaps we believe Zion is already built.

The same verse connects that fatal unbelief to vanity. Vanity is excessive pride or even conceit. When verse 55 connects "vanity and unbelief," one gets the idea that the reason we suffer from unbelief is because we are so proud of what we have accomplished that we simply can't accept the idea that we have anything left to achieve. We're "true," complete, and perfect. In our thinking, we are Zion already. In this simple way, we are indeed "lifted up" in the pride of our own eyes. Oddly enough, that's how Christ described us too:

> 10 And thus commandeth the Father that I should say unto you: At that day when the Gentiles shall sin against my gospel, and shall reject the fulness of my gospel, and shall be lifted up in the pride of their hearts above all nations, and above all the people of the whole earth, and shall be filled with all manner of lyings, and of deceits, and of mischiefs, and all manner of hypocrisy, and murders, and priestcrafts, and whoredoms, and of secret abominations; and if they shall do all those things, and shall reject the fulness of my gospel, behold, saith the Father, I will bring the fulness of my gospel from among them.

> 11 And then will I remember my covenant which I have made unto my people, O house of Israel, and I will bring my gospel unto them. (3 Nephi 16:10–11)

Notice that Christ doesn't say "if" the Gentiles sin against my gospel, he ways "when."

I know it is hard to believe that we are filled with the gross sins outlined above. None of us is in a position to judge such things accurately. Considering that we are a worldwide church with millions of members, it is not difficult to imagine that these things do happen to some degree. The dividing line seems to be when the Church "shall be filled" with these evil things. Let us pray with fear and trembling that this day never arrives. The mere fact that this scripture fell from the lips of a prophet is evidence enough that such a thing is possible.

It later allows that "if they shall do all those things," meaning the abominations listed above, and then in addition to these crimes "shall reject the fulness of my gospel," then He will bring the fulness of His gospel from among them. We are told that the gospel as we presently possess it will never again be destroyed or given to another people (D&C 138:44). So this verse can't be referring to non-LDS folks losing their opportunity to join this Church because that will never happen.

Who then are these slipshod gentiles? The term gentile has been used very differently over the years. Elder McConkie sums it up this way:

Thus Joseph Smith, of the tribe of Ephraim, the chief and foremost tribe of Israel itself, was the Gentile by whose hand the Book of Mormon came forth, and the members of The Church of Jesus Christ of Latter-day Saints, who have the gospel and who are of Israel by blood descent, are the Gentiles.[8]

We are the Gentiles. We are Israel both by roundabout blood descent and by spiritual adoption, but we are gentiles because we are not distinct members of the house of Israel. We must conclude that this warning is aimed at ourselves, not at the broader population of the non-LDS world. The feeling we are left with is that the real possibility, even the likelihood, exists that we will fall into this trap of sin and rejection.

How could we, the true Church, the true Saints, the true missionaries and light to the world, ever fall into such decay? The answer lies in that the rejection we are accused of is not of the gospel in its totality, but it is of the *fulness* thereof. We believe much of it—actually, we believe all of those things we are aware of, but we have for some reason rejected, or more understandably, aren't aware of a glorious portion of it. And, if we persist in unbelief and add to this the sins listed above, then this greater portion, this "fulness of my gospel" that includes the privileges of Zion and similar blessings, shall be taken from us and given to another.

All you have to do to take away the greater portion of the gospel from a people is to keep them uninformed that it exists.

We have already discussed what the fulness of the gospel means. There is little doubt that all is not well in Zion—because Zion does not presently exist (see 2 Nephi 28:21).

According to the divine record, we have already, through our unbelief, begun to reject that greater portion of the word.

> 13 Come unto me, O ye Gentiles, and I will show unto you the greater things, the knowledge which is hid up because of unbelief. (Ether 4:13)

> 54 And your minds in times past have been darkened because of unbelief, and because you have treated lightly the things you have received—

> 55 Which vanity and unbelief have brought the whole church under condemnation.

> 56 And this condemnation resteth upon the children of Zion, even all. (D&C 84:54–56)

It is a bitter pill to swallow, to think that the whole Church is under condemnation. It is tempting to assume that this sorry situation has since been rectified, that we are presently freed from that darkening shadow. Yet President Benson taught us in no uncertain terms that the condemnation of section 84 endures to the present day:

> In section 84 of the Doctrine and Covenants, the Lord declares that the whole Church and all the children of Zion are under condemnation . . . This condemnation has not been lifted, nor will it be until we repent.[9]

President Brigham Young, who was a personal friend with the prophet Joseph, and who himself lived through the failed attempt to establish Zion in its infancy, labored to establish Zion without success in Utah. He yearned for the day when Zion would be built and the curse taken off of the earth. This overarching curse will be lifted after we repent and lift the condemnation upon the children of Zion. Then, when we finally build Zion, the earth will rest. Brigham Young taught:

> We want all the Latter-day Saints to understand how to build up Zion. The City of Zion, in beauty and magnificence, will outstrip anything that is now known upon the earth. The curse will be taken from the earth and sin and corruption will be swept from its face.[10]

Now that we have considered how faith can be darkened by unbelief, let us reach toward the sunshine of faith and consider faith and belief.

FAITH AND BELIEF

One of the great obstacles to becoming Zion may be that we can't quite raise our belief structure to include viewing ourselves in Zion with firm desire and inspired hope. When we at last do conquer this unbelief we will find the heavens opening, for the Lord gives no commandment unto the children of men except He also prepares a way for them to accomplish it (see 1 Nephi 3:7).

If you can believe that God will open the way for you to be a righteous father, mother, or missionary, then you already have sufficient faith to become Zion. What you may yet lack is the ability to believe in your personal place in Zion. To understand how unbelief can rob us of the blessings of God, let us for a moment consider the interesting convergence between faith and belief.

Faith is a result of exposure to the Spirit of the Lord and is a gift of God. Faith does not naturally reside in man. When we obey some principle of truth, a commandment of God, or any whispering of the Spirit, the Spirit of the Lord touches our souls with a tiny increase of faith regarding that principle.

One can only have faith in things that are true (Alma 32:21). We can't have faith in a falsehood. Only to the extent that a principle contains truth can we exercise faith in it. For this reason, faith is always centered in Christ, because all truth flows from Christ.

Unlike faith, which is always pure, our belief structure includes both pure elements of truth and impurities of human assumption, tradition, false conclusions, and out-and-out lies. Most of what we believe comes from the experiences of our lifetime, all of which occur in the natural world, and most of which are in some way tainted. Such false beliefs are hostile to our progress unless overridden by revealed truth.

By so noting the difference between faith and belief, we are not assigning belief second-class citizenship. Belief, while very different from faith, is the sum total of what we think, both good and bad, true and false. Belief is extremely powerful and has a greater pull upon our lives than any other single force, because our belief literally defines our universe. Life is what we believe it to be. People are what we believe them to be. Our perception of our world, our belief structure, imposes so much distortion upon our vision that in many ways it creates the world we view.

Our every act is driven by a belief. Whether that belief is based upon truth, or upon a misconception, determines whether that act is righteous or evil. Often, our faith can be profound, while our belief about how that faith applies to us can limit, or even eliminate, our enjoyment of the fruits of our faith. Such faith-opposing believing is called "unbelief" in the scriptures. It is not necessarily an absence of faith and can coexist with faith quite companionably. But it is nevertheless an effective and often long-lived damnation of our faith.

An example of this might be: We may have faith that Heavenly Father loves us and has the power to heal an illness or disease we may have. But we may simultaneously believe (or assume because of what others have taught us) that Heavenly Father wants us to learn some lesson through our suffering, or that we must seek a medical solution first, turning only to Him as a last resort. Or, we may conclude that since we haven't personally seen this magnitude of healing with our own eyes, He may just not be doing healings of this degree nowadays, and thus, we doubt the will of God to heal us—not His power, but His intention to do so. We have great faith He can, we just don't believe He will, and thus uninspired belief (unbelief) smothers our faith.

Another example may be: We read the scriptures and have complete faith that the brother of Jared (or any other righteous figure) truly experienced the profound blessings, visions, revelations, and angelic visitations they record. And, even though the same prophet records that God is no respecter of persons and liberally grants the same blessings to all who righteously seek them, we believe that the scriptures are largely for our education and not a prototype of our personal spiritual potential. We may conclude that such things do not happen in this day, or if they do, they would happen to someone more highly placed or more obedient. We thereby doubt, not God's power, which is a by-product of our faith, but His will to grant us a place within His promises. Such doubt is by definition, unbelief.

We extinguish the fire of faith with the cold rains of unbelief. The Lord told Moroni:

> 7 And in that day that they [the latter-day gentiles] shall exercise faith in me, saith the Lord, even as the brother of Jared did, that they may become sanctified in me, then will I manifest unto them the things which the brother of Jared saw, even to the unfolding unto them all my revelations, saith Jesus Christ, the Son of God, the Father of the heavens and of the earth, and all things that in them are. (Ether 4:7; bracketed comment added)

This verse contains one of the most incredible pronouncements of promise this dispensation has ever been given. It is saying that when— notice it doesn't say if, it implies *when*—we rend the veil of unbelief and develop faith like unto the brother of Jared's, God will unfold unto us all of His revelations, which means that we will know all things, which would enable us to part the veil in many places and lay hold upon all promised blessings. This promise isn't being made just to the Quorum of the Twelve. This is a promise that is held out to every person who chooses to seek and obtain it. We have access to the same gifts in this day, in this priesthood, in this Church, as the brother of Jared used to rend the heavens in his day, which lit up his sixteen stones and his eternity.

So why aren't we doing so? Mormon's analysis of this incredible promise and why we fail to lay hold upon these vast things is illuminating:

13 Come unto me, O ye Gentiles, and I will show unto you the greater things, the knowledge which is hid up because of unbelief. (Ether 4:13)

So it is unbelief, not necessarily a lack of faith, but unbelief that keeps us captive in a state of wickedness. Does it seem harsh to characterize unbelief as wickedness? What is wickedness if not something that destroys our faith? False beliefs always send us off in pursuit of some path other than one that leads to exaltation. And pursuing a forbidden path is always the result of failure to heed His voice.

52 And whoso receiveth not my voice is not acquainted with my voice, and is not of me.

53 And by this [that they receive not my voice] you may know the righteous from the wicked, and that the whole world groaneth under sin and darkness even now.

54 And your minds in times past have been darkened because of unbelief, and because you have treated lightly the things you have received—

55 Which vanity and unbelief have brought the whole church under condemnation. (D&C 84:52–55; bracketed comment added)

The Lord here defines not receiving (not hearing and obeying) His voice, unbelief, and wickedness as the same spiritual malady. Furthermore, He states that our minds have been darkened because of unbelief—not sin or a lack of faith—but unbelief! "Darkened" implies a prior or even continuing presence of light that is being ignored or dimmed because of unbelief. Our minds are robbed of the light of our own faith through our inability to believe the truths that surround us. Further, we stand in darkness because we have treated lightly the things we have received.

BELIEF AND UNBELIEF

The genesis of belief—or in this case, unbelief—is an interesting puzzle. Part of this puzzle is revealed by Nephi while speaking prophetically of our day:

14 They have all gone astray save it be a few, who are the humble followers of Christ; nevertheless, they are led, that in many instances they do err because they are taught by the precepts of men. (2 Nephi 28:14)

The phrase "precepts of men" encompasses any uninspired thought, process, or belief. Anything uninspired is either partly, or wholly, untrue. Such uninspired beliefs could be as simple as "Miracles happen but not to me." Or it could be something more intimate like, "I just don't have much faith," or "I doubt I'll ever see a vision." Unbelief may also result from clinging to incorrect precepts that are the remnants of childhood, such as "I can't help myself. I'm just a naughty girl."

The precepts of men may also take the form of platitudes that seem true but are not scriptural and dangerously tainted. Such precepts of men may include things like, "You have to love yourself before you can love God," when in fact, the scriptures teach that we must love God first and foremost, and love of self comes from God, not from self-promotion.

Almost all concepts of self—self-esteem, self-love, self-fulfillment, self-sufficiency, and the like—are not scriptural and are largely uninspired. Even the concept of self-discipline as a primary process to perfection places too much emphasis upon self and too little upon obedience to the voice of God, which activates the enabling power of the Atonement and acknowledges our utter dependence upon Christ's grace to heal and uplift us.

King Benjamin taught that we are to consider our *self* as being even less than the dust of the earth (Mosiah 2:25). Why? Because our self, our natural self, is tainted with mortal impurity, and in that state it is forever excluded from the presence of God. There is nothing the self can do to change this except to yield to the enticings of the Holy Spirit and put off the natural self, and in so doing, become a Saint through the Atonement of Christ (Mosiah 3:19).

Elder David A Bednar made this timeless statement in general conference in October 2007:

> Remission of sin is not the only or even the ultimate purpose of the gospel. To have our hearts changed by the Holy Spirit such that "we have no more disposition to do evil, but to do good continually" (Mosiah 5:2) as did King Benjamin's people, is the covenant responsibility we have accepted. *This mighty change is not simply the result of working harder or developing greater individual discipline. Rather, it is the consequence of a fundamental change in our desires, our motives, and our natures made possible through the Atonement of Christ the Lord.*[11]

False beliefs often spring from the precepts of men, those seemingly ubiquitous gems of dirt that sputter in our thinking and teaching, those false beliefs which everyone apparently accepts simply because everyone accepts them. They are "the philosophies of men mingled with scripture." They are the toxic waste of uninspired or darkly-inspired thinking.

There is another body of the philosophies of men that contain truth but that have no saving value. An example of such a truth is math. Math is based upon truth but is not saving. No amount of math understanding will bring us to Christ or to salvation. Such truths cannot be elevated to the status of doctrine, or used to support or supplant truly saving principles.

Such non-saving truths include principles of positive mental attitude, wealth philosophies, laws of attraction, positive thinking, "correct" politics, and so on. These have a proper place in the natural world, but become dangerous when they are commingled with saving truths. Mortals have a tendency to quickly embrace philosophies that promise physical or financial success in favor of more spiritual truths that promise eternal rewards.

Philosophies of men have been commingled with scripture when we begin to tout works, good samaritanship, service, or charitable acts as a pathway to salvation. Salvation is in Christ alone, and no amount of good works can "earn" us a place in the eternities. Works will never displace Christ as our Savior, or bring us to the throne of God and bypass faith, repentance, baptism, and the receipt of the Holy Ghost.

The truth is, great and lasting works, the type recorded at the hands of Moses, Lehi, the brother of Jared, and Moroni, always flow *from* true faith in Christ. Outside of spiritual things, self-aggrandizement, popularity, and fame are generally the intended by-products of great works that have uninspired origins.

When we attempt to accomplish great things in the name of Christ through great works of un- or under-inspired origin, what we generate is frustration, fatigue, and a very disappointing interview come judgment day. The eternal value of any act is dependent upon the virtue of the underlying belief. If we perform works because we believe we must work ourselves to exhaustion to be saved, then our labors are tainted by a false underlying belief. If we, however, are acting upon a prompting from the Holy Spirit and correctly believe that we should perform some act of service upon Christ's request, then all such works are saving in their nature and have no residual element of fatigue or exhaustion, but are rejuvenating, empowering, and exalting.

The belief behind the act sanctifies or soils the result.

As we noted before, the power of belief is astonishing. Belief governs our every act, and for this reason, false beliefs can drain the life out of our faith. What is even more astonishing is that we are in absolute control of what we choose to believe. One can be in the hospital with a bullet hole in his body and still proclaim, "I just can't believe I've been shot!" We choose, as opposed to having it revealed to us, what we want to believe.

The thirteenth article of faith says, "We believe all things." What an astonishing statement! I believe that bold proclamation means that we must choose to believe all things our faith teaches us. Unlike faith, which is the fruit of revelation, belief is the result of choosing—sometimes in defiance of what we have been told, or even what we think we have experienced, but which the Spirit accords is true.

The best way to eliminate unbelief is to prayerfully, with divine help, reclaim control of our thinking and reshape it according to faith-inspired truth. This can be done by comparing what we believe with what we understand by faith, and where there is any disparity, we let our faith triumph. By so doing, we choose belief over unbelief. No matter what falsehoods may attempt to pollute our minds, we can and must choose to believe all things that our faith teaches us. We simply exercise childlike acceptance and believe. Such an act of sweet believing must occur whenever a precept of man contravenes some element of our faith.

Anything we choose to believe becomes unbelief when it contradicts our faith. Revealed faith is always true, but belief is only true when it uplifts and adorns our faith. In order for us to "believe all things," faith must always prevail.

Is it difficult to eliminate unbelief and simply believe all things? It can be very difficult for the natural man, because belief is based upon experience, and our experiences always seem true. The natural man and woman are reluctant to alter their beliefs because they feel well-founded upon experience. Beliefs protect us from further negative experiences. They are mortal man's means of coping and survival. A defining experience may only *seem* true, but in fact may be dangerously false.

As an example, a belief that God does not answer our prayers may arise after having prayed earnestly as a little child, or we may have prayed desperately and no answer became apparent for whatever reason. Perhaps the answer came but in an unrecognizable form. As a result we may feel betrayed or abandoned. Thereafter, to guard against this ever happening again, the belief is born that we alone must take care of ourselves because

God doesn't answer prayers. Such a conclusion feels rational and thus is true. It feels safe because it promises to keep us from experiencing previous pain over and over. It seems to put us in charge of our own destiny. For reasons like this, people cling to their false beliefs. The human psyche is littered with such refuse from the past, and without the workings of the Holy Spirit to cleanse and upgrade the soul, such thinking may well persist into and beyond the grave.

Of course, decision making and thus belief making are a natural part of development and survival. We may not be able to avoid tracking some mud onto our faith. Many such decisions serve a useful, even a powerfully important purpose until we can mature and learn a better way of relating to the world around us. It is very difficult to change what we have become thus far. What we can do is allow faith and the Spirit of Christ to refine and purify us. We can take all elements of our faith and "believe" them, thus letting them supplant useless and even damning remnants of childish thinking.

For spiritual individuals, correcting unbelief is more a matter of recognizing that we have dropped our beautiful white faith in the mud of unbelief, repenting, then picking it up and through repentance, restoring it to whiteness. Whenever the Holy Spirit directs us contrary to our belief, then our faith must triumph.

When a spiritual individual holds a false belief, the Holy Spirit will labor to purify the unbelief. This may take the form of repeated promptings, feelings of faith, and whisperings of the Spirit upon a single subject. Our part is to act upon these promptings and invite the Lord's intervention to cleanse us of these false beliefs.

An example of this may be reoccurring feelings of distrust of the opposite sex. Such feelings probably arose out of need and served a purpose in a challenging situation. But as a partner in an eternal marriage, such feelings are damning (meaning, they stop our progress). The Holy Spirit will repeatedly present us with urgings to trust, to have faith, and to be forgiving and understanding. Yielding to such promptings is a pure form of repentance—repenting of unbelief and repenting of false thinking. It is a milestone step toward purity.

Failure to repent in response to the quiet teachings of the Holy Spirit may be followed by a more urgent, or possibly even life-altering, experience where we have no choice but to trust the Lord to deliver us. Repentance at this juncture will teach us to believe our own faith, and thus to set aside our fears. The result is an experience that yields a purified belief. Such laboring of the Spirit is ubiquitous in our lives; it is ever-present.

A soul of lesser spiritual metal would merely shrug off the opportunity to change his thinking as impossibly vague and launch into a familiar, though uninspired, path. In so doing, they will feel safe, justified, and proud of their self-determination, even when destruction and death are the results. The once-popular song "I Did It My Way" is the world's proud anthem, and the inscription above the main gate of the telestial kingdom.

In time, the Holy Spirit ceases to strive with such individuals.

It is likely that the Lord, through the Holy Spirit, will labor with us year after year until we either unfetter ourselves from the chains of unbelief and embrace the truth, or prove ourselves unworthy of further inspiration, and thereby silence the Holy Spirit on that subject.

Like the Word of Wisdom, or tithing, or any other commandment, believing—for the sake of believing—is a true principle, and it is commanded.

We believe all things!

And, since it is a commandment, it is also deeply possible because of the grace of Christ.

As with Lehi's Liahona, which operated only after they believed that it *could* direct them (Alma 37:40), all principles of faith begin to fully function only after we also believe them. Until then, they function by hit and miss, by degrees and with apparent randomness. How many elements of our faith are hitting on half of their cylinders? We need no longer wonder why.

It is astonishing that faith can hibernate alive but dormant beneath the snows of unbelief, awaiting the springtime of our believing. It is almost frightening that we could surround ourselves with faith and testimony and yet be oblivious to the gray skies of unbelief blocking our view of the heavens.

The statement is "We believe all things," not "We believe what we have observed to be true." When we feel the gentle glow of faith warming some chilly part of our souls, we can choose to believe those things, no matter what we think our eyes may have taught us to the contrary.

In striving to implement this tenant of our faith we may invoke Nephi's promise that when God commands, He also prepares a way (1 Nephi 3:7). Thus, choosing to "believe all things" invokes heaven's blessings. In time sweet believing simply fills our souls. It is our Savior who makes such believing not just possible, but also a sweetly flowing river within the soul. When we believe that which is true, then that principle of truth becomes operative in our lives. When we at last are able to "believe all things," then all truth becomes operative now and forever.

Joseph Smith taught us that faith is the power by which Jehovah created all things. Thus, faith is "the power" of God.[12] When we, as mortals, possess faith in the same degree that God possesses it, then we will be endowed with that same creative power. Elder McConkie similarly notes: "To the extent that fallen men gain faith, they become like God and exercise his power."[13]

We also know that, at least in mortals, we taint our faith with unbelief. Elder McConkie taught this principle in these words:

> To the extent that they live in unbelief, they are without God in the world, do not exercise his power, are not in process of becoming like him, and cannot and will not be saved.[14]

God, knowing all things in their true and correct perspective, cannot experience unbelief, and thus has all power. Another way to say this is pure faith empowered by pure belief is the power of God. This is not an overstatement for the purpose of emphasis. The fact is that God stands supreme in the heavens, omnipotent and omniscient because He has perfect faith, which He couldn't have without perfect belief.

The scriptures refer to our almost universal inability to believe as "the veil of unbelief" (Ether 4:15). What an apropos description! Our unbelief is a soiled curtain which separates us from the fruits of our faith. It is impurity of the most damning kind because it is unseen. It is easier to recognize adultery than unbelief, yet it is probably true that more of the family of Christ will remain out of the celestial kingdom, and by extension, out of Zion, because of unbelief than some grosser sin.

Once an individual feels the Holy Ghost teaching him faith in the principle of Zion and yields his mind and heart to true believing about what Zion is and what his ordained part is there, the pathway to Zion will appear at the tips of his toes.

Even though the pathway to Zion is available for the whole world to walk, if they will, a mighty door guards the entrance to that path. The keeper of the gate is Jesus Christ, and the key that opens the door is faith and inspired belief (2 Nephi 9:41–42). There was no possibility of blindly or accidentally stumbling down the path into Zion. Now that the path is before us, true disciples of Christ will plot a course that unlocks the door and brings them into Zion.

FAITH IN CHRIST

Faith is the first principle of the gospel, but most people don't begin their career in mortality with faith. Most people aren't born with faith. It is acquired by obedience to commandments and law. Preceding this is a principle that must operate even before faith can begin. That principle is obedience to the Light of Christ as manifested by one's conscience. Once a person begins to recognize and respond to their conscience, faith will begin to grow. When a person acts upon their faith they will be led toward the restored gospel of Jesus Christ.

Faith is one of the gifts of the Spirit of Christ (D&C 46:19–20). It does not naturally reside in the soul of man. We receive incremental gifts of faith as a result of obedience to the Holy Spirit, which is the voice of Christ. It is not necessary to list here that we must obey the commandments, because all acts of obedience are prompted by the Holy Spirit, and all gifts of the Spirit come as a result of that obedience. Faith grows as we discipline ourselves to higher and greater obedience, which opens the heavens to higher and greater contact with the Holy Spirit. This process can occur, and often does, without an understanding of how or even why it occurs.

When the spiritual pilgrim realizes that this voice of truth within himself actually originates with Jesus Christ, his trust in that voice evolves into faith—living faith in Jesus Christ. It becomes much more than a general faith or a belief in Christ's love or grace. It becomes a living force in our lives. It is living because it originates from the living Christ. It is dynamic, sympathetic to our desires, and responsive to our needs. It empowers us to seek and find, ask and receive, knock and open. It is Christ Himself responding through the Holy Ghost to our pleas, our prayers, and our praise.

As we acquire faith through obedience we become more and more like Christ, until we become sufficiently like Him so that through faith we can work miracles, exercise priesthood power, call down the powers of heaven, and qualify for an interview with Him.

When asked what the difference is between someone who is saved and someone who is not, Joseph Smith replied:

We answer, from what we have before seen of the heavenly worlds, they must be persons who can work by faith and who are able, by faith, to be ministering spirits to them who shall be heirs of salvation; and *they must have faith to enable them to act in the presence of the Lord,* otherwise they cannot be saved.[15]

It is fascinating that Joseph uses the language "ministering spirits to them who shall be heirs of salvation," which is language that describes translated beings, as we discussed on pages 39 and 67. When we arrive at that high pinnacle of faith, then faith becomes the power that enables us to "act" in the presence of the Lord. The overarching message of Ether 12 is that it was faith that enabled all of the righteous to obtain the privileges of seeing the visions, visitations, and manifestations of deity that they enjoyed.

THE FRUITS OF FAITH

Faith is the very power of God and the power of creation. It is undeniably true that everything around us, seen or unseen, is a manifestation of faith. Every blessing we hope to obtain, every exaltation in the eventual kingdom of heaven, every angelic song, every fiber of joy and rejoicing in the heavens we ever experience will be a result of faith.

As we obtain faith through the processes of the gospel of Christ, we obtain every good and glorious thing. To acquire a full endowment of faith is to become like God. Thus Elder McConkie makes this sweeping summation:

"As faith, then, is the principle by which the heavenly hosts perform their works, and by which they enjoy all their felicity," our account continues, "we might expect to find it set forth in a revelation from God as the principle upon which his creatures here below must act in order to obtain the felicities enjoyed by the saints in the eternal world." How can mortals become either gods or angels unless they obtain the same powers, the same attributes, and the same holiness that such eternal beings now possess? God is God and angels are angels because they possess the powers and perfections that now are theirs. If men gain these same states of glory and exaltation, can they do it without becoming like those who already have so inherited?[16]

In the same glorious vein, when we do acquire saving faith, then we are inexorably drawn into the pathway to perfectness. Joseph Smith said:

> When men begin to live by faith they begin to draw near to God; and when faith is perfected they are like him; and because he is saved they are saved also; for they will be in the same situation he is in, because they have come to him; and when he appears they shall be like him, for they will see him as he is.[17]

Commenting upon the above statement by Joseph Smith, Elder McConkie penned these inspiring words:

> Manifestly there neither is nor can be anything greater than God. If men become like him, they ascend the throne of eternal power, are exalted to the highest state that exists in all the endless expanse of created things, and are themselves gods. Thus salvation is not only the greatest of all the gifts of God, it is also the chief and most glorious of all the fruits of faith.[18]

Exaltation is the most glorious of all the fruits of faith in eternity. Faith is also the principle that governs all the gifts of God in mortality. One of the great examples of faith embodied in a man other than Christ was Enoch. Through his great faith he obtained the fullest outcome any mortal may in this world. His faith was perfect, and since it was perfect, it was like unto God's, and with it he created a perfect society, a perfect city, and a perfect defense against evil. Ultimately Enoch's faith brought his entire city out of the telestial world and into the world of translated beings. Such is the greatest outcome of our faith while yet in mortality, that we may likewise be called into a world like Enoch's.

It is the greatest because it follows all other blessings, including being born again, calling and election, and the Second Comforter. The scriptures give us no greater accomplishment that a mortal may receive while yet a mortal. Of course, exaltation is the greatest gift of all, but this paramount gift is not offered to souls while yet in mortality.

> 30 For God having sworn unto Enoch and unto his seed with an oath by himself; that every one being ordained after this order and calling should have power, by faith, to break mountains, to divide the seas, to dry up waters, to turn them out of their course;
>
> 31 To put at defiance the armies of nations, to divide the earth, to break every band, to stand in the presence of God; to do all things according to his will, according to his command, subdue principalities and

powers; and this by the will of the Son of God which was from before the foundation of the world.

32 And men having this faith, coming up unto this order of God, were translated and taken up into heaven. (JST Genesis 14:30–32)

How did these of old acquire such faith? The answer is that they began as babes, naked and with nothing more than an inner voice of truth to guide them—just as you and I. They followed the true course laid out for them by their conscience. They loved and were obedient to truth, and in time were lifted from their natural strengths and made glorious through the Atonement of Christ.

10 Behold it was by faith that they of old were called after the holy order of God.

11 Wherefore, by faith was the law of Moses given. But in the gift of his Son hath God prepared a more excellent way; and it is by faith that it hath been fulfilled. (Ether 12:10–11)

16 Yea, and even all they who wrought miracles wrought them by faith, even those who were before Christ and also those who were after.

17 And it was by faith that the three disciples obtained a promise that they should not taste of death; and they obtained not the promise until after their faith.

18 And neither at any time hath any wrought miracles until after their faith; wherefore they first believed in the Son of God.

19 And there were many whose faith was so exceedingly strong, even before Christ came, who could not be kept from within the veil, but truly saw with their eyes the things which they had beheld with an eye of faith, and they were glad. (Ether 12:16–19)

In other words, "all things are possible to those who believe" (Mark 9:23).

Having thus obtained faith in Christ, or better stated, having begun the journey to perfect faith in Christ, the next step is a willingness to sacrifice our will, our time, and our possessions for the living Christ, even as He directs by His voice.

SACRIFICE

Such a scary term, sacrifice, yet a sublime principle lies hidden behind the images of supreme surrender and blood-letting.

Joseph described sacrifice as being essential to true religion and to true faith. The reason sacrifice holds this high office is because of the way truth is dispensed unto mankind. As we have discussed many times so far, our nexus with the heavens is the Holy Spirit, the voice of Christ. It is the most common means whereby the will of God is communicated from the heavens into our souls.

Being natural men and women as we are, we by nature pursue a course of life calculated to answer the needs and passions of the flesh. There is nothing inherently evil in the flesh, but it is through the flesh that Satan has power to tempt us, and thus the man of flesh, the natural man, is an "enemy to God." The tricky part is that we begin to interpret temptations as "natural" urgings when they are not. They are coming from an evil source outside of our natural selves. When the Holy Spirit speaks, it nearly always directs us into acts that fly in the face of what we interpret as natural urgings. Thus, to choose to obey the Holy Spirit is to sacrifice the will of the flesh to some degree, either lesser or greater. Choosing to fast as a means of spiritual attainment is a righteous form of sacrificing the needs of the flesh to the will of the Holy Spirit. Therefore, sacrifice is an everlasting and true principle of the gospel of salvation.

We do not often hear the call to lay down our lives, or to leave our loved ones to pursue some greater mission, or to die upon the long trail to Zion. Such sacrifices are not those of which we now speak, though such have been in the past and undoubtedly will be again in the future. The sacrifice that is essential to true religion and true faith is the sacrifice of the will of the natural man—the will of the flesh to obedience to the voice of Christ. To sacrifice the will of the flesh is to have a broken heart and a contrite spirit.

> 8 Thou shalt offer a sacrifice unto the Lord thy God in righteousness, even that of a broken heart and a contrite spirit. (D&C 59:8)

> 20 And ye shall offer for a sacrifice unto me a broken heart and a contrite spirit. And whoso cometh unto me with a broken heart and a contrite spirit, him will I baptize with fire and with the Holy Ghost, even as the Lamanites, because of their faith in me at the time of their

conversion, were baptized with fire and with the Holy Ghost, and they knew it not. (3 Nephi 9:20)

Notice that the end result of this sacrifice is the baptism of fire and the Holy Ghost. Ultimately, any person who makes these sacrifices will find that such great blessings flood into their lives that in due course these acts of selflessness are rendered no sacrifice at all but are an investment in a divine savings plan of eternal joy.

> 29 And every one that hath forsaken houses, or brethren, or sisters, or father, or mother, or wife, or children, or lands, for my name's sake, shall receive an hundredfold, and shall inherit everlasting life. (Matthew 19:29)

Beyond the eternal consequences of such obedience unto sacrifice lies the simple fact that all such obedience is rewarded with a divine acknowledgement of rightness. A feeling distills upon the soul that unimpeachably informs us that we are acceptable and on the strait course. It is an accumulation of these divine nods of approval that in time becomes "righteousness," which is to know, through revelation, that the course of life we are on is straight and true.

The prophet Joseph described it this way:

> An actual knowledge to any person, that the course of life which he pursues is according to the will of God, is essentially necessary to enable him to have that confidence in God without which no person can obtain eternal life. It was this that enabled the ancient saints to endure all their afflictions and persecutions, and to take joyfully the spoiling of their goods, knowing (not believing merely) that they had a more enduring substance (Hebrew 10:34).

> Having the assurance that they were pursuing a course which was agreeable to the will of God, they were enabled to take, not only the spoiling of their goods, and the wasting of their substance, joyfully, but also to suffer death in its most horrid forms; knowing (not merely believing) that when this earthly house of their tabernacle was dissolved, they had a building of God, a house not made with hands, eternal in the heavens.[19]

It is this knowledge, obtained through obedience and sacrifices of self that we make many times, that we may come to possess this actual knowledge, which will enable us, like the ancient Saints, to have saving faith in Christ. Joseph Smith taught in the Lectures on Faith that:

Nothing short of an actual knowledge of their being the favorites of heaven, and of their having embraced that order of things which God has established for the redemption of man, will enable them to exercise that confidence in him, necessary for them to overcome the world, and obtain that crown of glory which is laid up for them that fear God.[20]

As the following quote describes, every saint who has obtained this great faith obtained it this way. Failure to sacrifice the will of the flesh sufficiently to obtain this endowment robs us of the faith we require and eventually the adversary will gain power over us and destroy us.

Again, Joseph Smith:

All the saints of whom we have account, in all the revelations of God which are extant, obtained the knowledge which they had of their acceptance in his sight through the sacrifice which they offered unto him; and through the knowledge thus obtained their faith became sufficiently strong to lay hold upon the promise of eternal life, and to endure as seeing him who is invisible; and were enabled, through faith, to combat the powers of darkness, contend against the wiles of the adversary, overcome the world, and obtain the end of their faith, even the salvation of their souls.

But those who have not made this sacrifice to God do not know that the course which they pursue is well pleasing in his sight; for whatever may be their belief or their opinion, it is a matter of doubt and uncertainty in their mind; and where doubt and uncertainty are there faith is not, nor can it be. For doubt and faith do not exist in the same person at the same time; so that persons whose minds are under doubts and fears cannot have unshaken confidence; and where unshaken confidence is not there faith is weak; and where faith is weak the persons will not be able to contend against all the opposition, tribulations, and afflictions which they will have to encounter in order to be heirs of God, and joint heirs with Christ Jesus; and they will grow weary in their minds, and the adversary will have power over them and destroy them.[21]

There is another aspect of sacrifice that we need to explore, which is closely associated with purity. We have already discussed that purity is in part the result of the Holy Spirit cleansing us of the baggage of mortality. Quite often this cleansing process involves a form of bedrock humility which is not native to most mortals. What this means is that quite often this type of humility and willingness to lay aside our favorite and most entertaining imperfections is arrived at through divinely engineered life experiences that steamroll our pride. Eventually, such experiences either induce us to rebellion or into humble obedience to the will of God.

While being steamrolled is not a willing form of sacrifice, it does eventually, hopefully, yield humility and place our feet upon the correct path.

However, there is another form of sacrifice which *is* willing and righteous, and which yields the requisite purity without being flattened by dramatic events. This is when we offer up a broken heart and contrite spirit to the Lord, and in true humility lay all we are upon the altar and submit ourselves to any schooling needed to remake us into a Zion person.

This sacrifice is the sacrifice of our will, pride, fears, and mortal baggage. It is done in mighty prayer. What will happen after such an offering is a series of events that highlights our weaknesses, opening them to our view, and gives us a chance to repent and step away from them. If we are determined to serve God at all hazards, and if we enter with eyes opened by revelation and hearts truly joyful in the process, the price paid will not feel sacrificial, though it may tug at our hearts and fears. The price we pay will be to become pure, which is a far less dramatic process than to be compelled to humility and then be purified. The Prophet Joseph left this powerful insight:

> Let us here observe, that a religion that does not require the sacrifice of all things never has power sufficient to produce the faith necessary unto life and salvation; for, from the first existence of man, the faith necessary unto the enjoyment of life and salvation never could be obtained without the sacrifice of all earthly things. *It was through this sacrifice, and this only, that God has ordained that men should enjoy eternal life; and it is through the medium of the sacrifice of all earthly things that men do actually know that they are doing the things that are well pleasing in the sight of God. When a man has offered in sacrifice all that he has for the truth's sake, not even withholding his life, and believing before God that he has been called to make this sacrifice because he seeks to do his will, he does know, most assuredly, that God does and will accept his sacrifice and offering, and that he has not, nor will not seek his face in vain.* Under these circumstances, then, he can obtain the faith necessary for him to lay hold on eternal life.[22]

Notice that it is the sacrifice of all things which gives one sufficiently potent faith to seek the face of the Lord; and since a personal interview with Christ is the doorway into Zion, sacrifice takes its righteous place as the initiatory rite of Zion.

This is the eye of the needle, as it were, the birth canal of righteousness. This is the point at which hearts faint and knees weaken. No rational person seeks after ways to sacrifice. The saving principle here is that the ultimate object we must place on the altar is our broken heart and contrite spirit (see 3 Nephi 9:20). Since we *are* mortal and our lives depend upon mortal things, the only concrete way we can show that humility is to place everything we are, have, and hope to become upon the altar. The Lord doesn't need or want our "things." Material objects only get sacrificed when our mortal weaknesses attach themselves to physical objects; then the cleansing process can include watching those things go up in smoke so we can learn absolute purity and contrition of spirit.

In the process of Abraham's purification he was asked to sacrifice his son, who was Abraham's beloved son and his only posterity. Without unduly attempting to read between Abraham's lines, it appears that Abraham loved Isaac above all things, and therefore Abraham had to untangle his loyalties and his mortal pride in order to obtain the supreme blessings he had been promised. Abraham became the father of all righteous when he raised the knife over Isaac in complete faith, believing that in obeying God, he was doing a greater good than the obvious wrong of sacrificing his son. Abraham's faith was such that he did not know how God would fulfill His promises regarding Abraham's posterity, but believed that if necessary, God would raise Isaac from the dead (Hebrews 11:19).

With this faith in his heart and, I'm sure, fear in his hands, with tears and anguish, Abraham plunged the knife downward with every intent of sacrificing his son. And at that exact moment when he achieved his diamond-hard resolve to obey, Abraham overcame his failings and completed his sacrifice.

You see, what God wants isn't our beloved son or our home or our business, family, or marriage; those are only the things to which we attach our pride and weaknesses, and thus they can become the false idols of our lives. God wants us to sacrifice our impurities so we can see Him and become like Him. So, as soon as Abraham had triumphed, God sent an angel to save Isaac, and Abraham left the mountain with his son in his arms.

This test of Abraham's thus became the prototype of all such tests. For Abraham this was a terrible paradox. God had promised him great blessings through Isaac. It must have seemed to Abraham that it just couldn't be true that now God was asking for Isaac's life, yet He had. Abraham did not know how God was going to resolve the conflict. That was the paradox. No mortal logic, no brute force genius can unravel such a paradox. But faith can, faith did, and faith will. We will all walk away with our Isaacs if our own triumph of faith occurs as timely as did Abraham's.[23]

PRAYER

All of these principles of the gospel we are discussing are intertwined, and each depends upon the other for perfect application. They cannot be lived piecemeal and still enjoy the desired effect upon our souls. They operate upon us in concert. Through hearkening to the voice of the Good Shepherd we grow and learn. We learn to more clearly distinguish the voice of truth from that of the world.

In time the voice of the Holy Spirit, when obeyed, brings all mankind to the restored gospel, the ordinances, priesthood and temple, and the gift of the Holy Ghost, whose spiritual enhancements uplift, purify, and empower. As we walk by faith and by obedience to the ever-present Shepherd of our souls, a truth is quietly revealed, most often without fanfare, that we are within the narrow confines of the straight way. This divine assurance that we are living according to Christ's pattern bestows upon us a confidence that God will hear our prayers and grant our petitions. It enables us to "come boldly unto the throne of grace," not just in times of need, but in times of searching, yearning, and probing into the heavens (Hebrews 4:16). It is the means whereby we at last gain faith sufficient to part the veil in prayer.

Elder McConkie highlights the relationship between prayer and faith thus:

> Faith in its full and pure form requires an unshakable assurance and an absolute confidence that Deity will hear our pleas and grant our petitions. It requires a mental guarantee, sealed with surety in the soul, that what we ask is right and will be granted. Only then can we "come boldly unto the throne of grace," there to "obtain mercy, and find grace to help in time of need." (Hebrews 4:16) And it scarcely needs stating that no person can have this confidence and assurance when he knows he is not living in the way the Lord wants him to live.[24]

The mental guarantee Elder McConkie is speaking of is a gift of the Spirit and flows into the soul as we walk in obedience to the voice of Christ. The immediate result of that guarantee is "hope." We hope for great things all our lives, but *hope*, as a principle of the gospel, comes when the Holy Spirit reveals the knowledge that we are walking a course that is guaranteed to bring us the sought-after blessings.

It is my opinion that most higher spiritual events in this life begin as a prayer of faith and evolve into a glorious experience. Such seems to be the prototype laid down in the scripture. Rare it is that someone stumbles upon an angel by the way, or trips into a vision, or ambles upon the veil parting before him. Most grand spiritual experiences recorded in scripture began as a prayer. Thus, learning to pray with perfect faith is to learn to seek and obtain the spiritual desires of our hearts, whether they be pressing needs or glorious manifestations we earnestly desire from heaven.

REVELATION AND PRAYER

So much of what we do of our own intellect should actually be done by Christ utilizing our hands or our voice. Such was the perfect life of Christ that He did only those things which His Father showed Him (John 8:28–29). When we do any good thing without divine guidance and spiritual power, we may presume the act is counted unto us as good works; however, it only possesses a form of godliness, often lacking the power we are seeking.

Consider a priesthood blessing where a willing individual steps forth to perform that ordinance without having opened the channels of intimate revelation through the walk of his own life. For such an individual, the words will lack power and conviction, and the promises will be tentative and conditional—not unrighteous, but without power. Such blessings often include admonition, beseeching of the Lord, and escape clauses that give both the priesthood holder, and the recipient, a place to hang their faith if it doesn't come to pass. At the end of such blessings we are often not surprised, and oddly, not disturbed, when our desires are not realized as promised. We just accept that the answer from the heavens was no or that someone didn't have the faith necessary—and we're okay with that.

Consider this statement regarding haphazard priesthood healings:

Brother Joseph, while in the Spirit, rebuked the Elders who would continue to lay hands on the sick from day to day without the power to heal them. Said he: "It is time that such things ended. Let the Elders either obtain the power of God to heal the sick or let them cease to minister the forms without the power."[25]

Perhaps the most common "fine print" we use to give us a feel-good pass when a priesthood blessing does not materialize is "I guess it was just not the Lord's will." It may be the Lord's will that we not be healed at times. The contradiction here is that if we didn't take the time, live the life, or walk the walk that would have enabled us to understand the Lord's will in enough detail to use the proper words in a priesthood blessing, why are we then qualified to state that it was the Lord's will for us to continue to suffer? Without meaning to be at all judgmental, I ask, wouldn't it be more valiant of us to align ourselves with the will of the living Christ first, and then after we have spoken by authority, to be able to say with a resounding thunderclap of truth, "in the name of Jesus Christ, Amen"?

In line with Joseph's counsel, consider the same priesthood holder who has obtained the voice of Christ as his guide, has fasted and prayed diligently to obtain righteous priesthood power, is familiar with the workings of revelation, and is fearless in speaking the truths that come into his heart. As the blessing progresses, let us assume that the voice of heaven instructs him to invoke a powerful healing. To the extent that the individual receiving the blessing has faith in Christ and faith in his own ability to correctly hear the Holy Spirit, the resulting blessing will flow with power. Words of eternal worth will be spoken. Prophecy will tumble from his lips, and power will heal and sanctify the recipient of the blessing. There will be no fine print, no escape clauses, just the blessing and the palpable power. Both will walk away with greater faith, and the words will be fulfilled to the letter.

Prayer also fits this model perfectly. Prayer that our needs or uninspired thinking forces from our lips is often pleading, apologetic, filled with pathos, and at times begging. We don't feel the full power of prayer, so we use repetition and self-flagellation as a form of spiritual purgative. We include self-abuse and self-effacement to substitute for true humility and true faith that would have brought the healing power we seek. Such prayers have little power to call forth blessings; they just make us feel better because we have abased ourselves and bared our souls.

MIGHTY PRAYER

Of course, all forms of sincere prayer are delightful to Father, and even those that are forced and uninspired are counted in our favor. What we are striving to do is to take our sincere but sometimes less-inspired prayers and turn them into prayers in the power of the Holy Spirit, which calls forth great blessings from the loving heavens without stumbling over our mortal weakness.

True power in prayer comes in obtaining the mind of God through revelation during our prayers. Such revelatory guidance naturally leads us to offer powerful and effective prayer. The scriptures often refer to powerful praying as "mighty prayer" (2 Nephi 4:24; Enos 1:4; Alma 6:6; Alma 8:10) or praying in the Spirit (see D&C 46:28, 30). It might also be called revelatory prayer, or prayer guided by revelation. When the Holy Spirit is invited into the prayer circle, it acts as a loving tutor to guide us in our prayers. During such a prayer, all feelings of self-doubt, self-loathing, or even of self at all, depart. We no longer feel the need to apologize profusely, to self-denigrate or spiritually grovel to evidence feelings of humility.

In mighty prayer, feelings of self largely disappear. In other words, we aren't the important person in the conversation. God is, and we have sought His audience to feel His love and to sup at the banquet of His mercy. In true prayer, our primary feeling is an overwhelming sense of being loved, accepted, guided, and welcome in the divine court. The words flow and can at times exceed language and eclipse our natural speech, occasionally becoming song with meter, melody, and rhyme. Such prayers are sometimes described in scripture with words such as "singing the song of redeeming love" (Alma 5:26).

In such a prayer we will know what to ask, even when it is not what we may have expected or even hoped for, allowing us to offer prayers that transcend our ability to speak in words. Such prayers are "according to the will of God," because the words came from God.

The words are spoken, and because they came into our minds from a divine source, they are spoken with great faith. The heavens rejoice in our humility, purity, and faith, and the answer is always a resounding yes, even when the blessing we receive was not what we may have expected or thought we needed. We accept with faith because we know it came from God, and in time, we come to see that it was the only answer that was truly perfect. Our faith increases both in God and in prayer, and our lives change forever.

As was mentioned earlier, all sincere prayer is efficacious. It brings us blessings and sustains us. What is being suggested is, as in many things of the Spirit, that there is a greater way. There is a means whereby we can call down power, peace, and miracles into our lives more frequently and with greater effect. We can invite the heavens into our private chambers and into our homes. We can petition the Father and be admitted so that we seek and find, ask and receive, knock and see the gates of heaven opening.

So, how may we seek after mighty prayer? I believe there is but a single formula for this and all other spiritual blessings. It is so elegant that it may seem too simplistic. But nevertheless, it is true.

The formula is simply to obey.

The only way we may realign our lives to such powerful prayer is by simply living by the Spirit in our daily lives (Galatians 5:17). We become fluent, so to speak, in the spiritual tongue during the walk and talk of our mundane affairs, and then we take that same spiritual power with us into the private chambers of our asking, and the heavens open in solemn response to our "mighty prayer."

In the Name of Jesus Christ

True prayer occurs in the name of Jesus Christ. Not only are we instructed to pray in the name of Christ, but all other acts that affect our eternal hopes must also occur in the name of Christ.

All saving acts rely upon Jesus Christ to sanctify and empower them. It stands to reason that no act can truly be in the name of Jesus Christ unless it is performed under His direction, by His word, and according to His will.

Just as righteous acts must be assisted by the presence of the Holy Spirit to show us how to serve in His name, it follows that nobody can truly speak or pray in the name of Christ unless he speaks or prays by the power of the Holy Ghost. Elder McConkie made the same observation:

> In the pure and perfect and proper sense, no one can speak or pray in the name of Christ unless he speaks or prays by the power of the Holy Ghost.[26]

Thus it is that prayer in its most effective and powerful form is prayer which says the words, seeks the blessings, and worships the Father the same as if Christ himself had offered the prayer. In part, this is what is implied when we close each prayer "in the name of Jesus Christ."

The largest part of the meaning of this common ending to prayer is that we are relying upon Christ's grace and Atonement to plead our case before the Father.

The other part of that divinely sanctioned benediction is intended to establish in the record of heaven and in the minds of the hearers that the words spoken came by revelation and were in fact what Christ would have said had He uttered the prayer Himself. When we speak what Christ would have spoken, then Christ becomes our advocate with the Father because He has interceded in giving us righteous words and inspired requests to bring before our God. And in this way, we make the benediction "in the name of Jesus Christ" powerfully true.

While it is apparent that in our mortal weakness we do not always obtain the power of heaven before we pray either privately or in church, it is nonetheless commanded that we should conclude each prayer in Christ's name. While this is proper no matter how weak or hurried the words, it is more desirable that we should understand the impact of proclaiming a prayer to be "in Christ's name" and seek for the inspiration and righteousness that would make those words powerfully true.

Not only is this the most powerful form of prayer, but it is also made possible to us because we are hearers of the voice of Christ. The greater our obedience to the Holy Spirit, the more perfect becomes our spiritual hearing and the more clear and present becomes the voice of God. Each act, every prayer, and every obedience and service that we perform in response to His sweet voice has been truly done "in the name of Jesus Christ."

As the following quotation promises, when we ask in the Spirit, we are asking in perfect harmony with the will of God; therefore, it is done unto us even as we ask. And thus, we discover the great key to receiving answers to our prayers.

> 30 And it shall come to pass that he that asketh in Spirit shall receive in Spirit. . . .
>
> 31 He that asketh in the Spirit asketh according to the will of God; wherefore it is done even as he asketh.
>
> 32 And again, I say unto you, all things must be done in the name of Christ, whatsoever you do in the Spirit;

34 And ye must give thanks unto God in the Spirit for whatsoever blessing ye are blessed with. (D&C 46:28, 30–32)

To pray without the guidance of the Holy Spirit is not to perform some unrighteous act, but it is often to ask amiss.

Ye ask, and receive not, because ye ask amiss, that ye may consume it upon your lusts. (James 4:3)

This world is too complex and convoluted for the human mind to see any distance into our future. Thus, what may appear to be the obvious solution to some trial is often not to our betterment and occasionally damages us. We can't know what is best for us because we see through a glass darkly, as Paul said (1 Corinthians 13:12). But when the Holy Spirit speaks, we no longer walk in darkness on that subject, and revealed truth casts bright light upon a tiny spot of our world. In that one thing we can have pure and illuminated faith. In that one principle we may pray with great faith, and we can act with absolute confidence and safety.

26 Likewise the Spirit also helpeth our infirmities: for we know not what we should pray for as we ought: but the Spirit itself maketh intercession for us with groanings [Greek, a sigh: a sound rich in feeling, but without words] which cannot be uttered. (Romans 8:26; bracketed comment added)

Joseph rendered groanings as "with striving which cannot be expressed."[27]

Even with the spiritually profound—those who have been purified and sanctified and who receive everything they ask for in prayer—the instruction is that they shall be guided in their prayers.

29 And if ye are purified and cleansed from all sin, ye shall ask whatsoever you will in the name of Jesus and it shall be done.

30 But know this, it shall be given you what you shall ask. (D&C 50:29–30)

Thus, the pathway to mighty, efficacious prayer is the very process of taking the Holy Spirit to be our guide; it is learning to separate and hear the voice of Christ from all the noise and voices of opposition in this life. The challenge of prayer is the challenge of life, which is to hear and obey and thus receive blessings *beyond* our greatest yearnings.

In a pragmatic sense, it takes some discipline to pray in this way. We have been taught from our youth, and correctly so, to kneel and petition God according to our wants and desires. And so we do, year after year, with varying degrees of success. To change this acceptable pattern into greater prayer takes little more than recognizing that it is ours to claim, and being willing to pay the price to obtain it.

Here are a few ideas that may help. Each of us will want to petition the Lord to see if these are applicable to us.

- Develop the habit of preparing to pray. Set your world in order; make time; be willing to remain for as long as it takes.

- Kneel when possible.

- Don't speak immediately. Allow words to form around your feelings. Feelings flow from the Spirit; words flow from the mind.

- Don't multiply words. Begin by remembering who you are addressing. Ponder upon the idea that, as you truly pray in the Spirit, the most magnificent, powerful, and glorious Being in all of existence is going to stop and listen to your prayer and extend some portion of His glory in blessing you in your needs.

- If nothing happens, pray that the Holy Spirit will fall upon you. Cleanse your mind, forgive, repent, gird up your loins, and try again and again.

- Expressing gratitude for blessings, remembering Christ's sacrifice, pondering blessings received, and expressing love are all effective in opening the pathways of revelation through which mighty prayer flows.

- Wait upon the Holy Spirit to fall upon you. You will know when it comes because a sense of peace, power, and a quickening of understanding will flow over you. Words will flow into your mind a little quicker than your normal cognitive processes. It can take much experience to learn how to clear your mind and let the Holy Spirit fill it with thoughts and words of inspiration.

- Clear your mind of *your* desires, forget your needs, step outside of your mortal self, and let the words fill your uncluttered mind. Learn to remove your mortal will from the equation of prayer. God already knows what you want, what you need, and what you fear. And, He knows far better than you what is needed next in your righteous journey. Trust Him. Let yourself become unimportant until He wordlessly asks you "What is wanted?"

- Express flowing rivers of gratitude. Thank Him for every grace and gift in your life. The Spirit will fall upon you as you rejoice.

- Speak whatever words enter your soul. Don't edit them. Don't stumble over the placement of words. Don't worry if you don't feel in control. You can tell when the Holy Spirit is guiding you because your speech patterns will change. You will say things you have never considered, in ways and with words you would not normally use. Remember, the ideas come from the Holy Spirit, but the language is your own. The Holy Spirit doesn't speak English—you do. You are translating inspired feelings into language, and thus they may jumble together here and there or fail to express the exact meaning of your heart. Even if they are not perfect English, the Lord knows exactly what your soul is laboring to say. Language may be unnecessary at times of profound inspiration.

- Let your soul worship. Speak every loving and worshipful thought that enters your soul.

- Sing the song of redeeming love when moved by the Holy Spirit to do so. You will know how when it occurs.

- Weep, rejoice, worship, shout praises to God when so moved.

- Last—and least of all—ask for those things that you are instructed to request. If you are not given what to ask—ask for nothing.

- Remain upon your knees until instructed to end your prayer.

- End in the name of Jesus Christ. Speak His name slowly.

REPENTANCE

Repentance is much more vast than seeking forgiveness for an errant act or omission. When we enter mortality we become participants in the fall of Adam, and by nature become carnal, sensual, and devilish. Housed in mortal flesh, our perception becomes that we *are* our flesh. Spiritual things feel remote and mystic. We are unable to be in His presence and unable to pierce the heavens but for this tiny spark of the Holy Spirit we receive from Christ.

Repentance is the process of overcoming all things that separate us from God, including the nature, limitations, and foibles of mortality. We have a tendency to view repentance in a much more limited way, more like doing the dishes we've put off for a couple days instead of remodeling and redecorating the entire house.

Repentance is the means whereby we overcome our fallen nature, and through the grace and Atonement of Christ, we rise to the stature whereby we may in time become like God.

> 22 Adam did fall by the partaking of the forbidden fruit, according to the word of God; and thus we see, that by his fall, all mankind became a lost and fallen people. . . .
>
> 24 Nevertheless there was a space granted unto man in which he might repent; therefore this life became a probationary state; a time to prepare to meet God; a time to prepare for that endless state which has been spoken of by us, which is after the resurrection of the dead. (Alma 12:22, 24)

Notice that Alma viewed repentance as the means whereby we repent of our fallen nature inherited from Adam and whereby we prepare to meet God and eventually live with Him forever.

Of course it is true that we also repent of individual deeds of which we may at times become guilty, but saving repentance is an eternity broader than this. More than repenting of what we do, we are to repent of what we are—which is fallen man, unable to return to God. We are to become Saints in fact as well as in name.

Having become mortal, and as mortals subject to the conditions of the fall of Adam, we have become creatures of the flesh. By nature, or by our fallen state, we tend to obey the flesh and the needs it insists upon being fulfilled. We are tricked into thinking that the needs, lusts, and passions of the flesh are *our* passions and needs. The natural man is the tabernacle of flesh—our bodies. The natural man demands to be fed, housed, entertained, and its lusts obeyed. If it is hungry, we are compelled to answer the demands. If it is bored, we attempt to entertain it. If it lusts, we seek means to satisfy the call of the flesh. Such an individual is not necessarily evil unless their quest to satisfy the demands of the flesh harms others or disobeys known commandments. Even at their very best, they are natural, and the natural man is an enemy to God (Mosiah 3:19).

The natural man is an enemy to God mostly in the sense that the flesh has no built-in drive that leads it back to the presence of God. Since it is the work and the glory of God to exalt His children, and it is the work of the flesh to do everything but that, their goals and purposes are at exact opposites, and thus they are enemies.

The flesh is like an automobile designed to transport us from one destination to another. When we are born into mortality, we look around with infantile understanding, and we view the automobile we are seated in and say to ourselves, "Look, I'm a car." It never occurs to us until much later that the car is an added element to our being and that we are the driver of the car, rather than the car itself.

As we drive along, the passenger seat is often occupied by one or both of two passengers, the Holy Spirit, or the spirit of evil. The spirit of evil continually tries to obscure the distinctness of our soul from the car. It doesn't especially care where the car is going, as long as we think that every need of the automobile is a crisis that must be immediately satisfied. He can divert us from any meaningful destination if he can keep us from hearing the voice of the Holy Spirit. One of the ways he keeps us from hearing the Holy Spirit is by making the demands of the flesh too loud to ignore. When we are serving the flesh, the Holy Spirit departs for a time.

The Holy Spirit has a far greater purpose and desires for us a glorious destination, caring little about the immediate needs and lusts of our car. It urges us to properly maintain our vehicle, while ignoring its lusts and complaints at how rugged the road to the destination has become.

If we listen to the voice of evil we never truly separate ourselves from the car, and in time we just take our car anyplace it wants, to do anything it wants. Such an abandonment of our proper role initially feels like we are fully satisfying our needs, fully in control of a fulfilling life. The evil ones convince us that this path alone can render complete control of self, total fulfillment, and satisfaction of all our needs and desires. Those who choose this path begin with great gusto and verve.

When it becomes obvious that the aching need of their flesh always wants more and greater stimulus than any entertainment can provide, such a soul eventually feels cheated, out of control, frustrated, and may become angry, even suicidal. They feel cheated by life itself, because no matter how hard they have tried and how great a price they have paid, they feel less fulfilled than when they started. As time goes by, the world seems less and less able to fulfill their needs, and they feel compelled, even justified, in sacrificing other's needs to fulfill their own, which leads to immoral acts and even criminal activities. What initially felt like freedom and fulfillment ultimately reveals itself to be captivity and emptiness. When a mortal lets the car steer, he becomes a captive of the will of the car and the evil that amplifies its lusts, and his automobile becomes an extension of that evil.

When we listen to and obey the voice of the Holy Spirit we never abandon control, but our headlights become brighter and brighter until we can see far down the road. We see road signs that warn and advise. The Holy Spirit never promises instant gratification or thrills. It leads toward denial of bodily passions, service of others, and discipline. Beyond all of this, which seems like a poor bargain to the natural man, there is only a faith-based belief that somewhere down the road happiness, peace, and long after death, eternal life will result. To a faith-incapable collection of nerves and tissue, this does not seem reasonable.

When in defiance of our flesh, we choose to respond in faith to the Holy Spirit, our vehicle runs better because it has become an instrument of righteousness, and in time it ceases to resist the direction of our inspired choosing. The Holy Spirit invites other divine passengers to join our journey, and vistas open before our windshield that inspire and fill our souls with joy.

Then, something astonishing happens. The fulfillment and joy that the evil ones wanted to convince us that they alone could deliver and never could—begins to flow from the Lord. Sacrifices small and large are repaid a hundredfold. Joy and service tumble together in an unending river of peace and fulfillment. Our automobile becomes an eternally and perfectly joined part of our being, and all of our needs and desires flow to us as the dews from heaven, far in excess of our greatest yearnings.

Rather than us assuming our body's identity, as in the case of the flawed view of the natural man, our flesh has been subdued, even "crucified in Christ" (Galatians 2:20) and in surrender it assumes our righteous identity. In time it is changed and perfected until it greatly enhances our true self's evolution toward godhood. It becomes our eternal servant, a source of endless righteous sensory input and source of creative powers and everlasting joy.

> 28 And now, my sons, I would that ye should look to the great Mediator, and hearken unto his great commandments; and be faithful unto his words, and choose eternal life, according to the will of his Holy Spirit;
>
> 29 And not choose eternal death, according to the will of the flesh and the evil which is therein, which giveth the spirit of the devil power to captivate, to bring you down to hell, that he may reign over you in his own kingdom. (2 Nephi 2:28–29)

How is such a transition possible? How can we truly tame the beast of mortality, overcome the flesh, and begin living in power and righteousness? We do it by putting off the natural man. We cease to be a passenger in our own bodies. As the scriptures teach, we exercise our will by yielding to the enticings of the Holy Spirit and obeying its directed course for our lives. We discipline our bodies to do our inspired bidding. And in so doing, we put off the natural man by subjugating the will of our flesh to the will of the Spirit. In doing so we are "yielding to the enticings of the Holy Spirit" and aligning ourselves with the sanctifying power of the Atonement.

> 19 For the natural man is an enemy to God, and has been from the fall of Adam, and will be, forever and ever, unless he yields to the enticings of the Holy Spirit, and putteth off the natural man and becometh a saint through the Atonement of Christ the Lord, and becometh as a child, submissive, meek, humble, patient, full of love, willing to submit to all things which the Lord seeth fit to inflict upon him, even as a child doth submit to his father. (Mosiah 3:19)

And having become saintly, we receive from the Lord many gifts. These gifts are a portion of His divine attributes, which the above scripture notes is that we become as a child, submissive, meek, humble, patient, full of love, willing to submit to all things which the Lord seeth fit to inflict upon us, even as a child doth submit to his father. These attributes are granted to us through the grace of Christ, not as a result of personal discipline or determination. They are spiritual enhancements to our being.

Paul, who in his lifetime knew well the evils of bondage and forced servitude, gave us these words:

16 Know ye not, that to whom ye yield yourselves servants to obey, his servants ye are to whom ye obey; whether of sin unto death, or of obedience unto righteousness? (Romans 6:16)

We become the servants of whoever we obey; the evil one, or the Holy Spirit. We become the servants of God, or the servants of evil. Nobody wants to think of themselves as a servant of evil, yet when we choose to yield to a temptation, that is exactly what we are. If someone instructs you to do something and you obey them, then you are their servant, even if only for a moment. There are rewards for obeying God, and there are rewards for obeying the evil ones. Those dark dividends are generally physical fulfillment, thrills, fame, wealth, and worldly acclaim. These are but shiny copper pennies acquired at the expense of eternal wealth, with a final balloon payment of eternal damnation (meaning that person can no longer progress) due at death.

Another way to view this same concept is that we become an employee of whomever we obey, and we receive wages from that employer.

32 But, O my people, beware lest there shall arise contentions among you, and ye list to obey the evil spirit, which was spoken of by my father Mosiah.

33 For behold, there is a wo pronounced upon him who listeth to obey that spirit; for if he listeth to obey him, and remaineth and dieth in his sins, the same drinketh damnation to his own soul; for he receiveth for his wages an everlasting punishment, having transgressed the law of God contrary to his own knowledge. (Mosiah 2:32–33)

The reason such transgression is in fact contrary to our own knowledge is because we are transgressing, in every case, against the voice of our conscience. We are warned before every untoward act.

The true process of repentance thus becomes a conceptually simple matter of steering the vehicle of our being in an inspired direction, of hearkening to the voice of the living Christ, and choosing His course for our lives. It is conceptually straightforward because of its inspired simplicity. Obey—all else follows. Pragmatically speaking, it is a process of life arrived at through billowing flames of opposition, and usually with the bilious taste of sampled disobedience still on our tongues. Righteousness is often chosen as the humbling result of bitter experience and shattered self-will, conquered selfishness, and discarded dreams of self-aggrandizement.

When we choose such a lifestyle of obedience we enter into a progression of ever-increasing light, truth, and understanding. Every opportunity to sin, to be selfish, or to yield to temptation is met with faith, and the choice is made again and again to yield to truth.

Such a life is a life of right-ness.
Such a life is a life of faith.
Such a life is a life of joy.

Repentance is not limited to refusing to choose evil. It is also choosing to embrace godliness and to be Christlike in dispensing grace to others. It is, quite literally, to repent of the human condition.

EVERY GOOD THING

When we align ourselves with righteousness we lay hold upon every good thing. Does that seem impossible given what you think you know of mortal existence? Mormon proposed the same question: "And now, my brethren, how is it possible that ye can lay hold upon every good thing?" (Moroni 7:20).

Fortunately Mormon answers his own question. After discussing at length in the proceeding verses that all good comes from God and all evil from the devil, he tells us how to tell the difference:

12 Wherefore, all things which are good cometh of God; and that which is evil cometh of the devil; for the devil is an enemy unto God, and fighteth against him continually, and inviteth and enticeth to sin, and to do that which is evil continually. . . .

15 For behold, my brethren, it is given unto you to judge, that ye may know good from evil; and the way to judge is as plain, that ye may know with a perfect knowledge, as the daylight is from the dark night.

16 For behold, the Spirit of Christ is given to every man, that he may know good from evil; wherefore, I show unto you the way to judge; for *every thing which inviteth to do good, and to persuade to believe in Christ, is sent forth by the power and gift of Christ; wherefore ye may know with a perfect knowledge it is of God.*

17 But whatsoever thing persuadeth men to do evil, and believe not in Christ, and deny him, and serve not God, then ye may know with a perfect knowledge it is of the devil; for after this manner doth the devil work, for he persuadeth no man to do good, no, not one; neither do

his angels; neither do they who subject themselves unto him. (Moroni 7:12, 15–17; italics added)

In order to lay hold upon every good thing we must first perceive what good is. How can we gather good things to ourselves if we do not even know what those things are? Moroni tells us that all good comes from God. We can identify it because it always persuades us to do good and to believe in Christ. Moroni teaches us that we may know with a perfect knowledge that anything good that comes into our lives has its origin with Christ. Conversely, anything which encourages us to not believe in Christ, or to not serve God, is inspired of evil.

Here again we see the principle of repentance. We must repent of our failure to lay hold upon the good that Christ is flooding into our lives; and a little easier to understand, we must repent of indulging ourselves in those things that come of evil.

So, what does "lay hold upon every good thing" really mean? Aren't we speaking of more good than just the whisperings of the Holy Spirit, like a good job, or a good friend or eternal companion? The statement in verse 12 that "all things which are good cometh of God" includes, but is not limited to, promptings. All things—whether it is a good home, a good happening, a good marriage, or good health—all these things come from God.

So, again the question, how can we lay hold upon all these good things? The answer is startlingly simple.

19 Wherefore, I beseech of you, brethren, that ye should search diligently in the light of Christ that ye may know good from evil; and if ye will lay hold upon every good thing, and condemn it not, ye certainly will be a child of Christ.

20 And now, my brethren, how is it possible that ye can lay hold upon every good thing? (Moroni 7:19–20)

The answer is that we must search diligently in the light of Christ so that we can tell the difference between good things and bad things. If we can't tell the difference, we have a profound tendency to grab the shiniest and sweetest and call it good, only realizing much later that these things have harmed us. To know beforehand, by the light of Christ, what is good, even when it does not appear to be the biggest chocolate in the box, is to be able to lay hold upon every good thing.

21 And now I come to that faith, of which I said I would speak; and I will tell you the way whereby ye may lay hold on every good thing. (Moroni 7:21)

As Moroni then explains, it is by faith that we are enabled to lay hold upon every good thing. What he is saying is that when a prompting comes to us to do, say, or be something, we can't know how it's going to work out. Sometimes it can be quite scary to obey. It is seldom what we intended to do, and rarely convenient. If we choose to obey, it is an act of faith. We can only choose to obey because of our faith, and then let the Lord deal with the consequences, including blessing us for our obedience.

Often the outward appearance of promptings does not seem to be a straight pathway to quiet enjoyment of our lives.

Since we cannot see beyond the moment in which we live, we are blind to the future and even somewhat blind to the past. We remember poorly, and lessons learned blur into a jumble of feelings that may or may not serve us well in the present. Our jumbled emotions about the past and our often-jaded perceptions of the present do not cast much light upon the future.

Our natural response to the unknown, or the unknowable, is to walk away or to wait for more information. Our response to potential danger is to run away. When the Spirit whispers that we are to perform some act, such as to humbly ask for forgiveness of a person who has in fact harmed us, we are initially stunned by the unlikely correctness of such an act. We see the more probable damaging outcome more clearly than the potential good, and we are powerfully disinclined to act. After all, better safe than sorry, as we are want to say.

Having highlighted the place that faith holds in our ability to claim "every good thing," Moroni then acknowledges, as we always should, the central role of Jesus Christ in the very existence of every good thing. Not only do all good things come from Christ, but the faith that we rely upon to allow us to claim them is a glorious result of His Atonement.

22 For behold, God knowing all things, being from everlasting to everlasting, behold, he sent angels to minister unto the children of men, to make manifest concerning the coming of Christ; and *in Christ there should come every good thing.*

23 And God also declared unto prophets, by his own mouth, that Christ should come.

> 24 And behold, there were divers ways that he did manifest things unto the children of men, which were good; and *all things which are good cometh of Christ;* otherwise men were fallen, and there could no good thing come unto them. (Moroni 7:22–24)

Then this grand summation: that by angels, and by every word which proceeds forth from the mouth of God, which is the voice of the Holy Spirit, men began to exercise faith in Christ; and as a direct result, they grew in faith until they were at last able to lay hold upon "every good thing." So it was then, and so it is today.

> 25 Wherefore, by the ministering of angels, and by every word which proceeded forth out of the mouth of God, men began to exercise faith in Christ; and thus by faith, they did lay hold upon every good thing; and thus it was until the coming of Christ. (Moroni 7:25)

Yet, with faith in Christ, which is to say with faith in His voice, when such a prompting comes, no matter how improbable the outcome may seem or how hard the act may on its face appear, we may with absolute faith lay hold upon that good thing—knowing that it *is* good only by the fact that it came from Christ.

All "good material things" float upon the same tide as "good promptings," which is to say that they operate by the same principle. When some physical thing, event, or opportunity comes into our lives, we can know if these things are good by the Light of Christ, just as we must judge which promptings are good and from Christ. The yardstick we use for both is if that thing leads us to Christ and brings the Holy Spirit into our lives. If it blesses and uplifts others and fills us with peace, then it has its origins in Christ. If it does anything less, then it will harm us in the moment and in eternity.

Having become familiar with the workings of the Light of Christ in promptings, and knowing from experience what good promptings feel like, we can take that same sensitivity to truth and apply it when physical things, people, and opportunities come into our lives. Revelation has an essence, a flavor, a discernible texture that we come to recognize over time. We become familiar with the light by exposing ourselves to it. The taste of truth becomes both recognizable and delicious to us with repeated exposure. We become able to spot the tiniest speck of light within the tumble of the mortal mix. Then, when something comes along that is true yet disguised in worldly garb, we can sample for the now-familiar aroma of divine origin. If there is no light, only glitz, we humbly identify the counterfeit and walk away. We need never be deceived.

In time, through righteous experience, we learn that Christ's word is never wrong. It never leaves us standing alone. Happiness and peace always flow from obedience to His whispered commands. And thus we begin to not only have faith in Christ, but also to *exercise* faith in Christ, and in so doing we begin to lay hold upon every good thing.

Faith is the first principle of the gospel, which also implies that without faith we do not progress beyond the rudimentary and basic. Without faith, we can only lay hold upon those (apparent) good things that our eyes can behold and random chance can deliver, missing most of the greater blessings that come only to the faith-filled.

Armed with faith in Christ, the spiritual pilgrim now has the ability to see the everlasting value of being baptized by authority and of progressing to receive many other priesthood ordinances. We enter joyfully into these covenantal relationships because they are right and because we know by faith that they will bring us joy.

Although most people are sincere in requesting priesthood ordinances, we often participate in these ordinances without really understand what we are doing or what will be required of us to fully enjoy the promised blessings. In order for us to actually receive the full impact of these ordinances, they must be sealed by the Holy Spirit of Promise.

The Holy Spirit of Promise

Every ordinance of the gospel is dual in its nature. First, there is the ordinance itself, the act, performed when we decide we are ready to participate. Second, there is the effect of the ordinance, the blessings associated with righteous fulfillment of the conditions and covenants of the ordinance. These two elements are often far separated in years.

Due to the fact that we often choose to participate in ordinances when we are young and spiritually immature, we participate with imperfect understanding of what we are taking upon ourselves. Fortunately the Lord has granted us this right, and in fact encourages it. We act when we think we are ready. The Lord bestows the promised blessings when He knows we actually are ready. This functionality is called the Holy Spirit of Promise. It is a function of the Holy Ghost to bestow promised priesthood blessings when we at last arrive at a state of worthiness necessary to receive the promised blessings. Thus, even many years after the event, we can finally receive the blessings of prior ordinances.

Elder McConkie explains it this way:

> All covenants, contracts, bonds, obligations, oaths, vows, perfor-
> mances, connections, associations, or expectations (D&C 132:7), in
> which men must abide to be saved and exalted, must be entered into
> and performed in righteousness so that the Holy Spirit can justify the
> candidate for salvation in what has been done . . . An act that is justified
> by the Spirit is one that is sealed by the Holy Spirit of Promise, or in
> other words, ratified and approved by the Holy Ghost. This law of justi-
> fication is the provision the Lord has placed in the gospel to assure that
> no unrighteous performance will be binding on earth and in heaven,
> and that no person will add to his position or glory in the hereafter by
> gaining an unearned blessing.[28]

The Holy Spirit of Promise is also the merciful means whereby men and women may participate in priesthood ordinances when they deem themselves worthy and then fully receive the promised blessings when they finally are worthy. Without this provision in the gospel very few mortals could arrive at a state of full worthiness and determined obedi-ence prior to these saving ordinances, and thus the full blessings would almost universally be impossible to achieve.

This provision of the Holy Spirit of Promise also gives us time to repent, approach, receive, falter, and approach again. The blessings are bestowed when worthiness is manifest, even if it is for the second or third time.

Having made the above observation, it becomes obvious why the Lord allows us to baptize our children in their innocence at age eight. They reap the blessings of membership in His Church, receive the gift of the Holy Ghost, and grow in that brighter light until such time as they are truly worthy of the promises of baptism and the cleansing we must all have in the Blood of the Lamb prior to obtaining a place in His kingdom. When we finally and fully embrace and fulfill the covenants entered into as youth, then the Holy Spirit of Promise grants the full power of those blessings, even if it is decades later.

BAPTISM

As with all ordinances, baptism is dual in its nature. The first part is the holy immersion in water. This ordinance is an outward sign that the person has accepted Christ's gospel. It betokens cleansing, laying the old man of sin down in a symbolic grave, and arising new and reborn (Romans 6:1–6). It foresees and promises a remission of sins when worthiness calls forth the Holy Spirit of Promise to bestow that divine blessing. While it is possible in a mature individual, it is probably infrequent that the person being baptized fully receives the promised remission of sins at the moment of their baptism.

Of even greater impact is the fact that it is impossible that any person lives sinlessly from that moment on—and thus the operation of the Holy Spirit of Promise becomes indispensable in every person's case.

When the ordinance of baptism is ratified and sealed upon us, it is so powerful that it cleanses us of sin—not just a sin, but of all sin. It prepares us for the actual bestowal the Holy Ghost, which was promised in the companion ordinance of bestowing the gift of the Holy Ghost.

The prophet Joseph Smith made this comment on the necessity of both ordinances being in full effect:

> You might as well baptize a bag of sand as a man, if not done in view of the remission of sins and getting of the Holy Ghost. Baptism by water is but half a baptism, and is good for nothing without the other half—that is, the baptism of the Holy Ghost.[29]

THE GIFT OF THE HOLY GHOST

The reason baptism and the ordinance of the laying on of hands for the gift of the Holy Ghost occurs in concert is because they are essentially one ordinance. Baptism promises a remission of sins by the Holy Ghost—so reception of the gift of the Holy Ghost is an essential part of that promise. On the other side of the coin, receipt of the Holy Ghost as our constant companion requires a saintly state of sinlessness, which is promised at baptism. Thus, the two are essentially one.

Jesus proclaimed this fact when He taught Nicodemus that a man must be born of the water and of the Spirit to enter into the kingdom of heaven.

> 3 Jesus answered and said unto him, Verily, verily, I say unto thee, Except a man be born again, he cannot see the kingdom of God.
>
> 4 Nicodemus saith unto him, How can a man be born when he is old? can he enter the second time into his mother's womb, and be born?

5 Jesus answered, Verily, verily, I say unto thee, Except a man be born of water and *of* the Spirit, he cannot enter into the kingdom of God. (John 3:3–5)

The promised blessings of baptism and confirmation are twofold. They are first that we will receive a greater endowment of the Holy Spirit, which is the voice of Christ.

10 Now I say unto you, if this be the desire of your hearts, what have you against being baptized in the name of the Lord, as a witness before him that ye have entered into a covenant with him, that ye will serve him and keep his commandments, *that he may pour out his Spirit more abundantly upon you*? (Mosiah 18:10; italics added)

The second promise is that in time, when we have become worthy, we will receive the Holy Ghost as our constant companion, and thus be cleansed of our sins.

12 Yea, blessed are they who shall believe in your words, and come down into the depths of humility and be baptized, for they shall be visited with fire and with the Holy Ghost, and shall receive a remission of their sins. (3 Nephi 12:2)

The blessed reception of that glorious member of the Godhead is so profound upon the soul that it is proceeded by the candidate literally being immersed in spiritual fire which consumes the dross and burns away the unclean and impure thus making that person worthy of that holy companion, and consequently also worthy of a remission of his sins.[30]

The baptismal promise of a remission of sins waits upon the actual receipt of the Holy Ghost for fulfillment. That period of waiting lasts as long as it takes the spiritual pilgrim to find the obedience that will bring forth the requisite worthiness. When that divine member of the Godhead takes up residence in a soul, it purifies and sanctifies him.

20 Now this is the commandment: Repent, all ye ends of the earth, and come unto me and be baptized in my name, that ye may be sanctified by the reception of the Holy Ghost, that ye may stand spotless before me at the last day. (3 Nephi 27:20)

It is important to note that receiving incremental revelations from the Holy Ghost is not the same as receiving the full companionship of the Holy Ghost. As we progress in our journey, the Holy Ghost speaks upon those occasions when we place ourselves in harmony with divine law. We receive bursts of understanding, enhancements to our testimonies, doctrine, principle, and insight, line upon line from the Holy Ghost. Though these things are indeed glorious, a greater endowment awaits those who consecrate their souls to complete obedience, and who are determined to serve God at any cost. The Holy Ghost will become our constant companion, and we will thus be born again.

Being Born Again

The term "born again" has many levels of meaning and suggests powerful enhancements to the soul that extend beyond the potential of mortals and the duration of mortality. For our purposes, we will speak of that initial rebirth that lifts a person from the realms of the natural man, and into the world of the spiritual man.

> 14 Now I say unto you that ye must repent, and be born again; for the Spirit saith if ye are not born again ye cannot inherit the kingdom of heaven; therefore come and be baptized unto repentance, that ye may be washed from your sins. (Alma 7:14)

Being born again is not optional. In order to inherit the kingdom of God we are required to experience this mighty change.

> 25 And the Lord said unto me: Marvel not that all mankind, yea, men and women, all nations, kindreds, tongues and people, must be born again; yea, born of God, changed from their carnal and fallen state, to a state of righteousness, being redeemed of God, becoming his sons and daughters;
>
> 26 And thus they become new creatures; and unless they do this, they can in nowise inherit the kingdom of God. (Mosiah 27:25–26)

It is sometimes easy to view this requirement to seek and obtain the rebirth of the Spirit as a hardship or a requirement that is somehow beyond us. The truth is that it is well within our reach, and the effect upon us is so glorious that words are not adequate to describe it.

When King Benjamin's people embraced the gospel of Christ, they collectively experienced a mighty change. It is called the "mighty change" because it changes us in ways we couldn't accomplish by ourselves. We don't change ourselves to fit the pattern of a reborn soul; the rebirth changes us in a "mighty" way to fit the pattern of Christ. Through the grace of Christ, the Holy Ghost effects changes that upgrade and improve many aspects of our souls. We don't become perfect, but we become greater than our natural abilities allow. We love more purely, we serve more selflessly, we endure with patience and peace, and view our lives from an eternal perspective that previously was impossible.

> 2 And they all cried with one voice, saying: Yea, we believe all the words which thou hast spoken unto us; and also, we know of their surety and truth, because of the Spirit of the Lord Omnipotent, which has wrought a mighty change in us, or in our hearts, that we have no more disposition to do evil, but to do good continually. (Mosiah 5:2)

This "mighty change" is what changes us from a natural being to a spiritual being, and bestows mighty gifts upon us, even so that we have no more disposition to sin, but rejoice in doing good continually.

> 19 For the natural man is an enemy to God, and has been from the fall of Adam, and will be, forever and ever, unless he yields to the enticings of the Holy Spirit, and putteth off the natural man and becometh a saint through the Atonement of Christ the Lord, and becometh as a child, submissive, meek, humble, patient, full of love, willing to submit to all things which the Lord seeth fit to inflict upon him, even as a child doth submit to his father. (Mosiah 3:19)

As we have noted before, these are gifts to us. We become this way because we are beginning to become like Christ. The possible effects of having the mighty change are literally infinite. In addition to a general overlay of peace and joy which most people experience, every individual experiences unique gifts tailored specifically to their needs. For one, they might also experience an influx of patience. Another person may simply no longer feel a desire to stroke his pride. Someone else may at last find peace regarding what previously seemed to be insurmountable and looming trials. Another person may at last lay aside guilt for past follies. Every person who experiences this change eventually understands why the Lord calls it the "mighty change."

> 59 That by reason of transgression cometh the fall, which fall bringeth death, and inasmuch as ye were born into the world by water, and blood, and the spirit, which I have made, and so became of dust a living soul, even so ye must be born again into the kingdom of heaven, of water, and of the Spirit, and be cleansed by blood, even the blood of mine Only Begotten; that ye might be sanctified from all sin, and enjoy

the words of eternal life in this world, and eternal life in the world to come, even immortal glory;

60 For by the water ye keep the commandment; by the Spirit ye are justified, and by the blood ye are sanctified. (Moses 6:59–60)

Even with the manifest power of this change, it is interesting that few people realize what they have experienced until later in life.

20 And ye shall offer for a sacrifice unto me a broken heart and a contrite spirit. And whoso cometh unto me with a broken heart and a contrite spirit, him will I baptize with fire and with the Holy Ghost, even as the Lamanites, because of their faith in me at the time of their conversion, were baptized with fire and with the Holy Ghost, *and they knew it not.* (3 Nephi 9:20; italics added)

We are not told precisely why this is the case, but it seems to serve the purpose of quietly upgrading the soul without inflaming our pride.

Being born again is another sequential step on the straight path to becoming a Zion individual. What is also true is that the rebirth of the spirit is the result of a process and is more often received quietly, a little at a time, rather than as a noticeable event. It is most probable that far more people have experienced the rebirth than they themselves realize.

Thus, many people are born again and don't realize it. Some experience an event, or a startling realization that informs them of their new blessed state. Most simply experience it as a gradual influx of strength, determination, and dedication, and don't stop to analyze or put a name to what has happened over time.

Any time you meet someone whose face is filled with the light of righteousness, whose voice is softened and kind, who does not seek notice or applause, and who is possessed of true caring and kindness, these people have been born again. In fact, most of the people you know in the Church are like this.

People who have been born again become "as a child, submissive, meek, humble, patient, full of love, willing to submit to all things which the Lord seeth fit to inflict upon him, even as a child doth submit to his father" (Mosiah 3:19).

It is worth noting that persons who have been born again are not perfect. They still have failings. They will occasionally falter, or make poor choices. To be born again isn't to become perfect; it is to be changed, uplifted, and upgraded to be more like our Savior.

When a person with these gifts makes a poor choice or errs unintentionally, the gifts may cease for a time, and they may return to their "natural" state. They have the opportunity to repent and regain their spiritual footing and can return to their reborn nature fairly easily. It is expected that people will cycle in and out of the rebirth several, or even many, times before they are able to more permanently claim these gifts.

A word of caution however. If a reborn person chooses to grossly sin, to knowingly depart from righteousness, or to indulge in defiant transgression, it may well be very difficult to regain their favored stature. Actions such as these are open rebellion and are an insult to our Savior, who has purchased our grace-filled rebirth by the shedding of His blood. It may well take years to overcome such an uninspired choice and return to a state of grace.

The perfect pathway to Zion may be defined thus far as:

- Obedience to the voice of Christ / Holy Spirit
- Sacrifice
- Prayer
- Faith in Christ
- Repentance
- Baptism
- Gift of the Holy Ghost
- Being born again

After learning to retain these blessings that flow from the rebirth, a person gradually finds that their desires become specific and focused. They begin to acquire an eye single to the glory of God.

EYE SINGLE TO THE GLORY OF GOD

Jesus declared, "I am the light of the world: he that followeth me shall not walk in darkness, but shall have the light of life" (John 8:12). And again, "Behold, I am Jesus Christ, the Son of God. I am the life and the light of the world" (D&C 11:28; John 9:5; Alma 38:9; D&C 10:70, 11:28; JST Matthew 5:16). Christ placed himself in our lives as our light and often lamented that He is shining in darkness, and the darkness doesn't comprehend the light (D&C 6:21, 10:58, 34:2, 39:2, 45:7, 88:49).

But the promises associated with receiving His light and letting it grow in us are paramount. When we receive light into our souls, that light comes to us through the Holy Spirit. Even when the text we are reading is the scriptures, or the words are flowing from the lips of inspired teachers, it is the Holy Spirit which transports those immortal concepts into our souls.

When we let that light lead us in a continual path of righteousness, we receive more light, and that light grows brighter and brighter until the perfect day.

> 67 And if your eye be single to my glory, your whole bodies shall be filled with light, and there shall be no darkness in you; and that body which is filled with light comprehendeth all things. (D&C 88:67)

Bearing in mind that there is only one gospel and one effect of receiving more and more light, it becomes apparent that the following reference is also proclaiming the same principle.

> 36 The glory of God is intelligence, or in other words, light and truth. (D&C 93:36)

> 45 And whatsoever is truth is light, and whatsoever is light is Spirit, even the Spirit of Jesus Christ. (D&C 84:45)

As we have observed many times, it is the Spirit of Jesus Christ that fills our souls with truth and which is our connection with the divine throughout life.

This principle may be expressed in this way:

Light = Truth = Spirit of Jesus Christ = Glory = Intelligence

These words all mean the same thing when used in this context. To acquire the one is to acquire all of the others. To be obedient to one is to be obedient to them all. The verse just prior to that quoted above verifies this truth.

> 66 Behold, that which you hear is as the voice of one crying in the wilderness—in the wilderness, because you cannot see him—my voice, because my voice is Spirit; my Spirit is truth; truth abideth and hath no end; and if it be in you it shall abound. (D&C 88:66)

It thus becomes obvious that the glory of God to which we are to discipline our eye is the voice and light of Christ. Filling our lives with His light leads to brighter light and greater truths. His truth and His voice will lead us until truth abides in us and has no end—until we comprehend all things—until the perfect day.

24 That which is of God is light; and he that receiveth light, and continueth in God, receiveth more light; and that light groweth brighter and brighter until the perfect day. (D&C 50:24)

As we have observed previously, the "perfect day" is when He who is most perfect physically enters our lives. It is that moment when we enter the presence of God, and in the process of that interview we will be shown, among many other things, the vision of all and have our understandings opened to things we cannot otherwise comprehend in this mortal body. The next verse verifies that the perfect outcome of accumulating light upon light is that we may see God.

68 Therefore, sanctify yourselves that your minds become single to God, and the days will come that you shall see him; for he will unveil his face unto you, and it shall be in his own time, and in his own way, and according to his own will. (D&C 88:68)

No person arrives at the point where their eye is single to the glory of God in an instant, nor does it happen by our own virtue and strength. The only way that we may ever qualify for this most perfect of all perfect days, is that we become perfect *in Christ*.

BECOMING PERFECT IN JESUS CHRIST

The power of the gospel of Christ isn't that it points to a glorious outcome and cheers us on. The power lies in the fact that from the moment of our birth, through every decision and trial in our lives, to every necessary enhancement to our souls, to purging our sins, to lifting us beyond our mortal abilities, to cleansing, sanctifying, and purifying, Christ not only showed us the way, He *is* the way. It is through the grace of Christ that we can become these things which are far more than any mortal can achieve and be on their own.

He said, "Come follow me," not because He had a great idea and defined a pathway toward that goal, but because He became "the way" by the shedding of His blood and offered salvation to us at a cost that is well within our mortal budget.

It is within our reach because God does not require perfection of us per se. He requires obedience to His voice, which is His law (D&C 88:13), and in return He sanctifies, He purifies, and He changes us by virtue of His grace that we become like Him. It doesn't happen—it can't happen—as a result of our works, no matter how impressive they may seem to be. It is eternally beyond our ability to perfect ourselves by our works. It can only happen because we obey laws that trigger eternal gifts of grace that lift us to divine climbs.

We look upon Christ as the great exemplar because He is the Son of God—and so we do, and so we should. A possible perspective on Christ's life is that two notable things which Christ did occurred by virtue of his divine parentage. Everything else He did, He accomplished by obedience to the same laws He laid before us, and having lived His own plan flawlessly, he became perfect. He beckons us to follow Him and do the same.

Those two divine accomplishments are first that He lived a perfect and sinless life. He did this because He is the Son of God, He is Jehovah, and He was in His lifetime the greatest of all dwelling in a tabernacle of clay. This made Him different from us. It is not possible for us to duplicate this attribute.

The second thing is that Christ wrought out the perfect Atonement by the shedding of His blood. In that great atoning act He paid the price of sin infinitely (which means that there are no limits to its power) and eternally (meaning from the beginning of existence to the end of forever), and He broke the bands of death for all of the creations of the Father. He suffered and descended below all things to obtain all truth and all understanding so that He could become the only Light of Truth (D&C 88:2) that eternity will ever need or know. This only He could do because He *is* the Son of God. These are not things we can duplicate.

This perspective of Christ's life suggests that everything else Christ did, He accomplished by obedience to laws established by His Father, which Christ embraced within the gospel He established. This *is* something we can do. The mere fact that Christ said "come follow me" tells us that equipped as we are, and uplifted by His grace, we *can* follow Him.

> 10 The words that I speak unto you I speak not of myself: but the Father that dwelleth in me, he doeth the works.
>
> 11 Believe me that I *am* in the Father, and the Father in me: or else believe me for the very works' sake.
>
> 12 Verily, verily, I say unto you, He that believeth on me, the works that I do shall he do also; and greater *works* than these shall he do; because I go unto my Father. (John 14:10–12)

The point of Christ's words above is that He was not doing His work, but His Father's. He is here saying that the Father gave Him the power to do the works He did, and that when He returns to the Father that He, Christ, will empower us to do even greater works. He will distill into us the same power that the Father instilled in Him.

Elder Bednar taught us:

> All of our worthy desires and good works, as necessary as they are, can never produce clean hands and a pure heart. It is the Atonement of Jesus Christ that provides both a *cleansing and redeeming power* that helps us to overcome sin and a *sanctifying and strengthening power* that helps us to become better than we ever could by relying upon our own strengths.[31]

We have the same privileges "in Christ" as Christ had in His Father. Christ will show us all things whatsoever we should do and then empower us to do them. Thus, faith in Christ, works in Christ, and words spoken in Christ are the means whereby we may not only do as He did, but also do even greater things.

The great chasm that we must cross to follow Him and to do the works that He did and greater is to realize that we are not able in and of ourselves to be perfect, as He was. But we do have the ability to be perfectly and flawlessly obedient—as Christ was. The beauty and power of Christ's plan is that as we obey Him, He will provide all that we lack. He will close the great chasm we cannot cross by changing us so that we meet the standard of righteousness.

As the above reference teaches us, Christ did nothing of Himself. That doesn't mean that He couldn't put one foot in front of another, or that He had to be commanded to swallow food in His mouth. It means that, in all matters of His ministry, He relied upon the voice of His Father to direct Him. He did nothing more and nothing less than what the Father commanded Him to do. He spoke only the words the Father put in His lips. Elder Jeffrey R. Holland gave us this insight:

> Christ's final triumph and ultimate assumption of godly powers on the right hand of his Father came *not* because he had a divine parent (although that was essential to the victory over death) and *not* because he was given heavenly authority from the beginning (although that was essential to his divine power) but ultimately because he was, in his own mortal probation, perfectly obedient, perfectly submissive, perfectly loyal to the principle that the spiritual in his life must rule over the physical. That was at the heart of his triumph, and that is a lesson for

every accountable man, woman, and child who ever lives. It is a lesson for which Abinadi—and Christ—were willing to die. It is the lesson for which virtually every prophet has given his voice and his life: spirit over flesh; discipline over temptation; devotion over inclination; "the will of the Son being swallowed up in the will of the Father." [32]

To do as Christ did we must be as obedient to Christ's voice as Christ was to the Father's voice. This is well within our power. We can in all matters of our ministry speak every word that Christ puts to our lips and perform every service that He asks and directs us to do. And then comes the absolute power of the gospel of the Son of God: When we command such obedience of our hands, hearts, and lips, then Christ empowers us in that thing so that we "in Christ" can do that work just as He might if He were present.

Elder McConkie said:

> To gain salvation, men must come unto the Father, attain the faith that he exercises, and be as he is. Christ has done so; he is both a saved being and the perfect and only illustration of what others must do to gain like inheritances and be joint-heirs with him. He is thus the way to the Father; no man cometh unto the Father but by him and by his word. He is our Mediator, Advocate, and Intercessor, all because he wrought out the perfect Atonement through the shedding of his own blood. Through him, and through him only, fallen men may be reconciled to God if they repent and work righteousness. [33]

Notice here that the requirement to perfection is restated. We are to be perfect as the Father is perfect. We are to obtain faith as He owns it and to come unto the Father. But we are not in any way asked to plod along this path by our own steam. In fact, such a process is impossible. The following scripture highlights the only way it can work.

> 32 Yea, come unto Christ, and be perfected in him, and deny yourselves of all ungodliness; and if ye shall deny yourselves of all ungodliness, and love God with all your might, mind and strength, then is his grace sufficient for you, that by his grace ye may be perfect in Christ; and if by the grace of God ye are perfect in Christ, ye can in nowise deny the power of God. (Moroni 10:32)

Christ was the perfect man. He lived a perfect life, obtained this perfect faith, and then through the shedding of His blood, provided a perfect way for us to follow Him. That way is the gospel of Jesus Christ as it exists today. Through Him and through Him alone, we may come unto the Father if we will but walk the pathway that Christ defines by his voice every moment of our lives. That pathway consists of the entire gospel that bears His name. It may not be possible to reduce it to a single understandable paragraph. The purpose of the book you are now reading is to emblazon that gospel process across the skies of our souls, where we may rejoice in it, feel its glowing power, and luxuriate in the radiant warmth of the salvation He offers us.

Having then consecrated our souls to Christ by many acts of obedience, we begin to exercise living faith in Christ.

LIVING FAITH IN CHRIST

Faith, true saving faith, is always centered in Christ. The reason for this is as vast as eternity and all that Christ has done for us, and as small and seemingly tiny as that still small voice that speaks to our soul. To recognize that voice as the actual and literal voice of Christ is to learn one of life's great mysteries. To take that voice as our guide is to learn one of life's greatest truths—which is that our conscience is never wrong, that love and happiness, joy and peace always flow from such obedience.

This realization alone enables living faith in Jesus Christ.

Why is this so? It is because to have faith in an idea, or in a vast power that is largely disconnected from the intimacy of our lives, is only minimally efficacious. Having faith in the idea of Christ, with no realization that He is speaking to us hour-by-hour, is like having faith in a bottle of aspirin to cure a headache, but the aspirin still has the tamper-proof seal firmly in place. It takes us nowhere and has very little power other than to possibly motivate us to stare longingly at the bottle when we feel a headache coming on.

When we recognize the truth that Jesus *is* the Christ and the startling fact that He *is* speaking to us, we have literally opened the heavens above and invited the living, dynamic, intelligent, all-knowing, all-wise, and loving voice of the living God into our souls. Power flows from this one realization, and our faith thus becomes *living* and life-giving because it is animated by a living power. Without it, the heavens largely remain sealed, and our faith is theoretical in nature rather than living.

All other forms of faith flow from this one mighty seed. If you can believe and have faith in the Holy Spirit—the voice of Christ, to guide you in small things, then greater things will follow, and greater and greater still, until power flows unstoppable from God into your soul and into your life's ministry. You will find your bowels filling with charity toward all men; virtue will garnish your thoughts unceasingly, your confidence will wax strong in the presence of God, and the doctrine of the priesthood shall distil upon your soul as the dews from heaven. The Holy Ghost will be your constant companion and your scepter an unchanging scepter of righteousness and truth; your dominion shall be an everlasting dominion, and without compulsory means it shall flow unto you forever and ever (D&C 121:45–46).

To resolve to flawlessly obey that voice of Christ is to seize upon a process that will uplift, cleanse, sanctify, and perfect you. Note again that we do not perfect ourselves. We are made perfect in Christ. Our obedience brings us into the perfect pathway to Zion and places our feet upon the straight and narrow way. As we carefully walk as defined by His voice, Christ perfects us through the gifts of His Holy Spirit, by virtue of His Atonement. These gifts will make us like unto Christ and will bring us in due time into the presence of God.

In this simple, divinely-ordained and divinely-assisted process we are able to become as perfect as mortals may in this life. This process is the gospel of Jesus Christ. It is perfect, and it is available to all mankind. The beauty and power of it is that it does not require immense personal power and world-class discipline. It is designed for the weakest of the Saints, or even those who aspire to be Saints.

Joseph Smith said:

> God hath not revealed anything to Joseph, but what He will make known unto the Twelve, and even the least Saint may know all things as fast as he is able to bear them.[34]

If a university worked this way, we would go to our first day of class and the professor would hand us a small, one question quiz. The answer would be written on the board for all to copy onto their tests. It would be so easy that it might seem like a waste of time to even attend class. Many would stand up in disgust looking for a "real test" or a real teacher who really knew how to teach, because it couldn't really be that easy (see Alma 37:46). Yet, if we exercised a little faith and took the time to jot down the answer and hand in our test, something magic would happen. All of the underlying knowledge that underpinned and explained that answer would simply flow into our minds. As that knowledge distilled upon our souls we would be changed, uplifted, and empowered day by day, little bit by little bit.

Every day as we attended class, the question and answer would be magically applicable in our lives, satisfying immediate needs and answering pressing questions. Class would be over right after the quiz. No lecture, no explanation, just the quiz. We would return the next day and have the same experience over and over until we rejoiced in and looked forward to each new quiz and the resultant influx of knowledge and the incremental enhancements to our abilities.

The only homework that would be required would be that we apply each new bit of knowledge from class into our lives. If we faltered in our homework and returned to class the next day, the professor wouldn't be there; nothing would be on the board, and we would go home empty and unfed. Occasionally we might return in great need, hoping for help with something urgent and frightening; but having failed in our homework, no matter how desperately we searched, our professor would not be in class that hour.

However, as we repented and applied the answers we learned to our daily challenges, our professor would graciously return to class again and welcome us with loving acceptance each time, never upbraiding or criticizing our failures. He would just hand out a new quiz.

As we continued through the course we would begin to view life differently, and our service outside of class would rise above our native abilities. Our homework would be a joy, hardly a sacrifice at all.

However, if we failed to show up to class or decided that the answer on the board just couldn't be right and wrote something else down or insisted on our own answer, then the knowledge wouldn't flow, and we would begin to forget lessons of prior days. We would watch some students go from that simple arrogant assertion of self-will all the way to dropping out of the class altogether.

As we persisted day by day, our minds and souls would expand until we saw the beauty and power of what this amazing professor was trying to teach us. In time we would become not only educated in what he wished to teach us, be we would also become like him in every possible way.

In a far greater way, this is what Jesus Christ offers us in His divine classroom. He teaches us by providing answers to simple quizzes: "Say you're sorry. Drive the speed limit. Tell the truth. Say family prayers."

If we do our homework, which is to simply obey and do, then we are changed and gifted with abilities and attributes such as humble acceptance of our faults, prideless repentance, love, patience, faith, and a host of Christlike qualities that previously eluded us, which simply distill upon our souls. Not only this, but we also begin to understand the underlying truths such that these individual gospel truths and testimonies become "one great whole." By these simple things we are led to greater and greater strengths and sweeter purities until we are worthy to be in His presence. We become perfect by the fact that we are led by Christ, that He is in us, and we are one with Him.

In simplest terms, we become perfect in Christ.

Almost without noticing it, by our quiet enthroning of the voice of Christ as the guiding power in our lives, we have become prophets in our own world. We have almost effortlessly climbed the soaring peaks of personal revelation.

PERSONAL REVELATION

Having arrived at this pinnacle of growth that we may obtain truth from the heavens relative to our daily walk, we are now prepared to reach farther into the fountain of eternity and lay hold upon a far greater body of truth. These are principles of righteousness that eclipse our day-to-day needs, which teach of the eternities, of righteousness, and of Zion. It is our slowly-acquired ability to hear the quiet voice of the Holy Spirit that has given us "ears to hear" and "eyes to see" those things that are hidden from the world.

There is an intriguing relationship between the revealed word found in holy writ and personal revelation. One would assume that the natural process would be that we search the scriptures and find an example of promises we wish to claim or truths we wish to apply, gain a testimony of that principle through personal revelation, and then follow the course outlined in scripture that brings that blessing into our lives.

Obtaining promises can work this way. However, there is a less apparent way, which we apply much more often, even though we may not realize it. For Latter-day Saints, the process more often follows the pattern Joseph Smith was led to employ in restoring the gospel to the earth. He sought and obtained personal revelation regarding how the Lord wanted His kingdom organized. He then proceeded to do as the Lord commanded, and in the process, he observed that the scriptures taught that Christ had done the same thing in previous dispensations of the gospel. It would have been a great comfort to Joseph to observe this. The scripture in this setting acted as a second witness but would not have added to his ability to perform his high commission. The scriptures were not plain enough, indeed were not designed to be Joseph's blueprint to restore the gospel of Christ. But they were a perfect witness that what Joseph had been commanded to do was in harmony with the divine pattern. The holy writ bore witness—after the revealed truths were received—to the sacred and inspired work He was being called to perform.

Even the Book of Mormon did not instruct Joseph how to restore the Church. It did teach him the principles and doctrine, and occasionally did motivate him to ask pertinent questions and make special requests, but it did not teach him how to organize the priesthood, the temple, and many other things. Joseph learned all this by revelation and found testament to all these truths in the scripture—a witness after-the-fact, if you will, that he was acting in harmony with the eternal scheme of God's plan.

If one seeks to know how to establish Zion by searching the scriptures alone, one excludes the Holy Ghost from transporting the power and availability of Zion into the structure of our faith and personal beliefs. Such a one only reads these scriptural accounts as interesting snippets from history rather than as divine invitations to reach into the heavens and pull these blessings down onto our own heads. Thus, even understanding our place within the structure of Zion is a matter of revelation rather than of just reading about Zions past. This is not an inherent weakness in the scriptures but is rather a matter of divine design. God has ordained that all truth should come through Christ firsthand, and that the written word should bear testimony of those truths.

We call the scriptures the Old and New Testament because they "testify," or as the dictionary defines testament, it is proof of a pre-existing truth. The Lord instructed us to refer to the Book of Mormon as "Another Testament of Christ," because it is testifying and proving existent truth, not necessarily revealing it.

Even when we read something new to our thinking, it is not new to God. As the Holy Spirit implants this new principle of truth into our souls, the scriptures testify of its long and historic power.

However, if you flip the scriptural coin over, you will find that most personal revelation occurs as a result of studying the scriptures. So, not only do the scriptures act as a witness of the validity and virtue of revealed truth, but reading the scriptures is the primary way we prepare ourselves to receive that revelation.

This pattern is largely true in our personal search to build Zion in our souls. There is not enough information in the scriptures to tell each of us how to accomplish this incredible task. The scriptures inform us that many have sought and obtained these blessings, but the details of how they obtained them are not recorded in enough detail for us to imitate, assuming that mere imitation could bring about Zion. While reading about Zion the Holy Spirit bears witness that these principles are true, and that Christ offers these gifts to "even as many as have believed on my name" (D&C 38:4). Scripture establishes the pattern that these great patriarchs obtained these blessings during a personal interview with their God—though we are not told how they actually arrived at such a blessed state that they were invited into His presence.

While we read these scriptural accounts, the Holy Spirit informs us that we may likewise partake. We believe because of our faith in Christ. In our latter-day temples the promise of a personal experience with Christ is held forth. An inspired connecting of the dots informs us that one of the great gifts we may request beyond the veil is that of translation—but we aren't told plainly how to get to or through the veil that separates us from God.

Thus, personal revelation, largely obtained during scripture study, is our only means of obtaining a personalized step-by-step blueprint on how to arrive in Zion. As each step reveals itself before our newly-opened eyes, we look back through scripture and find the same flecks of gold scattered here and there, and the Holy Spirit assures us that we are on *the* pathway to Zion.

Stated personally, as you begin to receive your personalized blueprint through personal revelation—it is uniquely yours. The obvious truth here is that your blueprint will not work for anyone else. The less-obvious truth is that this is the very reason there is no blueprint in the scripture— because the one that worked for Enoch's personal journey could not work for anyone else. It couldn't work for many reasons, the chief being that the God of heaven has ordained that He and He alone will lead His children to all blessings, especially into His presence, and thus no amount of inspired words, brilliant speech, or powerful oratory can communicate either a testimony of Zion or the true pathway to Zion from one mortal to another.

Another underlying and less obvious principle is that as the Lord reveals to an individual their personalized straight path into Zion, they most often are not privileged to share that information with other people. For this reason, the holy word instructs:

> 12 And now Alma began to expound these things unto him, saying: It is given unto many to know the mysteries of God; nevertheless they are laid under a strict command that they shall not impart only according to the portion of his word which he doth grant unto the children of men, according to the heed and diligence which they give unto him. (Alma 12:9)

As a result, the pursuit of Zion is a personal and often lonely journey, though we shall in time become many, even cities populated by millions.

Christ alone is the fountain of truth, and though mankind may speak words of truth, Christ alone, via the Holy Ghost, can transport them to another's soul. Though this may seem odd, it is the order of all spiritual things. Even in far less grandiose truths, such as "the Church is true" or "Joseph Smith was a true prophet," no mortal can communicate that truth to another's soul. Only the processes of revelation can instill such truths into a human soul. Any missionary who has faithfully served in their calling will tell you than their greatest frustration is trying to get people to dine at the banquet of the restored gospel they lay before them. They quickly find that human language can only inform the ears, but the Holy Ghost must inform the soul.

There are two observable parts to personal revelation. The first is becoming worthy to receive it. This is done by repenting of sins and refusing to indulge in them. The second part as we have discussed is becoming familiar with the feeling, the tone, tenor, and flavor of revelation. It is not something that mankind does by second nature. It is an acquired ability and an acquired taste, something that in time becomes delicious.

Now that we have taken the Holy Spirit for our guide and attuned ourselves to personal revelation, we are ready to receive the personalized steps and guidance that is necessary to bring us to Zion. Since this process almost entirely involves a personal quest, it is important to understand how the living, latter-day prophets fit into this process.

Zion and the Living Oracles

It is tempting to excuse ourselves from the quest for Zion by saying something akin to "When the Prophet tells us to build Zion, I will begin." The flaw in this thinking is that the prophets have spoken about this dispensation and Zion for thousands of years. Our present prophets have dotted the landscape with temples, and within the temples we enjoy our greatest instruction on how to seek the blessings that bring us to Zion.

Is it possible that the next thing our prophet will say about Zion will be, "Sorry, too late," as the scriptures suggest he will if we persist in unbelief? (See Ether 4:13–15; 3 Nephi 16:10.)

At this very moment we have sufficient instruction to know that we can and should seek to become sanctified and to seek for an audience at the veil. If that audience leads us to Zion and translation, happy are we. If it leads us to other blessed climbs, happy are we just as completely. The paramount principle is that we do actually arrive at the veil and partake of these blessings.

Only the prophet can tell the Church when it is time to journey to any specific land and begin to assemble as a city. Only the prophet can tell us when it is time for the Church as an organization to focus upon any doctrine, or to begin to prepare to accomplish any goal. Only the prophet can say what doctrine will be included in priesthood manuals or taught in gospel doctrine classes. And only the prophet can tell us when it becomes time to start walking toward Missouri.

Nevertheless, it is the voice of living revelation that tells us as individuals when it is time to begin to establish Zion in the real estate of our souls.

The Paradox of Revelation

An interesting paradox of revealed religion is that personal revelation is both a solid, ascending stair and a slippery slope. When we learn to lay hold upon revelation and correctly apply it in our lives we climb upward into regions of spiritual blessedness that cannot be obtained any other way. On the other hand, if we release the iron rod of revelation and begin to willfully insist upon our own desires, then we can find ourselves quickly losing our footing and sliding backward.

The blessings, obligations, and glories that await us at the top are so intense and so godlike in their content that only the pure in heart can receive them to their eternal gain. To arrive there and then fall away would heap upon our souls punishments and even damnation that may endure beyond the scope of mortality. There are certain privileges from which one may not fall without becoming a Son of Perdition. So, when a person's heart and soul are not fixed upon righteous obedience to God at all hazards, then obtaining greater truth prematurely puts them at greater risk, and thus the mercy of God makes it easy to abandon climbs that we are not yet prepared to sustain.

This provision of revelation is merciful and also a little tricky. It means that by the time we finally arrive at the gate of Zion, we will have proven, again and again, that we are steadfast and unmovable in our determination, our faith, and our devotions, and that we belong in the divine presence. Like Christ, though in a much smaller way, we will have learned obedience through the things which we suffered (Hebrews 5:8), and we will have become pure in heart by the necessary abrasions to our ego and mortal will. It also means that arriving there will almost invariably include a few breathtaking slides backward to start over. The important consideration here is that we do learn from those painful, backward experiences and then actually do begin again with greater earnest and with greater ability.

The beginning process is gentle and form-fitted to each of our abilities and is molded to our desires. To dedicate ourselves to undeviating obedience to revelation is to be changed, reborn, and retooled into a likeness of Christ, taking upon ourselves the image of Christ. A process of increasingly more difficult obediences will bring us past many crossroads and along a straight course to power and purity.

False ideas will melt away. Impure thinking will taste sour to our souls. Uninspired entertainment will repel, and we will become pure in heart. In time, the voice of God will pronounce blessings indelibly, everlastingly sure, and we will know that our journey will end in glory. As individual obediences roll together into years of service, angels will attend, appear, and teach. In time the heavens will open to our view, and we will see as we are seen, and know as we are known (D&C 76:94–95).

We shall then be among those of whom the divine word proclaims:

55 They are they into whose hands the Father has given all things—

56 They are they who are priests and kings, who have received of his fulness, and of his glory;

57 And are priests of the Most High, after the order of Melchizedek, which was after the order of Enoch, which was after the order of the Only Begotten Son.

58 Wherefore, as it is written, they are gods, even the sons of God—

59 Wherefore, all things are theirs, whether life or death, or things present, or things to come, all are theirs and they are Christ's, and Christ is God's.

60 And they shall overcome all things.

61 Wherefore, let no man glory in man, but rather let him glory in God, who shall subdue all enemies under his feet.

62 These shall dwell in the presence of God and his Christ forever and ever.

63 These are they whom he shall bring with him, when he shall come in the clouds of heaven to reign on the earth over his people.

64 These are they who shall have part in the first resurrection.

65 These are they who shall come forth in the resurrection of the just.

66 These are they who are come unto Mount Zion, and unto the city of the living God, the heavenly place, the holiest of all.

67 These are they who have come to an innumerable company of angels, to the general assembly and church of Enoch, and of the Firstborn.

68 These are they whose names are written in heaven, where God and Christ are the judge of all.

69 These are they who are just men made perfect through Jesus the mediator of the new covenant, who wrought out this perfect Atonement through the shedding of his own blood.

70 These are they whose bodies are celestial, whose glory is that of the sun, even the glory of God, the highest of all, whose glory the sun of the firmament is written of as being typical. (D&C 76:55–70)

And:

94 They who dwell in his presence are the Church of the Firstborn; and they see as they are seen, and know as they are known, having received of his fulness and of his grace;

95 And he makes them equal in power, and in might, and in dominion. (D&C 76:94–95)

THE ENDOWMENT

It is difficult to speak or write of the temple because of the sacred obligation to not reveal holy things. We must speak in terms that those who have ears to hear may hear, and those who have eyes to see may see, yet leave in shadow those things which are sacred and are not to be revealed to uninspired eyes.

As we generally understand the term, "the endowment" is a temple ceremony. Several things happen in the endowment which can be discussed in this forum. We make solemn covenants, we receive promises of future blessings, and we are taught the process that will lead us to a personal experience at the veil if we are valiant. These future blessings are also an "endowment" in that they are a gift from Heavenly Father. It is through the temple endowment that we learn of and begin our journey toward a supernal endowment of power which will include all of the great and grand blessings that elevate us to the stature of a Zion individual. In this perspective, the temple endowment is a sacred ordinance that prefigures a greater Endowment, one of power from God that will occur much later, and as the sacred word indicates, probably outside of an actual temple.

Speaking of the Holy Order that both Enoch and Melchizedek entered, and which calling is offered to everyone who believes, the holy word says:

> 29 And it was delivered unto men by the calling of his own voice, according to his own will, unto as many as believed on his name. (JST Genesis 14:29)

Historically, that calling has occurred on mountaintops, in the wilderness, and in various locations outside of temples. The suggestion is that it can occur in any holy place that the Lord chooses.

The temple and the scriptures teach us that in time we may, if we are faithful, pierce the veil, enter the divine presence, and be allowed to request an actual "endowment"—a gift from the hands of God. As has been noted earlier, different people ask for different things. It is at this point that one may ask to be translated if it is our privilege to so ask. This gift from God is the fullest definition of the term *endowment*.

This gift and the divine event that surrounds it is the greatest outcome of mortality that occurs in mortality; a gift so glorious that nobody but God could bestow it. It is this endowment that the temple ordinance is prefiguring and which is the focal point of almost everything we experience within those sacred walls.

High Nibley, a noted LDS scholar, makes this same astonishing observation of what the endowment actually offers us: "*The Temple is teaching us (among many other things) to approach the veil and be 'endowed' with translation or some other gift.*"[35]

The temple ordinance is largely instruction geared to encode precious principles and instruction into the minds of the hearers, and to empower them to ultimately claim fantastic privileges when they finally catch the vision of what they have been promised. The whole experience is a shadow of greater things, shrouded in symbolism, buried within other themes that intentionally obscure greater truths from the unseeing, with its roots in antiquity so vast as to have literally emerged from the very mind of God.

Among many things, the temple accomplishes three important things:

- It provides living ordinances to prepare the living to enjoy eternal blessings.
- It teaches the living and prepares us to approach the veil where we may request our Endowment.
- It provides vicarious ordinances to link the generations in preparation for eternal blessings that bind us to the family of Christ.

If in our hearts we are primarily doing work for the departed, we are missing a large part of the purpose of the temple. Could it be that one of the reasons the temple experience is so repetitive isn't so much to bless the departed as it is to super-saturate the living with the message of how to righteously approach the veil?

The ceremony we call the endowment prefigures our mortal journey from the earliest stages of spiritual childhood in the premortal world to the loftiest stages of spiritual maturity in the natural world, which includes penetrating the veil, speaking with Christ, being endowed with power, and entering a special lifestyle beyond the veil.

The ideal journey through life of every mortal is being portrayed, not the journey of just one man and one woman. It is easiest to understand the things we see if we place ourselves into the lead role and see these things happening to us.

We needn't draw exclusively from our experiences in the temple to know what an ideal mortal life consists of. Through the restored gospel we know the following:

- We began in a state of premortal innocence where we made a decision to participate in mortality and, like Adam and Eve, we decided to partake of the knowledge of good and evil that through our experiences in mortality we might become like Heavenly Father.

Truman G. Madsen explained it this way:

> LDS doctrine provides two explanations that are uncommon in the Judeo-Christian tradition. First, all mankind chose to enter mortality with full knowledge of the great price that would be required of the Christ and of discipleship in his name. We chose knowingly to enter our present state or sphere of existence.[36]

- We were called, prepared and ordained to complete a mission in mortality. We chose good over evil before we were born, had great faith and good works (Alma 13). We made a covenant to be obedient to the light and knowledge we would be given in mortality. Other covenants were no doubt made, which involved spouse, family and individual callings. We understood that we must obey all truth which would come from Jesus Christ through His Holy Spirit, which we initially would recognize as our conscience.

> 3 And this is the manner after which they were ordained— being called and prepared from the foundation of the world according to the foreknowledge of God, on account of their exceeding faith and good works; in the first place being left to choose good or evil; therefore they having chosen good, and exercising exceedingly great faith, are called with a holy calling, yea, with that holy calling which was prepared with, and according to, a preparatory redemption for such. (Alma 13:3)

- We entered the mortal experience forgetful of our prior life and promises. With no memory of who we are or what glorious things we accomplished prior to mortality, our primary motivations come from the fabric of our souls, not from our life's experience. We immediately experienced right and wrong, and while our spirits have an inherent affinity to truth, our bodies are by nature attracted to evil (2 Nephi 2: 29). We instinctively try to remain faithful to forgotten covenants pre-mortally made.

- We learn in holy places that God sends angels to see if we are obedient to our covenants and potential. We can't see them of course, but they report the state of our lives and how we are dealing with the temptations and opposition of Satan.

- If we have been obedient, God sends representatives to teach us. These may take the form of parents, missionaries, a coworker, or perhaps a neighbor who presents us with the truths of the restored gospel. People born into the Church receive instruction from parents, teachers, and leaders.

- Those who are obedient to the voice of truth join the Church and learn the laws of the gospel. We attend church, pay tithing, and serve our fellowman.

- We learn to sacrifice in order to be obedient to the truth we possess. We begin to rejoice in the blessings those sacrifices bring us. At some point the gospel ceases to feel like a sacrifice at all because of the blessings that flow.

- We receive priesthood ordinations. We honor and magnify those callings. We enter the temples and receive greater ordinances and eternal marriage. We are taught to consecrate all that we have for the kingdom of God. In time we discover that consecration is not a sacrifice, but a joy, and we willingly, happily lay all we are on the altar.

- In the gospel household we are taught the sanctity of marriage and understand the consequences of infidelity and immorality. We make covenants to be chaste, because after we make covenants in the temple, sexual misconduct takes on eternal consequences.

- We begin to receive heavenly instruction that lifts and prepares us for our debut at the veil. Angels attend and in some cases appear. We are taught how to pray and receive everything we pray for, as the scriptures repeatedly promise. We learn about Zion, begin to understand our place within Zion, and yearn for the day when we will take our place within her walls.

- Worthiness and unflinching obedience at last invite us to the veil, and we speak with the Lord. He makes sacred pronouncements and promises us unconditional blessings. He plants a precious seed of truth into our minds that is barely understandable at the time, a true mystery of godliness, but which grows into an understanding of Zion and what our place within Zion means. We begin to yearn and labor unceasingly to obtain the fulfillment of those promises.

- In time we complete our preparations and, like the brother of Jared and all others of past righteous generations, purity prepares us to approach the veil once again, for the pure in heart shall see God (Matthew 5:8). We approach as one tried and true in all things, our preparations complete, our mind set upon a great purpose. We return to ask for our endowment which now blazes in the skies of our soul, lighting every part of the landscape of our being. We are invited into the presence of the Christ.

- Christ gives us personal instruction. We see "the" vision (1 Nephi 11:26; 2 Nephi 27:10; Ether 4:7, 15; Ether 3:22-27). We are ordained to a special calling (D&C 50:26).

- At last, we are asked what we would like from the Living Christ after He returns to the Father (3 Nephi 28:1-2, 4). We ask for the object of our rejoicing, that thing which the Spirit has taught us is ours to request; that which completes our mortal mission. For some, especially as the latter-day scenes evolve into Zion, that request will be for translation.

- We pass into a celestial form of mortality, which is to enter into the rest of the Lord (Alma 13:12; Alma 13:16; D&C 84:24). Through the grace of Christ we have now overcome the world. The laws of opposition are suspended (3 Nephi 28:7–10). All things are subject to our inspired command (D&C 50:26). We receive all that the Father hath (D&C 76:55). We have been changed into the Zion condition and dwell in the company of Christ (D&C 76:62). We have become a member of the Church of the Firstborn, and a citizen of Zion (D&C 76:54).

The list above may sound familiar to temple patrons, but it does not originate with the temple. This is common knowledge derived from the latter-day gospel and from the scriptures. Much cannot be included in this list which *is* unique to the temple.

The similarity between the ideal life noted above and sacred temple experiences is not accidental. The purpose of the temple is to instruct and empower us to successfully complete our journey through mortality and through the veil into the presence of Christ.

Without this essential instruction we could not derive from the written word what our privileges in the gospel actually are. Indeed, we can hardly perceive them even with temples dotting the land. Without the temple and the promises it continually lays before our eyes, most mortals could not develop sufficient faith to even conceive of a journey to the veil, let alone begin it. Without the empowerment of the temple and its covenants—which is to say, without the empowerment of Christ and His Atonement, flooding into our souls by virtue of covenants made and kept—we could never approach the veil that separates us from God. Consequently, we would never realize our privilege—our astronomical privilege—of returning to Christ's presence in this life, being endowed with power, and becoming Zion.

Catherine Thomas made this comment about this great privilege and quest:

> This was the very search for which [we] were put on earth: to rend the veil of unbelief, to yield to the pull of the Savior's sealing power, to stand in the Lord's presence, encircled about in the arms of his love (see D&C 6:20; 2 Nephi 1:15). This then is the temple endowment: having been cast out, to search diligently according to the revealed path, and at last to be clasped in the arms of Jesus (see Mormon 5:11).[37]

Last, it is exciting to note that the list above detailing the ideal life does not include death. The veil we approach in mortality that brings us face-to-face with deity is not death; it is the veil that separates mortals from God. It is this veil that we are to pierce to obtain our high station in Zion.

The celestial room thus represents the place prepared for mortals who qualify for His presence. It brings to mind eternal glories in the celestial kingdom for those who ultimately fulfill their covenants in the mortal world.

Since the veil of the temple does not represent death and the fulfillment of the promises at the veil are to be enjoyed in mortality, one can surmise that the celestial room also represents the type of life lived by those who progress beyond the veil and into the presence of God in mortality. It represents a mortal state of dwelling in the presence of God, of entering into the Church and kingdom of God, the City of the Living God, a state of rest and beauty—which are all descriptions of Zion.

The kingdom of God will be Zion during the Millennium, and Zion will ultimately be a translated society. The implication is that the celestial room also represents a glorious form of mortal life that flows from Zion. Can it be that where the temple experience is pointing us is not beyond the veil into a celestial realm, but into Zion?

POWER IN THE PRIESTHOOD

Before discussing how to obtain full priesthood power whereby we may move mountains and put at defiance the armies of nations, it is expedient to discuss the priesthood we hold today. Let's take a look at miracles as they do occur under the faith-filled hands of righteous administrators of the priesthood in our day.

There seem to be two classes of miracles today: those that we expect and commonly receive (such as healings, restoring sight and hearing, even raising the dead and similar things), and those that we do not expect, (moving mountains, walking on water, parting the seas, sealing the heavens, causing famine, restoring missing limbs, and the like). Interestingly enough, those that we do expect and do receive are listed as miracles of faith:

> 19 And again, to some it is given to have faith to be healed;
>
> 20 And to others it is given to have faith to heal.
>
> 21 And again, to some is given the working of miracles. (D&C 46:19–21)

From this it appears that we have taken some miracles that belong in the category of faith-powered and transplanted them under the heading of priesthood-powered.

In computer terms, we cut and pasted where we perhaps should have copied and pasted. By recasting such miracles as being by-priest-hood-only, we have excluded a high percentage of faithful members from believing it proper to command and receive such miracles by their faith, and even more problematic is that we have limited our belief regarding what miracles are available through the priesthood.

That these miracles belong to the priesthood is undeniable. We have all witnessed such things under the administration of righteous priesthood holders and can only believe that the fact that these miracles do occur, stamps them as approved of God.

What we have perhaps done is to overlook the fact that even priesthood miracles are a by-product of faith. Please note the following verse:

> 30 For God having sworn unto Enoch and unto his seed with an oath by himself; that every one being ordained after this order and calling *should have power, by faith*, to break mountains, to divide the seas, to dry up waters, to turn them out of their course. (JST Genesis 14:30; italics added)

Even when it is by the authority of the priesthood that someone places their hands on the sick and commands them to recover, it is faith that fuels the miracle from heaven. It is correct to say that the priesthood gives us the authority to command a certain outcome when properly inspired, but it is faith that makes the command efficacious. We are tapping into the power inherent in faith to fulfill priesthood blessings.

It also has to be correct to say that the same miracles can be obtained by non-priesthood holders who possess the same faith, with equal effect. Section 46 quoted above lists these miracles as the domain of all who have faith. The author of Mark recorded these same gifts as following "them that believe."

> 17 And these signs shall follow them that believe; In my name shall they cast out devils; they shall speak with new tongues;
>
> 18 They shall take up serpents; and if they drink any deadly thing, it shall not hurt them: they shall lay hands on the sick, and they shall recover. (Mark 16:17–18)

The prophet Joseph clearly taught this same principle to the Relief Society sisters at their first meeting.

> No matter who believeth, these signs, such as healing the sick, casting out devils, etc., should follow all that believe, whether male or

female. He asked the Society if they could not see, by this sweeping promise, that wherein they are ordained, it is the privilege of those set apart to administer in that authority, which is conferred on them; and if the sisters should have faith to heal the sick, let all hold their tongues, and let everything roll on.[38]

> Respecting females administering for the healing of the sick, he further remarked, there could be no devil in it, if God gave His sanction by [allowing a] healing; that there could be no more sin in any female laying hands on and praying for the sick, than in wetting the face with water; it is no sin for anybody to administer that has faith, or if the sick have faith to be healed by their administration.[39]

The only thing that has changed since 1881 is a point of procedure. To help avoid confusion, our inspired leaders have instructed that females performing healings by their faith should avoid "laying on hands," which is now reserved as a sign of priesthood authority. All else remains the same, except that it has become uncommon for non-priesthood holders to work miracles by their faith. We now consider such things to be the exclusive domain of the priesthood.

Returning now to the question of power in the priesthood, we are left to ponder the idea that if anyone can heal by faith, what advantage is holding the priesthood where a healing miracle is being sought?

There are several advantages that come to mind:

First, priesthood holders are literally commanded to administer to the sick. Otherwise it is probable that few priesthood holders would attempt such an audacious act.

> 14 Is any sick among you? let him call for the elders of the Church; and let them pray over him, anointing him with oil in the name of the Lord:
>
> 15 And the prayer of faith shall save the sick, and the Lord shall raise him up; and if he have committed sins, they shall be forgiven him. (James 5:14–15)

This fact alone has power not only to motivate, but to also generate the faith needed to successfully call down the blessings of heaven. By this command, healings have become a priesthood function, and rightly (albeit not exclusively) belong to the priesthood. By divine instruction, the priesthood's role is to administer the affairs and the spiritual blessings of the Church. Hence, the priesthood administers blessing of the sick and all other dispensations of power.

It has become a matter of common knowledge that priesthood holders (some more than others obviously) have power to heal. This knowledge is a fantastic support to our faith. Non-priesthood holders have no such legacy of success to draw from, even though the promises are the same.

It is also apparent that there is a category of priesthood miracle that does not follow all believers and which remains exclusive to priesthood power. Such miracles are those of legend: dividing the Red Sea, calling down manna, walking on the water, moving mountains, and the like.

Please refer back to the earlier discussion on the Holy Order on page 160. These greater Enochonian-like miracles seem to be the exclusive domain of those within the holy order of the priesthood which literally defines Zion. This is an order which we can seek and obtain, whose power we can share if we are willing to pay a similar price as those who previously obtained this great stature of righteous priesthood.

In the here and now of priesthood service, we may obtain a more pure faith in working priesthood miracles by doing this one faith-boosting thing: As we focus our lives upon obedience to Christ's voice, we become familiar with the feel and flavor of revelation. The nearer we attune our spiritual ears to His voice, the more perfect becomes our ability to ascertain His will.

Having obtained the voice of revelation then before a priesthood blessing, we may seek to obtain the will of God concerning what blessing we should deliver. Once we know what we are to say, then we can have great faith in the promised fulfillment of those things. Then, during the blessing, let us use the Christ pattern and say only those things which Christ, through the now-familiar Holy Spirit, puts into our minds and upon our lips. Thus, our priesthood blessings will truly be "in the name of Jesus Christ."

Let us review the Perfect Pathway to Zion as we now understand it:

- Obedience to the voice of Christ / Holy Spirit
- Sacrifice
- Prayer
- Faith
- Repentance
- Baptism
- Gift of the Holy Ghost

- Being born again
- Becoming perfect in Christ
- Personal revelation
- Temple endowment
- Power in the priesthood

Since our goal is to see Christ in person, and the pure in heart see God (Matthew 5:8), a necessary step in the pathway to Zion is that we become the pure in heart.

BECOMING THE PURE IN HEART

Becoming Zion pure is a task that reaches far beyond mortal ability. The road to Zion is such that we must engineer discipleship that brings us through the schooling of the restored gospel, relying upon the spiritual empowerment that flows from priesthood ordinances and the Atonement of Christ. We hearken to the voice of the Holy Spirit and school ourselves in righteous obedience. And then, by virtue of that purifying process, if we seek it and obey the associated laws, we may become the pure in heart and eventually all that Zion embodies.

Zion is the pure in heart, because we will have yielded ourselves to Christ and become Zion pure through the processes of Christ's grace.

> 18 And the Lord called his people ZION, because they were of one heart and one mind, and dwelt in righteousness; and there was no poor among them. (Moses 7:18)

> 21 Therefore, verily, thus saith the Lord, let Zion rejoice, for this is Zion—THE PURE IN HEART; therefore, let Zion rejoice. (D&C 97:21)

Nowhere in scripture is there a more concise formula for entering into the presence of God, and thus Zion, as we find in Matthew 5:8. "Blessed are the pure in heart: for they shall see God." It follows then that understanding what is meant by being pure in heart and how to achieve it is of vital importance in our quest for Zion. In commentary on this verse Elder McConkie stated:

> This promise is to be understood literally. Every living soul who is pure in heart shall see God, literally and personally, in this life, to say nothing of the fact that he shall dwell with and see him frequently in the celestial world hereafter.[40]

In my thinking there are two aspects to purity. The first and most understandable is an absence of sin. Little needs to be said about sinlessness, except to note that it is through the grace of Christ and through obedience to the voice of the Holy Spirit that we become as sin free as mortals may.

The second type of purity is more difficult to grasp and therefore to achieve. In my opinion, this type of purity may best be described as an unfettered soul, or a heart that is unpolluted by lies and false ideas.

This purity is more than an absence of sin. It is an inspired pattern of believing that is unpolluted by the mental refuse mortality dumps into our souls.

Throughout life, much of what we are taught by the world is lies. We are taught we're not popular because we're fat-skinny-tall-short-white-black-yellow-different, or we're unlovable, or we're a bad boy, or that we "have" a temper—and we believe these things, because big people told us so. These lies can fester in our being for years and years until in time we come to accept them as truth. "I'm just not good at . . ." is not seen as a lie that induces us to live down to someone else's expectation, but more of a statement of fact. These incorrect beliefs seem simple, but they are lies that originate from the evil one, and we can't approach the veil with lies in our heart.

If the pure in heart shall see God, then the *impure* in heart shall never see God. Other lies encompass relationships, body issues, philosophies of men, educational fallacies, corrupt politics, false doctrines, false religion, false tradition, and every aspect of our mortal experience and what we believe our world to be.

In the beginning our minds are like a beautiful white wall beside a busy road. Things get splashed on them by careless drivers, especially during rain storms and adversity. We only become impure when the mud sticks. We aren't only becoming impure by sin, but also through the unavoidable processes of mortal existence. To embrace the dirt as being a part of our structure is to not understand our true identity as spirit beings, or our true potential. To be able to view these smudges as pollution that is foreign to our most intrinsic goodness is to strip them of their power and to coat our souls with spiritual Teflon.

These lies have a damning effect when we do not understand where they came from. We most often just think that's "the way we are." These effects are the darker impurities of mortality—hate, fear, envy, jealousy, arrogance, pride, selfishness, anger, and an almost unending litany of darker human tendencies that Satan seeds into the voids of the soul. In one way or another, they all spring from deeply embedded falsehoods. Arrogance, for example, is often a by-product of feelings of inadequacy, of self-loathing, or of a need to prove our worth again and again. Such dark feelings and needs would melt if we correctly understood the truth about who we really are, how great our worth is, and how profoundly we are loved by God. Fear cannot exist when faith is present, and hate always yields its seat to love.

Eliminating these lies is an inspired step toward that purity of heart, which when achieved, allows us to see God. So, how do we acquire such an ethereal form of purity? How do we jettison the baggage of mortality that we may not even be aware of?

The answer is that such highly refined purity is a function of humility and of a willingness to let the Lord sequentially purge us of these impurities. Through the workings of the Holy Spirit He teaches us the truth about ourselves, and everything and everyone else. This process often involves experiences that bring the baggage to the surface where we proudly use it to hurt ourselves or others. The Holy Spirit then quietly corrects or chastises. If we chose to humbly comply, a tiny circle of pure white appears on our mud-spattered wall.

Over and over the Holy Spirit communicates truth in small things: Speak kindly, say you're sorry, ask for forgiveness, walk away, abandon your pride, put it back, pick it up, and on and on. Thus we conquer the impurities that have nothing to do with sin.

The wise man looks beyond the obvious and sees a larger process at work than just driving the speed limit when prompted to do so. The Holy Spirit is asking us to lay aside our pride, to submit to law or any of dozens of lessons that stand between us and purity. If they weren't important to our salvation, the Holy Spirit would be silent upon them.

Things like love, kindness, forgiveness, charity, mercy, service, and a correct understanding of who and what we are matter deeply to our salvation. Therefore, the Holy Spirit speaks. To abandon the arrogance of "this is who I am, deal with it" and to let the forces of divinity reshape us is to yield to the Holy Spirit and put off the natural man, replacing him with that purity which ultimately parts the veil.

There are two primary differences between ourselves and someone like the prophet Enoch, who achieved all that a mortal can in this life.

The first is, there are obviously truths that he understood and lived by, which we do not. The second is, there are errors and lies that he did not embrace, which we do.

In order to become Zion we must embrace all truth and jettison all the mental pollutants swilling in and around those truths.

I have a friend who for the last twenty-five years has lived just on the uphill side of poverty. He works hard and tries hard to succeed but has never managed to escape his situation. Many people have tried to give him advice on how to succeed at his ventures, but he continuously makes unwise decisions year after year and largely blames other people for failing him in some way or the other.

One time he was complaining bitterly about his circumstances. I asked him, "If you and the richest man in the world suddenly switched places, what do you think would happen?"

He thought about this and then said something very revealing. "I would have no idea how to run a big empire. I'd probably lose it all over time. Then I'd be right back where I am today, but with a lot more people mad at me than they are now."

I then asked him, "What do you think would happen to the rich guy after he was thrown into your situation?"

"Oh," he said, "he'd figure a way out and in ten years he'd probably create an empire again."

My friend's problem isn't an unwillingness to work. He actually works very hard day by day. His problem is his unwillingness, or inability perhaps, to think differently. He sees himself as stuck in the very circumstances that he himself has created, and so he stays there. His own belief system is that he cannot rise above where he is, even though he desperately wants to.

When our thinking is polluted by untruths we become like my friend. We keep ourselves stuck in the world our beliefs create. If our beliefs exclude a clear picture and bright hope of obtaining Zion, we are powerless to rise beyond our beliefs. If we cannot believe in and see ourselves luxuriating in the presence of God, then that impure belief alone—no matter what sinlessness we may otherwise obtain—is sufficient to keep us on this side of the veil.

That's the bad news.

The good news is that the very purpose of the Holy Spirit in our lives is to sanctify us, to uproot and purify even the very thoughts and beliefs of our hearts. It isn't necessary for us to intellectually identify our false beliefs, list them on a piece of paper, and sequentially eliminate them. In the first place, it's doubtful that we would be able to clearly identify them. And, in the second place, it's unusual for a mortal to see clearly enough into one's own mind to identify the falsehoods that are creating the offending beliefs. They are too deeply ingrained into our psyche. In most cases, we view them as perfectly normal and completely justified.

As an example, we might feel skeptical because our life has taught us that nothing works out the way you expected. So, we put our faith in a self-justified deep freeze of negative thinking. However, as we yield to the enticings of the Holy Spirit we become saintly, which is to say, sanctified by the Atonement of Christ. We become as a child, submissive, humble, meek, patient, full of love, and willing to submit to the will of the Father (Mosiah 3:19). The willingness to submit flows in large part from a deep sense of safety and love. We view life in its correct vista as being designed so that we might have joy (2 Nephi 2:25).

When we are at last fully changed by yielding to this process, then we will be the pure in heart, and blessed are the pure in heart, for they shall see God.

Elder Charles W. Penrose makes this connection between purity and Zion:

> The time will come when the servants of the living God will purify themselves before him until they will be fit to receive these blessings. When that holy temple is built in Zion God will take away the veil from the eyes of his servants; and the day is yet to dawn when the sons of Moses and Aaron, having become sanctified to the renewing of their bodies, will administer in that holy house, and the veil will be taken away, and they will gaze upon the glories of that world now unseen, and upon the faces of beings now to them invisible; but *it will be when they have purified themselves from the evils of this world, and are really the servants of the living God, and temples of the Holy Ghost.*[41]

CHARITY

As our purity grows we will find that two things happen with great impact upon our lives, first we will begin to experience a great love for our fellow pilgrims. That love is Christ's love which flows into us, and then out through us. This is Charity, the pure love of Christ, and it manifests itself as unselfish service to others.

> 47 But charity is the pure love of Christ, and it endureth forever; and whoso is found possessed of it at the last day, it shall be well with him.
>
> 48 Wherefore, my beloved brethren, pray unto the Father with all the energy of heart, that ye may be filled with this love, which he hath bestowed upon all who are true followers of his Son, Jesus Christ; that ye may become the sons of God; that when he shall appear we shall be like him, for we shall see him as he is; that we may have this hope; that we may be purified even as he is pure. Amen. (Moroni 7:47–48)

Charity is the highest expression of purity because it is that which motivates deity to save us. It is that which motivated the Christ to shed His blood in our behalf. It is a full endowment of charity which finally brings us to ask that we be allowed to remain upon the earth beyond the time allotted to man, to bring souls unto Christ. This is the ultimate meaning of love, and the bedrock attribute of those who become Zion.

The Perfect Pathway to Zion as we now understand it:

- Obedience to the voice of Christ / Holy Spirit
- Sacrifice
- Prayer
- Faith
- Repentance
- Baptism
- Gift of the Holy Ghost
- Being born again
- Becoming perfect in Christ
- Personal revelation
- Temple endowment
- Taught by angels
- Power in the priesthood
- Becoming pure in heart
- Charity

ENTERTAINING ANGELS

It is, of course, true that each people's journey will be unique, with different experiences in different order. The list above is not necessarily the order in which all people will, or even should, experience these things. This list only attempts to define the common events of the straight way, not the exact order.

Elder McConkie gave us a wonderful description of this same process. Although he was obviously not trying to be all-inclusive, he clearly defined the steps outlined above:

> After the true saints receive and enjoy the gift of the Holy Ghost; after they know how to attune themselves to the voice of the Spirit; after they mature spiritually so that they see visions, work miracles, and entertain angels; after they make their calling and election sure and prove themselves worthy of every trust—after all this and more—it becomes their right and privilege to see the Lord and commune with him face to face."[42]

We have already discussed the ministry of angels at length (see Zion and the Ministering of Angels, page 61). What may remain to be said is that angels *do* minister today, and we are those to whom they minister.

In the case of Enoch and his people, their present ministry is to be angels to those who are heirs of the terrestrial order, which order is their present state. Joseph Smith noted of Enoch and his people: "Their place of habitation is that of the terrestrial order."[43] Thus, they are ministering to people who are heirs of the same terrestrial order they now enjoy.

Elder Orson Pratt noted:

> They have been ministering angels during all that time. To whom? To those of the terrestrial order, if you can understand that expression . . . he granted to the people of Enoch their desire to become ministering spirits unto those of the terrestrial order until the earth should rest and they should again return to it.[44]

In other words, they are laboring among and with those who will become citizens of the latter-day Zion. According to Moroni 7:29–30 quoted above, those mortals to whom the angels from Enoch's Zion minister are those who are of a "strong faith and a firm mind in every form of godliness." These are the future inhabitants of Zion.

We learn in the temple that angels perform a vital function in the relationship of God and man. We may ascertain that, among many other things, they carry out assignments, deliver messages, report on their labors, check to ensure covenants are being kept, and deliver greater light and knowledge when we qualify for it. The also appear when the situation warrants it, either in or outside of their true identity. There are many accounts in LDS apocryphal literature of angels appearing as common mortals.[45]

So, we look around and think, I don't recall seeing any angels. Where are they? Why haven't I seen them?

First of all, we understand that most angelic labors are not performed visibly. Elisha had to pray to the Lord so that his servant could see the angels protecting Elisha. When his servant's eyes were opened, he saw that "the mountain was full of horses and chariots of fire round about Elisha" (2 Kings 6:17).

We also observe in the temple that angels are often sent with instructions to conceal their true identity. These are the "holy men" working among us that we "know not of" (D&C 49:8). The scriptures are full of angels doing marvelous works occasionally in plain view, but largely invisible to mortals.

> 29 And because he [Christ] hath done this [ascended into heaven], my beloved brethren, have miracles ceased? Behold I say unto you, Nay; *neither have angels ceased to minister unto the children of men.*
>
> 30 For behold, they are subject unto him, to minister according to the word of his command, *showing themselves unto them of strong faith and a firm mind in every form of godliness.* (Moroni 7:29–30; italics and bracketed comments added)

These examples are sufficient to suggest that most angelic works are performed behind the scenes, away from seeing mortals. The scriptures also plainly tell us that we can and will see them when our faith is strong, and our mind (suggesting our doctrinal understanding) is firm in every form of godliness.

Could it also be that belief plays a powerful role in whether or not we see heavenly visitors and visions? Consider this account of Joseph inviting two brethren to join him in a vision:

> Brother Joseph then said, "Now brethren, we will see some visions." Joseph lay down on the ground on his back and stretched out his arms and the two brethren lay on them. The heavens gradually opened.[46]

The astonishing element of this account is that Joseph was so proactive about it. He didn't just wait for angels to appear, he just went and did it, and he invited two other brethren to join him in the vision. He had seen many angels, and it was well within his belief structure that he could do it again. The brethren had confidence in Brother Joseph, and they surely approached the experience with excitement and expectation, which is a manifestation of true belief.

It also has to be true that the Holy Spirit had planted the appropriateness of this action into Joseph's heart, or he could not have approached it with sufficient faith to rend the veil. The unshakeable belief this event exhibits is astonishing.

The principle here is that most of having a "firm mind" on this subject of seeing angels is to believe that angels can, do, and will minister to us individually. Without this underlying belief, it is unlikely we will have much cognizant interaction with angels.

Calling and Election Made Sure

Elder McConkie included "after they make their calling and election sure . . ." in his wonderful description of how one qualifies for a personal appearance of Christ. Making one's calling and election sure is a subject of some obscurity in most of our minds.

What remains to be said is perhaps this: Having one's calling and election made sure is a natural progression in the quest for righteousness of all forms, including seeking Zion. It is not an obscure doctrine, nor is it mysterious—though it is rightly a "mystery" until we seek and obtain it. The way to experience this high and holy blessing is to walk the straight course as we have been discussing thus far. So far, our perfect pathway to Zion looks like this:

- Obedience to the voice of Christ / Holy Spirit
- Sacrifice
- Prayer
- Faith
- Repentance
- Baptism
- Gift of the Holy Ghost
- Being born again
- Becoming perfect in Christ
- Personal revelation
- Temple endowment
- Taught by angels
- Power in the priesthood
- Becoming pure in heart

- Charity
- Calling and election made sure

Like all of these potential steps, calling and election is not something that one can obtain out of context. It isn't possible to skip being baptized, for example, and yet seek the blessings of the temple. It also isn't reasonable to skip the rebirth, or the temple, or obtaining greater power of the priesthood, and yet yearn for and seek after the higher blessings, including Zion. The only way to walk the course is line upon line, precept upon precept, until the brighter day dawns incrementally upon us.

It is important to observe again that this list we are developing is a theoretical outline of the journey to these high and holy blessings. Different seekers may experience them in a somewhat different order, or perhaps with different emphasis. Some events will occur quietly, unnoticed for years until the Spirit of the Lord highlights them in our thinking. A possible postscript to this is that some steps may occur so personally and without fanfare that they may appear to have been skipped until greater light is shown upon our past.

The Lord may have a specific calling for you that necessitates a unique pathway other than what most will experience. I expect that Moses experienced spiritual growth somewhat differently than the typical Latter-day Saint will. What does not change is that all of these things are listed in the scripture as identifiable steps on the pathway to righteousness. Thus, no matter in what order they may occur, or how profound the individual experiences may be, we may not expect to skip any of them.

Let us make another minor observation at this juncture, which is that we may experience some of these things intermittently or even multiple times. The desired outcome is that we learn the laws associated with these blessings and set our lives into valiant observance, thus ending the mortal swings in and out of blessings. As an example, we may experience the rebirth multiple times, but at some point we must be changed into the Christ pattern and never depart therefrom. There are several things that we would not want to allow ourselves to slip in and out of that may well be dramatically harmful. These are on the upper reaches of our list, including temple endowment and onward. In point of fact, falling from calling and election may well make one a son of perdition.

The illustration that follows highlights this extraordinary journey in graphic form. What we see is that as time progresses, one principle builds upon another, each taking its proper order in our progression. Notice that

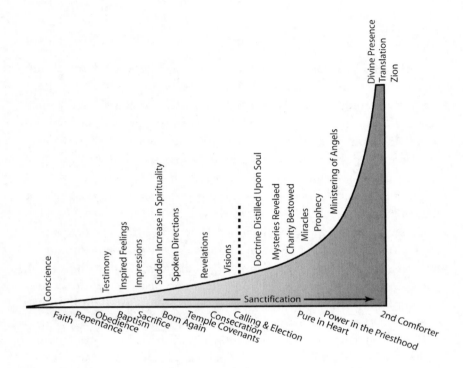

the relative power we experience in each step is only slightly elevated from the prior until we reach the greater things; then the rise becomes steep and profoundly upward. Until then, the upward progress appears slow and may be unnoticeable except in inspired retrospect.

Along the bottom of the chart are noticeable steps in progression, ordinances, and events. Along the top are the effects of those events and the spiritual outcome of so obtaining.

As you study the chart, you will observe that sanctification is a process that begins approximately at being born again and culminates at the throne of God. As it increases, we obtain greater righteousness, more revelatory privileges, and we begin to experience the gospel as it is detailed in the lives of the prophets, complete with attendant visions, miracles, and visitations. You will also observe the *vertical dashed line* between "Visions" and "Doctrine Distilled Upon Soul." This is the approximate limit of most Latter-day Saint's belief structure about what is possible for someone to experience during their lifetime. As spiritual infants the line of what is possible seems to be many steps to the left but moves upward as our faith and belief grows.

One might correctly call it the veil of unbelief.

It is also true that spiritual growth does not stop at the point that this chart does. This is merely the portion of our mortal journey that has been revealed to us, to which we can attach labels and read of in the lives of prior faithful. Beyond the Second Comforter lies the magnificence of being in the presence of Deity. As we have established, at that point we are "endowed" and may request translation and Zion or some other inspired gift.

Since we believe in eternal progression, there is no endpoint defined by death, or even by translation. The heavens keep opening before our eyes, revealing heavenly vistas newly within our grasp. Who can even guess what glories await the eyes, ears, and souls of those who are invited into that patrician general assembly and Church of the Firstborn, who company with translated souls, angels, the notable and profound of past generations, and our Savior? Who can imagine being a part of the 144,000 who reap the earth by miracles and openly manifest power, who receive their assignments from Christ's lips, and who move mountains at His command? What mortal mind can even conceive of the wonders of such a life: Sacrament meetings where John the Beloved might be the concluding speaker, where angels sing in choirs, and testimonies are illustrated by visions shared by all present? What mortal imagination can reach beyond the finite mind and understand the joy of living without fear, without opposition, and without possibility of failure; of being sent forth to do the impossible with prophetic visions of success? None can, and yet we do believe, and by faith we see through the glass of mortality dimly these profound blessings that await us.

Perhaps this is the reason the writings of Mahonri Moriancumer are sealed to our latter-day eyes—not that we aren't worthy so much as we simply aren't equipped to believe them.

Beyond those days of Zion quickly approaching, we will enjoy a celestial reward in an eternity that makes even Zion seem rudimentary and the exhilarating millennial day pale compared to the life that awaits us in the presence of the Father of us all.

THE SECOND COMFORTER

The Second Comforter eclipses calling and election, not only in attendant power, but also in the lack of understanding regarding what it is and why it is offered to us.

Elder McConkie taught us that this great privilege of seeing God and talking with Him face-to-face naturally follows calling and election:

> It is the privilege of all those who have made their calling and election sure to see God; to talk with him face to face; to commune with him on a personal basis from time to time. These are the ones upon whom the Lord sends the Second Comforter.[47]

Hyrum Andrus wrote of Enoch and how he obtained his blessings:

> He obtained power to take his portion of the earth and move out a little while, where he remains to this day. To do this, however, Enoch and his people first had to "enter into their rest"—into the presence of God as heirs of His glory. They developed in the plan of life and salvation until they made their calling and election sure to eternal life and were sealed by the power of the priesthood to those sacred family relationships by which they could be exalted in celestial society. They then acquired the right by covenant to enter into the presence of God and partake of His glory. Having brought his people to this state of spiritual excellence, Enoch obtained "power to translate himself and his people, with the region they inhabited, their houses, gardens, fields, cattle, and all their possessions."[48]

Notice the order:

- Calling and election
- Sealed in family relationships
- Enter the presence of the Lord's glory (Second Comforter)
- Obtained power of translation
- Enter into the rest of the Lord

The placement here of the sealing of family units after calling and election is correct, even though it seems it should be prior to it. The actual temple sealing is like all other priesthood ordinances in that we participate in the ordinance when we are prepared and then receive the outcome and blessing of the ordinance when we qualify for it perhaps much later in life. In order for eternal marriage to be of effect after this life, both participants must have their calling and election made sure, hence, the correctness of the order of these events in Brother Andrus' quotation. Commenting on D&C 132:26, Elder McConkie states:

> Then the revelation speaks of that obedience out of which eternal life grows, and still speaking both of celestial marriage and of making

one's calling and election sure says: "Verily, verily, I say unto you, if a man marry a wife according to my word, and they are sealed by the Holy Spirit of promise, according to mine appointment"—that is, if they are both married and have their calling and election made sure—[then they shall have eternal life].[49]

We covered the Second Comforter in "Priesthood and Seeing God." What we might yet say regarding this and all other principles of the "greater portion" blessings is its purpose. While there may be many just reasons that God shows himself to man in our day, we are taught of just one pure desire that will allow us to ask, seek, knock, and have the heavens open unto us.

Heavenly Father's house is a house of order, which not only implies orderliness and organization, but also sequentiality; line upon line, precept upon precept, in a divinely ordained pattern that is used again and again. Since this desire of which we speak has scripturally yielded this glorious blessing, it must do so every time it is righteously applied.

It may appear more obvious to desire the Second Comforter to exult in the presence of our Savior, to worship at His feet, to have the privilege of beholding His face, and tearfully thanking Him for the gift of His atoning blood shed for our expense. But as righteous as these things are, such a motivation is nowhere listed as sufficient to part the heavens.

There is a greater purpose even than that, one which powers the mighty mainspring of eternity and engages the gears of everlasting law. When that purpose becomes the only light that burns in our hearts—not just one of many flickering desires, but when our eye becomes single to this aspect of the glory of God—then our hearts will be pure indeed. Then the heavens will open, and the One whom holy writ calls Wonderful, Counselor, the Mighty God, the Everlasting Father, the Prince of Peace, will step through the veil.

The exact process to obtaining the Second Comforter cannot be annotated here, simply because it will be different for each of us, aligning with our premortally covenanted calling, and also with the immortal intelligence that uniquely defines us. But in addition to these indefinable specifics, there will be a common desire within the souls of those who enter Zion, like an exquisite melody whose harmonies are interwoven in the lives of the righteous. This shared desire is that we might, like John, whom the Savior called beloved, prolong our service to our master beyond the scope of mortality and beyond the ability of mortals to do far more than the laws of opposition allow; to sacrifice ourselves in Christlike grace to the cause of bringing souls unto Christ and preparing the world for His return in glory (3 Nephi 28:6).

Such pure and inspired (meaning eternally correct for you personally) desire to remain upon the earth to prepare the world for Christ's return cannot be arrived at in a moment, and not without the full blessings of priesthood, grace, and Atonement. Many will have other equally-glorious and inspired requests to make when that perfect moment arrives.

John arrived at this purity at least in part because of his great love of his Savior, and there can be no doubt that John's love was a reflection of Christ's love for him, who loved him first (1 John 4:19). This great love also earned him the eternal honorific "beloved." It is far more than interesting that Christ also referred to the Three Nephites as "his beloved disciples" (Mormon 1:16), seemingly elevating "beloved" to a revered description of all who so obtain. It seems thus apparent that of all the emotions and desires powering our soul as we ask, seek, and knock, as we petition God for the joy of His presence, as we humbly place our will upon the sacrificial altar of obedience, that the emotion that most powerfully parts the veil, is love: love for He who first loved us. That mighty river then flows into us from Christ, and outward from us as charity, the perfect desire to be of lasting service to our fellowmen beyond the normal time appointed to man.

ACHIEVING ZION AND 144,000

To my thinking, in this generation when Zion is the promised and ultimate mortal outcome of righteousness, such a pure desire humbly laid at the feet of the Master during our private interview with Him constitutes a request to become an architect and builder of Zion. Once within the walls of Zion we qualify to become one of the 144,000 who will be sent to gather out the elect into the safety of Zion.

Whatever songs have been written throughout history, whatever symphonies and grand orchestrations have praised the events of the past, as inspired and magnificent as they may have been—there is a masterpiece of such surpassing beauty yet to be sung that all previous symphonies shall be quieted in awe. This is the song the angels of Zion will sing as they bring the elect out from warring Babylon into Zion and into the Savior's arms. What a day of days that will be!

> 3 And they sung as it were a new song before the throne, and before the
> four beasts, and the elders; and no man could learn that song but the

hundred and forty and four thousand, which were redeemed from the earth. (JST Revelation 14:3)

Understanding that once we are in the presence of Christ we may request a place in Zion, and by extension, in the 144,000, our perfect pathway into Zion thus becomes:

- Obedience to the voice of Christ / Holy Spirit
- Sacrifice
- Prayer
- Faith
- Repentance
- Baptism
- Gift of the Holy Ghost
- Being born again
- Becoming perfect in Christ
- Personal revelation
- Temple endowment
- Taught by angels
- Power in the priesthood
- Becoming pure in heart
- Charity
- Calling and election made sure (elect of God)
- Second Comforter
- "Endowed" from on high
- Translation
- Zion / 144,000

CONCLUSION

Among the many things that are eternally true about the gospel of Jesus Christ, one of the most empowering is that *it works*. Yes, it is true, it is inspired, and it is led by a living prophet. Building upon this, and far more important in a pragmatic sense is that it functions; it works today with the same power and effect as it did in Enoch's day or in the brother of Jared's day. Every blessing, every privilege, every power and glory that God ordains for His righteous children is as available to you and I as it was to Enoch.

This is the dispensation of the *fulness* of times, a day when the *fulness* of the gospel is upon the earth. We, of all people, have upon the table before us the greatest spiritual banquet that has ever been spread before humankind. We have greater views because we can see more of the past, and thus possess more scripture than any other dispensation. We have greater views of the future because much of that scripture was either prophesying of or preparatory to this dispensation. We have more immediate and glorious privileges than perhaps any other era of time. The scriptures proclaim this day to be the greatest day of the history of man, a day when all things would be restored, when every fulness would be present, when Zion would be built and begin its unstoppable roll to fill the whole earth. This is our birthright and our obligation.

Let us raise our eyes in joy—joy in the promises, joy in the possibilities, joy in the approaching triumph of Zion, and joy in our Jesus.

> Israel, Israel, God is speaking.
> Hear your great Deliverer's voice!
> Now a glorious morn is breaking
> For the people of His choice.
> Come to Zion, come to Zion,
> And within her walls rejoice.[50]

NOTES

1. Joseph Fielding Smith, *Doctrines of Salvation*, 3 vols., 1:3; italics added.
2. McConkie, *Mormon Doctrine*, 314, parenthetical comments in original.
3. Ibid., 156–57.
4. Pontius, *Following the Light*, 20; bracketed comment added.
5. James E. Faust, "The Voice of the Spirit," *Ensign*, Apr. 1994, 7; bracketed comment added.
6. Pontius, *Following the Light*, 36.
7. Ibid., 38, bracketed comment added.
8. McConkie, *The Millennial Messiah*, 233.
9. Ezra Taft Benson, *A Witness and a Warning: A Modern-Day prophet Testifies of the Book of Mormon* (Salt Lake City: Deseret Book, 1988), vii.
10. Brigham Young, *Journal of Discourses*, 10:172.
11. David A. Bednar, "Clean Hands and a Pure Heart," *Ensign*, Nov. 2007; italics added.

12. Smith, *Lectures on Faith,* 1:15.

13. McConkie, *New Witness for the Articles of Faith*, 195.

14. Ibid., 195.

15. Smith, *Lectures on Faith,* 7:9; italics added.

16. McConkie, *New Witness for the Articles of Faith*, 194.

17. Smith, *Lectures on Faith,* 7:8.

18. McConkie, *New Witness for the Articles of Faith,* 195

19. Smith, *Lectures on Faith,* 6:2; parenthetical comments in original text.

20. Ibid., 6:4.

21. Ibid., 6:11.

22. Ibid., 6:7; italics added.

23. M. Catherine Thomas offers an insightful essay on this subject entitled "Hebrews: To Ascend the Holy Mount," from *Selected Writings of M. Catherine Thomas*, 145.

24. McConkie, *New Witness for the Articles of Faith,* 187.

25. *Autobiography of Parley P. Pratt* (Salt Lake City: Deseret Book, 1985), 254.

26. McConkie, *New Witness for the Articles of Faith,* 383.

27. Smith, *Teachings of the Prophet Joseph Smith,* 278.

28. McConkie, *Doctrinal New Testament Commentary,* 2:230.

29. Smith, *Teachings of the Prophet Joseph Smith,* 314.

30. Pontius, *Following the Light,* 97.

31. Bednar, "Clean Hands and a Pure Heart," *Ensign,* Nov. 2007, 82; italics in original.

32. Jeffrey R. Holland, *Christ and the New Covenant: The Messianic Message of the Book of Mormon* (Salt Lake City: Deseret Book, 1997), 193.

33. McConkie, *New Witness for the Articles of Faith,* 185.

34. Smith, *Teachings of the Prophet Joseph Smith,* 149.

35. Hugh Nibley, *Mormonism and Early Christianity,* ed. Todd M. Compton and Stephen D. Ricks (Salt Lake City and Provo: Deseret Book and FARMS, 1987, 72–73.

36. Truman G. Madsen, *The Radiant Life* (Salt Lake City: Bookcraft, 1994), 58.

37. Thomas, *Selected Writings*, "The Brother of Jared at the Veil," 389; bracketed comment added.

38. *Contributor* 3, no. 11 (August 1882): 322.

39. Ibid; bracketed comment added.

40. McConkie, *Doctrinal New Testament Commentary,* 1:216.

41. Penrose, *Journal of Discourses,* 21:49–50; italics added.

42. McConkie, *The Promised Messiah,* 575.

43. Smith, *Teachings of the Prophet Joseph Smith*, 170–71.

44. *Journal of Discourses*, 17:148–49.

45. For an interesting collection of such stories, see *Life Everlasting* by Duane S. Crowther.

46. *Writings of Early Latter-day Saints,* "Remarks of Zebedee Coltrin, Salt Lake City School of Prophets," 11 October 1883, 66.

47. McConkie, *The Promised Messiah*, 584.

48. Hyrum L. Andrus, *Principles of Perfection* (Salt Lake City: Bookcraft, 1970), 414–15.

49. McConkie, *Doctrinal New Testament Commentary,* 3:345; bracketed comment added.

50. *Hymns*, no. 7.

SELECTED BIBLIOGRAPHY

Andrus, Hyrum L. *Doctrinal Commentary on the Pearl of Great Price.* Salt Lake City: Deseret Book, 1967.

Andrus, Hyrum L. *Doctrines of the Kingdom.* Salt Lake City: Bookcraft, 1973.

Encyclopedia of Mormonism, 1–4 vols. Edited by Daniel H. Ludlow. New York: Macmillan, 1992.

Journal of Discourses, 26 vols. London: Latter-day Saints' Book Depot, 1854–1886.

McConkie, Bruce R. *Doctrinal New Testament Commentary*, 3 vols. Salt Lake City: Bookcraft, 1965–1973.

McConkie, Bruce R. *The Millennial Messiah: The Second Coming of the Son of Man.* Salt Lake City: Deseret Book, 1982.

McConkie, Bruce R. *Mormon Doctrine*, 2d ed. Salt Lake City: Bookcraft, 1966.

McConkie, Bruce R. *The Mortal Messiah: From Bethlehem to Calvary*, 4 vols. Salt Lake City: Deseret Book, 1979–1981.

McConkie, Bruce R. *A New Witness for the Articles of Faith.* Salt Lake City: Deseret Book, 1985.

McConkie, Bruce R. *The Promised Messiah: The First Coming of Christ* Salt Lake City: Deseret Book, 1978.

Nibley, Hugh. *Approaching Zion*. Edited by Don E. Norton. Salt Lake City and Provo: Deseret Book, Foundation for Ancient Research and Mormon Studies, 1989.

Pontius, John M. *Following the Light of Christ into His Presence*. 3rd edition. Springville, Utah: Cedar Fort, 1997.

Smith, Joseph. *Joseph Smith, History of The Church of Jesus Christ of Latter-day Saints*, 7 vols. Introduction and notes by B. H. Roberts. Salt Lake City: The Church of Jesus Christ of Latter-day Saints, 1932–1951.

Smith, Joseph. *Lectures on Faith*. Salt Lake City: Deseret Book, 1985.

Smith, Joseph. *Teachings of the Prophet Joseph Smith*. Selected and arranged by Joseph Fielding Smith. Salt Lake City: Deseret Book, 1976.

Smith, Joseph Fielding. *Answers to Gospel Questions*, 5 vols. Salt Lake City: Deseret Book Co., 1957–1966.

Words of Joseph Smith: Contemporary Accounts of the prophet's Nauvoo Discourses. Edited by Andrew F. Ehat and Lyndon W. Cook. Provo, Utah: Religious Studies Center, Brigham Young University, 1980.

OTHER SOURCES

References from the Bible are from the King James Translation published by The Church of Jesus Christ of Latter-day Saints.

Book of Mormon references are from the official publication of The Church of Jesus Christ of Latter-day Saints.

Many quotations were obtained through GospelLink 2001, by Deseret Book Company.

About John M. Pontius

On a personal note: I don't know how to write about what I do and what I am without sounding self-aggrandizing. Believe me when I say I don't mean to. Let the record show first and foremost that I glory in my Jesus. All else is just fluff.

I have lived in the pristine grandeur of Alaska's Matanuska Valley for thirty-three years. I am a business owner, oil industry consultant, and writer. I am very happily married to Terri Jean. We are the parents of eight wonderful children ranging in age from thirteen to thirty-four.

Terri and I are life-long members of The Church of Jesus Christ of Latter-day Saints. Terri was recently released as the stake music chair, which was the hardest job I ever had (if you know what I mean). She now serves as our ward choir director and compassionate service chair. She is a model of righteous womanhood.

I was recently released from the bishopric. I served for the second time on the high council before serving as stake executive secretary. My favorite job was teaching Sunday School, course sixteen. I just loved them and taught them the deep and peaceable things of the gospel. It was a wonderful experience.

Our recent list of exhausting projects include two stake plays, both Broadway musicals: *The Music Man* and *Annie*, as well as many talent shows and stake events. I have sung in or conducted our community performance of *Handel's Messiah* for nineteen consecutive years.

My hobbies include writing, inspirational speaking, piano, organ, conducting orchestra and chorus, wood working, oil painting, photography, landscaping, dreaming impossible things, moaning about politics, and listening to my kids say things like, "There's no way you could have known that!"

I have been blessed to publish five LDS books that are listed on page vi of this book. Like most obsessed writers, I have a file cabinet full of unpublished manuscripts waiting to be "discovered." Some of my books and essays are available for free on my website.

Brother Pontius can be reached through
www.followingthelight.org